A GLOBAL PERSPECTIVE OF VICTIMOLOGY AND CRIMINOLOGY

A GLOBAL PERSPECTIVE OF VICTIMOLOGY AND CRIMINOLOGY

YESTERDAY, TODAY AND TOMORROW

Festschrift for Professor Dr. K. Chockalingam
50 years of teaching in the Field of Victimology

Editors

Beulah Shekhar
Sanjeev P. Sahni

BLOOMSBURY
NEW DELHI • LONDON • OXFORD • NEW YORK • SYDNEY

BLOOMSBURY INDIA
Bloomsbury Publishing India Pvt. Ltd
Second Floor, LSC Building No. 4, DDA Complex, Pocket C – 6 & 7,
Vasant Kunj, New Delhi 110070

BLOOMSBURY, BLOOMSBURY PRIME and the Diana logo are
trademarks of Bloomsbury Publishing Plc

First published in 2020

ISBN: 978-93-89867-50-3

2 4 6 8 10 9 7 5 3 1

Printed and bound in India by Replika Press Pvt Ltd

To find out more about our authors and books, visit
www.bloomsbury.com and sign up for our newsletters

The book is dedicated to

Professor Dr. K. Chockalingam

Our teacher, mentor, role model, inspiration and
an institution builder

In Honour of Professor Dr. K. Chockalingam

Dr. K. Chockalingam, M.A., M.Litt. M.L., Ph.D., born in Kanniyakumari district in Tamil Nadu in India on 16 April 1945 is currently the chairperson of the Rajiv Gandhi National Institute of Youth Development, Ministry of Youth Affairs, Government of India, Sriperumbudur, Tamil Nadu, India. He was serving as Chair Professor in Criminal Law at the National Law University, Delhi until the end of February 2014 since May 2012. Earlier he was working as Professor of Criminology and Victimology at the Tokiwa International Victimology Institute of the Tokiwa University in Japan from September 2005 until the end of September 2011, after completing his three year term as the Vice Chancellor of Manonmaniam Sundaranar University, Tirunelveli in Tamil Nadu state in December 2004. During his stay of six years at Tokiwa University, Japan he worked as Deputy Director of the Tokiwa International Victimology Institute for two years and finally as Director of the International Centre of the Tokiwa University.

Prof.Chockalingam has received international and national awards for his contribution to progressive policy and programmes for crime victims and has been invited to lecture in universities in more than 30 countries (including Harvard and Oxford). He has more than 40 years of teaching and research experience at the University of Madras in India, at the Tokiwa University, Japan and later at the National Law University, Delhi in the field of Criminology, Criminal Law and Victimology. He is considered as pioneering the field of Victimology in India and was the Founder President of the Indian Society of Victimology and he held the position for 13 years

Dr.Chockalingam started his career as a Lecturer in the National Institute of Social Defence, Govt. of India, New Delhi from 1978 to 1983. In 1983, he was selected to head the newly established Department of Criminology at the University of Madras, Chennai. From 1983 to 2001, he started and consolidated a Master's and Doctoral program, established an exchange program with the University of Illinois, undertook an extensive series of research projects and lectured all over the world. He was a guest lecturer at the Indian National Police Academy for many years. Prof. Chockalingam has been a Life Member of the Indian Institute of Public administration for more than two decades and was elected as a Member of the Executive Council of Indian Institute of Public Administration (IIPA) for two terms. He was also elected/appointed to the boards of many national and international organizations. He was the keynote speaker invited by the Law Commission of Sri Lanka at Colombo to discuss the Draft bill on Victim Compensation and Assistance for Sri Lanka in June 2006.

In 2001, he was selected by the Government of Tamil Nadu to become the Vice-Chancellor of Manomaniam Sundaranar University in Tirunelveli in Tamil Nadu. He won significant grants for the buildings and infrastructure for the University, established a new work culture including a mission statement that focused on learning lawfulness, and launched a Master's programme in criminal. Prof. K. Chockalingam earned a name as an Institution builder through his vision, innovation and hard work insisting on the slogan 'Excellence in Everything' and created a new work culture among the faculty, students and non-teaching staff of the Manonmaniam Sundaranar University, Tirunelveli. Through his relentless efforts and dynamic leadership, he motivated the entire faculty and the administrative staff, and for the first time he submitted the university for NAAC assessment and earned the B++ level of accreditation with an institutional score of 80-85% in December 2003 by the National Assessment and Accreditation Council (NAAC) of India.

He has been a World Society of Victimology delegate to the Milan and Cairo UN Congresses on the Prevention of crime and the Treatment of offenders in 1985 and 1995. He has been a General Rapporteur for the 2000 International Symposium on Victimology of the World Society of Victimology (WSV) in Montreal. He presented papers in all the triennial conferences of the World Society of Victimology from 1985 until now. He participated in conferences in more than 30 countries in Asia and around the world. He was awarded the Max Planck Society's Research Fellowship at the Max Planck Institute for International and Foreign Penal Law, Freiburg in Germany three times. He was a Guest Professor at the Tokiwa University, Mito, Japan for four months in 1992-93. Subsequently he was Full Professor of Victimology at the Tokiwa International Victimology Institute of the Tokiwa University from September 2005 to September 2011, besides being the Director of International Centre of Tokiwa University from April to September 2011. He was a Visiting Expert of the United Nations Asia and Far East Institute for the Prevention of crime and the Treatment of offenders (UNAFEI), Tokyo at the 144th International Seminar in January 2010. Recently he was an invited keynote speaker at the National Conference of Victimology held in the University of Balikpapan in Indonesia and also lectured at the faculty of Law at the University of Indonesia, Jakarta in April 2017.

Foreword

It is a privilege for me to be asked to write a foreword for this book, 'A Global Perspective of Victimology and Criminology – Yesterday, Today and Tomorrow'. The most senior scholar Professor & Doctor K. Chokalingam, is a well-known criminologist, researcher and academician having more than 50 years of experience. He founded the Department of Criminology at Madras University. The book comprises chapters written by eminent professors, law enforcement experts, legal luminaries and research scholars of international repute. Skillful editing by Dr. Sanjeev P. Sahni, a professional and practical Psychologist, Professor and Principal Director, Jindal Institute of Behavioural Sciences, Jindal Global University, has made this publication highly readable and most relevant for students and teachers of criminology and victimology.

Civil societies have always strived to discover the causes and cures for the crime with a view to preventing victimization. The sufferings of the victim at the time of crime and also later are vital aspects bringing about double jeopardy. The chapter 'From the frying pan into the fire', portrays how the gullibility and vulnerability of hapless and helpless children is exploited. The chapter on 'Financial Criminology' explores a new dimension of Criminology expressing crime and criminal behavior under the realm of economic and financial offences. Cyber-crimes and repercussions arising from unfettered and unchecked use of the social media discuss 'victim precipitation' and suggest useful tools that can be adopted to protect individuals and institutions.

The book contains deeply researched articles, original thoughts and new ideas of the authors on subjects arranging from principles of victimology to fresher's victimization in educational institutions, money laundering, terrorism, and latest UN Conventions. The need to have speedy and effective criminal justice administration has been repeatedly emphasized. It is heartening to observe, that the contributions of these experts, will add great value to knowledge and literature on the subject. In addition, this publication will throw up materials and avenues for further research. A resourceful teacher can develop his teaching methodology based on trends perceived in various countries and the situations prevalent in his geographic jurisdiction.

It is a matter of honor for all of us, that this book is proposed to be released at the Fourteenth United Nations Congress on Crime Prevention and Criminal Justice at Kyoto (Japan) in 2020.

Dr. Ashwani Kumar, Indian Police Service (Retd)
PH.D.; MBA; PGDM (HR& Defence Studies)
Former Governor of the States of Nagaland & Manipur
Former Director, Central Bureau of Investigation, Government of India
Former Director-General of Police, Himachal Pradesh, Shimla

Acknowledgements

This book is an edited volume as a Festschrift for Professor Dr. K. Chockalingam towards his 50 years of teaching in the field of Victimology and is the result of substantial contribution and extensive efforts by the academicians, experts, and professionals who have authored the eighteen chapters of this book. All the chapters present topics related to the field of Victimology and Criminology from a global perspective. We would like to express our gratitude to the many people who saw us through this book; who provided support, talked things over, read, wrote, offered comments, and assisted in the editing, proofreading and design.

We as editors of this book and faculty member of O.P. Jindal Global University (JGU) and Manonmanium Sundarnar University (MSU) would like to extend our gratitude to the Jindal Institute of Behavioural Sciences (JIBS), JGU, for extending support in every possible way towards the successful completion of the book. We are immensely grateful to our Vice-Chancellor, Professor C. Rajkumar, for his continued guidance and support to Jindal Institute of Behavioural Sciences, JGU. We would also like to acknowledge our research associate – Vipin Vijay Nair – for providing technical and analytical support in editing the chapters of the book.

We would extend our thanks to all others who have not been mentioned here, but who took the initiative to provide ideas and insights for the book, in the process of shaping it. Last, but definitely not the least, we are indebted to our family members who provided us with the strength and motivation. It was their unconditional love, care and tolerance which made this book writing process smoother.

The book was shorlisted for its launch at the Fourteenth United Nations Congress on Crime Prevention and Criminal Justice at Kyoto, Japan but due to the global pandemic, the Congress is postponed.

Prof. Dr. Beulah Shekhar
Prof. Dr. Sanjeev P. Sahni

The editors are appreciative of extraordinary efforts of **Mr. Vipin Vijay Nair – Faculty of Jindal Institute of Behavioural Sciences**. He relentlessly edited, compiled and methodologically reviewed each chapter of the book. Without his support, this project would not have been completed.

Contributors

Aashish Srivastava (Aashish.Srivastava@monash.edu)

Dr. Aashish Srivastava is a Senior Lecturer in the Department of Business Law and Taxation at Monash University, Melbourne, Australia. He teaches undergraduate and postgraduate students in the area of commercial and marketing law. He completed his PhD in 2009 on 'Acceptance Issues in Electronic Signatures'. He researches and publishes his work regularly across his areas of interest, which include legal issues in e-commerce, bullying and hazing.

Arvind Tiwari (tiwari_a@tiss.edu)

Prof. Arvind Tiwari is well known Criminologist and a scholar in Criminal Justice Administration & Forensic Science, Human Rights, Police Studies & Public Security, Criminal law & Access to Justice, Victimology, Youth Justice and Crime & Development. Presently, he is the Dean, School of Law, Rights and Constitutional Governance since 2015 and Chairperson, Centre for Police Studies and Public Security at TISS. Previously, he served as Dean, Students Affairs, Chairperson, Nodal Centre of Excellence for Human Rights Education (NCHERE) and Coordinator, Centre for Socio-Legal Studies and Human Rights, School of Social Sciences at TISS, Mumbai.

D.K. Srivastava (profdkjgu@gmail.com)

Professor Srivastava has over forty years of academic experience. He started his teaching career at Monash University. He was Head of the Law Department at the University of Papua New Guinea and at City University of Hong Kong. At City University, he also served as the Associate Head of Law and Associate Dean, Faculty of Law. Professor Srivastava was also foundation Pro Vice Chancellor of OP Jindal Global University. Professor Srivastava specialized in torts, contracts, banking law, business and commercial law, Pacific Islands legal system and customary law. Professor Srivastava's works have been cited in judgments and by the Parliament of Australia.

Dick Daniel Taver'shima Andzenge (dtandzenge@stcloudstate.edu)

Dick D.T. Andzenge is a professor of Criminal Justice and Victimology and Director of Justice Research Center at St. Cloud State University. He is also a former Assistant Vice President for Academic Affairs/International Studies and Global Education. Professor Andzenge is a former member of the Executive Committee and Chair of the Scientific Committee of the World Society of Victimology (2003–2006). He is also co-director of the famous Post Graduate Course on Victimology, Victim Services and Criminal Justice and Dobrovnik, Croatia and in South Africa. Andzenge is a perennial resource faculty of the post graduate courses and education on Criminology, Victimology and Justice at Tokiwa University, Japan, O.P. Jindal Global University in India and several other universities in Africa, Asia, Europe and the Middle East.

G.S. Bajpai (gs.bajpai@nludelhi.ac.in)

Prof. G.S. Bajpai serves as Professor of Criminology & Criminal Justice; Chair Professor at K.L. Arora Chair in Criminal Law at National Law University, Delhi and also as the Chairperson at the Centre for Criminology & Victimology. Besides having a masters in Criminoloy & Criminal justice, he holds a doctorate in criminology & victimology and a post-doctorate in criminology as Commonwealth Fellow at the Department of Criminology, Leicester University, U.K. He is also the Registrar, National Law University, Delhi. Before this, he was serving (2007–2011) as Professor (Law & Development) & Chairperson at the Centre for Criminal Justice Administration, National Law Institute University, Bhopal (MP). He also had positions at the Indian Institute of Public Administration, (1989) Bureau of Police Research & Development, (1989–1995) Punjab Police Academy, Punjab and Department of Criminology & Forensic Science, University of Saugar, M.P.

Garima Pal (garima.pal@nludelhi.ac.in)

Dr. Garima Pal has been awarded Ph.D. in the field of "Drug Abuse and Alcoholism and role of Re-habilitation centers in Uttarakhand". She specialises in the field of Criminology and Victimology. She was employed as Assistant Professor in Symbiosis Law School, Pune, till July 2018. She is also associated with an NGO, Care Village Foundation, New Delhi as the Executive Director. She has also qualified UGC-NET for Lectureship in the year 2011. Prior to joining Symbiosis Law School, Pune, she taught UG/ PG students of Law at TMU University, Muradabad. She has previously worked as a Research Associate with Institute of Social Sciences, Vasant Kunj, New Delhi in research project sponsored by TATA.

Irvin Waller (Irvin.waller@uottawa.ca)

Irvin Waller is an internationally recognised expert on crime prevention and victim rights. He was a director general in the Solicitor General of Canada (now Public Safety Canada) in 1970's working on abolition of the death penalty, gun control, victim rights and crime prevention. His trail blazing work to get the UN General Assembly to recognize rights for victims in 1985 earned him multiple awards internationally and shaped 30 years working to persuade governments to end violence in crime ridden cities and provide rights for victims. He was the founding executive director of the International Centre for Prevention of Crime, affiliated with the UN. He has headed the World Society of Victimology and the International Organization for Victim Assistance, both in consultative status with ECOSOC. He is a member of the WHO Violence Prevention Alliance and participates in UNODC and Habitat meetings on violence prevention.

John Dussich (jdussich@csufresno.edu)

John Dussich has degrees in Clinical Psychology (BS), Corrections/ Criminology (MS), and Criminology/Sociology (Ph. D.) from Florida State University. He is the creator/founder of the National Organization for Victim Assistance (NOVA), which he launched in Fresno in 1976 serving as Executive Director for four years. He served in the World Society of Victimology (WSV) as founding Secretary General for three 3-year term; and as past President (2006-09). He taught 20 years in Japan (1993–2013) and was creator/director of the Tokiwa International Victimology Institute (TIVI) and editor-in-chief of its journal: International Perspectives in Victimology. He created the Mito Victim Support Center in Japan (now Ibaraki Victim Support Center) November 1994. He is Criminology Professor Emeritus from California State University, Fresno. He is an international volunteer disaster responder. He has published 16 books, 106 articles and made 204 presentations (mostly on victim support and victimology). His most recent international work was as chair of the WSV's United Nations Liaison Committee for victims' rights. On April 12th, 2016, he received the Ronald Reagan Public Policy Award from the US Attorney General.

K. Jaishankar (profjai16@gmail.com)

Karuppannan Jaishankar is an Independent Indian criminologist. He was earlier the Professor and Head of the Department of Criminology at the Raksha Shakti University (First Internal Security and Police University of India) Ahmedabad, Gujarat, India. Earlier, he was a faculty member at the Department of Criminology and Criminal Justice, Manonmaniam Sundaranar University, Tirunelveli. He is the editor in chief of International Journal of Cyber Criminology and the founding father of Cyber Criminology, an academic sub-discipline of Criminology. He is the founder president of the South Asian Society of Criminology and Victimology (SASCV), which works with motto to develop Criminology and Victimology in the South Asian region. He was a Commonwealth Academic Fellow during 2009-10 at the Centre for Criminal Justice Studies, School of Law, University of Leeds.

Marc Groenhuijsen (M.S. Groenhuijsen@uvt.nl)

Prof. Marc Groenhuijsen has been full professor of criminal law, criminal procedure and victimology at Tilburg University in The Netherlands since 1987. In 2005 he became the founding director of INTERVICT, the International Victimology Institute Tilburg, which developed into the largest dedicated research centre on victimology in the world. He is a member of the Board of Directors of the International Society for Criminology. From 1991 until 2004 he was President of the European Forum for Victim Services, later renamed into Victim Support Europe. From 2009 to 2018 he served as President of the World Society of Victimology. He also is a part-time judge in the Court of Appeals in Arnhem. Dr Groenhuijsen is a member of the Royal Netherlands Academy of Arts and Sciences. He was also elected as member of the Royal Holland Society of Sciences and Arts.

Michael O' Connell (Michael.OConnell@sa.gov.au)

Michael O' Connell AM APM MPubPol (with Distinction) BSocSc FGLF served as the inaugural Commissioner for Victims' Rights, South Australia (2006-2018). Prior, he served as that state's first Victims of Crime Co-ordinator and while employed as a police officer he was appointed the first Victim Impact Statement Co-ordinator. He is the Victim Advocate for Second Chances SA; a Member of the International Network of Services for Victims of Terrorism; and, a Foundation Board Member of Victim Support Asia. Further, Michael is a life member, current Secretary-General and chair UN Liaison Committee for the World Society of Victimology (WSV); and, a Vice President for the NGO Alliance on Crime Prevention and Criminal Justice, which is affiliated with the UN. In 1995 he was awarded the Australia Police Medal (APM) for his work to advance responses to the needs of victims of crime. In 2010 he received 'Victim Support Australasia' national award for advancing Victimology and promoting victims' rights; and, in 2017 he became a Member of the Order of Australia (AM). In 2018, the WSV presented Michael with an Irene Melup Certificate of Appreciation.

Miguel Abel Souto (Miguel.abel@usc.es)

Miguel Abel Souto is Professor of Criminal Law, University of Santiago de Compostela, Spain, President of the Ibero-American Association of Economic and Business Criminal Law, and Director of the Revista Cuatrimestral Europea sobre Prevención y Represión del Blanqueo de Dinero (European Quarterly Review for Prevention and Repression of Money Laundering).

Neerav Srivastava (nsneerav@gmail.com)

Neerav Srivastava recently completed his LLM at the University of Melbourne. He has previously obtained a B.Com., LLB and PCLL. He has published articles in distinguished journals including Oxford University Commonwealth Law Journal. Neerav's main interest is the intersection between law, technology and digital platforms. He has authored several book chapters in legal practitioners' texts and has been cited in judgments. Neerav previously occupied a senior position with a major legal publishing company.

P.M. Nair (nairpm@hotmail.com)

Dr. P. M. Nair served IPS for 35 years and retired as DGP of NDRF, Govt of India. He served Bihar Government, CBI, NHRC, CRPF, UNODC, NDRF and has the unique distinction of having worked with NGO, even while in government service. He was with the Institute of Social Sciences, on deputation, doing the National Action Research on Trafficking in Women and Children in India, a study for the NHRC, and the first of its kind in India. Dr. Nair is an acclaimed international expert on human trafficking. He has authored 17 books and several articles on professional subjects in law enforcement and justice delivery. He has received President's Medal for Meritorious Services as well as President's Medal for Distinguished services. He has undertaken research on trafficking issues for the UN, ADB, World Bank etc. Having set up the first nine AHTUs (anti Human Trafficking Units) in India, he is considered the father of this movement. He is the author of AHTC (Anti Human Trafficking Clubs in Colleges) in India, where he has mobilized the youth of the country against human slavery.

With MA in Sociology, LLB and PhD in victimology, he is also a graduate of prestigious academies like the FBI National Academy, Virginia, USA and the National Defence College, New Delhi as well as the Universities of Virginia, Delhi, Meerut and Kerala.

Rouguiatou Balde (rouguiatou.balde@umontreal.ca)

Rouguiatou BALDE is a PhD candidate in criminology at the Universté de Montréal, under the supervision of Dr. Jo-Anne Wemmers. Her thesis focuses on justice and reconciliation from the victims' perspective in the Republic of Guinea. Her research focuses on victimology, transitional justice, and international criminal justice. She also holds a master's degree in criminal justice, a master's degree in economics and a master's degree in chemistry.

Sam Garkawe (Sam.garkawe@scu.edu.au)

Sam Garkawe is an Associate Professor at the School of Law and Justice at Southern Cross University, NSW. Sam completed his Law Degree at Monash University, Melbourne, and is a Barrister and Solicitor of the Supreme Court of Victoria. He has been employed in a number of legal environments, including private practice, legal aid, as a research solicitor for the Victorian parliament, and has been an academic since 1991. He further holds Masters of Law degrees from both London University and Sydney University, and is also admitted as an Attorney-at-Law in California. Sam has taught International Criminal Law/Justice in a number of places around the world - Monash University (Melbourne); Hamline University School of Law, Minneapolis (Minnesota, USA); Tel Aviv (Israel); Whittier School of Law and Chapman University School of Law, (California, USA); and Murdoch University (Perth). In 2009 Sam was elected to the Executive Committee of the World Society of Victimology and has been an active member of their UN Liaison Committee since 2003. He has published widely in the field of victimology, particularly with respect to the role of victims in international criminal justice mechanisms, such as the International Criminal Court and the South African Truth and Reconciliation Commission.

Stacie A. Jergenson (Stacie.Jergenson@bemidjistate.edu)

Dr. Stacie A. Jergenson is an Assistant Professor at Bemidji State University, Minnesota, USA, with primary teaching responsibilities in Victimological Theory & Practice, Forensic Victimology, Global Perspectives in Victimology, Restorative Justice, and Directed Group Study (capstone projects).

Within a Criminal Justice B.S. program, she has created and delivered a new multidisciplinary Victimology Emphasis. Research topics include victim services, restorative justice practices, applied victimology, sex trafficking, prostitution, murdered and missing indigenous women, epidemiological criminology, homicides, and GIS analyses. She serves on an anti-sex trafficking task force, striving to build connections with three local American Indian reservations. Previous employment includes 15 years within a state judicial branch. She regularly travels and lectures internationally.

Van Dijk (Jan.vanDijk@uvt.nl)

Van Dijk is a former professor of criminology of Leiden University and emeritus professor of victimology and human security of the University of Tilburg, The Netherlands. Van Dijk was the co-founder and first chairperson of the National Organization of Victim Assistance in The Netherlands (1984–1989) and President of the World Society of Victimology (1997–2000). He authored over 200 articles on crime and criminal justice in academic journals. In 2011 he edited, together with Rianne Letschert, The New Faces of Victimhood; globalization, transnational crimes and victim rights, published in the Global Justice Series of Springer Press (2011). In 2012 he edited with A. Tseloni and G. Farrell The International Drop in Crime (Palgrave / Mac Millan, 2012). In 2012 he was awarded the Stockholm Prize in Criminology for his continued leadership of the International Crime Victims Survey. In 2014 the Ministry of Security and Justice of the Netherlands and the Dutch Fund for Victim Support jointly established the Jan van Dijk Award for the best master and PhD theses on victimology and victims' rights from students of Dutch Universities.

Vipin Vijay Nair (vvnair@jgu.edu.in)

Vipin Vijay Nair is a Lecturer and an In-Service Doctoral Scholar under the supervision of Professor Dr. Sanjeev P. Sahni at Jindal Institute of Behavioural Sciences, O.P. Jindal Global University. He received his Master's in Criminology from LNJN National Institute of Criminology and Forensic Sciences, GGSIPU, where he was awarded University Silver medal for his academic and research vigour. He has qualified UGC-NET lectureship (Criminology) in 2016 and was invited as a resource person at two-day National workshop on 'Career Advancement in Criminology'. He has presented papers in international conferences and has publications in the field of victimology, Criminology and Criminal Justice.

Wemmers Jo Anne (jo-anne.m.wemmers@umontreal.ca)

Jo-Anne WEMMERS (PhD) is currently a full Professor at the School of Criminology of the Université de Montréal, principal researcher at the International Centre for Comparative Criminology, and a member of the Canadian Partnership on International Justice. Former Secretary General of the World Society of Victimology (2006–2009), Professor Wemmers has published widely in the areas of victimology, international criminal justice, and restorative justice. Her books include Victimology: A Canadian Perspective, (University of Toronto Press 2017), which has been translated into French (Les Presses de l'Université de Québec, 2017).

Xin Ren (renx@saclink.csus.edu)

Xin Ren, Ph. D. is a Professor of Criminal Justice at the California State University, Sacramento since 1990. She graduated from the University of Pennsylvania with a doctoral degree from Wharton School in legal studies (criminology and criminal law). She was also an adjunct professor of the L.L.D. Program at the Institute of International Studies, Ramkhanhaeng University in Bangkok, Thailand between 2007 and 2014. As a life member of the World Society of Victimology (WSV), Dr. Ren served on the Executive Committee of WSV for six years (2006-2012). Recently, she was involved in the Organizing Committee to launch the Victim Support Asia and was subsequently elected to the Executive Board of VSA in 2019. In addition to teaching and advocating for victims' rights and support, she also worked with the UNICEF and the US Department of State on several human trafficking related projects.

Yoshiko Takahashi (ytakahashi@csufresno.edu)

Dr. Yoshiko Takahashi was appointed interim associate dean of the College of Social Sciences at California State University, Fresno in August 2019. Dr. Takahashi holds an M.S. in Criminal Justice and a Ph.D. in Public Policy from the University of North Carolina at Charlotte. Prior to joining the Dean's Office, she taught a variety of courses at Fresno State including victimology, family violence, juvenile delinquency, statistics, and research methods as faculty of the Department of Criminology. Her recent publications include a book with colleague Dr. Chadley James titled Victimology and Victim Assistance: Advocacy, Intervention, and Restoration. Dr. Takahashi is an elected Executive Committee member of the World Society of Victimology (WSV) and currently serves as the vice president of the WSV.

Contents

Chapter I

The Ascent and Decline of the Idea of Prioritizing a General UN Convention on Victims' Rights: A Case Study

MARC GROENHUIJSEN

Introduction

It is a pleasure and a privilege to write a contribution in a Festschrift in honor of professor doctor K. Chockalingam. The two of us have met in person some thirty years ago. I was instantly impressed by his professional standing in victimology, coupled with his personal charm. We saw each other at regular intervals during international conferences. For many years, he served with distinction in the Executive Committee of the World Society of Victimology while I was a member at the same time. As a consequence of these frequent face to face encounters, he offered me quite a few opportunities to visit him at his home ground at the University of Madras in Chennai. There, in Chennai, I saw first hand how much he meant for Indian criminology and victimology. Even back then, he was revered as the Head of the Department of Criminology since 1983. As the first Madras doctoral degree holder in the discipline of criminology, he exercised great authority among his staff and his peers. I found it hard to belief how someone who is celebrated because of his multiple accomplishments in his own country – and in international publications – could remain such a warm and modest person when he was in touch with colleagues abroad. He even extended his hospitality and his generosity by inviting me to give the prestigious annual V.R. Krishna Iyer Lecture in the year 2000 (an honor which was incidentally replicated by his successor in Chennai, Prof. Srinivasan, in 2018).

Everybody knows that Chockalingam was the founder of the Indian Society of Victimology. Interestingly, I found a small book, edited by Chockalingam in 1985. It includes a 'Foreword' written by the famous Indian judge, scholar and national hero Krishna Iyer whom I just mentioned. The text opens with the statement: 'Criminology is a Cinderella among social sciences and Victimology is a Cinderella of Criminology'. Whereas that allegation definitely had some merit when it was published in 1985, I seriously doubt whether the same observation could be credibly made today. Because of a lifetime of tireless efforts made by people like Chockalingam, I am convinced that victimology by now has emancipated as a fully accepted mature academic discipline in its own right.

Chockalingam has always had a keen interest in the activities of the United Nations on behalf of victims. He participated in the UN Inter-Regional Meeting of Eminent Persons hosted by the Indian Ministry of Social Welfare at New Delhi in 1985, which was preparatory to the Seventh United Nations Crime Congress held in Milan in Italy. He also took part in the Milan Congress later that same year. Which brings me to the topic of this contribution. The Crime Congress in Milan turned out to be the proverbial labour room for the 1985 United Nations Declaration of Basic Principles of Justice for Victims of Crime and Abuse of Power, unanimously adopted by the General Assembly only a couple of months later (GA Res. 40/34 of 29 November 1985). It was a fine document, significantly influential, and it rather quickly attracted the nickname 'Magna Charta of victims' rights'. However, one problem remained. The provisions contained in the Declaration were not properly implemented, no matter how hard the UN tried to improve the situation. Despite monitoring progress by sending out questionnaires, despite publishing a 'Manual on the use and application of the Declaration' as well as a 'Guide for policymakers' (1997), the state of affairs in many, many countries – the poor ones as well as the more affluent ones – remained unsatisfactory. Put shortly, in many regions there was no powerful steering group composed by relevant stakeholders, the attitude of responsible officials was not always conducive to reform, knowledge on victims' issues could not be sufficiently disseminated by adequate training programs, and quite often not enough resources were provided to allow authorities to assume additional responsibilities (Groenhuijsen 1999).

A New Idea: a United Nations Convention

Against this background some members of the World Society of Victimology (WSV) and the senior researchers from INTERVICT (the International Victimology Institute Tilburg) came up with the idea of adopting a novel approach. Instead of continuing to focus on making the UN Declaration work better, we felt that perhaps it could be more productive to aim for a stronger legal instrument on the UN level. Hence the option of a UN Convention became the new focus, even as a priority in our field of work.

At the time, there was a whole series of arguments supporting this new course of action. Garkawe (2005) summarized them as follows:

- A Convention would increase the visibility of victims' issues
- A Convention is a 'hard-law-instrument' (i.e. is binding on the State parties). As such, it might be taken more seriously by Governments and Courts than the Declaration, which is a soft-law-instrument
- A Convention would provide a new framework for analyses of any progress made: to evaluate developments (it has the function of a new benchmark)
- The ratification process, which is essential after adopting a Convention, may motivate States to question why they would not support new victims' rights
- Now that the UN had adopted quite a few other Conventions in the area of criminal law, the status of a 'mere' Declaration had been reduced.

On the other hand, there was also an awareness of some considerations pointing in a different direction. Two of these could be framed as arguments against the pursuit of a new UN Convention (Van Genugtencum suis 2006).

- The process of getting a UN Convention adopted (if and when successful at all) would take a long time. It is obvious that in the mean time, nothing serious would be done in order to improve the effectiveness of the Declaration
- In order to attain widespread support for a Convention, the risk had to be faced of completely watered down provisions. If that were to occur, than the benefits might be outweighed by the losses.

The Content of the Draft Convention

The only way to realistically assess the relative power of these arguments is to have a Draft in front of you and compare it with the content of the existing Declaration.

So the next step was that representatives of the WSV and INTERVICT met in December 2005, in Tilburg, The Netherlands, in order to produce the first version of the Draft UN Convention on Justice and Support for Victims of Crime and Abuse of Power. That happened according to plan. Subsequently, the resulting text was translated into various languages and posted on the Internet. We solicited critical comments in order to improve the operative provisions and to develop strategies for the adoption of the Convention. Some time after the Tilburg meeting, John Dussich and his colleagues joined our efforts. Dussich, Director of the Tokiwa International Victimology Institute in Japan and working there in collaboration with Chockalingam (and other accomplished victimologists like Gerd Ferdinand Kirchhoff), generated important new momentum for the project. In 2008, he organized a two-day Symposium at TIVI in which both content and strategy were exhaustively discussed by experts from the field (Dussich & Mundy 2008).

Turning to substance, seven major differences can be identified between the final wording of the Draft Convention and the 1985 Declaration.

The first one of these follows from the empirical finding that not all victims are the same. Since 1985, we had discovered that they differ substantially in needs and interests. This insight emanated from the more general concept of 'differential victimology'. Accordingly the Draft stipulated the non-discrimination clause (victims cannot be discriminated against on the basis of age, gender, sexual orientation, etc.), but added the vitally important disclaimer: '…without prejudice to provide special justice and support best-suited to victims who are particularly vulnerable because of age, gender, disability or other characteristics.' This reference to 'particularly vulnerable victims' was, like several other provisions, inspired by the 2006 Council of Europe's Recommendation Rec(2006)8 on Assistance to Crime Victims. Special vulnerabilities can be rooted in the nature of the crime, the circumstances in which the crime was committed, or personal characteristics of the victim (previous contacts with the criminal justice system included).

Secondly, the Declaration was completely silent on any kind of crime prevention. It is debatable whether crime prevention as such deserves attention in a protocol on victims' rights, since prevention is relevant for all citizens, whether or not they have been victimized. However, one thing is undisputable, and that is the special need to prevent repeat victimization. This concept, which was hardly known in 1985, turned out to be of paramount importance for crime victims. The numbers are staggering and apply to virtually all categories of crime (Farrel & Pease 2001). Consequently, the phenomenon was extensively addressed in the latest Draft in art. 8 section 6, subsection A under e ('protection from repeat victimization should be provided through the development of safety and security plans. This may include information on police surveillance, relocation, emergency communication and the like. It may also involve assistance with obtaining protection orders through the judicial system').

A third major deviation from the Declaration is that the Draft Convention provides for a right to appeal a decision by the prosecutor not to prosecute the case. Protection against inactivity by the government has long been sought in the instrument of 'private prosecution', allowing the victim to initiate criminal proceedings. However, experience has proved beyond any doubt that this just does not work. On the contrary, it exposes the victims to threats, to intimidation and to retaliation by the offender. And when private prosecution does not lead to conviction – which occurs frequently – the victim is usually financially liable for all sorts of costs. For these reasons, appealing to a higher authority is a superior mechanism of seeking redress for prosecutorial inactivity or mistakes.

The next improvement compared to the Declaration concerns enforcement of a judicial order and the decree granting financial awards to the victim. So whenever there is a court ordering the offender to pay restitution, the execution of such orders cannot be left to the beneficiary, but should be considered as an obligation of the government. It is impossible to overstate the relevance of this reallocation of responsibilities. When the victim is left on his own to collect court ordered damages, the likelihood of ever receiving any money is close to zero. Alternatively, when the State is charged with this duty, empirical evidence shows that the success rate will go up to over 80% (Brienen & Hoegen 2000).

Fifth, the informational rights for victims provided for in the Declaration were limited when regarded from a contemporary point of view. The basics were already there: victims were to be informed about their role and scope, the timing and progress of the (criminal proceedings and of the disposition of their cases, especially when serious crimes were involved and where victims have requested such information. Nowadays, higher standards apply, as is evidenced by several international protocols which have been adopted some decades after the 1985 Declaration. They all refer to a right to be informed about victim assistance, protection, how to report a crime, how to get legal advise, entitlements to compensation, and – very importantly – the right to know about the release of the offender from incarceration (including suspension of pre-trial custody). Another novelty in this area is the 'opt-out procedure', allowing victims to express their preference not to receive any information at all. The Draft Convention includes these state-of-the-art provisions.

The sixth main difference between the Declaration and the Draft Convention is the way these documents approach restorative justice. In the Declaration, the concept as such is absent. It speaks of 'informal mechanisms for the resolution of disputes, including mediation, arbitration and customary justice or indigenous practices', and it recommends these means 'where appropriate to facilitate conciliation and redress for victims'. In itself there is nothing wrong with this wording. However, since 1985 the awareness among victimologists has become more acute that restorative justice can be beneficial for crime victims, but – in the absence of adequate protective safeguards – it can also be highly disadvantageous or even dangerous for them. This sensitivity is reflected in the precise words used in the Draft Convention. It reads as follows: "States Parties shall endeavor where appropriate to establish or enhance systems of restorative justice that seek to represent victims' interests as a priority. (...) States Parties shall have the opportunity to choose or not to choose restorative justice forums under domestic laws, and if they do decide to choose such forums, these mechanisms must accord with victims' dignity, compassion and similar rights and services to those described in this Convention".

Finally, as is inherent in the legal nature of the two instruments, the Draft Convention provides for an elaborate enforcement and monitoring mechanism whereas the Declaration is completely devoid of any such construction. The main monitoring body suggested by the Draft Convention is a Committee on Justice and Support for Victims of Crime and Abuse of Power. Even though this Committee is modelled after some other UN Conventions, I am afraid this part of the Draft might be the least convincing and may give rise to objections by many States. Without going into detail, the costs of running the proposed Committee are probably prohibitive by themselves. On top of that, the far reaching powers of the Committee to investigate actual compliance with the Convention, including the power to conduct on-site visits, can not be expected to be acceptable for the large majority of Member States of the United Nations.

In conclusion, I can only state the obvious. Which is that the Draft Convention offers much better standing and protection for victims of crime and abuse of power than the level that was provided for since 1985 by the Declaration. The Draft Convention has cutting edge victims' rights which are evidence based. In preparing the draft, careful notice was made not to design a framework which can only attained by the very affluent countries, thus scaring off the lesser privileged nations. We included representatives of the group of poorest Member States and followed their wisdom whenever they assured us that some desirable reforms are just unaffordable.

All of which leads to some simple questions. Is it going to happen? Is the UN willing and able to adopt this Draft Convention? Or is it at least prepared to start further negotiations on the exact wording of any such document?

The Next Steps. Are There Any Realistic Prospects for Getting a UN Convention on Victims' Rights Adopted?

Some ten years ago my answer to these questions was: I just do not know (Groenhuijsen 2008). Today, I am more confident in making predictions. No, it is not going to happen. No, the UN is neither willing nor able to adopt this Draft Convention. The UN – as an international lawmaking entity – is not even prepared to discuss the exact content of a general Convention on victims' rights. I will try to explain what leads me to these sobering exclamations.

In order to understand the way the United Nations have worked during the past decade, we need to get back to the times directly following the publication of the Draft Convention.

There are two recurrent events where the United Nations deliberates policy in the area of administering criminal justice. One is the annual meeting of the UN Commission on Crime Prevention and Criminal Justice (hereafter: 'the Crime Commission'), in Vienna. The other is the UN Congress on Crime Prevention and Criminal Justice (hereafter: 'the Crime Congress'), held every 5th year in a different host country. It is only logical that the WSV primarily targeted these occasions to promote the idea of having a UN Convention on victims' rights. That was endeavoured right from the moment the first draft was finished at the end of 2005.

Initially it looked as if we were making some progress. With hindsight, I refer to this period of time as the era of the ascent of our aspirations, even though we only accomplished small steps at a time. At the 15th Session of the Crime Commission, in April 2006, we managed to get an important point included in the conclusions. It called for the Secretary-General to convene an Intergovernmental Expert Group Meeting (IEGM), mandated, amongst others, to study the ways and means of promoting the use and application of victims' rights. Obviously, this part of the remit included exploring the potentials of a UN Convention. Subsequently, later that same year, the first meeting of the IEGM was convened. Apart from agreeing on a questionnaire, the meeting included – following an initiative led by WSV representatives – three significant principles in its conclusions:

- Reference to a Draft Convention as a possible next step in the promotion of victims' rights.
- The idea of introducing voluntary peer review, meaning a process in which some countries volunteer to make an assessment of each other's performance with regard to respecting victims' rights (large countries like the USA and Japan were the first actual volunteers). This approach was meant to overcome resistance against the heavy-set monitoring procedure as described above in connection with the 'Committee on Justice and Support for Victims of Crime and Abuse of Power'.
- Motivating governments to seek the assistance of NGO's in completing the questionnaire. This was intended to improve the reliability of the ensuing information.

These conclusions were obviously encouraging. However, the follow up given to this meeting in 2007 was disappointing. The WSV set three goals when attending the 16th Session of the Crime Commission: (a) attaining higher priority for victims' rights at the level of UNOCD; (b) explore interest of national governments in supporting a Convention; and (c) ensure follow up on the IEGM recommendations. It turned out that the gathering exuded both 'questionnaire fatigue' as well as 'Convention fatigue'. The questionnaire was amended and adopted with little enthusiasm. However, the idea of a Convention was not supported. It was neither embraced by the UNOCD, nor by any country being willing to lead the way in getting the project through all the relevant channels.

In 2008, the WSV participated in the next Session of the Crime Commission (the 17th) with the same agenda as the previous year. More specifically, it aimed at targeting as many academics, civil servants and country delegations as possible to win them over. And it was agreed to focus on the next Crime Congress, to be held in Salvador, Brazil, in 2010. We wanted to have a reference to victims' issues included in the title of the Congress (Congress theme); and we aspired to have two workshops in the official program (out of a total of five or six) dedicated to victims' rights and interests. These goals were by no way modest. With hindsight, it has to be admitted they were sky high to the point of being unrealistic.

So, 2010 came and went without achieving any of these objectives. We did not even come close. Irvin Waller painted a dark – but not entirely incorrect – picture when he labeled the UN Crime Congress in April as "a throwback to the 1970's. No mention of victims in the program" (Waller 2009). What went wrong? Did we make serious mistakes? Had we been naïve about our own influence on such large machinery as the United Nations? After careful evaluation of our own performance, the WSV decided to expand the horizon of activities in this field. Even though the UNODC remained the focal point of entry, we would seek new alignments with the UN Human Rights Agencies based in Geneva. And apart from contacts with the Member States of the UN, we would explore ways to attract support from international entities such as the European Union (which had passed supra-national legislation on victims' rights during the years before); and with the South African Victim Empowerment Movement; and the assembly of poorest Member States within the UN. When it comes to the complexities of the UN as an organization, it was agreed that we needed solid advise from UN veterans and celebrities such as Eduardo Vetere, Irene Melup, Yael Danielli and Matti Joutsen, to name but a few. Obviously for Brazil we had been too late to have a fair chance to get our priorities included in the agenda of the Congress. Trying to avoid the same mishap occurring twice in a row, in 2010 we decided to immediately commence our efforts to timely influence the agenda for the next Crime Congress, to be held in 2015 in Doha, Qatar.

And, from that day on, the WSV adopted a different tone when advocating the substance of the Draft Convention. Subtly at first, more articulate as the years progressed. It became visible, for instance, during the 21st Crime Commission Session in 2012, when the Chairman of our UN Liaison Committee, John Dussich, approached the Draft Convention in a more contextualized way than we had done during the preceding years. He said: 'The World Society of Victimology accepts the informal role of "Guardian" for these two instruments (he referred to the 1985 Declaration and the 2005 UN Van Boven/Bassiouni principles) by continuing to remind the community of States about their existence and meaning; by offering to assist in their implementation; and, by promoting a stronger proposal than the Declaration based on the same principles in the form of a draft Convention on Justice and Support for Victims of Crime and Abuse of Power.'

The WSV delegation attending the 22nd Session of the Crime Commission in 2013 operated on the basis of a strategy which can be summarized as follows: to continue to mention our Draft Convention as an important resource document – but not to push for its adoption at this time, to be in active support of all appropriate instruments that mention victims, to offer partnership and support wherever possible with those States and NGO's which are trying to improve the status of various types of victims, and finally, to maintain a high presence for all members of the delegation being as active as possible in as wide a range of relevant events as possible. In my modest opinion this clearly marks the moment when the WSV had decided no longer to prioritize the adoption of the Draft Convention either as an end in itself or as a condition sine qua non for fulfilling its statutory objectives in the best way possible. This strategy of diversification immediately paid off. The WSV delegation met with the UNODC officer who was in charge of a project aimed at writing a new edition of the 1997 Manual on the Use and Application of the UN Declaration. This second edition was to become the new Handbook on, simply put, the effective implementation of the Declaration. Since the first draft of this updated and improved Handbook, which had been commissioned to a single victimologist with a background in victim assistance programs, turned out not to be satisfactory, two members from our WSV delegation were invited to take on editorial responsibilities. This recognition of the expertise within the WSV turned out to be mutually advantageous. Our members have been prominently involved in the extended drafting process, which continues to this day. It is expected that the new Handbook will be formally presented in 2020.

During the 22nd Session of the Crime Commission it further became clear that neither the overall theme, nor the agenda items or the topics for the workshops in the next Crime Congress in Qatar would have any direct reference to the position of victims (decided by General Assembly resolution 67/184 – adopted no less than three full years before the Congress took place). This did not deter the WSV from careful planning for the event, since several of the agenda items were widely enough worded to allow for significant input from the victims' perspective. Consequently, we defined our primary objective as to maximize the impact of the WSV resources to support all Congress instruments that relate to victims using the WSV UN Draft Convention as a primary resource. Secondly, we resolved to establish collaborative agreements with all States and NGO's that also support victim issues; and we planned to host and participate in all ancillary meetings where the interests of victims would be discussed.

And it so happened. One of the 'high level special events' was organized by the WSV in conjunction with Intervict and IOVA (the International Organization for Victim Assistance) in which we celebrated the 30th anniversary of the 1985 UN Declaration. During the session, the Draft Convention was not mentioned. Generally speaking, during the entire Congress the topic of crime victims was hardly addressed at all by the country delegations. As it has become customary during the past number of years, some attention was paid to trafficking persons, to the hardship endured by migrants, and to victims of some emerging crimes (cybercrime being the obvious example) (Groenhuijsen 2019). For the record, I have to report that John Dussich made an impressive speech at an ancillary meeting in which he explained the history and the still existing urgency of having our Draft Convention adopted (Dussich 2015). Likewise, Michael O'Connell, the then Vice President of the WSV, also strongly advocated this approach (O'Connell 2015). He convincingly argued that less than one out of ten victims of serious crimes who reported the crime to the police (which, as we all know, is only a quarter of all actual victims) received specialized help. Furthermore, he added, about four in ten of those who did not, expressed a need for support. Thus, he concluded, ex post facto the Declaration, the rhetoric cloaks the truth for many victims.

Concluding Remarks

In a way, the preceding sections represent the story of a remarkable journey. They recount the recent history of some academic victimologists who were also involved in victim advocacy. Colleagues who have advanced empirical research on crime victims and have contributed to theory formation in our field. On top of that, they contributed to policy making and to the drafting of supranational standards on victims' rights. Professor Chockalingam has been one of them. He has devoted his professional life to improve the position of crime victims. It was his generation of academics that has decisively influenced the adoption of the 1985 UN Declaration of Basic Principles of Justice for Victims of Crime and Abuse of Power. In those days, moral entrepreneurship could prevail in a community like the United Nations. I am afraid the world has changed since that time. Today, the UN has become more politicized. Good ideas no longer suffice. Humanitarianism has lost its natural foundation for marking the course to follow. Instead, power, blunt political force, has become the dominant moving factor. Such is the new habitat, the reality we have to deal with. It is easy to diagnose the current situation as a problem. However, that would not help any victim to improve their prospects. In line with contemporary vocabulary, it is more useful to describe the state of affairs as a challenge. Professionals of my age, as well as the next generations of victimologists, will have to deal with a much more complex geopolitical landscape. It will no longer be possible to get an international legally binding instrument adopted within a limited period of time. However, that should not deter us from setting goals, from pointing to dots on the horizon of our ideals. The one sustainable objective shared by all victimologists is to reduce avoidable misery for as many people as possible. Chockalingam has been an example in this respect which all of us have to try to emulate. In doing so, we will be worthy to protect his intellectual heritage.

References

Brienen, M.E.I. & Hoegen, E.H. 2000, Victims of Crime in 22 European Criminal Justice Systems. The Implementation of Recommendation R(85)11 of the Council of Europe on the Position of the Victim in the Framework of Criminal Law and Procedure, Nijmegen: Wolf Legal Publishers.

Chockalingam, K. (ed.) 1985, Readings in Victimology. Towards a victim perspective in criminology, Madras: Ravi Raj Publications.

Dussich, John P.D. & Mundy, Kieran (eds.) 1985, Raising the Global Standards for Victims: The Proposed Convention on Justice for Victims of Crime and Abuse of Power. *Proceedings of the 4th Symposium of the Tokiwa International Victimology*

Institute, February 15&16, 2008, Mito-shi, Ibaraki-ken: Tokiwa International Victimology Institute.

Dussich, John 2015, Introductory comments – History of the draft Convention and Introduction of the draft UN Resolution for a Convention on Justice and Support for Victims of Crime and Abuse of Power, speech made at the Ancillary Meeting, Session 37, April 15, 2015 at the Twelfth UN Crime Congress in Doha, Qatar.

Farrel, G. & Pease, K. (eds.) 2001, Repeat victimization, New York: Criminal Justice Press.

Garkawe, Sam 2005, 'The Need for a Victims' Convention', *The Victimologist*, p. 4-5.

Groenhuijsen, Marc 1999, Victims' rights in the criminal justice system: A call for more comprehensive implementation theory. In: Van Dijk, J.M., Van Kaam, R., Wemmers, J.A. (eds.), *Caring for Crime Victims: Selected Proceedings of the IXth International Symposium on Victimology*, Monsey, NY: Criminal Justice Press, pp. 85-114.

Groenhuijsen, Marc 2008, 'The Draft UN Convention on Justice and Support for Victims of Crime, with special Reference to its Provisions on Restorative Justice', *Annales Internationales de Criminologie/International Annales of Criminology. Annee 2008* (volume 46-1/2), pp. 121-136.

Groenhuijsen, Marc 2019, 'Recent past and immediate future challenges of victimology in a volatile environment', in: Robert Peacock (ed.), *Victimology in Africa*, third edition, Pretoria: Van Schaik Publishers, pp. 626-669.

O'Connell, Michael 2015, Cloaking the truth – ex post facto the UN Declaration of Basic Principles of Justice for Victims of Crime and Abuse of Power, speech made at the Ancillary Meeting, Session 37, April 15 2015 at the Twelfth UN Crime Congress in Doha, Qatar.

Van Genugten, Willem, Van Gestel, Rob, Groenhuijsen, Marc &Letschert, Rianne 2007, 'Loopholes, risks and ambivalences in international lawmaking: the case of a framework convention on victims' rights', in: *Netherlands Yearbook of International Law*, The Hague: T.M.C. Asser Press, pp. 109-154.

Waller, Irvin 2009, 'Post Graduate Course on Victimology. Inter-University Centre Dubrovnik', *Zvonimir Paul Separovic, 25 Years of Victimology in Dubrovnik*, Zagreb: Croatian Society of Victimology, pp. 29-31.

Chapter II

The International Crime Victims Survey: Update and Outlook

JAN VAN DIJK

Introduction

The ICVS is a standardized survey on the public's experiences with common crime and bribe-seeking by officials. Since its inception in 1987, the ICVS has been carried out in six main sweeps (1988, 1992, 1996, 2000, 2005 and 2010).Results were reported on in numerous reports, books and academic articles. From 2011 onwards, individual, standalone surveys using the ICVS methodology were conducted in, inter alia, Brazil, Georgia, Beijing, the Kyrgyz Republic, Luxembourg, Switzerland, five Caribbean countries and Kazakhstan. Altogether, the ICVS has to date been conducted once or more in over 85 countries, including all member states of the European Union, the USA, Argentina, Australia, Brazil, China (Beijing), India, Japan, South Africa and Russia (Moscow). Over a timespan of thirty years over 350.000 citizens have been interviewed in the course of this study using the same questionnaire (Van Kesteren, Van Dijk & Mayhew, 2013; Van Dijk, 2016).

The survey was conducted in Mumbai, India in 1992 with funding from the United Nations Crime and Criminal Justice Institute/UNICRI (Sing, 1995) and in four cities in Tamil Nadu, India (Madurai, Coimbatore, Trichy and Chennai) in 2002 with national funding. The latter survey was conducted under the energetic and effective leadership of my lifelong professional partner and friend, Prof. Chockalingam. Key results of the latter survey were published in *Forum on Crime and Justice*, a journal of UNODC at the time edited by me (Chockalingam, 2003).

In this paper we will present some updated, internationally comparative findings of the ICVS, and discuss the immediate and long term prospects for future rounds of the survey.

Results of the ICVS up till 2018

In 2010 the ICVS was repeated in Canada and in England/Wales, Denmark, Germany, The Netherlands, Sweden, Switzerland and the

Table 1: Percentages of the Public Victimised by Nine Types of Crime and by Crime Overall

	Year	*Nine Crimes Combined*	*Theft of Car*	*Theft from Car*	*Theft of Motorcycle*	*Theft of Bicycle*	*Burglary*	*Theft of Personal Property*	*Robbery*	*Sexual Offences (Women)*	*Assault and Threat*
One year previence rate		%	%	%	%	%	%	%	%	%	%
Average		15.3	0.7	2.9	0.5	4.4	2.4	4.5	1.5	1.4	3.8
Kzakhstan	2018	11.0	0.2	2.6	0.0	1.0	1.8	3.7	1.0	1.7	3.7
Astana	2018	13.4	0.4	2.7	<	1.2	2.0	4.3	0.7	2.1	4.7
Almaty	2018	17.2	0.3	5.2	0.1	1.9	2.8	5.1	1.7	2.3	5.4
Kyrgyzstan	2015	12.6	0.7	2.3	0.1	0.9	2.9	5.7	1.1	1.1	1.0
Bishkek	2015	22.8	0.8	4.2	0.2	1.7	5.1	11.1	2.0	1.4	1.7
Osh	2015	16.8	0.6	2.2	0.1	1.3	2.8	7.0	1.9	1.2	1.3
China											
Beijing	2014	33.0	0.2	3.5	4.5	22.1	2.2	4.1	2.9	0.8	2.2
Georgia	2012		0.0	<0.9	0.0	<0.2	0.6	0.2	0.2	<	0.3
Canada	2010	13.5	1.3		0.3	2.4	1.0	3.3	1.3	1.2	2.5
Denmark	2010	14.6	0.7	3.0	0.4	6.5	3.3	3.6	0.8	0.4	3.2
Germany	2010	11.0	0.2	1.8	0.1	4.0	1.2	3.3	0.8	1.5	2.8
Netherlands	2010	12.3	0.4	2.8	0.2	6.4	0.7	3.1	1.1	0.8	3.6
Sweden	2010	9.5	0.5	1.3	0.3	5.7	0.9	2.9	0.4	1.5	3.1
Switzerland	2014		<0.4	<1.5	<0.8	<3.2	3.7	4.4	1.0	2.8	4.7
United Kingdom	2010	11.7	0.4	3.2	0.3	2.0	1.5	2.5	0.6	1.2	3.2
Bahamas	2014		3.7				4.0	6.3	3.3		7.4
Barbados	2014		0.4				1.9	2.7	1.1		5.1
Jamaica	2014							8.9	5.2		10.9
Suriname	2014		0.7				4.6	3.5	1.8		5.6
Trinidad & Tobago	2014		1.3				3.3	3.7	1.4		3.9

< We do not have vehicle ownership rates for Switzerland and Georgia, the rates for the whole population are lower than for owners only.
Source: ICVS-based surveys 2010-2018

United Kingdom. Since 2010 ad hoc projects have been carried out outside Europe with support from various donors (in Beijing, Georgia, Kyrgyzstan and Kazakhstan). In the latest versions of the ICVS questionnaire the core items were retained but supplemented with new questions on cybercrime and on attitudes toward the police, modelled after the current victimization survey of England and Wales. In the Caribbean, the surveys, sponsored by the Inter-American Development Bank, used an abridged version of the ICVS questionnaire focussing on violent crime only (Sutton, Van Dijk &Van Kesteren, 2017). Table 1 presents an updated overview of regional results concerning victimization by nine types of common crimes from ICVS-based surveys carried out between 2010 and 2018.

In Table 1, presenting the most recent victimization rates available, Beijing emerges as the country/city with the highest overall rates. This position is largely caused by an extraordinarily high victimization rates for bicycle theft. In other respects, Beijing still qualifies as a relatively safe city. A comparison with the survey of 1992, levels of property crime have gone up, though, together with increased ownership of cars and other consumer goods. While the ICVS has empirically documented significant falls in crime across the Western world between 1995 and 2010 (Van Dijk, 2008), it has captured a rise in property crime in China's capital.

At the bottom of the table stands Georgia with very low rates across the board. In this Caucasian, post-soviet country, the ICVS has been repeated several times since its first conduct in 1992. From the ICVS rounds carried out in 1992, 1996 and 2000 Georgia consistently emerged as a high crime country. Between 2000 and 2010, however, the overall victimization rate suddenly dropped from 20% to 25%. In this country, then, the ICVS surveys have documented an unprecedented fall in levels of crime and corruption in a relatively short time span. This steep downward trend followed concerted and sustained efforts by successive administrations to clamp down on problems of organised crime and corruption (Van Dijk & Chantulia, 2011).

The criminological case history of Georgia reveals that levels of crime can successfully be driven down by massive governmental action. The government's harsh criminal policies were criticized by the media and international organizations. In 2015 the government was voted out of office. The case history of Georgia illustrates how crime control policies, however successful as such, can prove to be unsustainable if human rights standards are not observed.

Burglary levels are relatively high in the Kyrgyz Republic and, within Europe, in Denmark and Switzerland. A possible explanation for these comparative results is that levels of household security are for various reasons relatively underdeveloped in the latter three countries compared to, for example, The Netherlands and the UK (Van Dijk & Vollaard, 2012).

Finally, levels of victimization by violent crime – robbery and assaults/threats –appear to be by far the highest in Caribbean countries, most notably in Jamaica and the Bahamas (Sutton, van Dijk & Van Kesteren, 2017). Typical for Latin American countries is the high proportion of robberies and assaults involving knives or guns. The surveys in the Caribbean have shown that the ICVS methodology can be used to measure the level and nature of very serious crime, besides common crime.

ICVS 1992-2018

Up till now no comprehensive report has been produced on the overall, updated results of the ICVS up to 2018. Figure 2 presents unpublished results from the consolidated ICVS database on last year victimization by assault from all ICVS-based surveys conducted between 1992 and 2017. Presented is, besides the world regional rates, the country rate for India as a token of appreciation for Prof. Chockalingam.

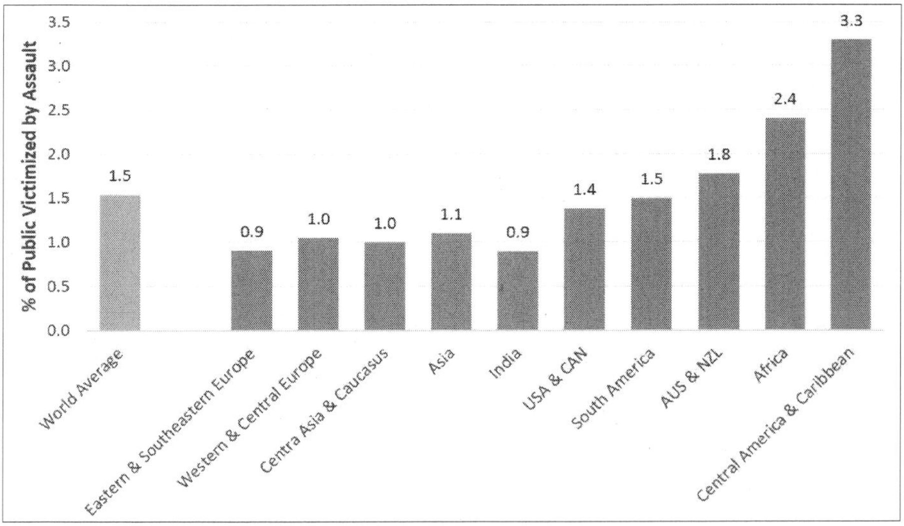

Figure 2: Percentages of the Public Victimized by Assault Last Year, Per World Region and Country (India); ICVS 1992-2018/Latest Results available Per Country (unpublished data)
Source: ICVS database.

The results show that in Europe and Asia victimization rates for assault are 1% or lower. This was also the case in Mumbai in 1992 (included in Figure 2), as well as in Tamil Nadu in 2002 (not shown). Medium high rates were found in North America, South America and Oceania (especially New Zealand). By far the highest rates were observed in Africa and, even more pronounced in Central America and the Caribbean.

An Asian Exception?

With regard to Asia, earlier publications on the global ICVS results have highlighted the comparatively low levels of most types of crime across the region (Van Dijk, 2008). From a global perspective, the average Asian country experiences low levels of common property and violent crime. Homicide statistics confirm that Asia remains a distinctly safe region from a global perspective (Alvazzi & Mugellini, 2012).

Although Asian countries show great variation in history, culture and wealth, they invariably enjoy relatively low levels of common crime. This persistent phenomenon has been dubbed the 'Asian exception' (Van Dijk, 2008). The modest levels of crime in Asian countries can be explained by their sustained high levels of family bonds and other forms of social cohesion (Van Dijk, 2008). Its relatively modest levels of inequality may also have contributed to lower levels of (violent) crime (Braithwaite, 2014).

Over the past ten years levels of affluence in Asia have gone up. In tandem, opportunities for theft and cybercrime have expanded and lifestyles have become more individualistic. Also, in several Asian countries' inequality has been on the increase. Building on these trends, a gradual rise of some common types of crime in the region may prove to be the inevitable price to be paid for rapid modernization. A case in point is the city of Beijing where, as discussed, levels of certain types of property crime such as car theft have gone up since the ICVS was first conducted in 1996. It remains to be seen whether the Asian exception will last much longer in the 21th century.

Victimization by Bride-Abduction in Central Asia

Bride-abduction, whereby the groom and friends kidnap the bride – a traditional phenomenon in parts of Central Asia – has been criminalized since Soviet times. Bride-kidnapping re-emerged as a growing problem in the Caucasus and Central Asia after the collapse of the Soviet Union (Werner 2009). Using as special mode of interviewing, questions on this practice have been put to married women in the ICVS studies in Kyrgyzstan and Kazakhstan. Table 2 shows results for both countries of this new experimental part of the ICVS questionnaire (Van Dijk, Van Kesteren, Trochev & Shade, 2018).

Table 2: Bride-abduction in Kazakhstan and Kyrgyzstan

(Asked to married women only)	*Kazakhstan*			*Kyrgyzstan*		
	Country	*Astana*	*Almaty*	*Country*	*Urban*	*Rural*
	%	%	%	%	%	%
Please indicate whether you have been kidnapped by the groom and his friends for marriage (bride kidnapping)?						
1 Yes	4.5	4	7	14	8	19
2 No	95	92	93	77	80	75
3 Do not know or cannot remember	1	3	0	2	2	1.5
4 Refusal	0	1	0	7	10	5
Did you agree to this kidnapping in advance?						
1 Yes	64	84	62	63	66	62
2 No	34	16	27	34	32	35
3 Do not know or cannot remember	2	0	11	2	2	3
4 Refusal	0	0	0	0	0	0
If you did not agree with this kidnapping, did you or anyone else report the incident to the police?						
1 Yes	0	0	0			
2 No	84	100	78			
3 Do not know or cannot remember	13	0	0			
4 Refusal	4	0	22			

Source: ICVS, 2016/2018

The results show that 14% and 4.5% of married women in Kyrgyzstan and Kazakhstan respectively say they have been kidnapped by their groom and his friends. In Kyrgyzstan the phenomenon is especially common in rural areas (one in five of married women). This is not the case in Kazakhstan where the rate was highest among married women in Almaty. Two thirds of the married women who said they had been kidnapped in both Kazakhstan and Kyrgyzstan indicated this was done with their advance agreement. This means that almost 5% of married Kyrgyz women and 1.5% of married Kazakh women have been kidnapped without their prior agreement. None of these women said they had reported their kidnapping to the police.

In an earlier part of the questionnaire all respondents were asked about their worries about the possible kidnapping of female family members (for results see Table 3). In Kazakhstan 29% reported being quite or very worried. In Kyrgyzstan the percentage seriously worrying about the kidnapping of female family members was twice as high (50%). The latter result suggests that, as with other common forms of crime, levels of concern roughly mirror actual prevalence. As expected, in Kyrgyzstan more people residing in rural areas were worried than those living in the capital Bishkek. By contrast in Kazakhstan inhabitants of Almaty were most concerned (36% were quite or very worried). Within the two countries local levels of worry about the phenomenon seem to reflect actual risks.

Table 3: How Worried are You that a Daughter/Granddaughter/Sister of Yours will be Kidnapped by Someone for Marriage (bride stealing)? In Comparison with Kyrgyzstan

	Kazakhstan	*Astana*	*Almaty*	*Kyrgyzstan*	*Bishkek*	*Osh*
	%	%	%	%	%	%
Not worried at all	37	30	26	29	30	22
A bit worried	20	26	20	15	20	17
Quite worried	11	11	10	17	16	32
Very worried	18	19	25	26	12	22
Don't know	7	8	8	3	3	1
Not applicable/ Refuse to answer (have no daughter/ granddaughter/ sister)	7	8	10	10	19	7

These survey-based results confirm anecdotical evidence of experts identifying rural Kyrgyzstan rather than Kazakhstan as the locus of bride-kidnapping in the Central Asian region (Werner 2009). They testify that the potential of the ICVS methodology to measure the prevalence of special types of serious crime. Bride-abduction is known to be common in, besides Central Asia, parts of Africa and Asia as well. At this juncture comparable results from surveys in other countries are not available.

Setbacks and Initiatives

As said, no collective sweeps of the ICVS have been conducted after 2010. In Europe a proposal for a Union-wide victimization survey modelled after the ICVS was prepared by Eurostat but ultimately rejected by the European Parliament in 2013. A British MEP of the Conservative Party argued that the project was expensive and superfluous since several member states including England and Wales carried out their own national victimization surveys. As a consequence, no comparative data on levels of types of crime in the EU are presently available. The only source of information on crime published by Eurostat are statistics on police-recorded crimes which, as duly admitted by Eurostat, are heavily influenced by inter-country differences in reporting and recording of crime. Within the EU rates of recorded crime are, for example, by far the highest in the United Kingdom, the Netherlands and the Nordic countries and the lowest in the countries of Eastern and Southern Europe, contradicting conventional wisdom and results of the ICVS. For lack of a proper Union-wide victimization survey, the truth about distribution and trends of common crime in the European Union is hidden in a pervasive mist of unreliable administrative statistics(Van Dijk, 2008; 2015; Van Dijk, 2016).

The Human Rights Monitoring Agency of the European Commission (FRA) has in recent years conducted large scale victimization surveys on violence against women and on hate crimes. But after 2010no surveys have been conducted on the prevalence of common crime, feelings of insecurity or attitudes towards the police. For the moment the political will to support and fund such project seems absent in Brussels, partly because of political deadlock and partly because decreased levels of common crime may no longer be seen as a primary public concern.

In the meantime, some promising initiatives have been taken elsewhere in the world. UNODC produced a manual for the conduct of victimization surveys, available in all five UN languages (UNODC, 2010). Japan has started preparations for a repeat of the ICVS in 2019. In India new ICVS-type victimization surveys are under preparation in several states.

In Latin America standardised surveys, partly based on the ICVS, have for some time been actively promoted by the Mexico-based regional Centre of Expertise on Statistics on Governance, Public Safety, Victimization and Justice, established by UNODC and the Mexican statistical Office, INEGI. One of the centre's key projects is the Latin American and Caribbean Crime Victimization Initiative (LACTI). Since 2010 victimization surveys have been conducted by national statistical authorities in Mexico, Bolivia, Colombia, Honduras, Panama, Guatamala, Argentina, Peru, Jamaica and Saint Lucia (Aebi & Linde, 2012; UNODC/INEGI, 2019). In parallel, Brazil continues with its national surveys modelled after older versions of the ICVS.

Although these regional and national initiatives are encouraging, they cannot from a methodological perspective be regarded as a continuation of the ICVS. Although a common set of core questions is used, neither the questionnaires nor the methodology of data collection is fully standardized. Inter-country comparisons remain therefore methodologically challenged. In the case of Latin America strikingly little comparative analyses of the results of the various national surveys have so far been carried out. Probably the governments of the countries of the region are hesitant to support comparative analyses resulting in a ranking of their countries in terms of crime.

For many governments across the world comparative crime statistics remain highly politically sensitive. In the course of three decades of ICVS, political opposition to the publication of comparative crime rates of countries has been a recurrent problem for the authors, surfacing in, inter alia, Spain, The Netherlands, Australia, New Zealand, and South Korea (Van Dijk, 2008). Due to these persistent political sensitivities, the governance of crime and security is uniquely lacking in comparative international metrics which have by now become commonplace in the fields of economics, health and many others. The crime and security sector is the Cinderella of international statistics. Those responsible for controlling crime, one of the most pressing humanitarian problems of our times, are in no position to benchmark their national or regional performance.

Demand and Supply of Survey-Based Crime Data

On the positive side, ineffective crime control is now generally recognized as major impediment of sustainable development (Wenmann, & Muggah, 2010)and this may finally mobilize international demand for better crime statistics. In 2011 the overarching theme of the World Bank's Development Report focused on the relationships between conflict, security and development (World Bank, 2011). The report presented evidence that high levels of serious crime impede economic growth by consuming scarce tax revenues and deterring foreign and domestic investment. In fact, the report shows that over the past 25 years, while poverty is declining globally, the countries most affected by organised crime and violence have been lagging behind in achieving development goals.

In august 2016, the United Nations' Economic and Social Council (ECOSOC) adopted the 2030 Agenda for Sustainable Development, comprised of 17 Sustainable Development Goals (SDG). Goal 16 specifically addresses the need for effective crime prevention and peace-building, to promote peaceful and inclusive societies for sustainable growth, provide access to justice for all and build effective, accountable and inclusive institutions at all levels. The adoption of this SDG is a ground-breaking acknowledgement by the world community of the pivotal importance of effective and humane crime prevention and control for sustainable human development. Fifteen years ago, such acknowledgment would have been unimaginable. In fact, crime prevention was not even footnoted in the Millennium Development Goals adopted in 2000. Subsequently, the UN Statistical Commission's Interagency and Expert Group on SDG Indicators (IAEG-SDGs) has adopted sets of indicators for each Goal to monitor progress made with its implementation. The chosen indicators reflect advances in the measurement of crime. Besides homicide statistics, statistics of police-recorded crime have for the reasons discussed above, been duly ignored as possible indicators of trends in (violent) crime. The indicators to measure SDG 16 include several key items of victimisation surveys such as those used in the ICVS, instead:

- 16.1.3 Proportion of population subjected to physical, psychological or sexual violence in the previous 12 months;
- 16.1.4 Proportion of population that feels safe walking alone around the area they live;
- 16.3.1 Proportion of victims of violence in the previous 12 months who reported their victimisation to the police;
- 16.5.1 Proportion of persons who had at least one contact with a public official and who paid a bribe to a public official, or were asked for a bribe by those public officials, during the previous 12 months.

The adoption of these indicators has raised the political stakes of a new standardized global victimization survey. To date this emerging global demand for survey-based international statistics on crime has not yet been met by concrete initiatives for their supply. The international police organization INTERPOL has expressed some interest in sponsoring such survey. Besides INTERPOL, the statistical unit of UNODC ranks as an obvious promotor and guardian of a relaunched ICVS. To our knowledge, unfortunately, no concrete action on such much-needed project has yet been taken.

By the private sector some new initiatives have recently been taken to survey public experiences with crime. Examples are the World Justice Reports, especially its Rule of Law Index and the World Internal Security and Police Index (WISPI, 2016). Perhaps most interestingly, Gallup International runs an annual population survey in over 160 countries with samples of 1,000 or more per country. Since 2007 this World Poll includes several items on crime and justice related issues covering feelings of safety in one's neighbourhood, personal experiences with theft last year and experiences with violent crime (assault or mugging) last year. The questions on crime experiences lack specificity, and therefore do not meet the standards of the ICVS or the UN Manual. On the other hand, its uniform data collection, geographical spread of sampling and periodicity make this poll potentially a unique instrument to generate regular international crime statistics at a global scale. In the absence of a full-fledged international victimization survey modelled after the ICVS, commercially run surveys like those of the World Justice Project or of Gallup deserve more attention from the international community as possible vehicles to monitor progress with implementing SDG 16 across the world. With some extra funding and an improved questionnaire design, these omnibus surveys could develop into valuable sources of international metrics on violence, crime and trust in the police.

References

[1] Aebi, M.F. & A. Linde (2012), The Growth of Victimisation Surveys in Latin America, In: M. Groenhuijsen, R. Letschert & S. Hazenbroek (eds), KLM Van Dijk: Liber amicorum J.J.M. van Dijk, Nijmegen: Wolf Legal Publishers.

[2] Braithwaite, J. (2014), Crime in Asia: Toward a Better Future, *Asian Criminology*, 9, pp. 65-75.

[3] Chockalingam, K. (2003), Crime victimization survey in four major cities in Southern India, *Forum on Crime and Society*, Vol. 3, No. 1 & 2, pp. 117-126.

[4] Dijk, J.J.M. van (2008), *The World of Crime*, Thousand Oaks: SAGE Ca.

[5] Dijk, J.J.M. van (2015), The case for survey-based comparative measures of crime, *European Journal of Criminology*. Vol. 12, 4, pp. 437-456.

[6] Dijk, J.J.M. van (2016), Illuminating the Dark figure of Crime: Victimisation Surveys and Beyond; Acceptance speech at the Award Ceremony of the European Criminology Award in Muenster, Germany, *ESC Newsletter*, 216/3.

[7] Dijk, J.J.M van, J. van Kesteren, A. Trochev & G. Shade (2018), *Criminal Victimization in Kazakhstan in en international perspective; new findings from the International Crime Victims Survey*, Astana: Delegation of the European Union to Kazakhstan/EUCJ.

[8] Dijk, J.J.M. van, & Chanturia, T. (2011), *The remarkable case of Georgia*. Tbilisi: Gorbi Institute/Ministry of Justice Georgia

[9] Dijk, J.J.M. & B. Vollaard (2012), Self-limiting crime waves, In: J. Van Dijk, T. Tseloni & G. Farrell (Eds), *The International Crime Drop*, Palgrave/McMillan.

[10] Gallup (2019), *Global Law and Order 2018*, available online at: insightcrime.org

[11] Van Kesteren, J., J.J.M. Van Dijk & P. Mayhew (2013), The International Crime Victims Surveys: A retrospective, *International Review of Victimology* 20(1): 49-69.

[12] Singh, D.R. (1995), The International Crime (Victim) Survey in Bombay, *Criminal Victimization in the Developing World*, UNICRI Publication No. 55 (Rome, United Nations Interregional Crime and Justice Research Institute, 1995), pp. 95-134.

[13] Sutton, H., J.J.M. van Dijk & J. van Kesteren (2017), The size and dimensions of victimization in the Caribbean, in: H. Sutton & I. Ruprah (Eds), *Restoring paradise in the Caribbean: Combating violence with numbers*, IDB Monograph 513

[14] UNODC (2010), *Manual on Victimization Surveys*, UNODC/UNECE, available at www.unodc.org

[15] UNODC/INEGI (2019), *Victimization Surveys Timeline*, available at www.gsj.inegi.org.mx

[16] Wenmann, A. & Muggah, R. (2010), More violence, Less development. Geneva: Geneva declaration secretariat, available at http://www.genevadeclaration.org/fileadmin/docs/MdG_Process/MoreviolenceLessdevelopment.pdf

[17] Werner, C. (2009), Bride abduction in post-Soviet Central Asia: marking a shift towards patriarchy through local discourses of shame and tradition, *Journal of the Royal Anthropological Institute (N.S.)* 15, pp. 314-331.

[18] WISPI (2016), World Internal Security Index 2016, 1th edition, available at: www.wispindex.com

[19] World Bank (2011), World Development report 2011: Conflict, security and development. Washington, DC: World bank, available at http://publications.worldbank.org/index.

[20] World Justice Project (2019), Rule of Law Index, available at: www.worldjusticeproject.org

Chapter III

Activist Victimology from Principles in 1985 to Practical Transformations by 2030

IRVIN WALLER

Professor K. Chockalingam's life work was as a model activist victimologist. He put victimology on the map in India but was not content to only be a researcher and teacher. He collaborated with supreme courts justices, helped develop the pioneering recommendations of the Malimath committee and much more. His activism fostered caring about victims, preventing victimization, compensation, reparation and rights for victims in Tamil Nadu, India and the world.

The next generation of Victimologists must be inspired by his exemplary role model and successful life work. Through the collaboration and innovation of so many Victimologists across the world, we have achieved so much but much more work is needed (Waller 2011; Waller 2019; Waller 2020). This chapter will highlight some of those achievements but it is a clarion call to Victimologists to be activists to accelerate progress towards dramatically reducing victimization and multiplying basic rights and services for victims. The opportunities for rapid advances are made possible by the extent of our knowledge, examples of good practice, and international exchanges but also by government commitment to act now to transform our world to get results through the Sustainable Development Goals. Getting action now is more possible than Victimologists think because of the new affordability of social media, modern ways to communicate and willingness of millennials to engage politicians.

In 1985, the UN General Assembly resolved to go beyond criminal justice to prevent victimization and provide victims with rights across the world. This resolution has become known as the Magna Carta for victims. It justified the action because of the magnitude of victimization and its consequences (UNGA 1985; Waller Martinez, 2015). While some governments in Europe and other rich countries have made significant progress, much more is needed and particularly in the countries with the most and highest rates of victimization. UN entities, governments and academic criminologists must transform their way of thinking consistent with the vision of dramatically reducing violent crime and closing the justice gap to which world leaders have committed in the Sustainable Development Goals.

The commitment to transformations in the Sustainable Development Goals (SDGs) is a first step, but we must help governments to put their laws and money where their mouth is. Victimologists must use science, model practices and social media to build on, and emulate. They must engage politicians and become policy leaders now to get transformations so that effective upstream prevention and victim rights become the new normal by 2030.

Tragic Consequences of Ignoring the Rights of Victims

Globally each year, half a million victims will be murdered (UNODC 2019), an estimated twenty five million women raped (extrapolated from Waller 2019, 9-10), and one billion children victims of violence (World Health Organization 2017). These are outrageous numbers given our knowledge and pathfinder successes. They are nothing short of a public health crisis for which we victimologists have many solutions.

These statistics reflect victims who suffer injuries, pain, trauma, financial loss and more. The victims are often the most vulnerable and disadvantaged. Where these tragedies have reached epidemic proportions, they threaten economic development and reduce the Gross Domestic Product. They threaten democracy and rule of law (Inter-American Development Bank 2018; Muggah 2019). These numbers reflect outrageous pain and loss that is preventable and often made worse by a flawed and often failed system of criminal justice.

Governments Agree to Dramatically Reduce Violent Crime by 2030

All major world leaders committed in 2015 at the UN General Assembly to achieve the Sustainable Development Goals, which include the commitment to reduce dramatically the numbers of victims of violent crime in SDGs 16.1, 5.2, 16.2 by 2030 (UNGA 2015b). 'Transforming Our World: The 2030 Agenda for Sustainable Development' (UNGA 2015a) requires a new way of doing business. There are essentially four new ways that we must get to know and understand. They are results based, build on progress in a network of domains, use evidence, and focus on transforming policies in both advanced and developing nations.

There are approximately 15 indicators in the SDGs for targets that are measuring whether violent crime has been significantly reduced (UN Sustainable Development Goals 2016). Six of the most important for this chapter are set out in the following tables for the subsections in SDG 5 for the reduction in victims of violence against women and in SDG 16 to the reduction of victims of violence and homicide and violence against children. They include access to justice but not yet clearly for victims of crime though one indicator is the proportion of victims who report to police in SDG 16.3.1.

Homicide in SDG 16	
'16.1	**Significantly reduce all forms of violence and related death rates everywhere**
16.1.1	Number of victims of intentional homicide per 100,000 population, by sex and age
16.1.3	Proportion of population subjected to (a) physical violence, (b) psychological violence and (c) sexual violence in the previous 12 months' (UN Sustainable Development Goals 2016)
Rape in SDG5	
'5.2	**Eliminate all forms of violence against all women and girls in the public and private spheres, including trafficking and sexual and other types of exploitation**
5.2.1	Proportion of ever-partnered women and girls aged 15 years and older subjected to physical, sexual or psychological violence by a current or former intimate partner in the previous 12 months, by form of violence and by age
5.2.2	Proportion of women and girls aged 15 years and older subjected to sexual violence by persons other than an intimate partner in the previous 12 months, by age and place of occurrence' (UN Sustainable Development Goals 2016)
Violence against Children in SDG16	
'16.2	**End abuse, exploitation, trafficking and all forms of violence against and torture of children**
16.2.1	Proportion of children aged 1–17 years who experienced any physical punishment and/or psychological aggression by caregivers in the past
16.2.3	Proportion of young women and men aged 18–29 years who experienced sexual violence by age 18' (UN Sustainable Development Goals 2016)

The indicator for homicide is measured regularly and considered reliable enough to make comparisons over time and between countries (UNODC 2019). So this is a clear example of a focus on results. The indicators on sexual violence and violence against children will require the use of surveys such as the gold standard victimization survey known as the Intimate Partner and Sexual Violence Survey developed by US Centers for Disease Control (2011; Together for Girls 2019a).

Goal 17 is a new concept for UN activities as it focuses on strengthening the means of implementation and revitalizing the Global Partnership for Sustainable Development. It includes knowledge sharing, capacity building, policy coherence, multi-stakeholder partnerships that mobilize and share knowledge, expertise, technology and financial resources, data monitoring and accountability (UN Sustainable Development Goals 2016). These are focused on Low and Middle Income Countries (LMIC) but have relevance for high income countries.

Governments must put their money where their mouth is

But the road to hell is paved with good intentions as governments have not acted to achieve them. 'Violence is on the rise in certain regions of the world, but it doesn't have to be. In fact, the world possesses the knowledge, tools, institutional structures, legal instruments, and data-collection capacity to halve violence, in all its forms, within a decade' (Locke and Steven 2019, 1). By 2015, the world had accumulated solid science on how to prevent violent crime and celebrated many national actions to provide victim rights (Waller 2019).

The movement known as SDG16 plus has provided remarkable leadership to get governments to accelerate the transformations to achieve the noble SDG goals. A growing number of pathfinder governments are signing up to collaborated but much more is needed (SDG16 plus 2019).

Decisive action is needed to accelerate action to use this science. The Under Secretary General, who is the head of the UN Office on Drugs and Crime (UNODC) stated that 'unless the international community takes decisive steps, targets under Sustainable Development Goal 16 to significantly reduce all forms of violence and related death rates by 2030 will not be met' (UNODC 2019, 1). This statement could equally be made about gender based violence and violence against children. So how can we help them they take decisive action now?

Victimologists must get to know the science, how to implement it and how to convince policy makers to invest in it. I have now written a book to share this knowledge with Victimologists, policy makers, faith based organizations and Non-governmental organizations, entitled the 'Science and Secrets for Ending Violent Crime' (Waller 2019). The book makes the evidence based case for a major shift from over use of criminal justice and incarceration to effective solutions that prevent violent crime and victimization before it happens. It is based in a careful analysis of the science available from many academic sources as well as websites like crimesolutions.gov of the US department of Justice and info violence from the World Health Organization (Waller 2019, 23-36). It explains the conclusions in terms that are easily understandable by politicians, victim advocates and the public. Here are some of the highlights.

Causes of Violence

Since 1985, significant knowledge has accumulated on what causes the violence and how to tackle these causes. There are several factors that lead to increased risk of experiencing or perpetrating violence, which are sometimes grouped under the labels of individual, family, community, and environmental (WHO 2002). Studies of life cycle development and the downstream impact of adverse childhood experiences – child victimization – have given us significant data on how the accumulation of negative life experiences, such as poverty, inconsistent and uncaring parenting, failure in school and lack of jobs correlates with persistent offending in adolescence and young adulthood (WHO 2002; Centers for Disease Control and Prevention 2019; Waller 2019).

Solid Sources of Knowledge about Effective Violence Prevention

The science of violence prevention is solid but not yet widely known or used by policy makers. My book can help victimologists and policy makers understand the policy implications.

We have accumulated significant proven and evidence-based knowledge about what is effective and cost effective in stopping interpersonal violence. This knowledge is endorsed by some of the most prestigious organizations in the world. It is freely available on websites, including that of crimesolutions.gov of the US Department of Justice (2015), violence-info the World Health Organizations (2017; 2009a; 2009b) and the tool kit of the British College of Policing (2019, pp. 23-32).

In 2017, WHO released the most international and extensive of these websites with its Violence Prevention Information System – Violence Info (WHO 2017). This is a 'global interactive knowledge platform of scientific findings about the prevalence, consequences, causes and prevention of various forms of violence. The tool contains global, regional and national homicide rates from WHO Global Health Estimates, and country-specific information on laws, policies, strategies and victim services to prevent and respond to violence' (WHO 2017).

These portals collectively access thousands of clinical trials that show which projects have stopped crime before it happens. In addition, national academic councils and commissions have reviewed the research to arrive at conclusions (Waller 2019, pp. 32-36). Further analyses of these projects available on a portal of the State of Washington in the USA shows these projects are remarkably cost effective by stopping harm to victims and saving the costs of reacting after crime has happened (Washington State Institute for Public Policy 2018; Waller 2019, pp. 31-32). These prove the adage that an ounce of prevention is worth a pound of cure.

Proven Solutions

The book explains solutions that violence prevention science shows are effective and cost effective and how to find out more (Waller 2019, 37-114), including both prevention and implementation of victim rights. It highlights and explains the solutions that have been proven scientifically to prevent violent crime before it happens. It shows these solutions to be more effective and cost effective than over-relying on a reactive criminal justice system after crime has victimized people.

The science shows that smart investment in prevention will avoid lives lost, trauma to victims and wasted taxes for all. It teases out programs that have been proven to reduce violent crime by 50% or better than our criminal justice system and explains them for politicians. These include some well-known but still little used programs that must be targeted to tackle factors of risk. The programs include outreach to youth such as Cure Violence, school curricula such as Becoming a Man, Hospital Interventions with victims, family support and early childhood, life skills training in schools and proactive policing (see Waller 2019, 63-70).

Smart Ways to Implement National and City Strategies

The book explains the essentials for this science to be applied. It focuses on guidelines, agreed at UN bodies such as UNODC (2019), UN Habitat (2019) and WHO (2016) that are little known but are essentials for governments to successfully implement that science and achieve sustained reductions in victimization. These have been integrated into an impressive model for national governments (EuroSocial 2015).

It shares some inspiring examples of cities that have acted consistently with these essentials to achieve dramatic reductions in homicides within as little as three years. It highlights the success of Glasgow in Scotland who achieved a 50% reduction within 3 years and has sustained the decline over much longer. The Glasgow model is being adopted by the Mayor of London, UK (2019). The largest Canadian Province now requires every municipality to have a community safety and well being plan (Ontario 2019).

It shows how cities have planned their ways to reduce street violence significantly and importantly why those cities succeeded when so many have not. The 7 Essentials for Success (Waller 2019, pp. 117-122) are:

- "Establishing a permanent violence and crime reduction board for the city;
- Being informed by violence prevention science and data;
- Having an integrated crime prevention plan;
- Mobilizing sectors able to tackle causes;
- Having adequate and sustained funding;
- Developing standards and training for human talent;
- Having public support and engagement."

How to Get Buy in

It identifies how to foster sustainable and smarter investments by policy makers. It make a giant step further forward to getting this knowledge used by using my several decades of experience in the USA and elsewhere, including India, to get buy in. Prevention is a big shift but includes the benefits of savings to taxpayers, reductions in mass incarceration, and meeting the visions of many victims to stop violence (see Waller 2019, 183-200).

So how do we make the transformations to make our communities safer (CMNCP 2019). Effective violence prevention is not only more affordable and successful than policymakers think; a modest equivalent of 10 percent of what they spend on police, courts, and corrections will do it and often before the next election! Violence prevention is achievable because voters, contrary to what the media tells us, want much more than reaction, they want prevention (see Waller 2019, 221-228). Yes they want tough on crime, but they also want tough on causes.

Think of a World where Victimologists Helped Reduce Violence by 50% by 2030

The stakes are high. The science and successes show that a 50% reduction in violent crime is achievable by 2030 (Waller 2019; Locke and Steven 2019).

Globally this reduction saves 250,000s lives from homicide for the target in SDG 16.1, more than ten million women from rape for the target in SDG 5.2 and half a billion children from violence for the target in SDG 16.2. Yes if we follow the life work of Professor Chockalingam, we can counter the crisis of epidemic proportions with getting policy makers to transform their policies, laws and investments.

The innovations needed are in the interests of governments by spending money better, managing cities to make cities safer, investing in disadvantaged families, and legislating support for affordable, popular and cost effective preventive solutions. In high violence countries and communities, it will increase GDP and well-being (Inter-American Development Bank 2018; Waller 2019).

The Challenge for Activist Victimologists

Victimologists now must get to know the science and model practices as well as use social media and political engagement. They must spear head decisive action, in partnership with UN agencies and pathfinder governments, by five initiatives:

1. get to know the science, the essentials for success, and how to get buy in;
2. raise awareness among politicians and the public of effective solutions and strategies, using modern communication tools;
3. train and foster the human talent to implement effective strategies successfully;
4. act locally to deliver effective solutions;
5. work collaboratively to convince policy makers to invest now, including policy proposals based on effective solutions and strategies (Waller 2020).

There are several movements with which victimologists can collaborate (Waller 2019, pp. 221-238). Most of these movements are focused on getting decisive actions now from governments to achieve the results agreed in the Sustainable Development Goals. Many of the movements are planning to advocate for transformations at the UN Congress on Crime Prevention and Criminal Justice in Kyoto in April 2020.

Across Latin America, ILANUD is working with seventeen or more Latin America countries and with cities within those countries to mobilise action to reduce their epidemic levels of violence, using science, tools and best practices (ILANUD 2019). ILANUD is the Latin American institute working on crime prevention and criminal justice as part of the program network of institutes associated with UNODC.

Peace in our cities campaign (2019) calls on mayors, local authorities, civil society, the private sector, and other partners to halve violent victimisation in their cities by 2030. They recognise that we now have the tools, evidence, and best practices to curb violence but also address the structural inequalities and injustices that perpetuate it.

The Coalition of Faith-Based Organizations, Spirituality and Justice Initiative (2019), held a major event in the Grace Cathedral in San Francisco where the UN Charter was first signed 74 years ago. It is exploring ways in which faith-based organizations can contribute to crime prevention and the criminal justice system. It will submit a declaration to the UN Congress on Crime Prevention and Criminal justice with a view to encouraging the transformations needed to achieve the objectives of SDG 16.

In the USA, several movements are pressuring governments to do something about gun violence (Waller 2019, pp. 233-235). March for our Lives for instance has proposed a plan for a Safer America (2019). In Latin America and increasingly globally feminists are calling for governments to pay attention and solve the issues of violence against women (Guardian 2019).

Conclusion

This chapter identifies the decisive action needed now to dramatically reduce violent crime by 2030 as required by SDG 16.1. 5.2 and 16.2. It shows how to cut violence in half and so avoid each year 25,000 homicides, 10 million or more rapes and half a billion child victims of violence. These reductions would increase GDP and decrease corruption and political instability. It is about shifting from (mis-)spending on what does not work to investing in the futures of young and disadvantaged people to save lives and taxes, while generating economic growth and political stability.

In 2019, we not only have the knowledge of what are effective solutions, successes in implementing them, and reasons for decision makers to shift investment, but we have social media and data analysis tools that were not available twenty years ago, we have cities that have been successful, we have guidelines agreed by governments. So we need to share the good news and get action now.

Victimologists can accelerate the transformations needed by partnering with UN agencies and pathfinder governments and cities, particularly by becoming active with the groundswell of movements calling on governments to shift from a failing criminal justice system to effective violence prevention. They must expand the leadership in the core network of those who already know the science, raising awareness of the strategies and the benefits to share this knowledge virally, develop the talent to make it happen, and help decision makers to see the benefits (WHO 2019; Waller 2020). We They can foster national prevention legislation and a shift from an agenda of punishment by the state to an agenda of prevention investing in people guided by science. To succeed, decisive action is needed from funders to develop these tools, talents and the momentum towards a world safer from violence by 2030.

References

[1] CMNCP (Canadian Municipal Network on Crime Prevention) (2017). SaferCities.ca

[2] Centers for Disease Control and Prevention, 2011, National Intimate Partner and Sexual Violence Survey, Summary Report, Atlanta, GA.

[3] Centers for Disease Control and Prevention (2019), Adverse Childhood Experiences, https://www.cdc.gov/violenceprevention/childabuseandneglect/acestudy/index.html

[4] Coalition of Faith-Based Organizations, Spirituality and Justice Initiative, (2019) https://gracecathedral.org/main_events/spirituality-justice-initiative/

[5] EuroSocial (2014), Regional Model for a Comprehensive Violence and Crime Prevention Policy, http://www.sia.eurosocial-ii.eu/files/docs/1461686840-DT_33-_Modelo%20regional%20Prevencion%20Violencia%20(ENG).pdf

[6] Guardian (2019) https://www.theguardian.com/world/2019/dec/06/chilean-anti-rape-anthem-becomes-international-feminist-phenomenon

[7] ILANUD (2019), https://www.ilanud.or.cr/encuentro-latinoamericano-y-del-caribe-sobre-prevencion-de-la-violencia-y-el-delito/

[8] Inter-American Development Bank (2018). 'Smart spending on Citizen Security: Beyond Crime and Punishment', https://flagships.iadb.org/en/DIA2018/chapter-7-smart-spending-citizen-security-beyond-crime-and-punishment

[9] Locke, R. and Steven, D. (2019), Fighting Violence with Evidence https://www.project-syndicate.org/commentary/sdg16-reducing-violence-conflict-homicide-by-rachel-locke-and-david-steven-2019-08

[10] London Mayor (2019), Violence Reduction Unit, https://www.london.gov.uk/what-we-do/mayors-office-policing-and-crime-mopac/violence-reduction-unit-vru/what-violence-reduction-unit

[11] March for our Lives (2019), A Peace Plan for a Safer America https://marchforourlives.com › peace-plan

[12] Muggah, R. (2019), Violent crime has undermined democracy in Latin America: When people are fearful, they are less likely to trust elected politicians. https://www.ft.com/content/7bbc9228-a09f-11e9-a282-2df48f366f7d

[13] Ontario Ministry of Community Safety and Corrections (2019), Community Safety and Well Being Planning: A shared commitment in Ontario. Toronto

[14] Peace in our cities campaign (2019), https://www.peacebuilding.live/peace-in-our-cities-press-release

[15] SDG16 plus (2019), Stevens, D. SDG 16+ Partnership on Peaceful, just and inclusive societies, Road Map, Center on International Cooperation. New York, New York University, https://www.sdg16.plus/

[16] UN-Habitat (2019), Twenty five years of the Safer Cities Program: Lessons Learned from Evolution of the Approach, Nairobi, in press.

[17] United Nations General Assembly (1985). Resolution 40/34 on Basic Principles of Justice for Victims of Crime and Abuse of Power, https://www.un.org/documents/ga/res/40/a40r034.htm (accessed 15 August, 2019).

[18] United Nations General Assembly (2015a), Transforming Our World: The 2030 Agenda For Sustainable Development sustainabledevelopment.un.org A/RES/70/1

[19] United Nations General Assembly (2015b), Sustainable Development Goals, Retrieved from https://sustainabledevelopment.un.org/

[20] United Nations Office on Drugs and Crime (2019), Global Trends in Homicide, Booklets 1-6. New York: UN, https://www.unodc.org/documents/data-and-analysis/gsh/Booklet1.pdf

[21] United Nations Sustainable Development Goals (2016), Final list of proposed Sustainable Development Goal indicators, https://sustainabledevelopment.un.org/content/documents/11803Official-List-of-Proposed-SDG-Indicators.pdf

[22] Waller, I. (2020), Reducing Violent Crime by 50% before 2030: Decisive Action Now to Achieve these SDGs chapter 16 in S. Redo and H. Kury, Crime Prevention and Justice in 2030 UN and the Universal Declaration of Human Rights, Springer in draft.

[23] Waller, I. (2019), Science and Secrets of Ending Violent Crime. Lanham, Maryland: Rowman and Littlefield.

[24] Waller, I. (2011), Rights for Victims of Crime. Lanham, Maryland: Rowman and Littlefield.

[25] Waller, I. & Martinez, V. (2019), Prevención inteligente: Pensar en las victimas, en ILANUD Violencias, Victimas y Sociedades Justas, Ministerio de Justicia y Derechos Humanos de Argentina, ILANUD, Libro Digital, pp. 25-47.

[26] Washington State Institute for Public Policy, (2018) Cost Benefit https://www.wsipp.wa.gov/BenefitCost

[27] WHO (2016b), INSPIRE: Seven Strategies for Ending Violence Against Children. Geneva, Switzerland: World Health Organization, https://www.who.int/violence_injury_prevention/violence/inspire/en/

[28] WHO (2017), Violence Prevention Information System (Violence Info). World Health Organization, http://apps.who.int/violence-info/

[29] WHO (2019), Violence Prevention Alliance. World Health Organization, https://www.who.int/violenceprevention/en/

Chapter IV

Revisiting Victimology: A Case for Scientific Victimology

D. DANIEL T. ANDZENGE & STACIE A. JERGENSON

The discipline of victimology has had a major impact in the world today. The World Society of Victimology has consultative status with the United Nations and the Council of Europe and is closely identified with the United Nations Declaration of Principles for Victims of Crime and Abuse of Power. Universities around the world have added victimology as an academic discipline and offer degrees or concentrations in victimology at both undergraduate and graduate levels. Local, regional and national policies and programs for victim compensation and services have been developed worldwide.

The increased interest in victimology and victim services is not driven as much by academic or scientific curiosity, however, as it is by advocacy for victims. Though interest-driven activism increases services for victims, it may neglect the need to provide services for victims of other crimes and natural disasters that do not attract any particular attention or popular appeal. The feminist movement and the perception that women are more likely to be victims have combined to focus more attention on female victimization than male, elderly and child victims. Likewise, more attention tends to be focused on victims of a targeted minority or cultural groups. The emphasis on victim advocacy and service rather than a critical examination of victimization incidents have also led to different definitions and perspectives of the problem. Mendelsohn's approach to victimization is a case in point. As a defense attorney interested in facts to aid in his defense of people accused of a crime, he was more interested in the context and facts related to criminal victimization than in defining a victim. This is in contrast to those attorneys and criminologists who tend to focus on victims and assume a general understanding of victims of crime. This poses difficulties for the recognition of persons whose victimization was not necessarily part of criminal activity.

This paper examines the historical development of victimology as a social science discipline that must first critically examine the circumstances and facts in victimization incidents before it can benefit society and victims. Limiting victimology to advocacy and service without assessing the facts and circumstances raises the risk that services may be offered to persons who are not necessarily victims and not in need of services. Advocacy and service alone without a critical assessment of victimization incidents also limits our ability to understand the true nature of victimization and of victims themselves.

Historical Overview of Victimology

The discipline of victimology features the contributions of a multitude of judicial and social science experts. It is helpful to review their contributions in order to better understand the historical developments, emphases, and current state of victimology.

Benjamin Mendelsohn. Victimologists trace their origin to Mendelsohn who as a Barrister at Law in 1937 began collecting information about victims for his law practice. As a barrister, he was assigned the role of a prosecutor in some cases or as defense counsel in other cases. The opportunity to look at both sides of cases in his routine practice enabled Mendelsohn to draw the conclusion that a successful defense is a result of well-documented facts and applying well-established law. Mendelsohn noted the importance of understanding the underlying facts of each case including a bio-social perspective that may reveal any social relations between the accused and the victim. Based on this theory, preparation for trial requires attention to the many facts regarding the case, the personality of both the accused and the victims, and the nature of relationships between them. He was interested in the dynamics of the interaction between the accused and the presumed victim. He developed a typology to aid in determining the degree of culpability in the criminal incident. Mendelsohn noted that many crimes resulted from interactions between the accused and the purported victim that must be understood before assigning blame or culpability. He identified six types of victims based on the degree of their role of participation in the crime:

1. The completely innocent victim who bears no responsibility for the criminal act; a victim who did nothing to contribute to her/his victimization, such as a child victim;
2. The victim with minor guilt for the criminal event; a victim who inadvertently places himself or herself in harm's way;

3. The victim who is as guilty as the accused party, e.g. co-conspirators;
4. The victim who is more guilty or culpable than the offender; a victim who instigates or provokes the conflict;
5. A victim most guilty who is hurt during the perpetration of a crime; an attempted robber who is shot in the process;
6. A simulating or imaginary victim; one who fabricates a victimizing incident (cf. Burgess, Regehr and Roberts, 2013; Daigle 2012; Doerner and Lab 2008; Wallace and Robertson 2011).

Based on this typology Mendelsohn suggested for example that in the case of rape or sexual assault there are factors and circumstances that must be accounted for in order to establish guilt and victimization. In his later work, Mendelsohn saw victimology as not limited to crime victims but also including victims of accidents, abuse of power and natural disasters. Mendelsohn's emphasis on assessing all facts and relationships relating to criminal acts and victim incidents offers greater credibility when the findings are based on an empirical, scientific process—a factor that places victimology as a legitimate discipline in the social sciences. For these reasons and the fact that he coined the term 'victimology' Mendelsohn is considered to be the 'father of victimology'. As a discipline parallel to but distinct from criminology, victimology is 'a theoretical study of or knowledge about victims' (Kirchhoff, 2005).

Hans von Hentig. In his book 'The Criminal and His Victim', first published in 1948, von Hentig observed that different professions approach crime from the unique lens of their professional interest. Sociologists look at social conditions that contribute to or respond to crime. Psychiatrists and criminal anthropologists look at physical or mental determinants and responses. With his professional lens as a professor of criminal law, von Hentig examined criminal behavior from four different perspectives; constitutional factors, sociobiological elements, geophysics, and crime victims. His elaborate and rich work has led many to consider him the founder of victimology, though his work on the subject came after Mendelsohn had already developed the concept and defined it as a study of victims. Von Hentigtitled his work, Studies in the Sociobiology of Crime. He first addressed what he referred to as constitutional factors of offenders by focusing on the individual physique, birth and lifespan, physical traits and peculiarities, psychological variables, and mental state or disorders. Von Hentig identified protective and pseudo-protective groups, crises in social and individual or group transition, occupations and religion or belief systems. In discussing geophysical aspects of crime, von Hentig examined delinquency and physical forces such as climate, seasonal changes, time of day, day of week and months of a year and other geophysical characteristics. The fourth major focus in his sociobiological examination of crime was a focus on victims as targets of crime. At the center of victims' attractiveness as the target of criminal victimization was their perceived vulnerability. The vulnerable characteristics of victims include thirteen categories: the young, females, the old, immigrants, the depressed, the mentally defective or deranged, the acquisitive, the dull normal, minorities, the wanton, the lonesome and heartbroken, the tormentors, the blocked, exempted and fighting victim (Von Hentig 1979).

Ezzat Abdel Fattah. Fattah contributed to the notion of victim typology through his identification of five types of victims: (1) Non-participating Victims who feel a denial or repulsion toward the crime and the criminal, and who do not participate in the origination of the criminal act; (2) Latent or Predisposed Victims, who have characteristics that predispose them for being victimized by certain offenses; (3) Provocative Victims, who precipitate the crime or even provoke it; (4) Participating Victims, who by their passivity or other similar attitude make their own victimization possible or easier; and (5) False victims, who are not victims at all or who victimize themselves (cf. Schafer, 1977). Fattah argued that victimology had undergone a metamorphosis from a 'victimology of the act' to 'the victimology of action'; and noted that the discipline had moved from a focus on specific crimes and criminal victimization to a concern with affirmative action for victims of crime. Victimology as science had become overshadowed by developments in the applied field intended to alleviate the plight of the victim (Fattah, 1979).

Marvin Wolfgang and Thorsten Sellin. Two criminologists produced another typology of victims which included: (1) Primary Victimization, referring to personalized or individual victims; (2) Secondary Victimization in which individuals or groups who are victims were not personal targets of offenders; (3) Tertiary Victimization in which the public or the administration of society are victims; (4) Mutual Victimization in which victims themselves are offenders in a given mutually consensual act; and (5) 'No Victimization' where there is no immediately recognizable victim (cf. Schafer, 1977). Marvin Wolfgang contributed further to the discipline with studies conducted with Menachem Amir. Wolfgang conducted the first major study of victim precipitation from 1948-1957 in which he evaluated 588 homicides in Philadelphia, concluding that 'the victim is often a major contributor to the criminal act' (Wolfgang, 1957; cf. also Wallace and Robertson 2011). Wolfgang made a persuasive case for victim precipitation in his Philadelphia homicide studies in which he found that in many instances of homicide, the victim was the first to use physical force against the perpetrator of the violent crime (cf. Doerner and Lab 2011). Efforts of Menachem Amir to apply the same reasoning to rape by examining the role of rape victims in their victimization created a negative reaction towards this approach to the study of victimization. Using Philadelphia police files to analyze rapes reported between 1958 and 1960, Amir argued that rape was victim-precipitated when males believed that females had consented to sexual acts, but then rescinded their original acceptance (cf. Eigenberg 2003; Doerner and Lab 2011). Amir's research and conclusions were largely criticized because they focused on the perpetrator's interpretation or claims about the victim's actions which essentially held the victim responsible for the perpetrator's actions. This fueled the notion of victim-blaming as a factor in dealing with and responding to victims. Today, researchers have become more focused on victims as innocent objects of their offender's abusive impulses.

Richard Quinney (1972). Quinney argued that people in power determine what is criminal with very little consideration for the actual impact or harm done by those acts. According to Quinney, 'the presence of a victim, the one officially designated, is an indication that the existing social order has been challenged' which according to Quinney is also to say that 'the rhetoric of victimization is one more weapon the ruling class uses to justify and perpetuate its own existence' (Quinney, 1972: 315-316). Quinney's argument is that victims, just like criminals, are socially created by those in power to determine that certain acts are criminal.

Stephen Schafer. After examining the work of Mendelsohn, von Hentig, Fattah, Sellin and Wolfgang, Schafer proposed a means to classify victims on the basis of responsibility instead of risk factors (Schafer, 1977). According to Schafer, 'the criminal-victim relationship may point to the genesis of a crime and a better understanding of its development and formation' (Schafer, 1977: 33). Schafer argued further that 'although one might disagree with the idea that proposes to assess the victim's responsibility, the concept (victim's responsibility) may operationally cover the pivotal issue in the criminal-victim relationship, that after all, is the critical problem of understanding and judging crime' (Schafer, 1977: 45). Based on this argument, he suggested the following victim typology:

1. Unrelated, no victim responsibility
2. Provocative victims, victim shares responsibility
3. Precipitative Victims, some degree of victim responsibility
4. Biologically weak victims, no victim responsibility
5. Socially weak victims, no victim responsibility

6. Self-victimizing, total victim responsibility
7. Political victims, no victim responsibility

The World Society of Victimology. Throughout the development of victimology as a discipline, the World Society of Victimology has played a leading role (Wemmers, 2009). Founded in 1979, the goals of the organization are to (1) promote research on victims and victim assistance; (2) promote the interests of victims throughout the world; (3) encourage interdisciplinary and comparative research on victimology; and (4) advance the cooperation of international, regional and local agencies, groups and individuals concerned with the problems of victims (cf. Wemmers, 2009). As a non-governmental organization that has consultative status with the ECOSOC of the United Nations and with the Council of Europe, the World Society of Victimology through its tri-annual symposia and other academic and consultative activities has influenced rapid development of the discipline and its contribution to research and policy. A key achievement of the WSV is the UN Declaration of Basic Principles of Justice and Victims of Abuse of Power. Professors Irvin Waller and LeRoy Lamborn, both members of the WSV, played a key role in the drafting of the UN declaration (Wemmers, 2009).

Parallel Developments

The Second World War and the Cold War. Wars have always brought out the worst in humans who engage in major acts of destruction against other nations. The Second World War revealed an unexpected extent of human cruelty: the holocaust. The passions associated with the holocaust may not have redefined the victim or victimology, but it contributed to a new perspective of victims not as active participants in their victimization but rather people who are targeted for victimization simply because of their identity: Jews, ethnic minorities; handicapped people; and other categories of people who were considered 'less than' or 'imperfect'. The suffering of these completely innocent people drew the attention of criminologists and victimologists to the distinction between perpetrators and victims as distinct groups and individuals. The need to protect the innocent and to hold offenders accountable for their evil, hateful thoughts and actions became the concern. The mere thought that victims might have a role in their victimization became offensive thus moving victimology away from its original premise. The perception that the holocaust was not a spontaneous or random expression of hate between groups or a government reaction to external aggression, but rather a systematic planned activity of an elected government against its own citizens appropriately shocked the world. The holocaust did not simply reveal ethnic hate and cruelty; it also exposed deliberate government use of science and technology to exterminate and to victimize, further increasing the passions in favor of victims and against perpetrators as distinct groups.

Following the end of the Second World War, despite the development of the United Nations and international agreement and unity against human victimization, the world evolved quickly into three major camps. A military alliance treaty signed on April 4, 1949, called the North Atlantic Treaty Organization made up of some North American and West European countries emerged as an exclusive group. As if it was feeling left out, the Soviet Union initiated an alternative treaty organization; the Warsaw Treaty Organization of Friendship, Cooperation and Mutual Assistance which was signed on May 14, 1955. The rest of the world was left out and became a target of courtship and manipulation by the two opposing military alliances. The issue of the welfare and rights of citizens in either of the camps became a major bargaining point in what became known as the Cold War.

The Civil Rights Movement in the U.S.A. The consciousness of global human rights aroused in the minds of many blacks in America a sense of urgency to demand the civil rights long denied them at home. The civil rights movement exposed to the world the hypocrisy of criticizing Nazi Germany while denying American black equal rights and liberties. Demonstrations against segregation in schools, public places including buses and restaurants, and housing, as well as the assassination of President Kennedy in 1963, led to a sense of urgency in the U.S. and resulted in the Civil Rights Act of 1965 and the voting rights act that outlawed discrimination in voting and other public institutions. President Lyndon Johnson followed by introducing and pursuing a campaign against poverty and urban decay. His campaign for a "great society" made the dream of equal rights real for minorities and hope for others who were victimized by tradition and law.

The Feminist Movement. Though women had always voiced concerns about their status in society in relation to the right to vote and to be treated equal, the response to these demands was weak. The success of the Civil Rights Movement gave new energy to the feminist movement. Now there was a broad demand for a constitutional amendment giving women equal rights in voting, employment, freedom from abuse, focus on crimes against women and other areas related to gender. Though the constitutional amendment did not pass, the laws have gradually changed in all areas. Both the Civil Rights Movement and the Feminist Movement contributed to a group-oriented focus of victim policies and activities, rather than on a neutral or objective study and policies on victims. As a result, victimology evolved as a social movement rather than the scientific discipline it is destined to be. Sociologists define a social movement as a collection of individuals who organize together to achieve or to prevent some social or political change (Fine 1985). According to the philosopher George Sorel, social movements unite a group of people, giving them a feeling of participating in a moral cause. It unifies individuals in a struggle for common ideals against their common enemies (Collins and Makowsky 1989). Victimologists find themselves united against perpetrators by the common goal of serving victims, whether or not they understand the victimization or even whether victimization actually occurred. Many who identify as victimologists find themselves dealing almost exclusively with crime victims, with very little interest or concern for 'non-crime' victims.

A Global Movement for Human Rights. While Victimology progressed professionally and academically, and while it helped promote victim interests scientifically, the victim's status reflected various political developments as well (Elias, 1986: 19). According to Elias, the post-World War II euphoria about human progress lost considerate momentum because of the Cold War and the Korean War, as the international concerns about promoting rights proceeded only very slowly. The Cold war was fought by appealing to the political interests of people in the developing countries as both sides of the war accused each other while promising a better life for citizens of the new nations scrambling for independence. Gradually, human rights interests were picked up by those interested in the well-being of segments of the population trapped in various social, economic and political circumstances. The United Nations and other regional and global organizations started emphasizing initiatives against public ills such as poverty, disease, starvation, civil liberty violations, abuse of power, child abuse, violations of women's rights, and economic exploitation. Victimologists' concerns for human rights has also grown to include other cultural practices such as female infanticide as a major victimological concern (K. Chockalingam, 2000). Chocklingam argues that female infanticide is a unique form of victimization because usually he killing is done by the family of the child and therefore there is no complaint as the perpetrators are either parent themselves or other relatives or family members with the active or tacit consent of the parents.

The Focus and Concerns of Scientific Victimology

Early victimologists saw in the discipline a science that would study victimization experiences in order to explain and prevent them. They viewed victimizing situations as comparable to criminology in that studying human interactions in victimization would help explain those human behaviors. The new science was able to study the behaviors of victims as well as offenders. As a science, they envisioned that victimology would address the following themes:

1. Theoretical developments and research that would help explain the causes of and contexts of victimization.
2. Theory-Based: To maintain a scientific identity, victimology must be based on a sound theoretical framework. This means that our knowledge of facts must be based on empirical testable assertions and not emotional sensitivities about victims. The concepts and definitions to be used must have empirical observable and measurable characteristics independent of personal biases or experiences and an acceptable degree of universal applicability.
3. Research Oriented: As a science, victimology must be based on and encourage rigorous research that takes into consideration all relevant factors related to its existence, characteristics, attributes and all related dynamics. Acceptance of facts must be based on empirical rather than emotional or socially expedient criteria.
4. Pure Research: Though there are many economic, social and political benefits and incentives for applied victimology research that relates to victim services, this should never be the primary purpose of victimological research. Pure research that is directed by an open-ended curiosity about the natural world and is not limited to inquiries of specific individual interests has led to new unexpected discoveries that have broadened our knowledge of the world and humanity today.
5. Applied Research: To suggest that victimology must emphasize pure research is not to imply that there should be limited or no focus on applied research. There is certainly a place for applied research for the purpose of understanding and responding to particular human and social needs. Many human victimological problems demand urgent policy responses. Research that provides policymakers and service agencies with findings and recommendations of the most effective strategies is necessary and must be pursued.
6. Research on the impact of victimization on individuals and on society is essential.
7. Research on effective ways of responding to and preventing victimization is essential.

Much of the early work in victimology shows the above as the promise of the new discipline.

Victimology as Advocacy for Victims: Benefits and Pitfalls

To argue that victimology has evolved as a social movement rather than a scientific discipline is not to undermine its contribution to knowledge and the improvement of service to victims. Victimology has, in fact, contributed immensely to increasing the awareness of the needs of victims globally, and also in making major improvements in responding to victims' needs and to the quality of care given to them. Contributions of the discipline are readily apparent to consumers of academic literature on crime and justice. Some are more obvious to policymakers than to average consumers.

Anyone familiar with criminal justice statistics is aware of the National Victimization Surveys and International Victimization Surveys. A major contribution of victimology as a social science is the victimization survey data that have helped researchers to gain a better appreciation of the magnitude of crime problems and the trends and characteristics of those involved in criminal activity. Daniel Glaser (1970) documented the advantage of victim survey data in assault; noting that in a third of the aggravated-assault cases and over half the simple assaults the victim did not report the assault to the police. This means that without victimization survey data, the official data would represent a small fraction of the actual amount of crime in society. This attests to the importance of the science of victimology, in contrast to the overabundance of texts and articles that limit victimology to social and political services and victim advocacy. Advocacy is commendable and needed with its emphasis on goals directed to solving problems or issues through political or social means – but advocacy is a service, not a science.

Philosophies of Services to Victims

Victim advocates understandably emphasized the philosophical and practical aspects of victim care. A major aspect of the development of victimology is to reclaim the place and role for victims that have been lost in the effort to create an objective or impartial approach to dealing with crime and criminals. According to Christie (1976), states and organized courts, have taken away the rights of individuals to sort out their conflicts. Irvin Waller (2011) observes correctly that the victim is almost forgotten in the courtroom and in the criminal justice system as we scramble to protect the rights of suspects and the protection of society. The United States Justice Department publishes a Victims' Rights and Services Guide for people working with victims. Many states in the US also have legislation on victims' rights and services. Office for Victims of Crime (OVC), Office of Justice Programs (OJP) and its sponsored publications include:

1. A clear articulation of victim rights
2. Public awareness of particular crimes and victimization trends such as identity theft, fraud, and other forms of awareness materials
3. Advancing and implementing effective survivor-driven advocacy
4. Financial support for victims of crime
5. Social Support to diminish the negative effects of elder abuse
6. Identifying and developing a multidisciplinary approach and best practices for sexual assault kits
7. Enhancing Police Responses to children exposed to violence
8. Other publications for general information to improve services to victims.

According to the Office for Victims of Crime, 'every crime has a victim, but not every victim has a voice within the criminal justice system. Victim advocates perform a myriad of functions for victims which may include speaking or acting on a victim's behalf, serving as a liaison between the victim and the court system to minimize the physical, psychological, emotional, and financial effects of the crime on the victim' (OVC 2018).

The move toward victim assistance has become a major focus of victimology and other organizations that have emerged over the years dealing with victims. The focus on victimology as a science that seeks to produce a greater understanding of victims, however, appears to have been neglected. We want to revisit the development of victimology and discuss its scientific promise in an attempt to make a case for reclaiming that promise.

Re-examining Definitions of Victimology

Early victimologists, (Mendelsohn, Von Hentig and Schafer) saw victimology as a study of victims and offender contexts and situations. They were concerned with victimization contexts, causes and typology and not victim care. Many who advocate for victims see their unique notion of victims without a clear definition of the victim or what the discipline of victimology does or should do. Karmen (2007) defines victimology as the 'scientific study of the physical, emotional, and financial harm people suffer because of illegal activities'. Karmen, like many victimologists, addresses victimology largely from the criminological and service perspective; by focusing on loss and harm. The truth is that victimology is not a limited concern for criminologists, human service and jurists. Many who study and intervene in working with victims come from diverse disciplines such as Social Work, Sociology, Psychology and Psychiatry, Medicine, Political Science, Business and of course Criminology and the Criminal Justice

Sciences. Too many of these professions, it is human suffering rather than a criminal activity that is important to them.

We define a victim as 'an individual who perceives himself or herself or is perceived by others as enduring an unwelcome pain and suffering.' From this definition, we see victimology as the study of victimizing contexts, processes, causes, theories pertaining to, victimological impacts and related issues, including all consequences of victimization and social, political, economic and other responses to said victimization. This definition returns to the original work of victimology's founding fathers and their expectation that the discipline will lead to increased understanding and prevention and not simply to provide relief for those who are presumed to be suffering. This call for a return to the victimology of the founding fathers forces us to re-examine the work of Mendelsohn. As a barrister who prosecuted and defended suspects of different crimes, Mendelsohn clearly saw the significance of objective or empirical facts in establishing victimization and culpability. He used the most sensitive and difficult forms of victimization to make his point, that of rape. Mendelsohn recognized that in almost every society rape is a crime or at least an offensive form of victimization. Like many sexual acts, most rapes occur where there are no eyewitnesses to provide evidence on what really happened. In many situations, the presumed suspect and victim have different explanations of what really happened. Not only do most rapes occur without third-party witnesses, but it also is ordinarily not an easy crime to commit. As morally offensive as forcible rape is, adjudicating it requires a comprehensive understanding of the contexts in which it is alleged to have happened and should not be based on moral outrage or sympathy for the alleged victim. Completing the criminal act requires the offender to overcome several physical and moral challenges.

According to Mendelsohn, the doctrine of victimology became more apparent to him while defending a suspect in a double homicide in 1945. That the accused killed his former wife and her new lover with premeditation were not in doubt. The facts of the case provided an important dimension to the understanding of the motive for the murder. Though the accused and his (ex-)wife, who had one daughter they both loved, were divorced and the wife now had a new lover, she would invite him back to the house under the pretense of preparing lessons with their daughter. She would feed him and keep him overnight and throw him out the following morning after she had taken all his money. In addition, her new lover, who was a soldier, ridiculed him. The accused cited the repeated exploitation, extortion and humiliation as the reason for killing both of them. These mitigating circumstances became relevant in his sentencing. In his discussion of the new doctrine of victimology, Mendelsohn differentiated himself from Hans von Hentig. According to Mendelsohn, von Hentig 'sees his study of the victim as a chapter in criminology' whereas he (Mendelsohn) considered victimology as a separate science which, because of its structure and its aim, should be an independent discipline (Mendelsohn 1963).

Implications of the Definitions

Perception of Victimization. Victims may perceive themselves correctly or incorrectly as a victim, and third-party witnesses may also perceive other people correctly or incorrectly as being victimized. Unfortunately, it is the perception rather than the actual act that determines victimization. In discussing of intergroup victimization, Dadrian (1972) argues that in such situations, 'victimization is not viewed as a unilateral but rather as a bilateral form of collective behavior in which the perpetrator and victim are discerned as interdependent units'. People may change their perception of who is a victim and who is a perpetrator based on increased awareness or other factors. The perception may also be influenced by others or by circumstances.

Third parties whose perception determines victimization may also be influenced by other factors related to or unrelated to the perceived victimization. Professionals with experience or history of dealing with victims may draw conclusions or develop perceptions of particular situations based on previous experiences, which may or may not be correct.

The factor of endurance is to experience pain or suffering for an extended time. Again, how long does one have to suffer or experience pain in order to constitute victimization? The argument herein is that not every unpleasant experience is victimization. If we are able to stop any unpleasant experience, it would not continue and so we would not have to endure it. As far as the perceived suffering continues beyond the ability of the person suffering it to end it, there is victimization.

The factor of being unwelcome means that the individual did not ask for the experience, does not want it and would stop it if they could. Pain is any physical, mental or emotional distress or injury. Suffering is any unpleasant experiences such as limited mobility, inability to function, loss or deprivation that is experienced.

A Future for Scientific Victimology

In order to evolve as a science, victimology must attempt to develop and to explore empirical-based theories and research methodologies that influence or shape academic and scientific work in the following areas:

Academic Pedagogies. The teaching of victimology as a science focuses on empirical observations, historical and contemporary observations and applications of related material. There are many victimology texts and classes at different universities, but few attempts to provide a sound definition or theory for understanding the discipline. Many simply define victimology as a study of victims. Karmen (2007) defines victimology as the scientific study of the victim's plight, the criminal justice system's responses and the public's reaction. He defines a victim as a person who suffers physical, emotional, and financial harm because of illegal activity. The definition of one who suffers as a result of illegal activity limits the definition of the existence of law and illegal behavior of others.

Our definition of victimology as those who endure unwelcome experiences leads us to argue that persistent or enduring situations are those that are not temporary or transient, and not necessarily a result of the criminal or illegal action of others. We argue further that the suffering is based on a perception that might change. A sound study of victimology must include the following: How do we study and understand persistent human situations? Next, in our definition of victim, is the idea of unwelcome experiences present? Painful or deprivation experiences may be welcomed or resented by those who experience or observe them. Individuals or groups consciously welcome or resent their experiences. Society might create standards of behaviors or experiences that are acceptable or unwelcome to the public. In many such situations, it is the unwelcome standards that determine victimization.

Victimological Symposia. Since the early founding of the World Society of Victimology, the society has met every three years on a different continent, where people interested in the discipline come to present their research and engage in discourse with each other about the directions of the discipline. This is a very welcome activity for a new discipline. It is probably the first discipline that at its infancy is global in nature and has not only envisioned a world view but has also had an immediate impact. Those who come to the symposia get excited about the prospects of service to victims, as they easily identify particular types of victims of injustice and discuss how the needs of such victims might be met. The focus on service to victims, though important, may disregard the necessary theoretical and substantive roots for the discipline.

Research and Publications. There have been a plethora of publications in the name of victimology. Many of them pay some homage to the founding fathers such as Mendelsohn, von Hentig, and Schaefer and then go on to write about particular victims, such as family, crime victims, victim legislation and victim services. Victim typologies and victim-offender relations that were central to early formulations of the discipline have become almost non-existent in publications, perhaps out of fear of victim-blaming, or simply a different parochial interest. Research and publications on victimology that is dedicated to the science should not be restricted in language and research curiosity out of fear of social reactions. Victimological problems such as family violence would be studied with an open examination of family dynamics and relations in which they occur. The role of all victims in the circumstances of their occurrence would be studied effectively and written about just like studies of etiologies of health and illness are done.

A central concern of the founders of victimology was the relationship between victims and their victimizers and other related contexts of victimization. They were not afraid to address the role 'perceived victims' played in their own victimization or the general contexts in which the victimization occurred. The role of victims in precipitating the conflict that produced the undesirable result was important in the treatment of victimization as a social event. This approach was very similar to what the medical profession does in its evaluation of etiologies of illness. Where had the patient been? What did the patient eat? With whom or what did the patient have contact? What had they been doing? All these questions contribute to diagnosis and treatment. A scientific study of victimology must address legal, cultural, social, psychological, personality, political and all other factors that contribute to the comprehensive understanding of victimization situations as well as victim experiences. This we believe was the vision of Mendelsohn. Just like the practice of medicine that focuses only on patient care and nursing without the understanding of causes, contexts and etiologies would be incomplete and probably ineffective, victim service without an adequate understanding of victimization would be incomplete and inadequate.

Contributions to Economic and Social Policy. Scientific Victimology should contribute to the policy by providing empirical facts untainted by group or factional interests. If victimology as a social science adds to the understanding of the social world, it would be very instrumental in helping to address different forms and causes of social and human suffering and help to improve human life and human conditions.

The Current State of Victimology. Available literature suggests that the intersection of victimology as a science and victim services has compromised the enthusiasm on victimology as a science. Victimology research has focused largely on finding relief for targeted victims often with less interest in understanding the contexts and processes of victimization. Understandably, advocacy for particular types of victims may make resources available for research that leads to effective responses to particular types of victims. People might contribute money for services in response to particular types of victims that generate particular interest. Unfortunately, service-oriented research that is based on empathy might ignore much-needed research on victims that do not generate the same empathy. Research the benefits children and elderly victims might attract more interest than research on immigrant, ethnic minority victims and inmate victims. Some individuals or groups may not generate research interest until they attract the attention of advocacy if research is based on the desirability of victim service. This dilemma is consistent with an earlier argument of Richard Quinney (1972) that power and interests can be said to influence the determination of who is a victim and which victims get the most attention and what type of attention they receive.

Suggestions for Aspiring Victimologists

Victimology has attracted the academic interest of scholars and students from academic fields who find that it interfaces very well with their field of academic interest. Victimology is not only inter-disciplinary, it is also global; so victimologists should endeavor to seek, find and accept international/ global partnerships. There are victims in every society and country. Wherever one happens to live and whatever they do, one can focus on possible victimization and the victims in those social contexts.

Concluding Remarks on Applied Victimology

Conceptual, Intellectual, and Theoretical Applications. More work is needed involving definitions based on observed social situations and evolving social norms regarding what is normal, what is not normal and the factors that contribute to those changes. Victimological understanding of what constitutes victimization can be studied. Also, applications of victimology will help inform scientific research and the dissemination of knowledge about victims and the services to benefit victims.

Social and Public Policy Applications. Social and public policies can be made using a shared understanding of victimization and victim-related understanding. Information on lawmaking, interpretation and enforcement based on victimological conceptions is needed. Victimological understanding can also be used in investigation and understanding of deviance related to victimization. Applied research can contribute to greater knowledge and understanding of victims to provide services to victims and to prevent victimization.

Medical and Clinical Applications. The use of victimological formulations and understanding can make significant contributions to diagnose, evaluate, assess and predict empirical understanding and prediction of victims and victimization. Finally, other applications of victimology in different related disciplines can greatly enrich understanding and knowledge that can improve the quality of victim work and services.

References

[1] Burgess, Ann W., Regehr, Cheryl, and Roberts, Albert, R. (2013). Victimology; Theories and Applications (2nd Ed) Burlington, MA: Jones and Bartlett.

[2] Christie, Nils (1976). Conflicts as Property, *British Journal of Criminology*, Vol. 17, No. 1 in Victimology by Paul Rock (Ed) Brookfield, USA: Dartmouth.

[3] Chockalingam, K. (2000). Female Infanticide-A Victimological Perspective in Victimology at the Transition from the 20th to the 21st Century a Festschrift for Hans Joachim Schneider by Friday, Paul C. and Kirchhoff, Gerd Ferdinand (Eds).

[4] Dadrian, Vahakn N. (1974). The Structural-Functional Components of Genocide: A Victimological Approach to the Armenian Case in Victimology by Israel Drapkin and Emilio Viano (Eds.).

[5] Daigle, Leah E. (2012). Victimology. Thousand Oaks, CA: Sage Publications.

[6] Davies, Pamela, Francis, Peter, and Greer, Chris (2017). Victims, Crime and Society. Thousand Oaks, CA: Sage Publications.

[7] Doerner, William G., and Lab, Stephen, P. (2011). Victimology. Boston, MA: Anderson.

[8] Fattah, Ezzat A. (1979). Some Recent Theoretical Developments in Victimology. *Victimology: An International Journal,* Vol. 4, No. 2, pp. 198-213.

[9] Fisher, Bonnie S., Reyns, Bradford W., Sloan, John J. (2016). Introduction to Victimology. New York: Oxford University Press.

[10] Glazer, Daniel (1970). Victim Survey Research: Theoretical Implications, in Victimology by Israel Drapkin and Emilio Viano (Eds.) (1974) Lexington, MA: Lexington Books.

[11] Hindelang, Michael, J., Gottfredson, Michael R. and Garofalo, James (1978). Victims of Personal Crime: An Empirical Foundation for a Theory of Personal Victimization. Cambridge MA: Ballinger.

[12] Karmen, Andrew (2007). Crime Victims, an Introduction to Victimology (6th Ed) Belmont, CA: Thompson Wadsworth.

[13] Kirchhoff, Gerd F. (2005). What is Victimology? Tokiwa International Victimology Institute.

[14] Mendelsohn, Beniamin (1963). The Origin of the Doctrine of Victimology, Exerpta Criminologica, 3, pp. 239-245. In Victimology by Paul Rock USA: Dartmouth.

[15] Schafer, Stephen (1977). Victimology: The Victim and His Criminal. Reston VA: Prentice Hall.

[16] Von Hentig, Hans (1979). The Criminal and His Victim, Studies in the Sociobiology of Crime. USA: Schocken Books.

[17] Wallace, Harvey and Roberson, Cliff (2011). Victimology: Legal, Psychological and Social Perspectives (3rd Ed). Boston, MA: Prentice Hall.

[18] Waller, Irvin (2011). Rights for Victims of Crime. Lanham: MD: Rowen and Littlefield.

[19] Wolfgang, Marvin E. (1957). Victim-Precipitated Criminal Homicide, *Journal of Criminal Law, Criminology and Political Science 48*(1), 1-11, reprinted in Victimology by Israel Drapkin and Emilio Viano (Eds.), pp. 79-92.

[20] Wemmers, Jo Anne (2009). A Short History of Victimology, in Victimology, Victim Assistance and Criminal Justice by Otmar Hagermann, Peter Schafer and Stephanie Schmidt (Eds.) Niederrhein University.

Chapter V

The International Criminal Court's Victim Participation Scheme – A Great Victimological Achievement, But What is Its Future?

SAM GARKAWE

Introduction

One of the key justifications in today's world for prosecuting people involved in very serious crimes such as genocide, crimes against humanity and mass war crimes, is to provide 'justice' to the victims of these crimes. The victims of such international crimes ('international victims') were in the past often marginalised after societies had returned to peace as the focus was more on the capture and then prosecution of the key offenders; reconstruction of effected societies and communities; and restoring order in the part of the world that suffered during the commission of these crimes. Prior to the establishment of the International Criminal Court ('ICC'), Courts instituted in order to prosecute offenders of these serious crimes also largely marginalised international victims for reasons made clear below. The innovative scheme for victim participation under the ICC, to be described in more detail below, was intended to provide a much better system of justice during court processes for international victims. The main purpose of this Chapter is to critically examine this claim, having the benefit of now seeing how the Court has operated in its first 16 years or more. There have been many critiques of the participation scheme, with some writers and commentators questioning the usefulness of the scheme and arguing that victims' interests can be better served in alternate ways to victim participation (Schabas 2011, 501), or that participation be more tightly controlled and the main focus of the system be on the traditional aims of criminal justice – namely, investigation, prosecution and punishment (McGonigle 2011, 357-360).

This Chapter will proceed as follows. Part II will discuss the concept of victim participation in the context of adversarial criminal justice systems, civil criminal justice systems and under international criminal justice mechanisms. In doing so, it will outline the main benefits of the concept of victim participation. Part III will then examine the ICC participation scheme in more detail and in doing so, will define what the scope of the scheme is for the purposes of this Chapter. This Part will also argue that the participation scheme is one of the great achievements of the modern victims' movement. The analysis of the scheme in this Part will lead into Part IV that will outline the main limitations, problems and criticisms of the scheme. The Conclusion will argue that provided there is continual monitoring and improvements where necessary, the benefits of the scheme outweigh the negatives and the scheme should continue into the future.

The Concept of Victim Participation in Criminal Justice – Why Should Victims Participate?

What do we mean by the concept of victim 'participation' in a criminal justice system and why is it a good idea? We will start by an analysis of the criminal justice system the writer is most familiar with – the modern adversarial, common law criminal justice system based upon British law and extended to many of Britain's former colonies. The 'modern' adversarial system came into operation largely from after the middle of the 18th century when State agents took over the prosecution of all serious crimes from individual victims. We start with this analysis not because the writer is most familiar with the British common law system, but as will be shown below, until the ICC was instituted, generally international criminal courts largely followed this model of criminal justice. Thus, to understand the origins of international criminal justice from a victims' perspective, a study of adversarial systems is necessary.

It is now well accepted that in such justice systems crime victims were considered and referred to as the 'forgotten' persons of the system because structurally they were no longer a party to court proceedings - only the prosecution and defence were parties and only they had the decision-making power that goes with being a party to court proceedings. Victims' involvement in a criminal case, until the rise of the modern victims' movement, was largely restricted to them being a witness in court proceedings only when and if called upon by the prosecution. Furthermore, even when they did testify, their testimony was largely restricted to a question and answer format in both their examination and cross-examination (especially where the trial involved a jury). While it is possible to regard a victim testifying as 'participating' in the criminal trial, this is not the sense in which this Chapter regards victim 'participation'. 'Participation' in the sense of this Chapter is much more than victims being witnesses in criminal trials; it involves victims' having agency and being able to make decisions independent of other justice professionals, with perhaps the ultimate in 'participation' being that of being entitled to have their own lawyer represent them in proceedings. It will be shown later that many civil systems of criminal justice allow for this; as does the ICC scheme.

So why is there a need for (the expanded view of) victim participation in adversarial systems? The positive arguments in favour are that it is a matter of procedural justice for the person(s) most impacted by the crime to have a structured input into proceedings – namely, the victim(s). This of course does not mean victims views are to be accepted – it is more a matter of the principles of natural justice (sometimes better described as 'procedural fairness') – that people effected by decisions should at least be able to present their perspective before a decision is made. Allowing victims some role may also contribute to their restoration, and perhaps will contribute to the prosecution by providing information to the court that the prosecution may have missed. The other way to look at the key arguments in favour of participation is to take the negative argument – what are the consequences of victims not being a party to a criminal trial, only being considered to be, in effect, pieces of evidence, and not being able to participate in the broader sense described above? There is much evidence and research to show that all too often victims in the adversarial system of justice never receive information about the progress of their case, and rarely receive any compensation or reparation for the crime inflicted upon them. They generally did not have the ability to put their point of view to the court on issues affecting them. Even when they are called upon to give evidence in Court, this has not proven satisfactory in many instances. Not only has their ability to tell their 'story' been restricted due to the formal question/answer format of criminal proceedings, but also it has been shown that testimony can result in further trauma for victims, especially when they are vigorously cross-examined by defence lawyers. Without someone to directly protect their interests in court victims are more likely to suffer secondary victimisation by the system itself. This notion of 'secondary victimisation' goes to the heart of why victim participation in criminal trials is mainly advantageous – while it may not necessary result in total 'satisfaction' for victims (given the nature of crime), it has the potential to help victims emotionally by overcoming their feelings of powerlessness and preventing the excesses of defence cross-examination. Of course, any potential therapeutic benefit must be balanced with the potential that participation might lead to false or unrealistic expectations for the victim that may end up being counter therapeutic. Schemes for participation must always be done sensitively and there is clearly a need to educate victims and victim communities on how the Court works and what are the choices victims can exercise in their dealings with the Court, so that expectations can be kept realistic.

Another argument in favour of participation is that it will also benefit victims financially as their claims for reparation will be better advocated, and an integrated reparation procedure within the criminal trial (like the ICC and many civil law criminal justice systems) may be more efficient and beneficial. All these positives should assist in their satisfaction levels and consequential greater cooperation with the criminal justice system. This then leads to direct benefits for the system itself – more reporting of crimes as victims would be more prepared to come forward. Victims and their family/friends very often provide the necessary trigger to invoke criminal justice; if they are not happy with the system more crimes will go unreported. Needless to say this is particularly true for vulnerable victims - entitlement to participation would have direct benefits in particular for women and child victims, with domestic/family violence, sexual assault and child abuse prosecutions being well-established problematic subjects of criminal trials, especially in adversarial justice systems.

It should be stated that the modern victims' movement in adversarial justice systems has seen improvements in the position of victims. These include matters such as state funded compensation, heightened relationships with prosecution Departments, enhanced rights during the justice system including information rights and protections against aggressive victim cross-examination by defence lawyers at court, and the introduction of victim impart statements during sentencing. There is no doubt these improvements need to be expanded and consolidated as they offer the best chance for victim satisfaction within the constraints of the adversarial justice system. However, overall, at a structural level their position will remain weak and an entitlement to have a lawyer directly representing their interests at Court will remain unlikely due to the nature of the adversarial system. While there is some scope for private victim prosecutions in adversarial systems where the state refuses to prosecute, this is often a limited right and is at the cost of victims, and is rarely used as a result.

On the other hand, in civil law systems of justice (often also referred to as the 'inquisitorial' system; a prejudicial label the writer prefers to avoid), victims do have a much wider range of participatory rights, often including the right to have a lawyer represent them in court proceedings. Furthermore, in some jurisdictions, there is legal aid available for this right to become a reality for indigent victims. Such systems are based on models such as the partiecivile French model (Doak 2008, p. 310); and the 'adhesion' or

Nebenklage German/Austrian system, whereby victims become subsidiary prosecutors (McGonigle, 2011, 82-83). While there is considerable variety in the details of these systems, they have been extended in one form or another to many continental European justice systems, and to many former colonies of these European powers in other parts of the world. These models certainly are structurally better for victims in theory than the adversarial model, but they have not been without criticism by victim advocates. In practice a low number of victims utilise their rights under this system (see McGonigle 2011, 83 for research on the German system), and also even when they do, their rights to be represented are at times constrained by the purpose of their representation, which often linked to their civil claims for compensation as an adjunct to the criminal trial. There is no doubt, however, that consideration of such justice systems was high up in the minds of those drafting the ICC Statute and the later Rules of Procedure and Evidence ('RPE') – many of the founders of the ICC were of course distinguished lawyers from such systems of justice. Having said this, it needs to be pointed out that such a right of victims to representation at Court could not be replicated easily when it came to drafting the ICC scheme. There is one very big difference between these European civil law schemes and the ICC that is fundamental to understand and lies at the heart of any analysis and criticism of the ICC model. This is that these European civil criminal justice schemes were established in a domestic criminal justice setting where there is commonly only one victim, or maybe a handful of victims at most, involved in the criminal trial; whereas in an ICC trial, given the nature of the international crimes prosecuted, there will often be hundreds, if not thousands or tens of thousands of potential international victims in a court proceeding. Thus, a model of an automatic right to representation was simply not possible in the drafting of the ICC model – to have hundreds or thousands of international victims with their own representation could not possibly be allowed in the interests of efficiency of the process, preventing massive delays and costs, and ultimately bearing on the right of defendants to a speedy and fair trial. How the ICC scheme has dealt with this issue of multiple victims will be examined in detail below, but it is important to recognise at the outset the difficulties of introducing a victim participation scheme where so many multiple victims have the potential to be involved.

Let us now turn our attention to victims and international criminal courts. The notion of the 'forgotten person' also very much in the past applied to international victims in the court mechanisms meant to provide justice in the aftermath of the atrocities committed against them. The first modern international criminal court, the Nuremberg International Military

Tribunal (the 'IMT'), set the tone for this as although doing justice to the victims of the Nazi regime was one of the primary reasons for the trial, in fact few victims testified; they certainly did not have their own lawyers; and victim compensation was not on the agenda. The main reason for the relative lack of victim testimony was that they were not really needed as the crimes could be proven without their testimony due to both admissions by some of the defendants, and the voluminous and detailed documentary evidence the Nazis had compiled that was often more than adequate as proof of their crimes (Garkawe 2006). After a long hiatus due primarily to the Cold War, the UN Security Council was finally able to agree in the early 1990s to form ad hoc international criminal Tribunals – the International Criminal Tribunal for the former Yugoslavia ('ICTY') in 1993 and the International Criminal Tribunal for Rwanda ('ICTR') in 1994, following the terrible violations of international law in the former Yugoslavia and Rwanda respectively. These Tribunals also largely excluded victims from having their own lawyers, adopting the traditional adversarial model where victims would be witnesses for the prosecution if and when called upon. However, there was now a major difference with the IMT – here concrete measures were needed in order to encourage victims to testify, as unlike the IMT victim testimony was needed for convictions – in particular, for international crimes involving sexual violence. These measures involved a number of major advances – the formation of Victims and Witness Units to assist and support victims in their dealings with the Tribunals, and the development of special procedural rules and/or measures of protection for victims, with special rules being adopted for women and child victims. These measures mirrored many of the advances made for victims in modern times, particularly in adversarial systems of justice (described above). However, victim participation was not part of the structure of these Tribunals.

This changed with the agreement of the world community at the Rome Conference in June/July 1998 to the formation of the ICC Statute (1998), which entered into force on 1 July 2002 following the necessary 60 ratifications and two month waiting period. The Statute includes the innovative victim participation scheme that is the main subject of this Chapter and is described and analysed in more detail below. However, the scheme is one aspect, albeit the most innovative one, of the many victim-related provisions that form part of the overall structure of the ICC (Garkawe 2001). This includes not just the Statute, but also the very significant, from a victims' perspective, RPE that were agreed to by a Preparatory Commission after the Statute was drafted (Schabas 2017, 21-22), and some of the Court's Regulations. The contrast between the lack of victim provisions in previous international mechanisms and those of the ICC is well summed by distinguished international criminal law expert William Schabas:

> The attention given to the role and rights of victims by the Rome Statute of the International Criminal Court, and by its subsidiary instruments such as the Rules of Procedure and Evidence, is quite stunning when set aside the very secondary role they have been given historically by international criminal law and international humanitarian law. (Schabas 2017, 337)

Later criminal courts with an international element (including 'hybrid' type courts that have a mixture of international and domestic criminal justice aspects) established to bring to justice perpetrators of international crimes, have also placed far more emphasis on the rights of victims and some, such as the Extraordinary Chambers of the Courts of Cambodia ('ECCC') (McGonigle 2011, 173-177) and the Special Tribunal for Lebanon (McGonigle 2011, 159-163) allow for forms of victim participation. This perhaps indicates that victim participation is becoming an international norm, emphasising the significance of the ICC participation scheme, which the writer will argue in the next Part has been one of the great triumphs of the modern victims' movement.

A Description of the ICC Participation Scheme

This Part will explain in more detail the ICC victim participation scheme and how it defined for the purposes of this Chapter. As stated already, the writer does not regard a victim testifying in court as being a 'participant' in the criminal justice system, rather it is where the victim has some agency and ideally is even legally represented at Court. It should be noted that is entirely possible for a victim to be both a witness in court and a participant in ICC proceedings, or for a victim to just be a witness (not wishing to participate or being ineligible to do so), or for a victim to just be a participant (being unwilling or unable to provide testimony).

The main provision in the ICC Statute that allows a victim to be a participant in ICC proceedings is found in article 68(3) of the ICC Statute:

> Where the personal interests of the victims are affected, the Court shall permit their views and concerns to be presented and considered at stages of the proceedings determined to be appropriate by the Court and in a manner which is not prejudicial to or inconsistent with the rights of the accused and a fair and impartial trial. Such views and concerns may be presented by the legal representatives of the victims where the Court considers it appropriate ...

This innovative provision is the foundation to victim participation, but in order to fully understand the scheme one needs to also examine the RPE as this provides for a definition of who is a 'victim' under this provision; how a person applies to become a victim participant; and the mechanics of how a Chamber of the ICC decides these and many other issues that involve victims. What is also important is how the ICC has interpreted the key phrases in Article 68(3) and the RPE that specifically relate to victims.

Despite there being a vast jurisprudence related to the above issues, some preliminary points need to be made. First it is essential to understand that article 68 (3) represents a compromise between adversarial and civil systems of criminal justice. There is no automatic right of a victim to become a participant as there largely is in civil systems of justice; rather it is a matter for the ICC's discretion in each case. While ICC procedure, especially with respect to the trial stage of proceedings, has much in common with adversarial systems of justice, this is mitigated by many civil system elements being included, such as victims having the possibility to participate. The ICC system is a truly unique system – a Sui generis blend of adversarial and civil criminal justice.

This then leads to an important second point – that the provision is very discretionary in every sense. A Chamber of the ICC (part of the pre-trial structure of the ICC) must rule on almost all victim issues – and of course this is quite time consuming and demanding of resources. Even setting aside the many issues found in the RPE (such as when does a person qualify as a 'victim'?), just focusing on the above words of article 68 (3) indicates many critical questions that a Chamber must decide: for example, what are a victims' 'personal interests'? What is meant by their 'views and concerns'? What are the 'appropriate' stages of the system they can participate? And when is this participation not 'prejudicial to or inconsistent with the rights of the accused', and to 'a fair and impartial trial'? And finally, when will the Court consider it to be appropriate to allow a victim their own legal representation?

This in turn then leads to the third point – the ICC judges that will have to make such decisions come from different backgrounds – from both adversarial and civil justice systems (and possibly others) – these have conflicting systems with respect to the role of victims, so surely their views on victims issues will be very much influenced by the role of victims in the system they have been educated and operated within. Thus a judge from a civil law background is likely to be open to a broad approach to victim participation, whereas a common law background judge is more likely to take a narrower approach. Not surprisingly, inconsistency has turned out to be a problem between different Chamber decisions. It should be noted that the ICC has no strict formal system of precedent, and until a Chamber decision is referred to the Appeals Division and that Division makes an authoritative judgment, other Chambers are free to make their own decisions on victim issues.

Due to time and word limitations this Chapter will be mainly focused on victim participation during the trial stage of the proceedings, this being the heart of any criminal justice system. This is not to downplay the potential importance of victim participation in other significant stages of the system, such as pre-trial procedures (which includes the framing of the charges), sentencing, appeals, and reparations hearings. Furthermore, there is in most situations a clear relationship between the trial stage and these other stages in terms of victim participation; for example, a good victims' lawyer of course ideally will be able to follow through and bring continuity to represent their client(s) throughout each stage of the system. Another limitation of this Chapter due to time and word limitations will be that it will focus on when the second sentence of article 68 (3) is invoked and the victim(s)is/are able to have a legal representative appointed to act for them. While not denying that a victim may be given permission by the ICC to present their views and concerns themselves to the court without a legal representative, and this is also a form of victim participation under article 68 (3), the ICC has only given such permission in few cases (Kendall & Nouwen 2013, 251). It is perhaps trite to also point out that unless a victim is particularly articulate and knowledgeable and is not suffering significant trauma, it is far from ideal for a victim to attempt to participate during the trial stage of proceedings in this manner anyway.

Why is the ICC victim participation scheme such a major victimological advancement? That the ICC even got off the ground after so many years of international stalemate is in itself a remarkable achievement in international law making – keeping in mind that it is the first permanent international criminal court in human history that potentially at least covers international crimes committed anywhere in the world. For 120 nations or so to also agree in Rome in 1998 to the Statute of the ICC that contained such a wide range of victim-related provisions and the victim participation scheme was clearly a strong acceptance and endorsement of much of the work of the modern victims' movement. While of course there were many differences amongst nations over the terms of the ICC Statute, after much negotiation compromises were reached, but it is fair to say that the victim provisions were of much lesser concern in obtaining agreement than the myriad of other issues the Rome Conference had to deal with. It should also be pointed out that a considerable number of these 120 or so nations had common law criminal justice systems,as a result of which they may have been uncomfortable at least with the victim participation aspect of the ICC Statute, yet they were prepared to signal their consent. And finally, not only did 120 nations agree to the terms of the ICC Statute in Rome but the same number (more or less) went on to then make the commitment at a later stage of ratifying the Statute and thus formally agreeing to its terms, no small matter given these States had to make changes to their own laws in order to comply with the terms of the Statute.

It is true that there was and still is significant opposition to the ICC by a number of major powers (Russia, USA and China in particular), and other key nations have not ratified the Statute (India for example), but this has largely been due to other reasons than the victim-related provisions. In general, one can say that it has been the small and medium states that have been the biggest supporters of the ICC; these states particularly being interested in a global world order based upon the rule of law rather than power politics prevailing. It needs to be highlighted that the ICC Statute and its RPE set out in elaborate terms the rights of accused persons, while at the same time providing for the care and rights of victims like no other previous international criminal court had ever done, or for that matter any type of criminal court. This detailed articulation of the rights of both defendants and victims in the ICC Statute and its RPE and the authoritative jurisprudence being expounded by the Court on many of the issues surrounding these rights make the ICC a great model by which all domestic and other international (and hybrid) type courts can benefit.

Given all the above factors, the writer would thus argue that the widespread acceptance of the victim-related terms of the ICC Statute by States primarily interested in the rule of law is probably the second best victimological international achievement in recent times, behind the agreement of the UN General Assembly to the 1985 UN Declaration of Basic Principles of Justice for Victims of Crime and Abuse of Power.

Limitations, Problems and Criticisms of the ICC Scheme

The discussion to date has focused on the definition and the structure of the ICC victim participation scheme as primarily found in article 68 (3) of the ICC Statute, and to date all seems very positive about the scheme, culminating in the claim that it is one of the great achievements of the modern victims' movement. In this section we will look more closely at how the ICC participation scheme has actually worked after over 16 years of the

ICC's operation. The focus will be on the negative aspects and criticisms of the scheme, which has led to some questioning its future viability.

We will start with the limitations of the scheme. For a start, there are a number of issues that relate to the manner in which the ICC has defined a 'victim' for the purposes of being able to participate under article 68 (3). Rule 85 (a) of the RPE states that: 'Victims' means natural persons who have suffered harm as a result of the commission of any crime within the jurisdiction of the Court'. There are many issues with regard to this definition (and for that matter the application process, including proof of identity (see McGonigle 2011, 240-257), but the most important is probably the requirement of a link between harm suffered and 'any crime within the jurisdiction of the Court'. On a broad reading of the phrase it would seem a person can be considered a victim provided they have suffered due to any crime under the Statute, with no need for it to be a crime a defendant has actually been charged with. However, the clause has been interpreted in a far narrower manner, and this has serious ramifications. The ICC Appeals Chamber has ruled that '[f]or the purposes of participation in the trial proceedings, the harm alleged by the victim and the concept of personal interests under article 68 (3) of the Statute must be linked with the charges confirmed against the accused' (Lubanga 2008, para. 2, 64). McGonigle (2011, 249-250) states that 'This judgment of the Appeals Chamber once and for all determined that only those victims who can show a causal link between the harm and the charges against an accused can participate in trial proceedings' (see also Baumgartner 2008, 422-423).

This ruling invokes a number of critical limitations on which international victims can participate in the trial. It must first be understood that the ICC is not meant to prosecute all potential offenders involved in the commission of international crimes in any given situation being investigated by the ICC. Due to time and resource limitations the ICC will generally only attempt to prosecute the most senior persons responsible for the particular crimes that it is investigating. In most situations of mass international criminality there are many potential defendants, and not surprisingly the ICC could not possibly prosecute each one; quite rightly it is selective to choose the highest ranked or the most responsible and/or the ones who they have the best chance of gaining custody of and then securing a conviction. Many of the 'high ups' prosecuted might not commit the crimes themselves; more likely it is their foot soldiers and others down the chain of command who actually physically carry out the crimes. The limited number of defendants indicted by the ICC in a given situation will mean that crimes committed against many international victims will simply not be prosecuted, and this in turn means that these international victims will be very unlikely to be declared as 'victims' for the purposes of the participation scheme as per the above ruling of the ICC Chamber. Their chance to participate are extinguished very early on. Furthermore, even where victims are recognised as being eligible for participation, they will be unable to use their participatory rights until the Court is able to physically take possession of the defendant that is theoretically 'before' the ICC. A substantial number of the defendants indicted by the ICC remain at large. For example, victims of the Ugandan Lord's Resistance Army ('LRA'): '…enjoy formal status before the court, but because the defendant members of the [LRA] have not been arrested, the victims substantive participatory rights have been deferred' (Kendall & Nouwen 2014, 247). Note that this is still the case today, over 5 years since this statement was made, and in fact, some of the defendants have died in the meantime!

A second limitation is that even where the international victim's alleged perpetrator is being prosecuted and is before the court, time and resource limitations may well restrict the areas of a conflict the Prosecutor is prepared to investigate and then prosecute – it may save its resources for those areas where investigation is easier, or where there is better quality evidence, or where the commission of international crime is more obvious. In fact, there may not even be a logical reason to leave out certain areas – it may be a necessity to choose some areas given resource limitations and the fact that the prosecution believes there is plenty of evidence in the areas focused upon to obtain the necessary convictions against the chosen defendant(s). The consequence of this is that if you are an international victim of a crime committed in an area that the prosecution has chosen not to investigate/prosecute you again probably miss out on being a 'victim' for the purposes of the participation scheme.

A third limitation is that even where both the international victim's alleged perpetrator is being prosecuted and the crimes investigated are in an area where the international victim was victimised, the international crimes that the prosecutor chooses to actually charge the defendant with may not include those that are of particular concern to the international victim involved. The ICC Statute makes it clear that the ICC shall only have 'jurisdiction over persons for the most serious crimes of international concern' (ICC Statute, Preamble and article 1), and the 'most serious crimes' may not include the very ones that an international victim may be most affected by. Furthermore, the Prosecutor, for various reasons such as lack of sufficient evidence to convict, may decide not to proceed with some charges, even though 'serious'. There are some pre-trial procedures that victims' representatives can utilise to attempt to change the list of charges brought (this issue being beyond the scope of this Chapter), and some trial procedures as well – namely the use of ICC Regulation 55. If these fail to change the charges this means that while the victim might be able to participate, it may not be in respect of a crime that the victim is most concerned about. A good example of this is found in the first historical prosecution (and conviction) brought by the ICC – namely that of Thomas Lubanga Dyilo. The charges drafted by the prosecutor and confirmed by the ICC focused on the conscription, enlistment and use of child soldiers (ICC Statute, articles 8(2) (b) (xxvi) & 8(2) (e) (vii)). However, victim advocates:'long voiced their annoyance and indignation over these narrow set of charges' (McGonigie, 2011, 294), and wanted crimes involving rape and other sexual crimes included in the charges. Part of the problem was that child soldiers were perpetrators of such crimes, but could not be charged. The request to include sexual violence related crimes was ultimately denied, although the ICC did ensure that discussion of such crimes were part of the proceedings and were acknowledged as having occurred – this was still not entirely satisfactory (McGonigle, 2011, 294-296).

There are further limitations of the scheme from a victim participation perspective which stem from how the ICC Rules attempt to deal with the potential problems of having multiple victims wishing to participate. In cases where there are hundreds, if not thousands of victims wishing to participate, the ICC clearly must strike a balance in finding workable procedures that will not be overwhelmed by the numbers of victims' representatives wishing to participate, the fair trial rights of defendants and the right of victims to have their say and participate. The RPE attempt to strike this balance in two ways – first, by limiting the number of victim representatives and then, secondly, placing limitations on the involvement of victims' representatives. In regards to the second limitation, cases to date show that victims' lawyers have been allowed to 'participate in eight ways: to attend hearings; make oral motions, responses, and submissions; file written submissions; access evidence; ask questions; submit evidence; call witnesses; and be notified' (Moffett 2015, 268). While this list seems comprehensive, victims' representatives must generally apply each time to a Chamber of the ICC in order to make any specific intervention. Only when the ICC Chamber has examined the application (including any responses to the application by the defendant's lawyer and the prosecution) and decided in favour of it can the lawyer be assured they can do what they wish to do during the trial. This process is obviously time-consuming and there is no certainty beforehand in the result of their application given the Chambers do not operate on a strict precedent system. Results of applications have been known to vary considerably on the permitted scope of a victims lawyers role, perhaps depending on the different judge's background who make up Chambers.

With respect to the first method of limitation, the RPE in Rule 90 (2) allows an ICC Chamber to 'request' victims or groups of victims to choose a 'common legal representative', and goes on to suggest that it may request the ICC Registrar to choose one or more common representatives where victims cannot agree (Rule 90 (3)). In such situations, the Rule goes on to say 'The Chamber and Registry shall take all reasonable steps to ensure that in the selection of common legal representatives, the distinct interests of victims... are represented and that any conflict of interest will be avoided'. (Rule 90 (4)). While this sounds all well and good, conflicts of interest are hard to avoid when there are a large number of victims to be represented by one lawyer, even where that lawyer is from the same cultural/ethnic/racial/religious background. Can one lawyer really represent a multitude of victims? Naturally, the problems of whether there is fair representation is multiplied when the lawyer is not from the same background as the victim.

Leaving these difficulties aside, there are many more problems whereby the seemingly worthwhile concept of legal representation becomes increasingly diluted as one lawyer may be needed to represent more and more victims. While the number of victim participant applicants started at low levels, not surprisingly, the numbers have increased exponentially over time (Schabas 2017, 340), although they have plateaued over recent years. A Report by the International Federation of Human Rights (2014) has suggested in their recommendations to improve victim participation that meetings with legal representatives be restricted to a maximum of 50 victims. But even if there are a maximum of 50 victims per meeting, is this sufficient for a victim to feel represented? Can a victim actually get to talk to their 'own' lawyer in such circumstances? Another big problem is where victims live remotely (as many of the African international victims do) and there are difficulties in victims attending meetings. An even larger issue is where the victim lives in Africa (as to date all ICC victims do as all cases have African defendants) and the victims' lawyer is based in Holland – can there really be a relationship between the lawyer in Holland and the victim? Another problem is that victims' lawyers increasing are being represented by other lawyers, making representation even more indirect. For example, victims' lawyers in the Kenyan situation are based in Kenya, but are represented by lawyers at the seat of the ICC in The Hague. In the Bemba case about 5000 victims applied to be represented, but the Court only allowed there to be two victims' lawyers at Court - while victims' could have their own lawyers, these lawyers were only allowed to be represented at Court by two lawyers. This is similar to how the ECCC dealt with multiple victims in case 002 (the pivotal case of the leaders of the Khmer Rouge) – victims could have their own lawyers, but only two victim lawyers could address the Court. This idea of your lawyer being represented by other lawyers makes representation indirect at best, and a dubious form of representation at worst. One starts to wonder whether this is really representation that would satisfy the basic right of victims to have their 'views and concerns' put to the court?

All the above discussion points to two more very obvious problems with the victim participation scheme. One is the scheme, given all the extra victim issues that the ICC must decide, adds to the time in finalising cases. Delay is one issue on which defendants, victims and almost everybody associated with the Court can agree –they are bad and should be kept to a minimum. This is particularly so for international criminal trials which notoriously already go for inordinate lengths of time. Too much delay is also a violation of the fair trial rights of the defendant. With respect to the victim participation scheme the potential for delay is manifest and manifold –first, the victim application process by which a new branch of the Registry – the Victims Participation and Reparations Section ('VPRS') – has been instituted in order to check applications by persons wishing to be considered as 'victims', and make recommendations to Chambers on their suitability, has at times left victims having to wait for a long time just to find out if they would be recognised by the Court as victims. Then there are the questions around article 68(3) ICC Statute when those declared as 'victims' apply to participate – the Chamber must decide what are a victims' 'personal interests' and what is meant by their 'views and concerns'? What are the 'appropriate' stages of the system they can participate? And when is this participation not 'prejudicial to or inconsistent with the rights of the accused', and to 'a fair and impartial trial'? And finally, when will the Court consider it to be appropriate to allow a victim their own legal representation? Assuming a lawyer is appointed, then there are all the Chamber decisions surrounding the scope of what they might wish to do in court (see above), and the Court then having listen to and take into consideration their arguments. And in each of these Chamber decisions, the Chamber must seek and allow for the views of the defence and prosecution (adding of course to a strain on their resources as well).

As well as the problem of delay there is of course the obvious associated problem of the extra costs involved with the victim participation scheme. Not only are there the direct costs to the court of a new section of the Registry to deal with victim applications (VPRS); the new Office of Public

Counsel for Victims ('OPCV') to overview and organise the scheme for victims' lawyers, including the cost of legal aid for victims' lawyers; and the cost of mechanisms to provide reparations to victims. There are also, however, a multitude of indirect costs which are very hard to quantify. These include the extra costs of all the Chamber applications and any written submissions (which may also involve the need for language translation) the Court must deal with in respect of victim participation – these also throw a greater burden onto the defence and prosecution as they have the right to object and/or comment upon each application, and thus must are forced to allocate resources to read and analyse them. The total cost is potentially huge, and '(u)nfortunately, no adequate study has been conducted assessing the full cost of victim participation and placing this alongside the value of the contribution that the unique and unprecedented feature of the Rome Statute makes to the proceedings.' Schabas (2017, 349). Schabas goes on to ask rhetorically whether victims themselves have been surveyed if they would prefer the money involved to be spent on this or whether the money might be better utilised to give them forms of direct assistance (given there is generally insufficient ICC funds for victim reparations).

On the other hand, it is always easy to question the costs and delays involved with an innovative initiative such as the new ICC victim participation scheme and question if they are value for money. The International Federation of Human Rights (2014, 6-13) takes issue with these negative arguments. In respect of delay, it points to the opinion of judge Sir Adrian Fulford (2010) who states that victim participation did not add to the length of the Lubanga case he presided over. In respect of costs, it estimates the cost of the quantifiable aspects of the victim scheme – the VPRS, OPCV and legal aid for victim lawyers represents only 4.15% of the total ICC budget. These costs, as well as the indirect costs discussed above must of course be balanced against the advantages of victim participation articulated in Part II above. Costs also cannot be the sole determinative of a justice system – bringing justice to those most effected by the crime and involving them in a meaningful way must involve some costs.

The final problem of the scheme is its potential effect on the rights of defendants to a fair trial. In a detailed section of her book, McGonigle (2011) argues that victim participation schemes have potential risks for the rights of defendants in respect of a number of fair trial principles – the presumption of innocence (the term 'victim' is used in documentation when no one has yet been convicted, and where crimes are not yet admitted); defendant's right to have adequate time and resources for their defence (the need to read and analyse potentially a multitude of victim applications); the right to an expeditious trial as articulated in articles 64 & 67 ICC Statute and in the qualifying clause of article 68 (3) itself; right to trial by an Independent and Impartial Court (danger of Chambers authorising victims lawyers to directly lead evidence); equality of arms (defendants must face not one, but multiple lawyers likely to be arguing for conviction and generally taking a position opposed to their arguments); and the lack of legal uncertainty (vagueness of the procedural rules concerning victims and of the diverse Chamber decisions) (McGonigle 2011, 349-357).

Conclusion – Will the Participation Scheme Survive?

All the limitations, problems and criticisms of the ICC victim participation scheme discussed in Part IV has led some writers to suggest that ICC trials should revert back to the traditional adversarial model, with victims benefiting from separate reparations and restorative justice mechanisms (Schabas 2011, 501), and the money saved from not having the victim participation scheme going into much more money being available for these mechanisms. Of course, there is still strong ongoing support for the victim protection measures used in modern adversarial systems, including the ICTY and ICTR, to be continued and which are even strengthened in some ways by the ICC – namely the Victims and Witness Unit/Section to assist and support victims in their dealings with the Court, and the development of special procedural rules and measures of protection for vulnerable victims such as children when testifying (except perhaps on the issue of anonymous victims/witnesses).

But not only is their opposition to the ICC victim participation scheme by some writers/academics, but also from professionals associated with the Court itself. Defence lawyers and advocates of course are concerned with the impact of the victim participation scheme on the various principles that make up the right to a fair trial as discussed by McGonigle above, and particularly do not like being outnumbered at Court by victim lawyers. Furthermore, extra delays mean their clients stay in custody longer during the proceedings, an injustice if they are eventually acquitted. Prosecutors are concerned that the victim participation scheme means they may lose control of their case as victims' lawyers may disagree and thus undermine their presentation of the case on many issues – such as which defendants to proceed to charge, the actual charges, any 'plea bargain', and what sentence to recommend. Some judges, particularly those from an adversarial legal system, find victim participation and the extra time, costs and effort required, difficult and perhaps unnecessary. Other bureaucrats of the Court are also concerned by the delays and costs that the volume of victim applications bring.

Overall, it is clear that there is major concern and opposition to the victim participation scheme to the extent that many are questioning if it will continue into the future, or at least be significantly be curtailed. Of course, all the criticisms must be balanced against the positives of victim participation referred to in Part II above. The writer remains optimistic concerning the continuation of the scheme. Eliminating or significantly changing the scheme would necessitate some amendments to the ICC Statute (very difficult to achieve), and a major re-write of many of the RPE. It would also make all the discourse coming out of politicians, supporters of the Court and diplomats about the importance of prosecuting international crime for the sake of victims, almost a contrivance, exposing a wide gap between the rhetoric and reality of victims in international criminal justice. Changing the scheme would also re-enforce what writers such as Kendall & Nouwen (2014) have called the gap between juridified (i.e. what happens in practice at the ICC) and abstract victimhood, and be a continuation of paternalistic international justice, whereby victims are invoked symbolically to legitimate international prosecutions (Moffit, 2015), but are not treated well by the system.

Naturally, a continuation of the scheme means that the mostly valid above mentioned limitations, problems and criticisms would all need to be tackled, and improvements to the scheme need to be constantly made as new issues arise. With goodwill and hard work many of the problems have already and can into the future be contained and addressed. One good simple example of this was that the application form that needed to be filled out by a person that wished to participate as a recognised 'victim' was, prior to 2010, a complex 17-page document. In 2009 the Court reviewed the form after many complaints as to its complexity and the difficulties many victims had in filling it out. In 2010 it was changed to a simpler 7-page document (and consolidated with reparation applications) (McGonigle 2011, 240). Furthermore, over time the ICC relaxed proof-of-identity requirements, acknowledging the difficulties of victims in post-conflict areas in providing some documents (McGonigle 2011, 244). Both these changes have made the application process simpler and fairer, although the Court is aware that it needs to guard against fraudulent claims, especially when it comes to claims for reparations (McGonigle 2011, 257).

Let us quickly examine the groups of limitations, problems and criticisms in Part IV above. First, the many international victims who might miss out on being able to participate attributable to resource, geographical and personal limitations beyond their control, and due to lack of arrests of defendants, can receive some measure of justice by being allowed to be involved in collective reparations. An increased use of intermediaries and technology can reduce the distances between international victims and their legal representative. Sufficient, well-trained victims' legal representatives should be appointed in each case so that victims can establish a good connection with their representative. Delays and costs will always be a problem, but must be seen as the necessary cost of giving victims a meaningful voice. Steps should be taken to minimise these, such as reforming the RPE to embrace more developed and certain rules and procedures, and Appeal Chambers rulings should be increasingly sought to add more certainty to their interpretation. Finally, fair trial principles are paramount and should always be upheld. The ICC should ensure that the participation scheme will not jeopardise these – certainly article 68(3) is very clear on this.

The writer's conclusion is that rather than 'throw the baby out with the bath water', the ICC victim participation scheme, with appropriate monitoring and continual reform, should endure and be supported by victimologists. While this Chapter can only scratch the surface of the many issues surrounding this innovative scheme, overall the benefits of the scheme, including advancing victims' procedural and substantive justice, trump its admittedly many problems.

References

[1] Baumgartner, E (2008), 'Aspects of victim participation in the proceedings of the International Criminal Court', *International Review of the Red Cross*, Vol. 90 (870), pp. 409-440.

[2] Doak, J. (2008), Victims' rights, human rights and criminal justice: Reconceiving the role of third parties (Hart Publishing).

[3] Fulford, Sir Adrian (2010), 'The reflections of a Trial Judge', http://www.iccnow.org/documents/Reflections_of_a_Trial_Judge_ASP_New_York_6_December_2010.pdf

[4] Garkawe, S. (2006), 'The Role and Rights of Victims at the Nuremberg International Military Tribunal' in Reginbogin H & Safferling C (eds), *The Nuremberg Trials: International Criminal Law Since 1945* (KG Saur Verlag), 86-94.

[5] Garkawe, S. (2001) 'The Victim-Related Provisions of the Statute of the International Criminal Court – A Victimological Analysis', *International Review of Victimology*, Vol. 8(3), 269-289.

[6] International Criminal Court ('ICC') Statute (1998), [also known as 'the Rome Statute'], adopted by the Diplomatic Conference of Plenipotentiaries on the Establishment of an International Criminal Court (A/Conf. 183/9, 1998).

[7] International Federation for Human Rights (December 2014), Five Myths About Victim Participation in ICC Proceedings.

[8] Kendall S. & Nouwen S. (2014), 'Representational Practices at the International Criminal Court: The Gap Between Juridified and Abstract Victimhood', *Law and Contemporary Problems*, Vol. 76(3) & (4), 235-262.

[9] Lubanga (2008), The Prosecutor v Lubanga, No. ICC-01/04-01/06-1432, 11 July 2008.

[10] McGonigle Leyh, B. (2011), Procedural Justice? Victim Participation in International Criminal Proceedings (Intersentia).

[11] Moffett, L. (2015), 'Meaningful and Effective? Considering Victims' Interests Through Participation at the International Criminal Court', Criminal Law Forum, Vol. 26(2), 255-289.

[12] Schabas, .W (2011), 'The International Criminal Court at ten', Criminal Law Forum, Vol. 22(3), 493-509.

[13] Schabas, W. (2017), An Introduction to the International Criminal Court (5th ed, Cambridge University Press).

Chapter VI

Crime and Development: A Criminological Study

G.S. BAJPAI & GARIMA PAL

The inter-relation between development and crime has been studied and written about for a long while now. It is viable and interesting for legal academia to study the criminal behaviour of the society from a variety of vantage points (Fisher, 1987), and one such interesting avenue happens to be the impact of development on the crime rates of the country. The empirical testing of this complex relation has produced mixed results. Kick and LaFree who conducted cross-national studies have found that economic development contributes to increases in property crime and reductions in violent crime (LaFree, 1985).

The Human Development Index Report 2018 ranks India at 130 out of 189 countries, as opposed to HDI rank 131 in the previous year. This means that the HDI has improved by one level for India. Further, India's annual GDP as per 2018 is at 7.1%, which has increased from 6.1% annual GDP in 2017. This shows that growth rate is also increasing. On the other hand, crime rate in India has been recorded 367.5 in 2014, 374.1 in 2015, and 379.3 in 2016 (NCRB, 2017). It shows 3% increase from 2014-2015 and 2.6% increase from 2015- 2016. Thus, taking a holistic view, all these indices reflect an upward shift in the rate of crime with the increase in growth and development.

Generally, there are three factors discussed in this paper for the increase in crime rates with the increase in development. Firstly, with development, the literacy levels increase in the society and the marginal groups are more empowered, which encourages them to approach the law enforcement agencies, when necessary. Hence, the number of reported crimes increases (Saikia, 2018). Secondly, because of rapid development directly affecting industrialisation, migratory patterns indicate inflow of large number of populations shifting to urban cities from their rural dwellings. This creates an unstable and congested set up and concentration of a very large population at one place, which leads to increase in conflicts (Husain, 2009). Thirdly, unemployment is yet another factor which influences crime rate to a great extent (Husain, 2009). Criminologists suggest that during tough economic times more people tend or rather are willing to commit crimes. The effects of development on crime and indeed, the effects of crime on development, remain important topics for future criminological research. This is due to the fact that countries in the global South continue to experience rapid economic, social, political, and cultural changes as a result of their particular development trajectories (Jarrett Blaustein, 2018).

The purpose of this paper is to analyse the impact of development on crime in India. Due to the multiplicity of factors which represent the level of development in the society, the paper shall concentrate upon only three of such parameters, which are, literacy rate, urbanisation statistics and unemployment levels of the country.

Objectives

- To evaluate scope of economic development with crime rate of India.
- To analyse extent of development affecting crimes of 28 states in India, using Human Development Index.
- To draw out relationship of socio-economic developmental factors with respect to various types of crime.

Research Question

- Is rate of crime affected by growth rate in India?
- Do socio-economic factors of development affect various types of crime?
- Should the parameters of development include rate of crime in its ambit?

Research Methodology

The methodology used for the purpose of this article is doctrinal and descriptive, and the empirical data analysed is based on secondary sources.

Sources of Data Collection

The paper involves the analysis of empirical data available from secondary sources, in order to establish their inter-relation with the entities under consideration. Suitable framework for such an analysis is created where the data has been acquired from National Crime Records Bureau (NCRB) 2011 and Open Government Data (OGD) Platform India. The data has been extracted between the years 2001-2011, even though data from the NCRB 2016 statistics was available. This is because data for indicators of development were in decadal format, i.e. last 10-year data, which was till 2011.

Due to the reason of maintaining consistency in analysis of data taken from a specific time set, i.e. years till 2011, data for HDI is taken uniformly with the rest of the data. HDI or Human Development Index for 28 states has been taken from the National Institute of Public Finance and Policy data base (Sacchidananda Mukherjee, 2014).

Data Interpretation and Analysis

The researchers have tried to present the data and develop a relationship between the variables discussed via Line, Scatter, and Bar graphs. Further interpretation was done using analytical and statistical induction method using SPSS Version 25 and MS-Excel. Further interpretation is done using Correlation and Regression equation for better understanding and deduction.

Factors Affecting Crime Rate with Reference to Development in India

An analysis of the trend in crime rate over the study period reveals an overall increasing trend, with a sharp decrease in 2005 (Fig. 1). The rate of decrease in 2011, however is modest being less than 10%. This figure represents an average trend indicating increase in the crime rate.

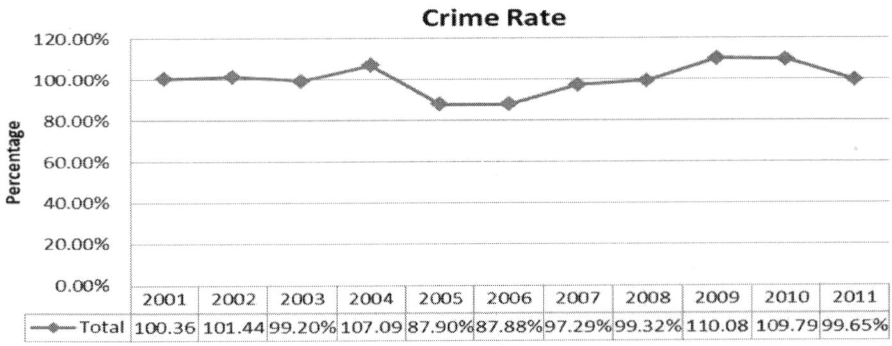

Figure 1: Crime Rate

Another point of significance is the comparative relationship between crime rate and growth rate in Figure 2. This is the major premise of this paper and is graphically depicted in the figure given below. According to the below finding it can be observed that growth rate, as calculated from the GDP growth of India, has drastically increased from the year 2003 and has maintained an upward change except a decline in the year 2008. When it comes to crimes in India, an upward frequency indicating increase in crime rate can be observed, excluding a few years in between and the year 2011.

Table 1: Year-wise Percentage of Growth to Crimes in India, 2000-2011

Year	*GDP*	*Crime Rate*
2001	73.34%	100.36%
2002	48.47%	101.44%
2003	107.55%	99.20%
2004	94.30%	107.09%
2005	119.67%	87.90%
2006	120.81%	87.88%
2007	117.65%	97.29%
2008	84.83%	99.32%
2009	108.43%	110.08%
2010	112.47%	109.79%
2011	112.47%	99.65%
Grand Total	**100.00%**	**100.00%**

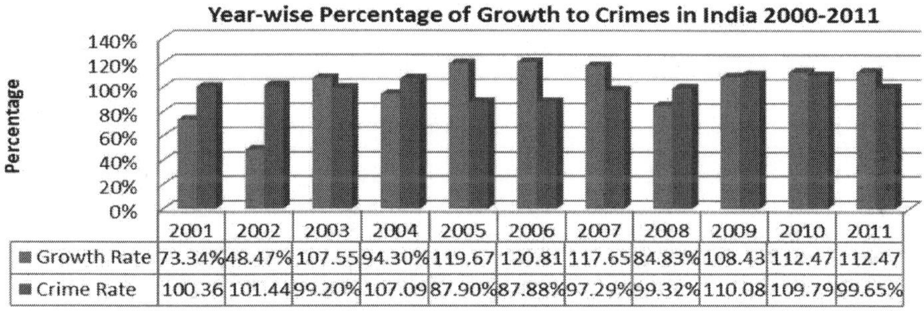

Figure 2: Year-wise Percentage of Growth to Crimes in India, 2000-2011

* In the above figure, relationship between the GDP and the crime rate is graphically presented. GDP is taken as the measure for growth. Both the variables are taken in the histograph so as to measure the difference in value in the subsequent years from 2001-2011.

Interpretation

For the purpose of establishing a relationship between crime rate and developmental growth of a Nation, it is very important that its economic growth is taken into account. GDP is the appropriate indicator for analysing the nexus between crime and development. When examining the variables separately, it can be clearly observed that crime rate is rising along with GDP of the country. This is explained below using Human Developmental Index (HDI) and Crime rate separately, firstly.

In (Fig. 2) above the researchers took GDP as the growth parameter. This economic function to growth is quite important; however other parameters cannot be ignored. One of the major parameters is the HDI i.e.

the Human Development Index. So, in order to analyse the relationship between development and crime, the following segment has taken the variables, HDI and crime rate into focus. HDI for 28 states of India has been taken for data analysing through the software, SPSS version 25.

For analysing the relationship between HDI and Crime Rate, simple scattered graph with fit line has been shown in the figures below separately for each year, i.e. 2001, 2005, 2010, and 2011. HDI taken is the state-wise data for four years of 28 states. (Data for the same is tabulated in the Annexures)

Simple Scattered Graph with Fit line for the Year 2001

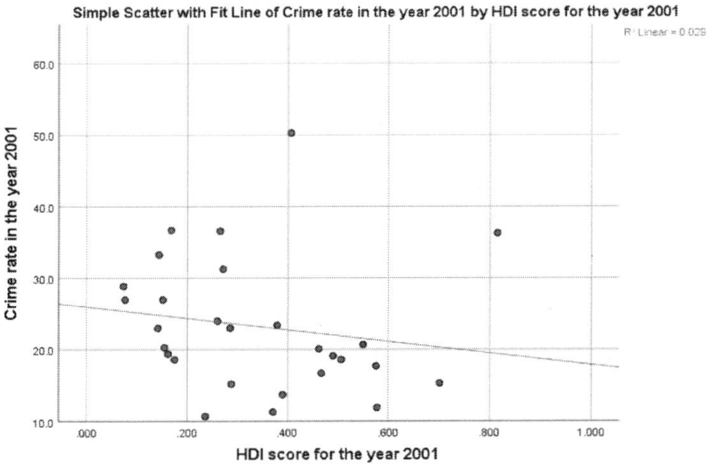

Figure 3: Simple Scatter with Fit Line of Crime Rate in the Year 2001 by HDI Score for the Year 2001

Figure 3 graphically demonstrates the relationship between HDI in 2001 and Crime Rate in 2001 of the 28 states in India. In this equation, crime rate is dependent on HDI. This means to say, the paper seeks to find a relationship wherein when HDI changes, crime rate also changes. So, we can say that crime rate is the dependent variable and HDI is the independent variable.

Crime rate = function of (HDI), i.e. $c = f(H)$

Interpretation

The two variables are plotted on the graph on the basis of their nature. Independent variable is always placed on the x axis and dependent variables are placed on the y axis. Because of this, Figure 3 represents the two variables on x and y axis. Scattered dots represent correlation or the weak relationship present between the variables. In Figure 3, crime rate data is plotted by the y axis and HDI data is plotted by the x axis. The average of the values so obtained is used to craft a fit line showing the direction of their relationship, this called '*a line of regression*', as shown in the Figure 3. A correlation is obtained which is not so a significant correlation. This means in the states where HDI is low, the crime rate is high; and where the HDI is comparatively higher, the crime rate is indicated to decline for the year 2001.

Regression and Correlation Analysis

ANOVA[a]						
Model		*Sum of Squares*	*Df*	*Mean Square*	*F*	*Sig.*
1	Regression	66.349	1	66.349	.769	.389[b]
	Residual	2243.772	26	86.299		
	Total	2310.121	27			

a. Dependent Variable: Crime rate in the year 2001
b. Predictors: (Constant), HDI score for the year 2001

Correlations			
		Crime Rate in the Year 2001	*HDI Score for the Year 2001*
Pearson Correlation	Crime rate in the year 2001	1.000	–.169
	HDI score for the year 2001	–.169	1.000
Sig. (1-tailed)	Crime rate in the year 2001	–	.194
	HDI score for the year 2001	.194	–
N	Crime rate in the year 2001	28	28
	HDI score for the year 2001	28	28

Coefficients[a]						
Model		*Unstandardized Coefficients*		*Standardized Coefficients*	*t*	*Sig.*
		B	*Std. Error*	*Beta*		
1	(Constant)	25.978	3.605		7.207	.000
	HDI score for the year 2001	–8.098	9.236	–.169	–.877	.389

a. Dependent Variable: Crime rate in the year 2001

Here the p value is 0.389 which is more than alpha (.05), we say that the model is not so significant.

To predict whether there is certain effect due to developmental factors on crime rate, Regression Analysis was done, Denoted by $y = mx + b$

Where: m = slope, x = observations, $b = y$ intercept

The slope is negative (-8.098) is very small, thus stating that HDI is a negative predictor for crime rate. The Pearson's correlation coefficient is (r), which is –.169 and significance level is 0.389; thus, suggesting that there is negligible relationship between the variables.

For the Year 2005

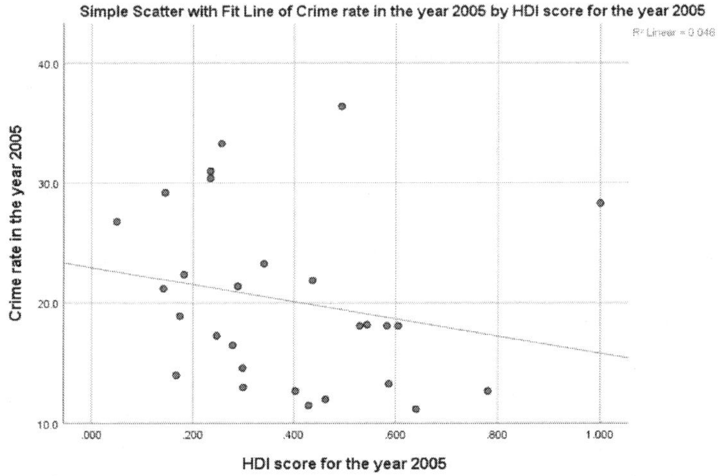

Figure 4: Simple Scatter with Fit Line of Crime Rate in the Year 2005 by HDI Score for the Year 2005

Interpretation

Similarly, for Figure 4, data for the year 2005 is taken. The variables are HDI and Crime Rate, wherein HDI is the independent variable and Crime Rate is the dependent variable. Relationship between the two is shown in Figure 4 by way of graphical presentation of the scattered graph with fit line. The fit line so constructed can be easily deciphered by observing the direction that has been plotted with the help of values of the dependent and independent variable. It shows that HDI and Crime Rate have a not so significant correlation in 2005 also. This means when HDI rises in a state, the crime rate is lesser as compared to states where HDI is low. This can be seen in the table discussed below:

Regression and Correlation Analysis

ANOVA[a]						
Model		*Sum of Squares*	*Df*	*Mean Square*	*F*	*Sig.*
1	Regression	65.328	1	65.328	1.262	.272[b]
	Residual	1346.050	26	51.771		
	Total	1411.379	27			
a. Dependent Variable: Crime rate in the year 2005						
b. Predictors: (Constant), HDI score for the year 2005						

Correlations			
		Crime Rate in the Year 2005	*HDI Score for the Year 2005*
Pearson Correlation	Crime rate in the year 2005	1.000	–.215
	HDI score for the year 2005	–.215	1.000
Sig. (1-tailed)	Crime rate in the year 2005	–	.136
	HDI score for the year 2005	.136	–
N	Crime rate in the year 2005	28	28
	HDI score for the year 2005	28	28

Coefficients[a]						
Model		*Unstandardized Coefficients*		*Standardized Coefficients*	*t*	*Sig.*
		B	*Std. Error*	*Beta*		
1	(Constant)	22.971	2.811		8.171	.000
	HDI score for the year 2005	-7.149	6.364	-.215	-1.123	.272
a. Dependent Variable: Crime rate in the year 2005						

Here the p value is 0.272 which is more than alpha (.05), we say that the model is not so significant.

To predict whether there is certain effect due to developmental factors on crime rate, Regression Analysis was done, Denoted by $y = mx + b$

Where: m = slope, x = observations, b = y intercept

The slope is negative (-7.149), which is very small, thus stating that HDI is a negative predictor for Crime Rate. The Pearson's correlation coefficient is (r), which is -.215 and significance level is 0.272; thus, suggesting that there is weak negative relationship between the variables.

For the Year 2010

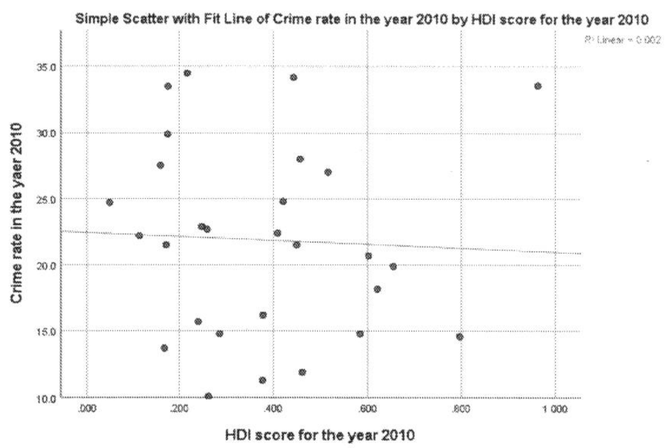

Figure 5: Simple Scatter with Fit Line of Crime Rate in the Year 2010 by HDI Score for the Year 2010

Interpretation

For the purpose of analysing the relationship of crime and development between multiple years, data for 2010 is also taken into account. In Figure 5 shown above, similar process has been followed, wherein independent variable, i.e. HDI is plotted on the x axis and Crime Rate which is the dependent variable is plotted on the y axis. After obtaining a scattered data on the graph, fit line is obtained by finding average data of the two variables based on the plotting done. It shows in Figure 5 that crime and development have a not so significant relationship, wherein in the case where HDI is low, the crime is high and where HDI is high, the crime is low.

Regression and Correlation Analysis

ANOVA[a]						
Model		*Sum of Squares*	*Df*	*Mean Square*	*F*	*Sig.*
1	Regression	2.731	1	2.731	.050	.825[b]
	Residual	1418.903	26	54.573		
	Total	1421.634	27			

a. Dependent Variable: Crime rate in the year 2010
b. Predictors: (Constant), HDI score for the year 2010

Correlations			
		Crime rate in the year 2010	*HDI score for the year 2010*
Pearson Correlation	Crime rate in the year 2010	1.000	–.044
	HDI score for the year 2010	–.044	1.000
Sig. (1-tailed)	Crime rate in the year 2010	.	.412
	HDI score for the year 2010	.412	.
N	Crime rate in the year 2010	28	28
	HDI score for the year 2010	28	28

Coefficients[a]						
Model		*Unstandardised Coefficients*		*Standardised Coefficients*	*t*	*Sig.*
		B	*Std. Error*	*Beta*		
1	(Constant)	22.442	2.850		7.873	.000
	HDI score for the year 2010	-1.460	6.528	-.044	-.224	.825

a. Dependent Variable: Crime rate in the year 2010

Here the p value is 0.825 which is more than alpha (.05), we say that the model is not so significant.

To predict whether there is certain effect due to developmental factors on crime rate, Regression Analysis was done Denoted by $y = mx + b$

Where, m = slope; x = observations, b = y intercept

The slope is negative (–1.460), which is very small, thus stating that HDI is a negative predictor for crime rate. The Pearson's correlation coefficient is (r), which is –.044 and significance level is 0.825; thus, suggesting that there is negligible relationship between the variables.

For the Year 2011

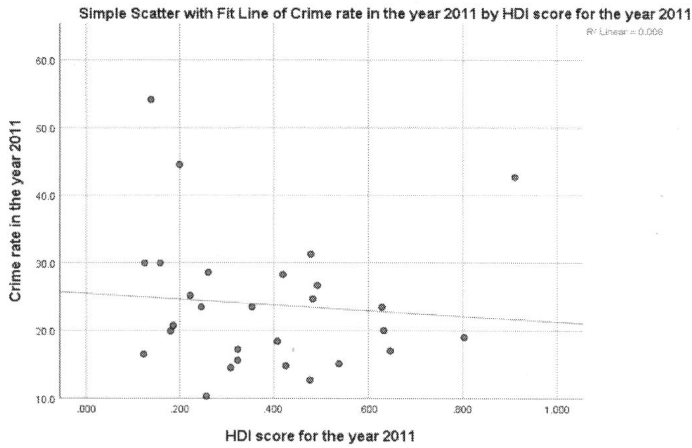

Figure 6: Simple Scatter with Fit Line of Crime Rate in the Year 2011 by HDI Score for the Year 2011

Interpretation

In Figure 6, the same method has been applied like in the above three graphs. Scattered graph has been plotted taking into account the independent variable, i.e. HDI and the dependent variable, i.e. Crime Rate for the year 2011. HDI is placed on the x axis and Crime Rate is placed on the y axis. The fit line so plotted with the help of average of values of the variables indicates that there is a not so significant relationship between the variables. This means in the case where HDI is high, the crime rate is low and vice versa in other cases.

Regression and Correlation Analysis

ANOVA[a]						
Model		*Sum of Squares*	*Df*	*Mean Square*	*F*	*Sig.*
1	Regression	20.987	1	20.987	.200	.659[b]
	Residual	2731.165	26	105.045		
	Total	2752.152	27			
a. Dependent Variable: Crime rate in the year 2011 b. Predictors: (Constant), HDI score for the year 2011						

Correlations			
		Crime Rate in the Year 2011	*HDI Score for the Year 2011*
Pearson Correlation	Crime rate in the year 2011	1.000	–.087
	HDI score for the year 2011	–.087	1.000
Sig. (1-tailed)	Crime rate in the year 2011	.	.329
	HDI score for the year 2011	.329	.
N	Crime rate in the year 2011	28	28
	HDI score for the year 2011	28	28

Coefficients[a]						
Model		*Unstandardized Coefficients*		*Standardized Coefficients*	*t*	*Sig.*
		B	*Std. Error*	*Beta*		
1	(Constant)	25.505	4.129		6.176	.000
	HDI score for the year 2011	-4.246	9.498	-.087	-.447	.659
a. Dependent Variable: Crime rate in the year 2011						

Here the p value is 0.659 which is more than alpha (.05), we say that the model is not so significant.

To predict whether there is certain effect due to developmental factors on crime rate, Regression Analysis was done Denoted by $y = mx + b$

Where: m = slope, x = observations, b = y intercept

The slope is negative (-4.246), which is very small, thus stating that HDI is a negative predictor for crime rate. The Pearson's correlation coefficient is (r), which is -.087 and significance level is 0.659; thus, suggesting that there is negligible relationship between the variables.

Cumulative Interpretation and Analysis

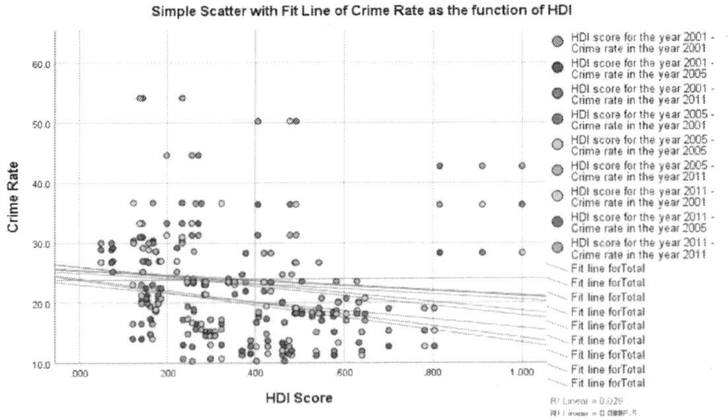

Figure 7: Simple Scatter with Fit Line of Crime Rate as the Function of HDI

Interpretation

Figure 7 is the cumulative depiction of 3 years of data comparing HDI and Crime Rate. HDI is the independent variable, and so data for three years is placed on the x axis. Also, Crime rate for three years is placed on the y axis. Plotting of the two variables is done as in the same way when only one year was taken into account. In the above graph, different colours are used to differentiate between the data of the different years. Upon analysis of the above graph, direction of the Crime Rate and HDI can be measured for different years. Here, HDI and Crime Rate of all the three years show almost a similar result as to the relationship between the two variables. The states where HDI is growing, the crime rate is declining.

In short, interpreting Figure 7 entails to the result that the above-mentioned indicators of HDI have a role in changing the crime dynamics of a society. This means to say that the average of all the factors contribute in influencing the crime rate in a state.

The slope so constructed that is seen from the graph from Figure 3 to Figure 7, is denoted from the fit line. This fit line moves from upward left to downward right side of the graph. This indicates a not so significant relationship between the variables on x axis and y axis, and the slope is less than 0. This result can be further explained from the regression analysis discussed in the next segment.

Relationship between Determinant Variables of Development with Various Types of Crime

In this section of the paper, the researchers aim to take socio-economic factors, which are one of the driving forces in ascertaining development of a nation. These factors include literacy level, urbanisation, and employment. So, these individual indicators are studied separately from the year 2000 to 2011, since the data for these factors are decadal in nature. Apart from this, different crime types are studied, namely – crime against women, crimes

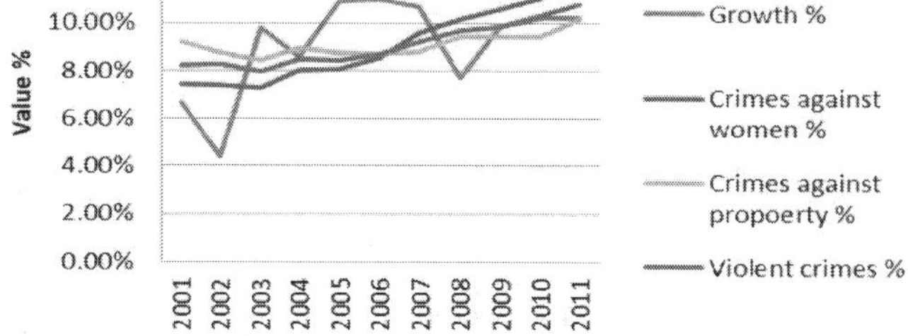

Figure 8: Evolution of Crime (%) and Growth (%) in India

against property, and violent crimes. An interrelation is analysed between the three socio-economic factors and the different types of crimes in order to evaluate the parameters of development in depth.

In Fig. 8, crimes against women, crimes against property, and violent crimes have been analysed with respect to economic growth, i.e. the GDP of India from the 2001 to 2011. It shows even though GDP is on the rise, crimes against women, crimes against property and violent crimes are increasing with the subsequent years. This is not the complete picture for the researchers to measure the relationship between crime and development. For this purpose, three socio-economic developmental factors, i.e. Education, Urbanisation and Unemployment is analysed with respect to the three crime types, i.e. crimes against women, crimes against property, and violent crimes, in the section below. Following are the three factors discussed and evaluated according to the data collected from OGD and NCRB.

Education

Literacy levels gravely impact the crime rate in a society. Increase in the education levels may give rise to both positive and negative effects, thereby affecting crime rate. One of the positive effects of education is the 'civilization effect', which means moral behaviour and other virtues of hard work and honesty can be attained through education, which might be incidental in reducing crime in a society (Husain, 2009). There is a fact that education widens the mind and perspectives about various elements in the society, and a literate person develops enough intellect through education so as to build a solid case for violence (Pani, 2018). Tables below illustrate percentage of crime against women, crimes against property, and violent crimes from 2001-211 in comparison with education, urbanisation and unemployment.

Interpretation

Figure 9 is a clear representation of the scenario as to how crimes against women are affected by the literacy levels in India. From the above scattered data plotting, both education and the said crime is said to have a rising trend, as seen in Fig 9. These are said to be indirectly related to each other, which means changes in the independent variable does not put a direct impact on the direct variables. In such a case, it can be deduced that with the increase in literacy levels, crimes against women are also increasing. It means rise in crimes against women is not completely dependent on the literacy rate. Other than that, this graph is indicative towards the Indian scenario denoting that increase in education is not helping towards reducing crimes against women. This graphical presentation holds true since it is an

Table 1: Education to Crimes against Women

Year	*Crime against Women*	*Education (in %)*
2001	7.45%	61
2002	7.41%	
2003	7.29%	
2004	8.00%	
2005	8.06%	
2006	8.54%	
2007	9.61%	
2008	10.15%	66
2009	10.56%	
2010	11.07%	
2011	11.85%	74.04
Grand Total	100.00%	67.01333333

* *Please note:* Missing data of education is on account of the data being decadal in nature.

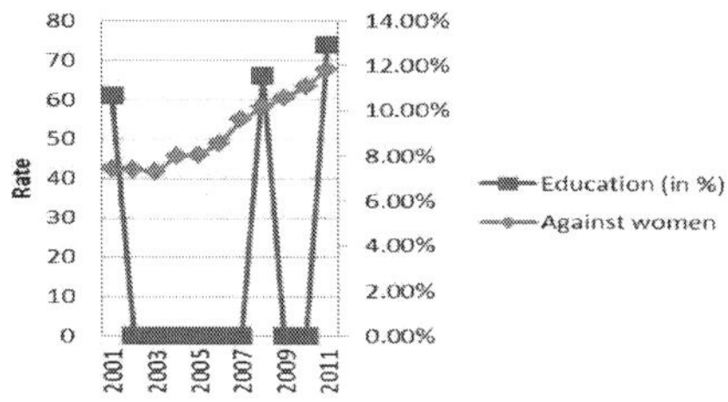

Figure 9: Education to Crimes against Women

* The line-graph points out to a not so significant relationship between crime against women and education as shown in figure. X-axis, i.e. the independent variable has plotted years and the dual Y-axis which plots the dependent variable shows the education, i.e. the literacy rate and crimes against women. The tabular data is plotted in the graph with the values as taken from government data sources.

Table 2: Education to Crimes against Property

Year	*Crime against Property (in rate)*	*Education (in %)*
2001	37.16	61
2002	35.28	
2003	34	
2004	36.08	
2005	35.26	
2006	35.04	
2007	35.47	
2008	38.05	66
2009	38.15	
2010	38.02	
2011	41	74.04
Grand Total	36.68272727	67.01333333

* *Please note:* Missing data of education is on account of the data being decadal in nature.

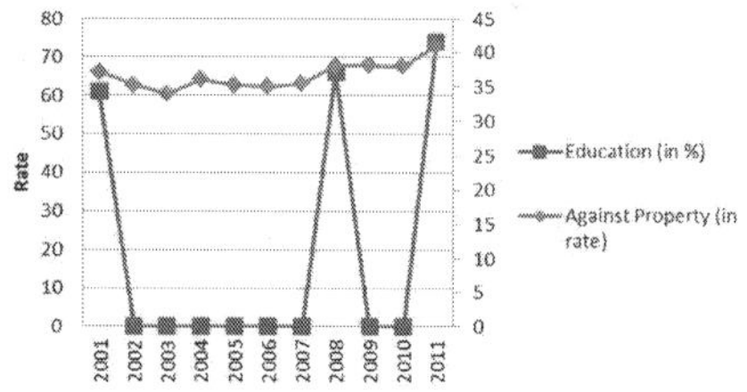

Figure 10: Education to Crimes against Property

* In the above figure, relationship between crime against property and literacy level is plotted. The two variables are plotted along the y axis, with subsequent years on the x axis. This has been plotted along the values obtained of the years 2001-2011.

Table 3: Education to Violent Crimes

Year	*Violent Crime*	*Urbanization (in %)*
2001	8.21%	61
2002	8.26%	
2003	7.96%	
2004	8.50%	
2005	8.46%	
2006	8.71%	
2007	9.23%	
2008	9.71%	66
2009	9.84%	
2010	10.32%	
2011	10.79%	74.04
Grand Total	100.00%	67.01333333

* *Please note:* Missing data of education is on account of the data being decadal in nature.

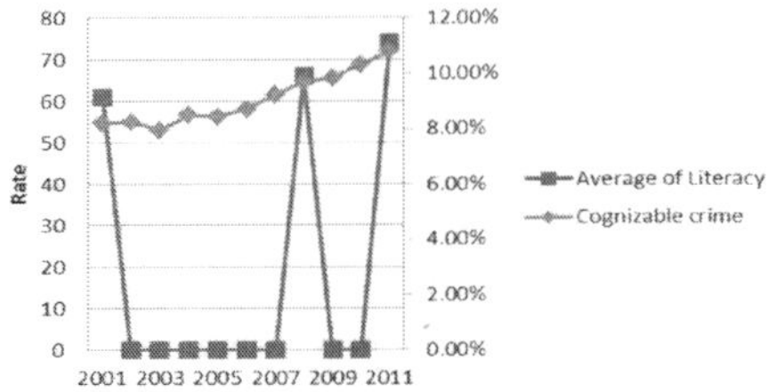

Figure 11: Education to Violent Crimes

* Above Figure is the graphical representation of violent crimes in relation to literacy levels in the society for the years 2001 to 2011. Both the variables, i.e. violent crimes and literacy levels are plotted on the y axis and the subsequent years are plotted on the x axis since it is the constant variable. Violent crimes data taken into consideration are the cognisable crimes committed in India.

unbiased statistical deduction of the data taken from authentic websites of the government.

Figure 10 showcases a not so significant relationship between education and the said crime. The reason why the researchers deduce this representation as a weak relationship is because data of crimes against property is less affected by the independent variable. It is clearly visible from the graph that as literacy levels are rising over the years, crimes against property are increasing along with it.

Figure 11 is a clear representation of the scenario as to how violent crimes are affected by literacy levels in India. From the above scattered data plotting, both education and the said crime is said to have a rising trend, as seen in Fig. 11. These are said to be indirectly related to each other, which means that independent variable is weakly affecting dependent variable. In such a case, it can be observed that as education increases, violent crimes are also increasing in India. Other than that, this graph is indicative towards the Indian scenario, denoting that increase in education is not helping towards controlling violent crimes in the society.

Urbanisation

Urbanisation leads to restructuring of a society at the molecular level. Such inclusion into an urban set-up increases crime rates because of various reasons (Fisher, 1987). Resources remain the same but the mouths to feed increases, hence there is congestion and occurrence of insanitary living among the migrated living because of less space in comparison to large number of people. This leads to social tension, thereby erupting violence and crime (Shelley, 1981). This may result into erosion of community and socio-religious norms already existing in that society to curb crimes (Kumar, 2013).

Interpretation

Figure 12 is a clear representation of the scenario as to how crimes against women are affected by the migration levels in India. From the above scattered data plotting, both urbanisation and the said crime is said to have a rising trend, as seen in Fig. 12. They are said to be indirectly related to each other, which means independent variable weakly affects dependent variable. In such a case, with the increase in migration levels, crimes against women are also increasing. From the above graph, it can be clearly seen that migration to cities has increased from 2001 to 2011. Crimes against women was less in 2001, however, with the increase in the urbanisation levels, the said crime has also increased. It can be said that migratory patterns are affecting crimes against women.

Table 4: Urbanization to Crimes against Women

Year	*Crime against Women*	*Urbanization (in %)*
2001	7.45%	27.78
2002	7.41%	
2003	7.29%	
2004	8.00%	
2005	8.06%	
2006	8.54%	
2007	9.61%	
2008	10.15%	
2009	10.56%	
2010	11.07%	
2011	11.85%	31.14
Grand Total	100.00%	29.46

* *Please note:* Missing data of education is on account of the data being decadal in nature.

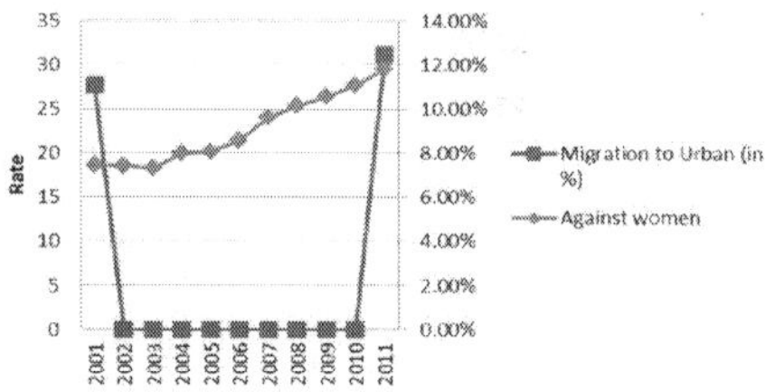

Figure 12: Urbanization to Crimes against Women

* The line-graph draws out relationship between crime against women and urbanisation as shown in Figure. X-axis i.e. the independent variable has plotted years and the dual Y-axis which plots the dependent variable shows urbanisation and crimes against women. The tabular data is plotted in the graph with the values as taken from government data sources.

Table 5: Urbanization to Against Property

Year	*Crimes against Property (in rate)*	*Urbanization (in %)*
2001	37.16	27.78
2002	35.28	
2003	34	
2004	36.08	
2005	35.26	
2006	35.04	
2007	35.47	
2008	38.05	
2009	38.15	
2010	38.02	
2011	41	31.14
Grand Total	36.68272727	29.46

* *Please note:* Missing data of education is on account of the data being decadal in nature.

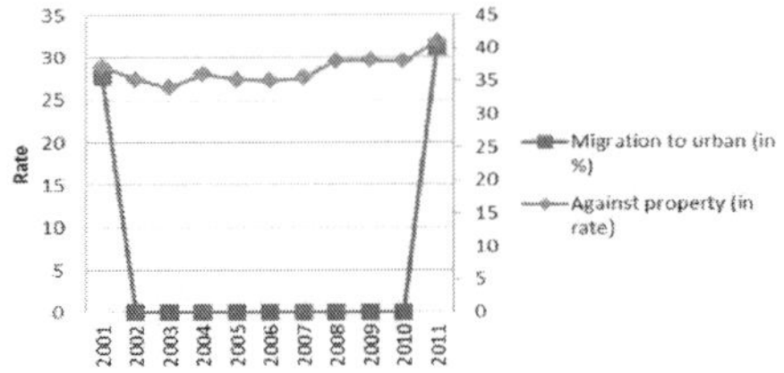

Figure 13: Urbanization to Against Property

*In the above Figure, relationship between crime against property and urbanisation is plotted. The two variables are plotted along the y axis, with subsequent years on the x axis. This has been plotted along the values obtained of the years 2001-2011.

Table 6: Urbanization to Violent Crimes

Year	*Violent Crimes*	*Urbanization (in %)*
2001	8.21%	27.78
2002	8.26%	
2003	7.96%	
2004	8.50%	
2005	8.46%	
2006	8.71%	
2007	9.23%	
2008	9.71%	
2009	9.84%	
2010	10.32%	
2011	10.79%	31.14
Grand Total	100.00%	29.46

* *Please note:* Missing data of education is on account of the data being decadal in nature.

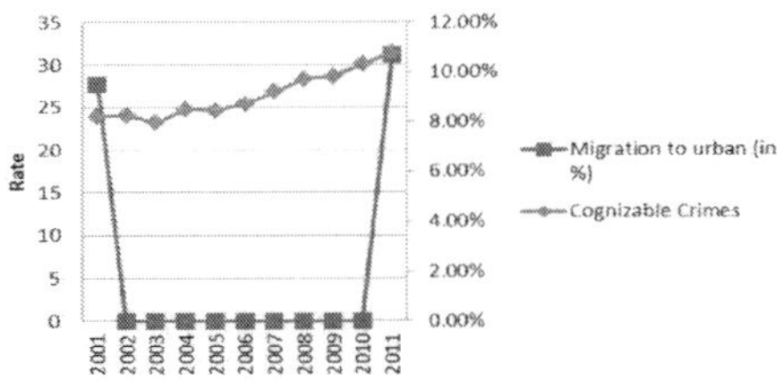

Figure 14: Urbanization to Violent Crimes

*Above Figure is the graphical representation of violent crimes as to urbanisation in the society for the years 2001 to 2011. Both the variables, i.e. violent crimes and migration levels to urban cities are plotted on the y axis and the subsequent years are plotted on the x axis since it is the constant variable. Violent crimes data taken into consideration are the cognisable crimes committed in India.

Figure 13 showcases a not so significant relationship between urbanisation and the said crime. The reason that the researchers deduce this representation as a weak relationship is because increase in independent variable negatively affects the dependent variable. However, it is clearly visible from the graph that as the literacy levels are rising over the years, crimes against property are increasing along with it. This means that with more and more people migrating to urban cities, crime against property is on the rise.

Figure 14 is a clear representation of the scenario as to how violent crimes are weakly affected by the city-migration levels in India. From the above scattered data plotting, both urbanisation and the said crime are said to have a rising trend, as seen in Fig. 14. Thus, can be clearly observed from the graph above that in a scenario where urbanisation levels are rising, crime in that particular area inevitably rises. The data represents a not so significant relationship between the variables. This is mostly because of the social tensions that develop around the people that have migrated.

Unemployment

A firmly established relationship is that of between crime and work status, viz., whether employed or unemployed. Increase in employment opportunities can be expected to have two distinct effects on crime. The first is the negative influence that higher levels of employment or work-force participation exerts upon crime due to the increase in available wealth, because of the higher return from the activity. The second effect is reducing the negative impacts brought about by unemployment through a reduction in the agent's income, as well as by the depreciation of human capital due to the period of absence from the labour market. Also, the longer the agent remains unemployed, the greater the probability of taking part in crime, as shown in Fig.15.

Interpretation

Figure 15 is a clear representation of the scenario as to how crimes against women are affected by the unemployment levels in India. From the above graph, it can be seen that unemployment levels have come down from the year 2001 to the year 2011. This is a positive developmental effect that a society should have. However, crimes against women are constantly on the rise in the subsequent years. It can be observed that as the unemployment rate is decreasing (or employment among the people is rising), rate of the said crime is rising exponentially. It is the general notion that when employment rises, rate of crime tends to decrease. However, from the above

Table 7: Unemployment to against Women

Year	*Crimes against Women*	*Unemployment (in %)*
2001	7.45%	52
2002	7.41%	
2003	7.29%	
2004	8.00%	
2005	8.06%	53
2006	8.54%	
2007	9.61%	
2008	10.15%	
2009	10.56%	
2010	11.07%	37
2011	11.85%	38
Grand Total	100.00%	**45**

* *Please note:* Missing data of education is on account of the data being decadal in nature.

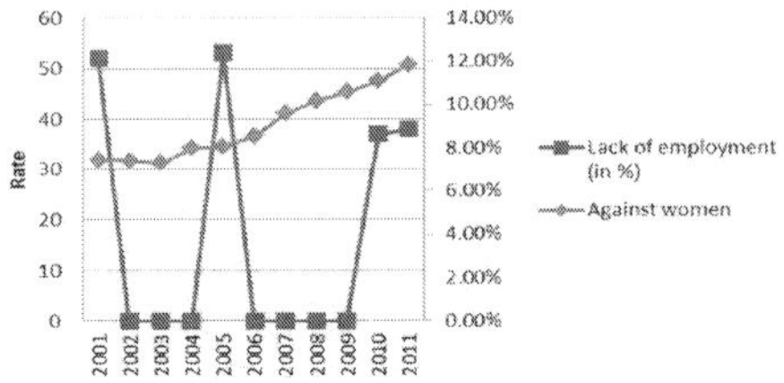

Figure 15: Unemployment to against Women

* The line-graph points out relationship between crime against women and unemployment as shown in Figure. X-axis i.e. the independent variable has plotted years and the dual Y-axis which plots the dependent variable shows unemployment level and crimes against women. The tabular data is plotted in the graph with the values as taken from government data sources.

Table 8: Unemployment to Crimes against Property

Year	*Crimes against Property (in rate)*	*Unemployment (in %)*
2001	37.16	52
2002	35.28	
2003	34	
2004	36.08	
2005	35.26	53
2006	35.04	
2007	35.47	
2008	38.05	
2009	38.15	
2010	38.02 37	
2011	41 38	
Grand Total	36.68272727	45

* *Please note:* Missing data of education is on account of the data being decadal in nature.

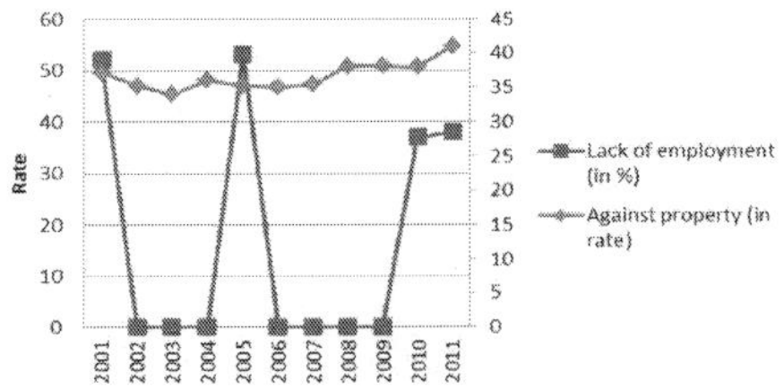

Figure 16: Unemployment to Crimes against Property

* In the above Figure, relationship between crime against property and unemployment level is plotted. The two variables are plotted along the y axis, with subsequent years on the x axis. This has been plotted along the values obtained of the years 2001-2011.

data and Fig. 15, it can be observed that when employment is rising in India, crimes against women are also rising.

Figure 16 showcases a relationship between education and the said crime. This means to say that, as per the graph and the data, property crimes of 2011 have risen and surpassed the maximum level of unemployment as seen in the year 2005. Although the unemployment levels have considerably decreased in the year 2011, crimes against property have increased to an alarming position. The inverse relationship that can be seen between unemployment and crimes against property indicate towards how the Indian society is reacting to the increase in employment levels. This is a negative over-shadow of rising employment levels over the property crimes in the society.

Figure 17 is a clear representation of the scenario as to how violent crimes are affected by the unemployment levels in India. From the above scattered data plotting, both unemployment and the said crime is said to have a relationship as seen from the Figure. From the above graph, it can be seen that unemployment levels have come down from the year 2001 to the year 2011. Although this is indicative of development in a society, but it is negatively influencing rate of violent crimes in the society.

Table 9: Unemployment to Violent Crimes

Year	*Violent Crimes*	*Unemployment (in %)*
2001	8.21%	52
2002	8.26%	
2003	7.96%	
2004	8.50%	
2005	8.46%	53
2006	8.71%	
2007	9.23%	
2008	9.71%	
2009	9.84%	
2010	10.32%	37
2011	10.79%	38
Grand Total	100.00%	45

* *Please note:* Missing data of education is on account of the data being decadal in nature.

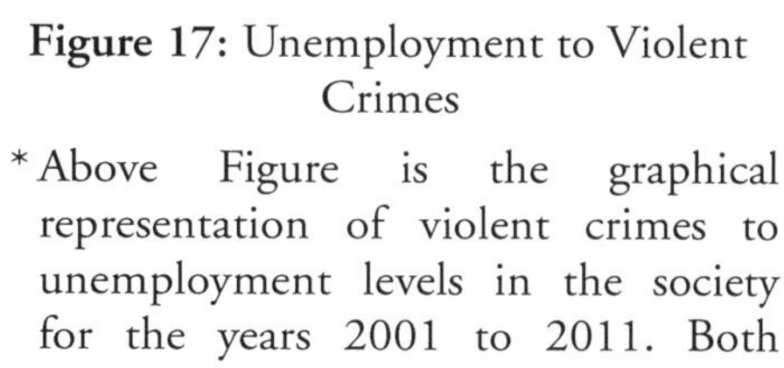

Figure 17: Unemployment to Violent Crimes

* Above Figure is the graphical representation of violent crimes to unemployment levels in the society for the years 2001 to 2011. Both the variables, i.e. violent crimes and unemployment levels are plotted on the y axis and the subsequent years are plotted on the x axis since it is the constant variable. Violent crimes data taken into consideration are the cognisable crimes committed in India.

Discussions

The empirical results show that developmental factors have not so significant and negative correlation with Crime Rate of various states in India, as per data of the years 2001-2011. In the first part, the HDI of the year 2010-11 is highest in the state of Kerala (0.911) followed by Goa (0.803) and Tamil Nadu (0.633). Whereas in the year 2009-10, HDI of Goa and Tamil Nadu was less, and HDI of Kerala was higher than in 2010-11. Surprisingly, Crime Rate rather than decreasing in these states have increased – Kerala (42.7 in 2010-11, 33.6 in 2009- 10), Goa (19 in 2010-11, 14.6 2009-10) and Tamil Nadu (20 in 2010-11, 18.2 in 2009-10). The researchers through the empirical data discussed above have tried to individually study the relationship of developmental factors and crime rate between the years 2001-2011. The researchers in Figures 3-7 have thus tried to draw out the relationship and the effect of crime on development across 28 states in India. In the second part of this paper, the researchers have individually analysed developmental measures, like education, urbanisation and unemployment of India. Figure 9 to Fig. 11 state how education affects crime. Even though education percentage has increased from 2001-2011, it does not decrease the percentage of crimes committed against women, property, and violent crimes. This is being justified by negative correlation deduced from the slope. Education should have played the key factor in decreasing the percentage of crimes committed, however, the empirical data suggests otherwise. Figure 12 to Fig. 14 analyses urbanisation as one of the factors contributing towards development of India. However, the graphs portray a different picture. As the urbanisation percentage increases between 2001 and 2011, the crime percentage against women, property, and violent crimes also increases. Figure 15 to Fig. 17 established a weak negative relationship between unemployment and crime. The graphical representation shows that even though there is decrease in the percentage of unemployment between 2001 and 2011, the percentage of crime still increases.

Recent Trends

The researchers have also compared current GDP and crime rate to understand trends between 2001 to 2019, as depicted in Fig. 18. It can be interpreted from Fig. 18 that as the GDP changes, crime rates get affected. The current scenario states that there is a dip in the GDP of India and as a result crime rate is increasing. If every state across India has preventive strategies to control crime to a minimum level, the predicted annual GDP could be improved.

Table 10: GDP to Crime Rate

Year	*Average of GDP*	*Average of Crime*
2001	77.85%	105.89%
2002	51.46%	107.03%
2003	114.17%	104.67%
2004	100.10%	112.99%
2005	127.03%	92.75%
2006	128.24%	92.73%
2007	124.89%	102.66%
2008	90.05%	104.79%
2009	115.11%	116.15%
2010	119.39%	115.84%
2011	119.39%	105.14%
2012	70.22%	101.31%
2013	73.16%	109.96%
2014	85.63%	74.78%
2015	99.29%	76.12%
2016	107.20%	77.18%
2017	109.48%	NA
2018	96.08%	NA
2019	91.25%	NA
Grand Total	100.00%	100.00%

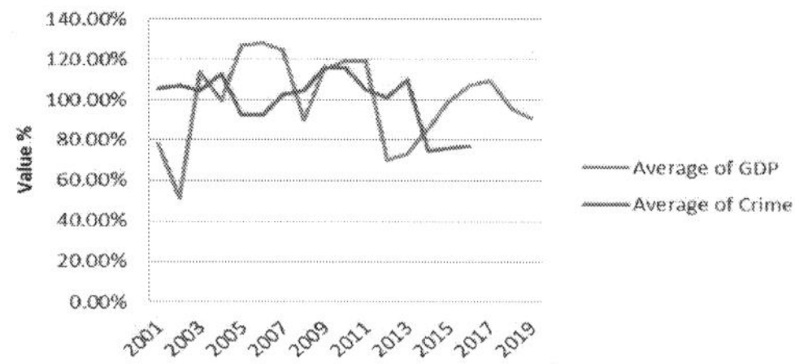

Figure 18: GDP to Crime Rate

* The above data and line graph are the representation of the relationship between GDP of the Indian economy and the Crime Rate in India. It shows the relationship between the two variables in percentage. There can be seen a relationship between GDP and Crime Rate.

In the above Figure, researchers have taken the data from the years 2001-2019. The GDP index of India has been taken from IMF World Economy Outlook (GDP Growth of India, 2019) and the Crime Rate data has been taken from the National Crime Records Bureau. Crime rate is limited to the year 2016, since it is till this year that NCRB has been published. Fig. 18 shows the graphical relationship between Crime Rate and GDP and showcases that in the years where GDP was on the rise, i.e. in the years 2005 to 2014, Crime Rate was considerably decreasing; however, when GDP deteriorated, i.e. in the years 2001 to 2004 and 2015 to 2016, the frequency of crime also started increasing. This denotes an inverse relationship between the two variables. Hence, this negative relationship is indicative of the fact that economic development of the country also affects its crime rate.

Conclusion and Suggestions

To draw a certain kind of relationship between socio-economic developmental factors and crimes in India, the researchers applied bivariate methods. To test the robustness of various parameters chosen, the researchers used correlation tests. In the first section of the paper, the researchers found a negative relationship between GDP and Crime Rate across India. In the second section, the researchers found negative and statistically a not so significant relationship between Crime Rate and Human Development Index across 28 states. In the third section, the researchers individually analysed socio-economic developmental factors, like Education, Urbanisation, and Unemployment with crimes against women, property, and violent crimes. The results show that socio-economic developmental factors also haves' important effects on crime per se. Though, this does not rule out the fact that other developmental factors like legal, political, and other social factors may also play an important role in influencing the level of crime. This paper is a small attempt to take necessary steps in helping curb crimes in India. The researchers through statistical representation have tried to develop a rough picture of the current standing of our country. The Criminal Justice System of our country needs to be more modernised and reformed given the magnitude of forgone economic offences. Also, the social and economically inclusive development restrains the crimes committed in our country.

References

Abbott, M.C. (1973). *Crime in Developing Countries: A Comparative Perspective* . New York.

Bureau, N.C. (2017). *Crime in India 2016.* Govt. of India, Ministry of Home Affairs, New Delhi.

Fisher, S. (1987). Economic Development and Crime: The Two may be associated as an adaption to Industrialisation in Social Revolution. *The American Journal of Economics and Sociology, 46*(1).

GDP Growth of India. (2019, 7 17). Consulté le 1 8, 2020, sur Statistics Times: http://statisticstimes.com/economy/gdp-growth-of-india.php

Husain, M.D. (2009). Determinants of Crime Rates: Crime, deterrence and growth in post-liberalized India . *Munich Personal RePEc Archive* .

Jarrett Blaustein, N.W. (2018). Crime and Development in the Global South. *The Palgrave Handbook of Criminology and the Global South.*

Kumar, S. (2013). Crime and Economic Growth: Evidence from India. *Munich Personal RePEc Archive* .

LaFree, E. &. (1985). Development and the social context of murder and theft. *Comparative Social Research, 8*, 37-58.

Lynch, R.B. (1996). Towards a Caribbean Criminology: Prospects and Problems. *Caribbean Journal of Criminology and Social Psychology, 1*(1), 8-37.

Nations, U. (1970). *Social defence policies in relation to development planning: Working Paper of the Fourth United Nations Congress on the Prevention of Crime and the Treatment of Offenders.* Kyoto, Japan.

Pani, N. (2018, 1 21). *Education does not deter violence.* Consulté le 1 2020, 8, sur The Hindu Business Line: https://www.thehindubusinessline.com/opinion/education-does-not-deter-violence/article10045300.ece

Roser, M. (2014). *Human Development Index (HDI).* Consulté le 1 8, 2020, sur Our World in Data: https://ourworldindata.org/human-development-index

Sacchidananda Mukherjee, D. C. (2014). Three Decades of Human Development across Indian States: Inclusive Growth or Perpetual Disparity? *National Institute of Public Finance and Policy.*

Saikia, K. (2018, 2 24). *Crime and Prosperity.* Consulté le 1 8, 2020, sur *The Indian Express*: https://indianexpress.com/article/opinion/columns/crime-and-prosperity-ncrb-data-assam-crime-5075945/

Shelley, L. (1981). *Crime and Modernization.* Southern Illinois University Press.

Social defence policies in relation to development planning: Working Paper of the Fourth United Nations Congress on the Prevention of Crime and the Treatment of Offenders. Kyoto, Japan: United Nations.

Soares, R. (2004). Development, crime avd punishment: Accounting for the international differences in crime rates. *Journal of Development Economics, 73*(1), 155-184.

UNDP (s.d.). *Human Development Index (HDI).* Consulté le 1 8, 2020, sur UNDP Human Development Reports: http://hdr.undp.org/en/content/human-development-index-hdi

UNDP (s.d.). *Technical notes.* Consulté le 1 8, 2020, sur HDR UNDP: http://hdr.undp.org/sites/default/files/hdr2016_technical_notes.pdf

Chapter VII

Fresher's Victimisation: Failure of Law or Educational Institutions

D.K SRIVASTAVA, AASHISH SRIVASTAVA &
NEERAV SRIVASTAVA

Introduction

Ragging is one of the biggest problem facing higher educational institutions. In India, US, and Australia, the problem is endemic. It is the result of the perceived superiority of senior students over new students or freshers. It includes physical, psychological and sexual ragging and acts of humiliation, violence and acts constituting mental trauma to freshers. Seniors assault freshers in every possible way; murder, rape, assault, causing of grievous hurt and wrongful confinement. Some freshers commit suicide. Apart from committing serious offences new students or freshers are forced to strip naked, consume large quantity of alcohol and coerced into performing unacceptable tasks; writing assignments for their seniors. They are also forced to pay money to seniors (*Deccan Herald*, 2019).

However, higher educational authorities shy away or deliberately ignore ragging complaints. They are conflicted in that they wish to preserve their image and steady flow of students. Also the myth that ragging is benign persists. The atrocious behaviour of higher educational authorities and senior students has led to the passing of regulations and criminalisation of ragging.

This brief article (*Dhaka Tribune*, 2019) examines how the University Grants Commission Regulation on Curbing the Menace of Ragging in Higher Educational Institutions (2009 Regulations) and the UGC Promotion of Equity in Higher Educational Institutions (2012 Regulations) makes significant *attempts* to control ragging. Besides the UGC 2009 Regulations and 2012 Regulations 14 out of 29 states have also declared ragging a criminal offence. This is in addition to the Indian Penal Code (IPC), which applies throughout the country, and proscribes many criminal activities committed in the name of ragging. Apparently neither any the

2009 nor 2012 Regulations or criminal legislation have stemmed the tide of ragging. In fact, ragging is at an all-time high. Criminalisation of ragging in the US has not had an impact either. In the 1990s, the US courts ruled that higher educational institutions owed students a duty of care in negligence to take reasonable care to control ragging.

The failure to control ragging is both (a) a failure of social reform and (b) an aspect of the social failure is legal failure. This paper is concerned with the latter. It explores some of the deficiencies in written law and the problem of poor enforcement.

UGC 2009 and 2012 Regulations

Both the UGC 2009 and 2012 Regulations are comprehensive pieces of legislation designed to prevent ragging in higher educational institutions.

2009 Regulations

The 2009 Regulations apply to all higher educational institutions, including universities and its colleges. The objective is to eliminate ragging. The Regulations are detailed and prescriptive. Ragging includes both words and acts used against a fresher that has the effect of teasing, treating or handing him with rudeness, any rowdy or indiscipline activity which cause or is likely to cause annoyance, hardship or psychological harm or raise fear or apprehension or 'asking a new student to do any act which has the effect of causing or generating a shame, or torment, or embarrassment so as to adversely affect the physique or psyche of such fresher'. It also includes 'exploiting the service of a fresher or any other act for completing the academic task of another individual or a group of them and any act of financial extortion, any act of physical abuse including sexual abuse, homosexual assault, stripping, forcing of doing obscene and lewd acts, gestures, causing bodily harm or any danger to health.

The 2009 Regulation implore higher educational institutional authorities to take all prohibitive and preventive measures necessary to eliminate ragging. Prohibitive measures require authorities not to permit or condone any ragging activity within the boundaries or jurisdiction of the institution.

Preventative measures include, but are not limited to, printing of UGC Regulations in the students admission brochure; obtaining affidavits from students as well as parents or guardians that the student was not involved in any ragging activities in the past; convening a meeting by the head of the institution before the start of the academic session with hostel wardens, student representatives, parents, guardians, representatives of district administration authorities to discuss measures to prevent ragging and steps to identify those indulging in or abetting ragging; constitute anti-ragging squad and anti-ragging committee; strengthening security on the campus by lighting and patrolling and round- the- clock vigil of areas vulnerable to ragging and; the head of the institution to register an First Information Report (FIR) within 24 hours if breaches of any penal law has been committed by the student.(UGC Regulation, 2009)

In case the above measure do not work, and ragging is committed, the institution must take appropriate administrative actions against the ragger as outlined by the 2009 Regulations. These include suspension, withholding or withdrawing of scholarships, withholding of results, cancellation of admission, rustication or expulsion of the ragger from the institution for one to four semesters. The Regulations also make provisions for punishing the recalcitrant institution: withdrawal of institutional affiliation, withholding of grants, and declare the institution ineligible to seek general or special financial assistance from the UGC.

2012 Regulations

Caste and religious discriminations are prevalent in India and sometimes that is the underlying cause of ragging. To give one example, in 2016, a first-year nursing student was verbally abused by her seniors for belonging to a lower caste and was asked to clean the toilet. When she refused, toilet-cleaning liquid was forcibly poured into her mouth causing extensive damage to her food pipe. The police charged two seniors with attempted murder. The 2012 Regulations are specifically designed to prohibit discrimination on the grounds of caste and/or religion as the2009 Regulations did not refer to these. On the other hand, the 2009 Regulations are much wider in scope. The Regulations spell out various preventative measures that every higher educational institution is required to take. Second, the 2009 Regulations list various administrative machineries to enforce the provisions of the Regulations, including formation of anti-ragging committee, anti-ragging squad, involvement of district authorities, and the police. In contrast the 2012 Regulations merely proposes the constitution of equal opportunity cell.

Criminalisation of Ragging

Concomitant with the increase in number of ragging, violence at higher educational campuses have been on the rise. More and more students are losing their lives, committing suicide, being raped or physically assaulted or suffering from mental trauma.

Anti-ragging statutes are directed at punishing raggers for their wanton and wilful misconduct, not acts of mere negligence. There is a lack of uniformity amongst state statutes. When it comes to defining ragging, some refer to causing mental or psychological harm; others to only physical injuries and assault; a handful of them refer to causing social harm and annoyance. Andhra Pradesh provides maximum sentence of life imprisonment or up to 10 years of imprisonment and/or fine for ragging. At the other end, Assam provides imprisonment for only six months. Given this lack of uniformity, it is perhaps not surprising that a lack of a common understanding, and serious as to what is ragging persists.

It cannot be said that criminalisation of ragging by statutes has achieved any success. Recent statistics on ragging suggest that it is at an all-time high. If the anti-ragging statutes, in imposing lesser sentences, were designed as a backstop to the IPC, this does not seem to be well known. Further, the lower sentences can confuse the ragger and administrators. The confusion is perhaps evident in more lenient sentences being imposed. A 19-year old fresher was severely beaten by his seniors and died. The case was brought against the wrongdoer under the IPC but the punishment given was only four years imprisonment. Such decisions send the wrong message.

Indian Judicial Approach to Ragging

Even judges have not reached a consensus on how serious ragging is. Ragging cases reach the courts in two ways. First, the matter goes to the court under the IPC or under a state anti-ragging criminal statute. Second, the matter is brought before the court to challenge the institutional decision made under the 2009 Regulations and/or the 2012 Regulations. The directive of the highest court of India, the Supreme Court is that punishment for ragging must be exemplary and harsh to serve as a deterrent. Unfortunately, as noted above, lower courts have failed to comply with this directive; surprisingly. this failure extends to serious cases such as abetment to suicide and grievous hurt.

Where ragging has resulted in suspension or rustication of the ragger the attitude of the courts at the High Court level is lenient. The authors have examined a number of High Court decisions to get a sense as to how the State level judiciary is handling ragging cases. The approach is lenient and the following are examples of this. In *Akshay Chaudhary & Another v university of Delhi* the Vice Chancellor of Delhi University expelled the petitioners for one year. An FIR was filed on the victim's complaint. Petitioners then reached a settlement with the victim. The FIR was quashed by the Delhi

High Court and the Vice Chancellor's order of expulsion for one academic year was revoked as the petitioners would have 'remained without a Degree of Graduation,' and their future career marred. In another case suspension orders on students were revoked by the High Court of Allahabad, after it took into account that the raggers were studying at a distinguished institute and were potential national assets. The problem with that view is so were the victims. The Karnataka High Court cautioned against imposing harsh and cruel punishments on students. In its view the relationship between the head of institution and student is like that of a parent and child; there is no scope for any retribution or giving vent to a feeling of wrath. Similar views have been echoed by the Gujarat, Guwahati, Kolkata Odisha and Uttarakhand High Courts.

Imposing Duty of Care in Negligence for Protecting Freshers

In the US the emerging judicial trend is to impose civil liability or economic sanction on higher educational institutions for their failure to protect students. In *Furek v University of Delaware* it was held that universities owe a duty to students to take reasonable control to prevent ragging. In a striking example, liability was imposed for student suicide where the institutional authorities could foresee that a student might attempt to commit suicide but didn't take any preventive measures. *Regents of the University of California* v *Superior Court of Los Angeles* decided in 2018 is another striking example of US courts holding higher educational institutions to account. There the complainant was stabbed by a fellow student. The University was aware of the dangerous propensities of the fellow student. The court held that public institutions have special relationship with students to protect them from foreseeable risk of injury on university premises. Likewise, a girl student succeeded in her claim for rape committed in her dormitory run by the University.

In India, we have argued, universities also owe a duty of care to prevent ragging. It is clear that student-university relationship is similar to that of the US:

> A university and its students are clearly in a proximate relationship. Students are identifiable group of persons...it is fair just and reasonable to impose such a duty on an Indian university. The Supreme Court of India has described ragging as human rights abuse. The UGC Regulations make universities directly responsible for policing ragging. (Srivastava, 2018)

Conclusion

Ragging cannot be controlled by just passing regulations and legislation. As far as the 2009 Regulations are concerned there are problems. The UGC mandate is not being adhered to. Higher educational institutions need to make sure that anti-ragging committees and anti-ragging squads have been set up and they are functioning properly and implementing 2009 Regulations as regards security of students on the campus. Some institutions have not set the required committees nor they are aware of them. Higher educational institutions are not taking their task seriously. Higher educational institutions must proactively enforce 2009 and 2012 Regulations and develop a culture among students of reporting ragging.

Consideration should be given to criminalising non-reporting of ragging. Even when it is reported ragging complaints are treated lightly by the institution. A judge of the Gujarat High Court wondered how many institutions were aware of the 2009 Regulations. Institutional ARCs are largely non-functional. University-student relationship is being revisited in countries where ragging is much prevalent. It is interesting that an Australian report fixes responsibility on reforming the culture firmly on universities.

The attempt of criminalising ragging does not achieve much. Rather it causes confusion and creates problems of interpretation. Where ragging is defined as causing social harm, or annoyance or insult to a student, these terms must be interpreted objectively. The 2009 Regulations proscribes certain unacceptable practices. A common form of exploitation of freshers is to get them complete their seniors' assignment. Despite all the publicity about 2009 Regulations and criminalisation such inequitable practices continue to grow. In 2011 a Tamil Nadu fresher was killed for refusing to write the ragger's assignment.

The Supreme Court directions to the lower courts have not been followed. As we have noted the state level judiciary does not award proper punishment to raggers. That sends the wrong message. We can understand the courts concern that raggers are our future. But what about the victims? The sentencing has become misaligned with the Supreme Court's directive and policy. To use a Hindu mythological analogy, like the rakshas Raktabīja, whenever a ragger is spared it may spawn ten more raggers. Raggers and victims alike are our future. Justice must be equitably dispensed with.

References

[1] Gkvk student found dead after alleged ragging. (24 October 2019), Deccan Herald. Retrieved from https://www.deccanherald.com/city/bengaluru-crime/

gkvk-student-found-dead-after-alleged-ragging-770662.html, accessed 6 Nov. 2019.

[2] Torture the other name for ragging. (11 October 2019), Dhaka Tribune. Retrieved from https://www.dhakatribune.com/bangladesh/dhaka/2019/10/11/torture-the-other-name-for-ragging, accessed 4 Nov. 2019.

[3] DK Srivastava,Aashish Srivastava, Neerav Srivastava 'A hazy shade of liability': Duty of care ofuniversities to prevent hazing' *Journal* Vol 2 (2) 1-36; *Torts Law Journal* (2018) Vol. 25, 25-48.

[4] *Mullins v Pine Manor College* 449 N.E.2d 331 (Mass. 1983); *Furek v University of Delaware* 594 A.2d 506 (1991); *Regents of the University of California v Superior Court of Los Angeles* 413 P 3d 656 (Cal) 2018.

[5] UGC Regulation on Curbing the Menace of Ragging in Higher Educational Institutions (2009). University Grants Commission, New Delhi.

[6] Two Students Charged in India Dalit "Ragging" Incident (23 Jun. 2016) *BBC News*, retrieved from https://www.bbc.com/news/world-asia-india-36604360. accessed 21 Oct. 2019.

[7] *Maharashtra Prohibition of Ragging Act* 1999, Tamil Nadu Prohibition Act 1997, *Himachal Pradesh Educational Institutions (Prohibition of Ragging) Act*, 2009.

[8] *The Tripura Educational Institutions (Prevention of Ragging) Act*, 1990; *Haryana Prohibition of Ragging in Educational Institution Ordinance 2012.*

[9] *The Assam Prohibition of Ragging Act, 1998,* s. 3; The Goa Prohibition of Ragging Act 2008.

[10] s 2(e); The *Haryana Prohibition of Ragging in Educational Institution Ordinance 2012.*

[11] s 2(f); *The Andhra Pradesh Prohibition of Ragging Act 19972*(e).

[12] *The Andhra Pradesh Prohibition of Ragging Act 1997.*

[13] *The Assam Prohibition of Ragging Act, 1998, s. 4.*

[14] Ragging in Educational Institutions—4696 Cases Registered in Last 7 Years, *Amar Ujala*, 13 June 2019 retrieved from https://www.amarujala.com/india-news/ragging-in-educational-institute-4696-cases-registered-in-last-7-years-in-ugc

[15] Aman Kachroo Ragging Death Case: All Accused Freed on "Good Conduct", *Zee News*, 22 August 2013 retrieved from http://zeenews.india.com/news/himachal-pradesh/aman-kachroo-ragging-death-case-all-accused-freed-on-good-conduct_870868.html

[16] *University of Kerala v Council of Principals of Colleges in Kerala and Others* (2009) SCC 301; *Mahatma Gandhi University and Ors v Sherin, S. and Ors* 2010 (4) KHC 261.

[17] Aman Kachroo Ragging Death Case: All Accused Freed on "Good Conduct"', *Zee News*, 22 August 2013retrieved from http://zeenews.india.com/news/himachal-pradesh/aman-kachroo-ragging-death-case-all-accused-freed-on-good-conduct_870868.html

[18] W.P.(C) No.1897/2010 & CM No.9422/2010

[19] *Abhinav Kumar and Ors v Union of India and Ors* (2018) (4) ADJ191.

[20] *TT CharavarthyYuvraj v Principal, Dr. B R Ambedkar Medical College* AIR 1997 Kar 261.

[21] *Sk Nur v Director College of Engineering and Management and Ors* WP No 199 (W) of 2005, Kolkata High Court.

[22] *BasudevSethi and Ors v State of Odisha and Ors* AIR 2018 Ori 80.

[23] *Sandeep Panwar v Govind Ballabh Pant University* WP (M/S) No 2914 of 2016.

[24] *Furek v University of Delaware* 594 A.2d 506 (1991).

[25] *Eisel v Board of Education of Montgomery County* 597 A.2d447 (Md 1991).

[26] 413 P 3d 656 (Cal, 2018).

[27] *Mullins v Pine Manor College* 449 N.E.2d 331 (Mass. 1983).

[28] Neerav Srivastava, Aashish Srivastava, DK Srivastava, A Million Winslows: Private Liability of universities for ragging in India, *Oxford University Commonwealth Law Journal*, Vol 2(2), 1-36; 16-17.

[29] Anti-ragging committees in Mumbai colleges to be upgraded' *Times of India* (03 Jun. 2019). Retrieved from https://www.mid-day.com/articles/anti-ragging-committees-in-mumbai-colleges-to-be-upgraded/21067190, accessed 4 Nov. 2019.

[30] *Jwalant Jitendra Wadhwa v Institute of Infrastructure Technology Research and Management* 2019 (2) SCT 369 (Gujarat) [42].

Chapter VIII

The Need for Financial Criminology in India Over Changing Global Scenario

SANJEEV P. SAHNI & VIPIN VIJAY NAIR

Introduction

"White collar crimes" are categorized as crimes that are non-violent and fall directly or indirectly under the domain of financial gain or avoiding gain to any individuals. These crimes usually involve professionals or working class in any organization, business, or government. There is no single definition of "white-collar crime" that exists reflecting the various facets of financial crime. Police personnel appears to concentrate dedicatedly on wrongdoing among the "lower class," while overlooking violations submitted among business and expert men.

Edwin H. Sutherland was the first to coin the term White Collar Crime in his speech at the American Sociological Society in Philadelphia on December 27, 1939. Sutherland's idea of white-collar crime has envisioned various laws and regulations in financial crime across the globe. The Federal Bureau of Investigation (FBI) states a simplified explanation of white-collar crime as"lying, cheating, and stealing." There have been numerous cases of financial fraud reported across the globe, including the Wall Street crisis in 2008, bringing multiple prosecutions for fraud and other financial abnormalities, although many critics argue that the number of trials was limited in terms of financial loss.

Mehta (2009) expressed that financial wrongdoing happens as a deviation from the violator's work profile. Additionally, the vast majority of the laws instituted or violated are not part of the customary criminal code. Such crimes are corporate misrepresentation, financial extortion, tax avoidance, monetary forms imitation, Mastercard extortion, licensed innovation encroachment, and with the newest addition of Cyber Crime. A criminal perpetrating financial wrongdoing takes an enormous amount of cash and utilizes innovation and correspondence to do unlawful business exchanges, manipulate a database, or arrange massive cheats. Another attribute of commercial, business, corporate, or professional violations is that they are a great business: and great business frequently requires cutting corners. Legal infringement by organizations constitutes a significant aspect of the business framework, much like modern spying or mentally intriguing promoting methods. Those exercises are an expansion of the entrepreneur framework dependent on benefit and a specialized adherence precisely instead of the actual intent of the law. Financial violations influence society overall. For example, bogus promoting actuates people, in general, to put resources into items that don't have the ideal impact. Risky medications, pesticides, and nourishment increases influence the wellbeing of thousands. Introduction to modern perils, for example, dangerous hardware and harmful materials and discharges adversely affect laborers' longevity.

Furthermore, a noteworthy extent of transnational organized violations expects the idea of worldwide monetary wrongdoing. Records of cross-border breaches, for example, drug dealing, blackmail, pollution, tax avoidance, arms sneaking, psychological oppression, and misrepresentation, should be notified and requires relevant actions. The universal financial risk, presented worldwide sorted out wrongdoing, in a worldwide economy is among the significant "new" dangers to national security. Worldwide Economic Crime doesn't merely influence a select gathering of money related organizations or local regions; it affects universal monetary systems and economies at a national level. Laundering billions of dollars in organized wrongdoing declines civic obligation because of the enormous aggregates of cash lost as assessment income to that country's government. Worldwide organized wrongdoing can damagingly affect political structures, particularly delicate vote based systems and growing economies. As individuals feel that the administration is weak to stop composed wrongdoing, they go to wrongdoing pioneers for security, and political organizations start to fall apart. There are various legislations to manage such wrongdoers explicitly to deny guilty parties of the returns and advantages got from the commission of offenses illegal of the nation. It accommodates the reallocation or relinquishment of the profits or resources utilized in associations with the commission of specific wrongdoings.

The Compositional Structure of Financial Crime

Financial crime is malpractices that involve wrongdoings that are contrasting to the traditional crimes and includes modern-day technologies and techniques. Michel (2008) contends that money related wrongdoing is opportunity-driven. Opportunity is an adaptable attribute of financial wrongdoing and shifts relying upon the kind of offenders included. Types of financial wrongdoing can shift as much as the criminal associations and criminal experts included. The prospects develop while finding a shortcoming in a method. Gaps show up when a hazard exists. When looking at legitimate and illegal operations, Michel (2008) contends that the reasons why agents hold the administrations of specialists in the money related market are equivalent to those of lawbreakers. Their competency defines the legitimacy of the task.

Pickett and Pickett (2002) stated that there are various elements of white-collar crime that separates itself from traditional wrongdoing.

- *It is devious.* Individuals involved in financial crime tend to state lies, cheat, conceal, and maneuver the facts.
- *It is premeditated.* Any wrongdoing in financial crime is not usually an error or fluke but involves purposeful attempt to receive advantages or gains. Therein, it resonates with an act that is premeditated by the offender.
- *It is a breach of trust.* Organizations principally run on trust. Mutual trust is the binding glue in the working environment for organizational performance. It is this trust that violated to defraud other individuals.
- *It entails costs or profit reduction.* Financial crime leads to obtain illegal gains or to curtail any profit to be received by any individual. These crimes involve a quantum of loss or disadvantage towards assets owned by individuals other than the perpetrator. White-collar crime reflects a draining impact of the resources of the economy.
- *Generally hidden.* One of the critical features of White-collar crimes is the possibility of non-reporting. The tendency of altering, customizing, and suppressing the facts to represent a false reality is prominent after the commissioning of financial crime. Unless detected by experts in the field, the errors are a challenge to be traced by a common man
- *Respectable professionals.* The perpetrator is usually an employee or employee at an upright position and reflects an excellent social status, making it difficult for the identification of a white-collar criminal compared to a traditional criminal.

The Status of Financial Crime in India

The occurrence of financial crime in any government or private organization depends on the weakness in an organization exploited by the perpetrator. The distinct categorization of financial crime is difficult due to the greater magnitude and opportunity of crime. Crime in India report by the National Crime Records Bureau notifies that the reporting of Economic offenses has fluctuated over the year from 142560 cases in 2014, 150170 in 2015, 143524cases in 2016, and 148972 in 2017 (NCRB, 2014; NCRB, 2015; NCRB, 2016; NCRB, 2017).

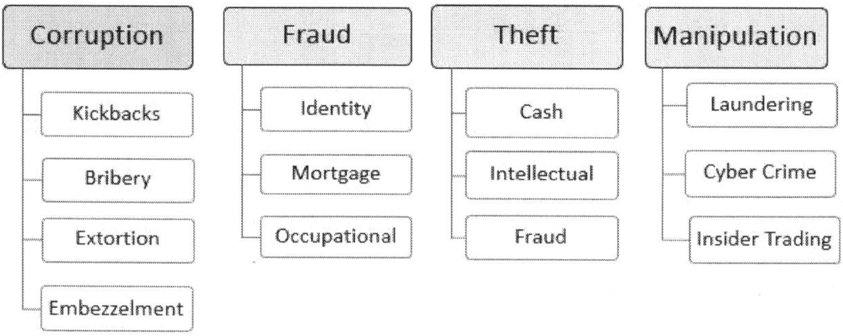

Source: Gottschalk, 2010.

Corruption

Corruption is defined as the giving, demanding, getting, or tolerating of an inappropriate preferred position identified with a job, office, or task. The benefit need not be connected to a specific act or not acting. It is ample evidence to be associated with a work profile. (Okokrim, 2008). Corruption as a crime inflicts harm over the goodwill and reputation of the individuals. These involve various offenses like Kickbacks, Bribery, Extortion, Embezzlement, etc.

- *Kickbacks:* An employee who, with due influence over a particular agreement, receives benefits and gains for assisting the contractor of the transaction.
- *Bribery:* An employee fetching over-the-counter income through an illegal activity in the job profile.
- *Extortion:* An employee/ individual minting monetary avenues through coercive measures.
- *Embezzlement:* Activity to retain resources with the end goal of the transformation of such funds from the owner to another for explicit purposes.

Fraud

Fraud is any activity that deceives another individual to achieve financial or personal gains. These involve various offenses like Credit/Debit Card fraud, Cheque fraud, Identity fraud, Mortgage fraud, Occupational fraud, etc.

- *Credit/Debit Card fraud:* The misuse of credit/debit card of an external source for illicit financial gains or profits.

- *Cheque fraud:* Illicit financial gains or profits by an external party through misuse of the cheque.
- *Identity fraud:* Activity that violates the identity, dignity, and privacy of an individual without his permission to achieve illicit gains.
- *Mortgage fraud:* Documentation or procedural violation to make one's desirable gain through the illegal procedure.
- *Occupational fraud:* Activity that procures or hire logistics against the norms and conduct of the profession. These activities manipulate the employee or potential employee and achieve illegal gains.

Theft

These crimes involve the transfer of ownership of any resources without due permission or consent of the owner. These include various offenses like Cash Theft, Intellectual Property Crime, Art Theft, etc.

- *Cash Theft:* The act of stealing monetary finances directed through the victim to the perpetrator. This transaction leads to the loss of cash, assets, property with or without proper approval.
- *Intellectual Property Crime:* The modern-day crime that involves a violation of copyright, trademark, or any other literary or scientific content.
- *Art Theft:* The crime that involves stealing or smuggling of creative forms owned by another individual without proper authorization.

Manipulation

These crimes involve activities that sway factual data into malicious evidence for future actions like Laundering, Cyber Crime, Insider Trading, Income Tax Crime, Counterfeit currency, Ghost employees, etc.

- *Bid Fixing:* These crimes involve providing undue advantage to an external source by the initiator of the contract. These activities violate the code of conduct of any contractual agreement.
- *Laundering:* The act of money laundering involves the conversion of illegitimate finances into legal transactions
- *Cyber Crime:* These crimes are high-tech and modern-day crimes involving electronic and computer devices. The offenses are committed mostly in the digital world without the direct presence of the offender at the crime scene.
- *Insider Trading:* This activity induces the action of buying or selling stock of the company with a piece of non-public information to make profits. Insider trading involves loss to the listed company due to a single

transaction leading to irregular financial functioning. These transactions can cause considerable damage or burden towards the company.

- *Income Tax Crime:* The action of manipulation in paying legitimate income tax towards the company through various means like manipulating actual data, forging documents, etc.
- *Counterfeit currency:* The action of forging actual currency notes, coins, and denomination into fake money with close to legitimate features. This activity ensures that individuals utilize phony currency for a valid transaction without much of legal trouble
- *Ghost employees:* The action of reflecting employees and recruits in a company without actual personnel on the ground. The database of employees created guides in the manipulation of various financial transactions in the name of these employees. The same concept resonates with *Shell Company,* and these companies reflect as a functioning asset on paper without any actual presence on the ground. Tax evasion, financial fraud, laundering are one of the few core motives of ghost employees and shell company.

The Outlook towards Financial Crime in India

India is among those nations that have an ample number of laws and organizations deterring economic offenses. The primary law that governs underlying crime like cheating, fraud, breach of trust, and counterfeit is the Indian Penal Code (IPC) and Criminal Procedure Code (CrPC) that regulates the procedural aspect of criminal activity. The Companies Act 2013 (Companies Act) also contains provisions that aim at preventing fraudulent activities by and in companies. Other statutes such as the Prevention of Corruption Act 1988 (PCA) and the Prevention of Money Laundering Act 2002 (PMLA) also contain provisions dealing with corporate and business fraud. Furthermore, laws such as the Securitisation and Reconstruction of Financial Assets and Enforcement of Security Interest (Sarfaesi) Act, 2002, the Recovery of Debts Due to Banks and Financial Institutions Act, 1993, and the Prevention of Money Laundering Act, 2002, theorize the assigning of assets as a punishment. Various economic offenses are group-based and commissioned in an organized mode. Maharashtra Control of Organised Crime Act (MCOCA), 1999, regulates any illicit activities associated with organized crime. Various legislations that penalize fraud, manipulation in different transactions, and respective territorial jurisdictions are:

1. Public Gambling Act of 1867 running or owning a gambling house
2. Explosives Act, 1884 & Explosive Substances Act,1908 dealing with illicit trafficking in explosives

3. Passport Act, 1920 functions to discourage racketing of false travel documents
4. Central Excises Act, 1944 deals with the evasion of excise duty
5. Import & Export (Control) Act,1947 to prevent illegal foreign trade
6. Banking Regulation Act, 1949 to deter fraudulent bankruptcy
7. Prevention of Food Adulteration Act, 1954 avoid fraud and deception in food items
8. Essential Commodities Act, 1955 deals with provision preventing any obstruction through hoarding or black marketing of certain items
9. Companies Act, 1956 and The Monopolistic and Restrictive Trade Practices Act, 1969 provides the provision to deter company frauds
10. Wealth Tax, 1957, caters with filling for wealth tax over the net wealth of individual, Hindu Undivided Family, or a company.
11. Copyright Act, 1957 (Amendments 1984 & 1994) deter infringing Intellectual Property Rights
12. Arms Act,1959 dealing with illicit trafficking in arms and ammunition
13. Income Tax Act, 1961 dealing with tax evasion
14. Customs Act, 1962 and COFEPOSA, 1974 coping with illicit trafficking in smuggled goods
15. Foreign Contribution (Regulation) Act, 1976 dealing with manipulation in foreign transactions
16. Narcotic Drugs and Psychotropic Substances Act, 1985 & NDPS Act, 1988 reflecting provisions against drug trafficking
17. Prevention of Corruption Act, 1988 dealing with corruption and bribery in public office
18. Transplantation of Human Organs Act, 1994 regulating trading in body parts
19. Foreign Exchange Management Act, 1999, and the Money Laundering Act 2002 dealing with money laundering
20. Information and Technology Act, 2000, reflects various provisions to deter cybercrime
21. Lotteries (Regulation) Rules, 2010, prohibits the sale of lottery by the central government

The regulations mentioned above have periodically amended to cater to the latest modus operandi. The newest addition to the lost list of economic offense laws is Fugitive Economic Offenders (FEO) Act, 2018 establishes various provisions dealing with the economic offenders listed under multiple cases. This law consolidates different legislation into a wholesome comprehensive law.

Various organizations that monitor different economic offense laws and knows as a regulatory mechanism are:

1. State & Central Police Personnel oversees economic offenses following the law of the land
2. Serious Fraud Investigation Office has the responsibility to investigate major corporate frauds involving the financial sector, capital market, customs, corporate law, etc.
3. The primary role of the Central Bureau of Investigation is to investigate massive scale smuggling of drugs, firearms, foreign exchange violation, etc.
4. Enforcement Directorate is an enforcement agency accountable for strict implementation of economic offense laws.
5. Central Vigilance Commission is a governmental institution to monitor any corruption-related matters under the central government.
6. Central Economic Intelligence Bureau is an intelligence agency in charge of gathering information and observing the economic health of the country over economic offenses.
7. Economic Intelligence Council is responsible for coordination, information sharing, and strategy creation amongst various institutions in the country to combat economic offenses.
8. Competition Commission of India eliminate any practices and procedure that curtal fair competition and promote the interest of the customers.

The Risk of Financial Crime in India

The Crime in India report of National Crime Records Bureau, India included the terminology of financial crime via-a-vis Economic crime, corruption, and cybercrime only from 2014. The case of Criminal Breach of Trust has substantially increased from 18708 in 2016 to 20371 in 2017, and the offense of Counterfeiting has reflected a downward trend in the case of registration from 1476 in 2016 to 1171 in 2017. The instances of Forgery, Cheating, and Fraud have shown an upward trend in cases reported from 123340 in 2016 to 127430 in 2017. These crimes don't just reflect the increase in crime but also showcase the dent in the economy with the financial loss to such a substantial extent. More than 4,970 people committed suicide, given liquidation or debt in 2018. These represented 3.7 percent of the total number of suicide in the year. Strikingly, this is somewhat lower than the 5,151 such suicides found in the earlier year, which represented 4 percent of the complete suicides in 2017. (NCRB 2016, NCRB 2017).

The growing menace of trafficking has also contributed to smuggling and money laundering across various nations (Bell, 2001). The impact of money laundering and trafficking in drugs, arms, and humans has not just impacted the economy but the social structure of the society. The ever increasing dependency on electronic devices and the virtual world have led to the emergence of cybercrime. The case reported under Cybercrime in the National Crime Records Bureau has substantially increased over the years with 11592 cases in 2015, 12317cases in 2016 and 21796 cases in 2017.

Various offenses under cybercrime and monitored through Information Technology Act, 2000 are tampering computer source documents, computer-related attacks, dishonestly receiving stolen computer resources or communication devices, identity theft, cheating by personation, violation of privacy, cyber terrorism, publication/transmission of obscene/sexually explicit act in electronic form, unauthorized access, data theft, abetment to suicide, cyberstalking, fraud, cheating, forgery, defamation/morphing, fake profile, cyber blackmailing, fake news. The above-stated offenses comprise of both violent and non-violent crimes. The act of fake news, violation of privacy, cyberstalking, etc. have impacted not just the financial position of the position but also the mental and psychological state. Cases of suicide, depression, anxiety and other psychological disorder are reported consequences over various economic offenses.

Financial Criminology

Criminology is a discipline that has reflected upon the study of crime and criminal behaviors. There have been various sub-division of criminology describing different facets of misconduct ranging from Positivist Criminology by Cesare Lombroso, Environmental Criminology by C. Ray Jeffery, Cyber Criminology by K. Jaishankar. These sub-disciplines explained the importance of the by-product in criminology and continued there work in the respective field and were taken forward by their colleagues and scholars. In spite of the emphasis on various economic and financial offenses across the globe, there was no dedicated discipline under criminology that dedicated a greater focus on studying crime and criminal behaviour under economic crimes. A specialized subject in financial criminology would provide greater importance in training, education, and awareness in financial crime.

The layman's definition of financial criminology following the discipline of criminology narrates itself as, "*The study of Crime and Criminal behaviour under the realm of economic and financial offenses.*"The ambit of such crime is different from traditional crime in terms of operation, magnitude, behaviourism and other related characteristics of misconduct.

The only offered course across the globe in Financial Criminology is at the Universiti Teknologi Mara, Kuala Lumpur, Malaysia, under Masters and Ph.D Curriculum. The ongoing changing scenario in the financial diaspora should emphasize more on education and professional development in financial criminology. The scarcity of courses, program and certification under financial criminology globally has resonated with the lack of experts and professionals in the field of financial crime.

Conclusion

Financial criminology as a discipline in criminology would act as a promoter into the research and studies of financial crime. The ever-growing financial frauds ranging from money laundering, smuggling, corporate frauds, tax evasion, cybercrime has emphasized in a dedicated discipline with courses creating a pool of experts and professionals contributing to control the menace of financial crime and deterring the potential criminality in economic offenses.

The need for financial criminology in Indian scenario is on an ever-rising stage with the increased reporting of various financial crimes over the years without many prosecutions and justice delivery and cases of corruption, frauds, tax evasion, cybercrime has seen headlines with the figures extending into thousands of crores. The reported crime has seen the face of criminal trials without any financial recovery to individuals, organization or the economy. The dedicated workforce in the field of financial criminology would contribute to research and investigate the root cause of such crime and would expertise in combating economic offenses.

References

Bell, R. E. (2001). Sex trafficking: A financial crime perspective. Journal of Financial Crime, 9(2), 165-178.

Gottschalk, P. (2010). Categories of financial crime. Journal of financial crime, 17(4), 441-458.

Gottschalk, P. (2010). Theories of financial crime. Journal of Financial Crime, 17(2), 210-222.

Michel, P. (2008), "Financial crimes: the constant challenge of seeking effective prevention solutions," Journal of Financial Crime, Vol. 15 No. 4, pp. 383-97.

Mehta, D. (2009) Economic Crime in a Globalized Society: Its Impact on the Sound Development of the State –An Indian Perspective.126th International Senior Seminar, India

National Crime Records Bureau (2014): Crime in India, New Delhi: Ministry of Home Affairs, Government of India.

National Crime Records Bureau (2015): Crime in India, New Delhi: Ministry of Home Affairs, Government of India.

National Crime Records Bureau (2016): Crime in India, New Delhi: Ministry of Home Affairs, Government of India.

National Crime Records Bureau (2017): Crime in India, New Delhi: Ministry of Home Affairs, Government of India.

Økokrim (2008), Annual Report 2007, Norwegian National Authority for Investigation and Prosecution of Economic and Environmental Crime, Oslo.

Pickett, K.H.S. and Pickett, J.M. (2002), Financial Crime Investigation and Control, Wiley, New York, NY.

Chapter IX

Victim Damage Assessment and Its Role in Criminal Justice System

P.M. NAIR

The Plight of a Victim of Sexual Exploitation

Let us consider a teenage girl child victim of sex trafficking. She has been exploited physically, sexually, or by removing organs from the body. She has been enslaved or subjected to practices similar to slavery or servitude. She has been displaced from her safe constituency by abduction or kidnapping; criminally confined; criminally restrained; physically and mentally tortured; sold by somebody and purchased by somebody else, like a chattel; modesty outraged; raped repeatedly and for several days with no end till rescue; sometimes subjected to gang rape; battered with pervasive sexual exploits and subjected to bondage of sorts. The conspirators and abettors have unleashed multiple abuses on her at several places starting from the source, through all the transits which continued at different destinations, till she was rescued. The right to redressal has been denied at each stage of exploitation. Therefore trafficking is a 'basket of crimes' (Nair, 2010), a continuing crime and a crime of crimes. It is a borderless crime as the offenders have no jurisdictional limitations.

The Deprivation of Human Rights

The list of human rights abuses and exploits unleashed by the various criminals, who constitute the organized network, on the victim is long and winding, starting with the core and basic fundamental rights enshrined under the Constitution of India, not to be trafficked (Art 23) and the right to life (Art 21). The deprivation includes the right to life of dignity, with the slave like conditions; deprivation of the right to security; deprivation of the right to privacy; denial of the right to health services; denial of the right to self-determination, as the victim has no place in the scheme of things; denial of the right to return to one's community, as she is confined and restrained as per the will of the exploiters; denial of the right of representation, as she has no voice even in deciding her fate; denial of the right to be heard before decisions are made on her and on her behalf; denial of the right to access to justice; denial of the right to think; denial of the right to rest; denial of the right to enjoy; denial of the right to peace; denial of the right to education (especially in the case of children under 14 years who have a constitutional right for free education); etc. The list is, in fact, further long.

Colossal Damage

The Constitution of India, which has been given by the people of India to the people of India, as the preamble reads, enshrines a glorious principle, under Article 23, that human trafficking, in every form, is prohibited. If a person, say a women of 23 years of age or a child of 12 years, is likely to be trafficked, that person has a constitutional right not to be trafficked and every other citizen of India has a constitutional duty to ensure that the person is not trafficked. Therefore, in every trafficking crime, whatever be the purpose, this fundamental and cardinal principle that is constitutionally assured to the person, has been denied, rejected and trampled upon. This means that despite there being a constitutional protection, as against a legal protection or an ordinary administrative protection, yet the victim of human trafficking is denied and deprived of this guarantee enshrined upon under the Constitution. Therefore I deem human trafficking as a crime against the Constitution.

Identity Lost

The victim remains a commodity at the hands of the traffickers, abusers and exploiters. She loses her individuality and even identity. She becomes a body. She is transformed into a body of nobody (Bhamathi, 1996). She becomes a commodity and is sold and purchased like any commodity. Therefore the golden principle of humanness, individuality, respect for human being and human kindness to fellow beings are all lost. She becomes an object, which can be bartered and transferred anywhere and anytime, with impunity. Her dignity is ravished. The commoditization of human beings debases the victim irreparably and irrecoverably. She is no more a she. The she in her is demolished and distraught. The soul in her is lost for ever.

Commercialization

Human trafficking is crass commercialization, where the exploiters make huge profit by selling the victim. The sale does not start or end with one transaction. The process continues unabated and multiple times, by several offenders who are part of the trafficker's network. The 'cost' and 'price' depends on the market, dictated by the 'demand'. More the demand, more the price. Therefore, as research has shown, children are much in demand. This is the first criteria of demand (Nair, 2005). This is followed by other parameters, which quintessentially means the likes of the 'customers', like 'skin colour, body shape, body features, ethnicity, and above all, submissiveness'. These parameters are not always static, as they may vary from place to place and from 'customer' to 'customer', even though the essential features of demand remain almost the same.

Demand

Therefore the linkage with demand decides the source and transit. This is the truth, even though, the general perception is that it is the source that decides the destination. The research referred to above demolished this and many other myths. Oftentimes, poverty was considered to be the root cause of trafficking. Study exploded this myth too. Many a poor were not trafficked and could not be as they were not available for sale. Despite being poor, they were under good parental protection, or were empowered, well aware of the rights and well capable to assert and access to the rights. Poverty, by itself, was not a causative or aggravating factor. It is definitely a baseline but not the be all and end all. The real story is that trafficking is a product of vulnerability of the victim on the one side and the demand on the other side. The vulnerability factors include socio-cultural oppression, illiteracy, ignorance and access to rights (Nair, 2010), lack of care at home, economic deprivation, poor law enforcement, etc. Even if the person is vulnerable, there is no trafficking unless there is demand. Therefore, it is not the victim who decides trafficking. Victim is a pawn in the game played by those who create, perpetuate and sustain demand. As a corollary, if there is demand, the traffickers will locate the vulnerable and therefore there will be trafficking, come what may. The role of demand remains cardinal to trafficking. Demand dictates trafficking (Nair, 2010).

The Organized Network of Traffickers

In order to assess the victim's plight in the world of human trafficking, the understanding of the opposite side, ie the world of offenders, is essential. The truth is that the victim remains a pawn in the organized network of the traffickers. This network is well established and well oiled. Yet, this is a world often unfathomed, unmeasured and unassessed. Here lies the main challenge in assessing the harm to the victim that these offenders have caused.

The network starts with spotters and recruiters, who fan out and locate the vulnerable localities and persons. The vulnerability, as discussed above, may be shifting over a period of time.For example, if the law enforcement becomes effective, the vulnerability gets reduced. If the victims and probable victims are empowered, vulnerability comes down drastically. Therefore the recruiters will assess the situation and then only indulge in their work.

Once recruited, the core elements of trafficking come into operation. Several offenders swing into action. The buyers will bargain and 'buy' human beings, whereas the sellers will 'sell' them, the transporters will transfer them to the destination may be directly or through transit places. The transit will require harbourers who provide safe houses, where safety means that of the offenders and not so much of the victims. Well, the victims have to be kept I safe custody so that they do not venture to escape or make noise about their plight. Oftentimes, transits are also places of exploitation, including sexual abuse. More often, transits are places of 'collection', 'collation', segregation' and decision on further course of action accordingly. Many times, especially in case of trans-border trafficking, transits may also require long stays, if travel documents are not ready or when border crossing is challenging due to difficulties in the terrain or due to vigil by border guarding forces. In a case of 2018 of trafficking of more than 160 women and children of Nepali origin to Myanmar and beyond, the traffickers chose to move them out through More, on the Manipur border with Myanmar. Thanks to a few victims blowing the whistle and timely interference by NGO and prompt response by local police, the whole racket got busted and the victims were saved before being moved across the border. The inquiries showed that the victims were made to stay over at More, for more than a month, so that the travel documents could be fabricated and got ready. Luckily for the victims and unluckily for the traffickers, this process took more time than expected and this led to the expose. This shows that the harbouring can be for long periods too, depending on the place and requirements of the situation. It also shows that the role of harbourers is significant in the trafficking network.

The transporters, the money lenders, the agents (dalals), the conspirators, the abettors, etc. are all part of the organized network and all of them together ensure that the demand is sustained and perpetuated. The nexus with certain officials dealing with law enforcement, border guarding, immigration, etc. are also contributory to the crime. This nexus facilitates and promotes trafficking, wherein the traffickers are able to attend to their business with impunity. The list of offenders is incomplete without the men who exploit the victims, usually called 'customers'.

The 'Customer'

The person who buys sex and violates the trafficked woman or child is generally referred to as 'customer'. The term has been probably coined by a smart person to protect oneself and pass the blame to the victim, branding her as a prostitute. Research has shown that the right coinage is not 'prostitute', but 'prostituted woman' (Nair, 2005) and not 'child prostitute', but 'prostituted child'. The terminologies have to be redefined from a right's perspective. In this context, the victim of trafficking cannot be said to be a prostitute at all. She is not indulging in 'flesh trade', nor is she a 'fallen woman', nor is he 'indulging in the business of selling sex'. All these terminologies are indeed violative of the rights of the victim and will only demolish her further and exacerbate harm and damage perpetrated on her. As a corollary, the man who violates her is not a 'customer', nor is he doing the 'business of sex' with her, as the entire act is not that of any business, but is a serious crime perpetrated on the hapless victim. Therefore the right word for the oft used word 'customer' should be 'criminal', 'rapist', 'abuser', 'exploiter' or 'sex-offender'. He could be the abettor or the conspirator too, depending on the context. Terminologies decide the orientation of thought, action and response and, therefore, one has to necessarily adopt a rights-based approach. Only such a rights-based paradigm will bring home the damage such persons cause to the victim. Prejudiced and biased views and perceptions have to be dispensed with, while assessing the harm and damage to the victims of trafficking. Therefore let us be clear that such a person is not a 'customer', but is the criminal, the offender.

The Offender's Might

Irrefutable is the fact that the offenders form a strong and dominant force against the victim, where the latter become completely helpless. As against the usual perception that the world of sex trafficking is all fun and frolic, it is a world of power and authority. It is not just sex, but it is an onslaught. It is not simple pleasure but it is vicarious pleasure. It is not paid sex, but the payment is a sugar coat for the right to exploit the victim in any manner, any form and ant extent. Instances are plenty, where the offender injures the victim, physically and sexually. Emotional blackmail and deprivation are very common.

The payment has several meanings in the world of sex trafficking. Firstly, comes the perceived 'right' of the offender. The offender thinks he has 'right' over the victim, as he has 'purchased' her and that the right is unbridled. This perception is the core to exploitation. Secondly, 'payment' is perceived to mean the silence of the victim. Since the 'customer' has 'paid', the victim has to oblige. She loses her right to deny whatever be the demand. Her silence has been purchased. The master-servant relationship is held to be non-negotiable and the sufferer is the victim. No doubt, several victims have tried to resist or avoid, but all of them have met with serious violence being unleashed on them by the 'managers', their henchmen, security personnel employed by the owner of the brothel or the place of exploitation, which may be functioning under the façade of massage parlour or tourist circuit or bar tending and so on.

Physical exploitation

Inevitably, the might of the offender is showered on the victim by physical assault. Bodily injuries of torture in different forms like beating, cigarette burns, biting, pushing things into the private parts, etc. are the commonly seen manifestations of physical assault. Even silent and submissive victim may also be subjected to torture as this is often linked to excitement and demonstration of power and authority.

Sexual Exploitation

The sexual acts indulged in by the offenders include barbaric and despicable ones, which can beat even the hardest pornos. The exploits range from making the victim surrender and subjugate to sexual acts of sorts and extend to perverse and violent acts that cause irreparable damage to the private parts of the victim. Though they often suffer in silence, the impact is colossal. Medical care not wanting, the injuries get worse and at times dangerous. Further, even the protective systems like condom are not preferred by many men who indulge in sex. The NHRC study referred to earlier presents case studies of such 'customers', who had different reasons for involving and insisting in unsafe sexual activities. Whereas the adolescent 'customer' said he was trying to test his masculinity and thought that one odd act would not be a health hazard for him, the bestial minded 'customer' said that it was for the women to protect herself if she wanted and that as a male his priority was to let go on her as he wished and as long as he wanted, where he has no patience or consideration for things like condom. Such things had no place in his scheme of things. The result is that the victim of sex trafficking has several abortions, many suffer UTIs, many contract HIV, some die of AIDS and so on. The lack of health care systems at such places, the expensive medical care, lack of medical insurance, undue interference of money lenders who capitalize the situation and make money out of the victim, making her further bonded, all add to the list of sufferings of the victim. Rudimentary health care facilities and safe sex methods especially condoms are available at many such brothels, thanks to the activists working on HIV prevention, but their utilization is fully dependent on the will and wish of the 'customer', where the victim has no say at all. The harm to the victim is colossal.

Financial Exploitation

The victim of human trafficking is in eternal bondage. The offenders make out a convincing case of debt so that the victim remains bonded. The money lenders, who are the part of the organized nexus, add fuel to the fire. Every time a victims is injured, it adds to her burden as she has to fund for her treatment. Health issues create a heavy burden on the victim, almost a perpetual bondage. Anytime the police 'picks' her up as a 'prostitute' and prosecutes her, she is further harmed financially too. The brothel madam or her cohorts will put up defence and lawyer to get her on bail and this expenditure is construed as additional bondage. The victim is made to suffer more 'customers' to make up the additional bondage. The financial burden that accrues to the victim after such an ill planned rescue, makes her more distraught and poor.

There is one more disturbing side to the economic exploitation of the victims by the traffickers. This is in respect of sharing the revenue and income generated in selling innocence. The share of the income generated from the commercial exploitation of the victim that accrues to the victim is very nominal. Often, the brothel keeper, usually called Madam, or the manager, takes the cake as the money is collected by them. The victim gets a small share, usually 10% to 40% and rarely 50% and beyond. In the world of exploiters, there is no scope or thinking of anything like equality, equanimity or due diligence as they are the ones who decide how much the victim should get. The fact that it is only because of the victim that all of them prosper is never a consideration. Their interest, at best, is to keep the victim healthy enough to have more and more 'customers', 'please the customers as they want' and 'be servile, silent and obedient'. The victim is, therefore, deprived of her rightful share of money that they make by selling her! In this way, humongous is the damage to the victim.

In a rapid assessment on the brothels in Kamla market, Delhi, during 2004, undertaken in the NHRC study referred to earlier, it came out that the profit that the exploiters make out of approximately 1500 women and children in sexual exploitation runs into several crores of rupees, whereas the share that these women and children received was a few thousands! In another assessment undertaken during 2012, BBA found that 360 billion USD, which is equivalent to INR 21 Lakh Crores (Satyarthi, 2014) is generated by enslaving children in exploitation in India, which is equivalent to one fifth of India's GDP. The study concludes that this black money propels capital corruption and sustained exploitation of children in India.

The fact that the enormous illegal revenue generated by the traffickers remain unaccounted for and yet enters the mainstream revenue of the Nation is another damage that affects not only the victims but also the Nation and all its citizens. Unfortunately, the response systems have not matured enough to trace the illicit and seize, confiscate and bring it to the licit. Therefore the huge profits that the traffickers and their coterie make out of selling any buying of human beings remain under the carpet and always to their advantage.

Damage to Health

The discussion of the health issues that the trafficked victims who are prey to commercial sexual exploitation is another chapter by itself, even though this is also an area which has not been probed much, except reports of some NGOs and certain other stakeholders. The health issues that are common are UTIs, HIV, AIDs, influenza and several otherviral, fungal and bacterial infections, gynaecological issues, bleeding, long lasting injuries on different parts of the body, especially due to anal/oral sex, perverted/ violent sex, and so on. The ailments often get complicated due to lack of treatment or poor care. There have been deaths also due to over infections and related complications. The common ailments like cold, cough and fever etc. get attended to by over-the-counter medicines, as the offenders want the victims to be ready for the next 'customer' and in no time. Such medicines also worsened the issues and many victims develop complications in body systems like sleeplessness, indigestion, excitement, anaemia, cough, pneumonia etc.

Health complications are further exacerbated by addictions which are prevalent in such brothels and places of exploitation. The victims are forced to cheap drinks, smoke, drugs and so on at a very early age. The purpose is to 'reign them in'. This is another accompaniment of the 'breaking-in ceremony', usual to most of the brothels, wherein the newly acquired girl, i.e. the newly trafficked victim, is forced to have sex with the boss or the lead manager of his henchman. The victim is demolished at the entry time itself. Added to this, she will be forced to drinks, smoke, drugs etc so that she is 'naturalized' to these addictions, which, in turn, would make the victim servile to the offenders. Drinking, drugging and smoking related health complications are too many. The victim loses interest in food and is able to survive on minimum, as the brother keepers want it to be. The victim remains under rigid control and becomes willing to accept all perversions and violations that are unleashed on her by the 'customers'. This is a catch 22 situation. More the addiction, more the exploitation and more the silence and servility of the victim. Many times, the rescued victims are unable to sustain without drinks, smoke or drugs as they have been so much indoctrinated and habituated. Hence the care givers have to go for deaddiction care as an essential requirement before any other act of rehabilitation. This explains the tremendous harm that the trafficked victims had been subjected to.

The Psycho Social Problems

The victims of sex trafficking are completely destroyed by the continuous and incessant types of exploitation of sorts. They develop serious psycho social complications. Withdrawal symptoms, stress, trauma, PSD, loneliness, mental instability etc ate just a few of the long list of issues in their lives. It has been observed that many get attached to the man who comes up as a regular 'customer', and sometimes they even marry. So long as they are happily married this looks fine, but that is not the story. The offender finds this as a springboard to exploit her further and therefore even such relationships are at a great disadvantage to the victim. Several rescued victims have been seen to be suffering from serious mental disorders requiring psychiatric care for long, only to get them some relief. The psychosocial damage to a victim of sex trafficking is immeasurable. Imagine the plight of a teenage girl, who had "23 Customers" one night and had eventually died of AIDS after being in the brothel for less than three years. Each day was a nightmare for her. Each 'customer' was a demon on her. Each event was ravishing her. Where on earth and how can one assess the damage to such a person? Nobody except the victim knows the extent of the damage to her. Nobody except the victim had listened to her tribulations. And now that she is dead, nobody has any record of what all went through her. It is her story only and remains dead with her. The damage to this young lady is the sum of the pleasure and money made by all those who trafficked her, sold her, purchased her, bartered her and raped her, calling themselves as 'customers'. The merchants of human dignity and human body have no idea of the monumental harm and damage to the lives of innocent souls.

The Bondage

All these activities coupled with the helplessness of the victim makes her bonded for ever to the traffickers and other offenders. The bondage remains a Damocles' Sword on her head and she is not able to move out. If she ventures to do, the goondas will get her back and will inflict aggravated harm on her, including physical assault. Seeing the case of several such instances, other victims do not dare to venture out or even speak out.

The "Trusted Offender" and the Offender Dependency Syndrome

The bondage is not only financial, but also physical and emotional. The victim will have nobody else to speak out her part of the story, except a manager of madam from the offender's fraternity. There she might find some solace and this brings in another bondage. The optionlessness leads the victim to a state of bondage with the offender. It is a creation of the situation. The lack of law enforcement and the distorted law enforcement would only exacerbate the situation and such a scenario makes the victim to be fully dependent of the offender as the friend and philosopher. The only flicker of hope for the victim is the offender. The criminal who had been exploiting her turns out to be her only hope. Offender dependency syndrome is a hallmark of extreme deprivation and exploitation that the victim has been subjected to. Had there been some hope or scope for relief from the law enforcement agencies or civil society or any public spirited person, this syndrome would not have been in the scheme of things. The lack of redressal of grievances, coupled with the complete despair to reach out to any such grievance redressal systems, cemented by the stories that they are told repeatedly about further violations and sufferings at the hands of police who are meant to redress the grievances, the victim remains shrunk to herself and finds company only in this "trusted offender". Therefore this syndrome is directly linked to the poor response systems and the lack of faith and trust in the response systems. The trusted offender is by no means a messiah, as she continues to be a mercenary indulging in the commercial sexual exploitation of the girl, but with minor adjustments of time and number of 'customers', etc.

Where is the Relief?

The variety of exploitations and the lack of redressal mechanisms, make the victim, howsoever strong mentally she is, as a distraught and demolished person. The distortions in the response exacerbate the challenges.

Response efforts also have several challenges within. To cite a few examples, if the police or NGO rescues her, there will be a lot of obstruction at the scene to prevent this and in the process the victim often suffers too. However, if the follow up actions after rescue are not in place, the victim may languish in some 'Home', where she remains in isolation or further exploitation. Victims are briefed well in advance by the traffickers on such issues, picturising gory tales about police custody, further torture and exploitation etc. and therefore the victims also may try to avoid bring 'picked up' by police and NGOs. These activities leave a lot of frustration and desperation in the mind of the victim. Such rescue operations, without effective post-rescue care is more harmful to the victim, than rescue. The sufferings at the rescue process, post rescue procedures and lack of care, coupled with the isolation, lack of freedom and often abuses at the 'Homes', have created a situation where many victims are happier to be confined and exploited in the brothel rather than being confined and harassed at the 'homes'. Improper and inefficient post care adds to the harm to the victim. The civil society runs several 'Homes'. Some are good whereas some do not adhere to even the minimum standards of care. In the year 2017, many such Homes were found to be exploitative camps on a study by TISS and the matter is now under investigation and subjudice.

At the same time, a few NGO run Homes have developed tie ups with other stakeholders including Corporates and are providing skilled rehabilitation, leading to a life of dignity. In such cases the harm to the victim, the damage that she has suffered, gets mitigated to a large extend. Similarly, there are sterling examples of government run initiatives across the country, wherein the women and children in exploitation have been rescued and have been provided with appropriate vocations, like security guards, industrial stitching, housekeeping, drivers, masons, elderly care services, beautician, spa services, shop vendors, etc., where they lead a life of respect and freedom, with sustained income. Though the damage and harm to the persons due to their being trafficked earlier cannot be washed away, there has been good amount of mitigation of the damage. A case in point is the "Green Police" in Kolkata, started by the Kolkata Police, along with SANLAAP wherein several trafficked victims were rescued, trained as security guards and are manning the vigilance work in malls and industrial establishments. Another example is that of industrial stitching in Odisha, where women rescued from extreme levels of sexual exploitation in the challenging heartland were trained by CRPF and Maghar, and are employed in stitching garments, living a life of earning, dignity and freedom.

There is another school of thought which argues that the institution based rehabilitation should be replaced with community based rehabilitation, so that the recued victim gets acceptance in the community. The essential principle behind this thought is the fact that even after rehabilitation, often the person continues to face social ostracism. The social stigma is a dangerous weapon which can harm the rescued person. When the community brands her as a 'prostitute' and outcasts her, she has nowhere to go. At the brothel, where she had to face all abuses and exploitations and yet she was accepted as part of the fraternity and was made wanting. But the community which outcasts her will throw up serious challenges for her very survival itself. Therefore, whether one goes for institutional care or community care, the harm to the victim remains endless, even after rehabilitation. This is a typical feature of human trafficking victims, as against the victims of other crimes.

To conclude on a positive note, one should place on record several good practices, outstanding initiatives, and sterling efforts with positive impact, undertaken by government and civil society. Many police officers, whose services have been recognized by the Government and the United Nations and have been working against human trafficking since 1982, have made strident improvements with lasting impact. Several institutional structures like AHTU (Anti Human Trafficking Units), AHTC (Anti Human Trafficking Clubs in Colleges) and Nodal Officers in the States etc. have been set up by these police officers, starting from 2002. They have made great impact in the redressal of grievances, made a paradigm shift in improving the response systems and even in preventing human trafficking. Many of these initiatives have been replicated, evaluated and institutionalized. So is the case of several NGOs and civil society organizations across the country, many often unsung and even unnoticed, which have made positive, innovative and strident steps in the rehabilitation and re-integration of the thousands of victims rescued from the world of commercial sexual exploitation. Therefore the response systems cannot be rated as poor across India, rather it remains uneven. However, the good practices, sensitive response, adherence to minimum standards of care and attention, responding to the needs and ambitions of the rescued person etc. are the hallmarks of the developments that have been of great help in redressing the harm to the victims and probable victims.

Unless the victim's plight is fathomed, there cannot any meaningful response. The Police Official need to know the depth of the harm and damage so as to document the same and bring it before the courts of law and also the rehab agencies. The understanding of the extent of the damage is crucial as evidence against the exploiters and also to obtain relief and compensation to the victim. The prosecutor need to know the same so as to place it before the court and other adjudicatory agencies. The judiciary need to know so that a well-considered decision of the crime disposal as well as for justice delivery can be arrived at. The care givers need to know the same so that they can orient trauma care, relief, protection and rehabilitation accordingly. The political leaders need to know so that they orient the policies and programmes accordingly. The media need to know so that they ensure that the victims are not further victimized and that their anonymity is assured and that the agencies concerned realize the problem and act accordingly. The Nation need to know so that they citizens uphold their constitutional mandate of preventing human trafficking. All are duty holders in the process. Hence a clear victimological understanding and assessment of the damage and the harm to the victim is of utmost importance in preventing and combating human trafficking.

References

[1] UNODC, New York, 2010, Manual for Criminal Justice Practitioners on Anti Human Trafficking.

[2] UNODC, ROSA, New Delhi, 2007, Manual for Psycho Social Interventions in Respect of Human Trafficking.

[3] Nair PM, Human Trafficking: Dimensions, Challenges & Responses, Konark Publishers, Delhi, 2010.

[4] Nair PM and Sen. S, Trafficking in Women and Children in India (study for the NHRC), Orient Longman, Delhi, 2005.

[5] Nair PM et al, Handbook for Police in Crimes Against Children, BPRD and TISS, 2017.

[6] Nair PM, Handbook for Police in Investigating Sex Trafficking Crimes, UNODC and UNWOMEN, 2007.

[7] Nair PM, Handbook for DM to address Human trafficking, NLUO Cuttack, 2017.

[8] Nair PM et al, SOP on Video Conferencing in the Trial of Trafficking Crimes, IJM, Mumbai, 2017.

[9] BBA, Missing Children on India, Delhi, 2013.

[10] BBA, Capital Corruption: Economics Behind Child Labour, 2014.

[11] Surendra Kumar, Role of Duty Bearers in Child Protection, NLUJA, Guwahati, 2019.

[12] IJM, A Guide to Good Practices, Mumbai, 2019.

[13] Nair PM, Rights Based Investigation, TISS Mumbai, 2017.

[14] Elizabeth Qiunn Right, Sarah Brightman, Crime Victimization, Carolina Academic Press, USA, 2018.

[15] Siddhrath Kara, Sex Trafficking- Inside the Business of Modern Slavery, Columbia University Press, 2017.

[16] Kevin Bales, Disposable people- New Slavery in the Global Economy, University of California Press, 2012.

Chapter X

From the Frying Pan into the Fire? Victim Turned Offender

BEULAH SHEKHAR

Scientists do not aim at immediate results. They do not expect that their advanced ideas will be readily taken up. Their work is like that of the planter, or the future. Their duty is to lay the foundation for those who are to come, and point the way.
– Nikola Tesla

Introduction

"From the frying pan into the fire?" expounds the concept of the victim turned offender. The author had conducted numerous studies among the incarcerated persons, juveniles in conflict with the law and young offenders to illustrate how a victim, his victimization and his experiences in the aftermath of his victimization, contribute to his offending behavior. According to Buckl (1897) 'Society prepares the crime, the criminal commits it'. It implies that the environment plays a vital role in the creation of a criminal. However, not everyone affected by the environment becomes a criminal. Human choice also matters in becoming an offender (Brennen, 2011). The researcher has conducted n studies covering retrospective information on previous victimization. This paper is an outcome of a decade of research among incarcerated persons and young offenders in juvenile homes, delving into the past of these offenders to see if there was any victimization. An attempt was also made to see whether any victim assistance was provided in the aftermath of their victimization and to see if there was any residual anger as a result of not having received timely assistance. Following victimization, is there a causal path towards criminalization? Is a victim who is not reconciled with his/ her victimization more susceptible to becoming a criminal? Can the knowledge about this causal relationship, be used in the treatment of offenders and assist in preventing recidivism or reoffending?

It would be most appropriate, to begin with a story of a little village boy, Munna (Burke, 2013) who was the oldest of five children, a victim of neglect and deprivation, whose father was an alcoholic and consequently he became a victim of physical abuse, he was sent to a village school where he was a victim of corporal punishment. So, he dropped out of the school. When he was thirteen years old he washed plates in a local eatery, a victim of child labor. After two years of washing plates, he befriended a man and moved with him where he started washing buses for a bus company. He then moved to the capital city, New Delhi with his new found friend and worked with another bus company there, still cleaning buses. On December 16th 2012 he boarded the bus with five other co-workers, for some fun and the rest is history. The little boy was the sixth perpetrator in the notorious Delhi gang rape case. Finding prima facie evidence against the 17-year-old juvenile, Principal Magistrate ordered framing of charges under various provisions of the Indian Penal Code, dealing with gang rape, murder, kidnapping, unnatural offences, attempt to murder, dacoity, destruction of evidence and conspiracy. Earlier the police had in its PIR (police investigation report, which is equivalent to charge sheet) filed before the juvenile justice board, slapping charges of gang rape, murder, unnatural sex, dacoit, criminal conspiracy and destruction of evidence among other offences under the Indian Penal Code against the minor.

So, now let's analyze the past experiences of this young offender, in the light of his previous history of victimization and answer some pertinent questions. Was Munna a victim of abuse? To answer this, the Article 19 of the convention on the rights of the child comes in handy. The Convention on the Rights of the Child defines a child as anyone below the age of eighteen and affirms the child as fully possessed of human rights. Every child has the right to be protected from being hurt or badly treated. Article 19 of the UNCRC makes it clear that children and young people have the basic human right to dignity. This means they have the right to be protected from violence, just like everybody else. What is this violence? The UNCRC considers violence to happen when someone's mind is hurt as well as their body. Because of this, verbal abuse and intimidation are included in its definition of the term. As well as being protected from violence, children and young people should be protected from all forms of exploitation, sexual abuse and neglect. As member States who have ratified the convention, the government of India is duty bound to guarantee and to ensure the implementation of the 54 articles of children's rights. Especially in this context, the right to protection, which guarantees the safety of children, will be covering specific issues such as abuse, neglect, and exploitation. Having said this, was Munna in our story a victim of abuse? What is abuse? The dictionary defines abuse as, to use or treat so as to injure or damage.

Now again, was Munna used? Was Munna treated so as to injure him? Permanently for life? Tamil, the most ancient language, defines abuse as உரிமைமீறல் or URIMAI MEERAL which simply means violation of rights. Now let's relook at the initial question: Was Munna a victim, a victim of abuse and neglect? Was Munna an offender? Was Munna a victim turned offender?

Theoretical Discussion

The causal mechanisms of crime have been studied in depth over the last two centuries. Agnew's (1992) general strain theory and Akers' (1985) social learning theory too, emphasize the role of former victimization within societies which provide motivation and specific training to commit crimes. The other theory providing a foundation for the correlation of victimization and offending is low-self control (Gottfredson & Hirschi, 1990).

In 1941, a German criminologist, Hans von Hentig was seeking to develop better crime prevention strategies. Having researched the factors that predisposed one to criminality (the tormentor), Von Hentig was referring to the abusive parent. In contemporary terms, there are abusive caretakers, intimates, and family members of all kinds. Hans von Hentig made a series of hypothesizes about the role of the victim in someone committing a crime. And he also believed that studying it could prevent more crimes to happen and more victims to be hurt in future crimes.

Hans Von Hentig developed a typology of victims responsible for their harms His classification schema was based on psychological, social and biological factors. In 1948, he developed three broad categorizations of victims namely: 1. the general victims, 2. the psychological victims, and 3. the activating sufferer. He also approximately at the same time as Mendelssohn, the father of Victimology, suggested that there is an interconnection between 'killer and the killed, duper and the duped'. According to von Hentig, the victim is not just a passive figure but rather an activating sufferer. Victim turned offender or the activating sufferer is one of the class of Hans Von Henting's classification on the victims. Sometimes this victimization acts as a predisposing factor and turns the victims into offenders.

Suppportive Literature

Scholars may opine that research in the direction of causality between victimization and offending is still in its infancy. However a plethora of empirical evidence of most published studies on the victim offender overlap focus on how victimization is influencing offending. The overlap between victims and offenders is not well understood in criminology, and is even widely ignored, although it has been well documented since the early contributions by von Hentig (1941, 1948) and Wolfgang (1958). According to a survey (Shaffer, 2004), results in the literature indicate that victims are two to seven times more likely than non-victims to be offenders. This can also be seen from the example of one of the most quoted articles in the literature on the victim offender overlap, (Singer, 1981),Akers (1985) and Agnew (1992) employ the explanatory power of former victimization on offending.

In Von Hentig's typology of victims, the 'tormentor,' was a victim of attack from the target of his abuse, such as the battered woman (Kreuter, 2006). In a ground breaking study on battered women, Walker (1979) reported that that there is a relationship between battered women and child abuse. Men who beat their women were themselves beaten as children. Rivera, Beverly; Widom, Cathy Spatz (1990), Widom (1989) examined the relationship between childhood victimization and violent offending using prospective cohort design and found that childhood victimization increased overall risk of violent offending, particularly for males and blacks.

The Lorena Bobbit case of 1994 (Crime Library.com) demonstrated how intense and continuous physical and emotional abuse drove a woman to the extreme violent act of severing the perpetrator's penis. A similar case has been reported from rural India where the wife resorted to the same violent act subsequent to physical and emotional torture and marital rape by the husband (Express News Service, 2009). Hartline (1997) proposes that a battered woman is a caring agent who has repeatedly suffered a violation of basic rights at the hands of her perpetrator and believes her life to be in danger. In these types of cases, the victimization experienced by the wife maybe an overt manifestation of impact of victimization in the form of vigilantism. Smith and Thornberry (1995) report a significant relationship between child maltreatment and self- reported and official delinquency that remained even when controlling for other factors. Their results also suggested that more extensive maltreatment is related to higher rates of delinquency. A study by Fagan (2005) demonstrated that adolescent physical abuse has immediate and enduring effects on the prevalence and frequency of a variety of self-reported offenses, including violent and non-violent crimes, drug use and intimate partner violence. Furthermore, the study revealed that while victimization increases the prevalence of offending for victims of varying backgrounds, the frequency of offending is moderated by family income, area of residence, and family structure. Mustaine and Tewksbury (2000) found that individuals who are both victims and offenders showed similarities in demography, social activity, neighborhood, exposure, illegal activities, and alcohol and drug use variables. Thus previous empirical research has already confirmed the existence of a strong overlap between victimization and offending (Broidy et al., 2006; Klevens, Duque and Ramirez, 2002).

In a survey of existing results on 'Victimization causes subsequent offending' Ousey et al. (2011) report mixed results regarding this direction of influence. Hay and Evans (2006), Cullen (2008), Cullen et al. (2008) and their studies characterized as 'intergenerational transmission of violence' find that former victimization is positively related to future offending. Based on evidence from a meta analysis, Farrington et al. (2012) find highly significant links between school bullying and later offending. In their review of the 'reciprocal' literature, Ousey et al. (2011) mainly refer to two studies, Schreck et al. (2006) and Wilcox et al. (2006), who both use repeated panel waves to study the dynamics of the victimization offending victimization feedback. Both studies confirm what Ousey et al. call the 'reciprocal escalation hypothesis', i.e. victimization increases offending, which in turn provokes higher victimization (Ousey, 2011). On the other hand, however Ousey et al. (2008) and Jacques and Wright (2008), propose a contradictory view 'victimization termination' rationale according to which victimization represents a shaping traumatic turning point which causes individuals to reassess their involvement in risky activities such as frequenting bars, alcohol and drug abuse and ultimately control their committing property and violent crimes. Contributions in the field of psychology also focus on school bullying (perpetration and victimization) and their consequences later in life.

In depth interviews with street criminals (Jacobs and Wright, 2010) have shown that retaliation is not necessarily addressed against the perpetrator but that random redirection might lash out at any available victim, leading to and reinforcing a climate of urban violence. In recent surveys on behavioral economics of crime (McAdams, 2009) point at the preference for fairness which may underlie certain crimes of 'self help' retaliations against their perpetrators: People gain utility by acting altruistically toward those who treat them fairly and by acting spitefully against those who treat them unfairly (Fehr & Gächter, 2002; Garoupa, 2003). Using survey data on the German resident population, some author's new econometric evidence on the mutual dependence of victimization and offending results indicate that both variables are affected by a long list of social, demographic, economic and further criminological factors. As regards the mutual interdependence of victimization and offending, recursive bivariate probit analysis suggests endogeneity of victimization and exogeneity of offending (Entorf, 2012).

(Eitle David & Turner, 2002) reported that recent exposure to violence in the community along with a history of receiving traumatic news, direct victimizations in the community, recent life events, and associations with criminal peers increase the risk for young adult criminal offending. Nofziger and Kurtz (2005) argue that exposure to violence is indicative of a lifestyle of violence. Molnar et al. (2005) reported that violent victimization was an important risk factor for subsequent violent behavior by girls. Schreck, Stewart, and Osgood (2008) observed significant differentiation between the tendencies to be an offender versus the tendency to be a victim which was stable overtime. Estevez and Emler (2011) found that being a victim of crime may be a predictor of offending irrespective of gender. Pauwels and Svenson (2011) in a study of urban delinquency report that victimization has a significant positive effect on offending, independent of background characteristics, low self-control and lifestyle risk. Many juvenile sex offenders are also victims of sexual abuse said Muster N (1992).

Also the overlap of victimization and offending, anger seems to be a major motivation of retaliatory behavior, as also stressed by many criminological and psychological research papers (Agnew, 1992; Kubrin and Weitzer, 2003; Jacobs and Wright 2010; Simons & Burt, 2011). Anger in response to perpetrated injury, frustration and unfair treatment is a triggering event that motivates 'striking back', not necessarily to the perpetrator himself but also to non-involved bystanders and other available victims, also at some later point in time. Such behavior is often consequence and origin of norms of honor and respect, prevailing and potentially escalating in sub cultural societies (Anderson, 1999; Kubrin and Weitzer 2003; Kubrin, 2003).

The findings of a study among incarcerated persons, who were victims of crime, suggest a new perspective that victimization can also be the cause of crime. The background of the juvenile in conflict with the law in the brutal gang rape at Delhi also leads to the premise that victimization can also be the cause of crime. Shekhar stated that crime victimization could also be a cause of crime. She further proposed that this be included as one of the factors influencing the volume and type of crime in the Uniform Crime Report of the Federal Bureau of Investigations (Shekhar, Sundar & Somasundaram, 2014).

82.2% of the respondents perceived that if the previous victimization had not occurred they would not have committed a crime (Raja & Shekhar, 2012).

A study in a prison also revealed that out of 272 offenders, 194 had a previous history of victimization. The researchers now attempted to view the data along these two classifications. For this purpose visual binning process was carried out for two variables, crime committed and type of victimization. Petty crimes and property crimes were combined into a single category, Crimes against property and the remaining three categories constituted Crimes against persons. Consequently the 5 types of victimization were also combined into two categories, victims of property offences and victims of crimes against persons. Data was then subjected to Spearman correlation which was significant ($\rho = 0.147$, $p = 0.05$) a positive correlation between victimization and offending (Shekhar, 2012).

In yet another finding there was a strong indication that there might be an association between type of crime and type of victimization. In order to delve into this association, putting aside data with no victimization, the sample of 194 victimized inmates was subjected to Chi Square test. This was done by cross tabulating the categories of the two variables – the type of crime and the type of victimization and calculating the observed and expected frequencies. The test revealed that crime committed by the offenders varied significantly by the type of victimization (74.80, $p = 0.001$). (Shekhar B., 2014)

A study by Shekhar & Somasundaram (2009) on incarcerated persons revealed that childhood victimization in the incarcerated persons had severe psychological, financial and physical impact which subsequently led them to commit crimes in adulthood and Victimization could lead to criminal behaviours in adulthood. (Shekhar & Somasundaram, 2009)

Shekhar B. (2012) on crime as the cause of crime showed that crime does not happen in a vaccum. Crime is the outcome of a process, crime is not an action but a reaction (or an overreaction) to external and environmental stimuli (Hentig, 1948). Some of these stimuli emanate from the victim or victimization (Fattah, 1999)

Shekhar B. (2015) on victimization survey in the prison – the victim turned offender showed that 75% previous victimization and related anger and frustration had led them to commit a crime. 82.2% opined that if the previous victimization had not occurred this crime not has been (B S., 2015).

Shekhar B. (2015) stated that victim assistance and crime prevention are two sides of the same coin. It showed that Delhi rape and the involvement of a juvenile and their troubled histories of the accused.

The findings of a Study by Shekhar B. (2015) on victimization as a cause of crime showed that physical abuse in childhood increases the propensity to commit criminal violence later in life. Secondly the degree of victimization is related to the seriousness of the offence.

Shekhar B & Somasundaram, conducted a victimization survey among adolescents of three districts in Tamilnadu. The findings showed that 469 adolescents had experienced crime victimization at least once in their life time. (Somasundaram & Shekhar, 2016)

A study by Kumar S. & Beulah (2018) on a comparative study of the victimization among the institutionalized juvenile in conflict with law and the non institutionalized juvenile showed that there is a difference between juvenile & non juvenile in their victimization. There is difference between the groups with regard in witness of violence (hurt/riot/ murder). There is relation in the victimization of the juvenile & non juvenile with regard to physical abuse.

Shekhar B (2019) suggests as a method of preventing recidivism and reoffending by delving into the past and addressing the victimization. (Shekhar B., 2019)

Indirect victimization, peer and sibling victimization, crime victimization and sexual victimization are predecessors to criminal behavior. (Shekhar B., 2019)

Outcome of These Studies

Based on the findings of these studies for the past decade, three models were evolved for victimization prevention, crime prevention and reoffending / recidivism prevention.

- First outcome was the prevention of childhood victimization (Model 1)
- Second outcome providing victim assistance in the aftermath of victimization, to help the victim reconcile with his victimization, to prevent the victim turning into an offender, victim assistance is crime prevention. (Model 2)
- Third outcome was a model to more specifically reduce recidivism among offenders by identifying their childhood victimization, addressing their childhood victimization, and incorporating this into the treatment of offenders namely in the reformation, rehabilitation and resocialization of offenders. (Model 3)

Models for Victimazation Prevention, Crime Prevention and Recidivism/ Reoffending Prevention

A diagrammatic representation of the three models have been reproduced here in this paper.

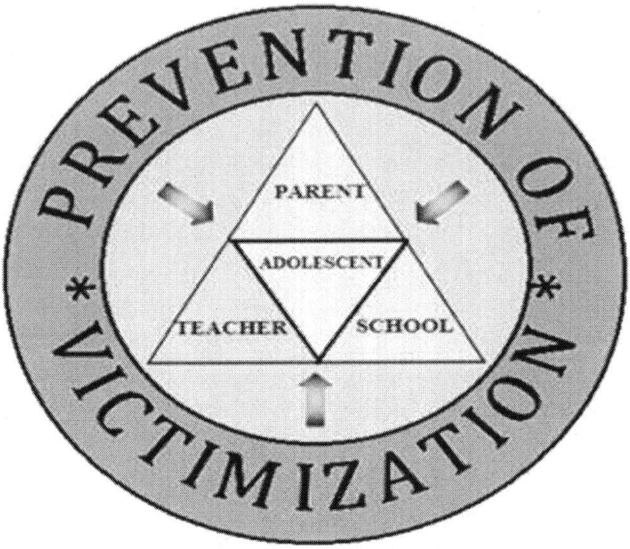

Figure 1: Childhood Victimization Prevention

Mechanism for Prevention of Victimization (Somasundaram & Shekhar, 2014).

Figure 2: Crime Prevention

Timely victim assistance is crime prevention (Shekhar, 2014) or lack of victim assistance leads to offending behavior or crime.

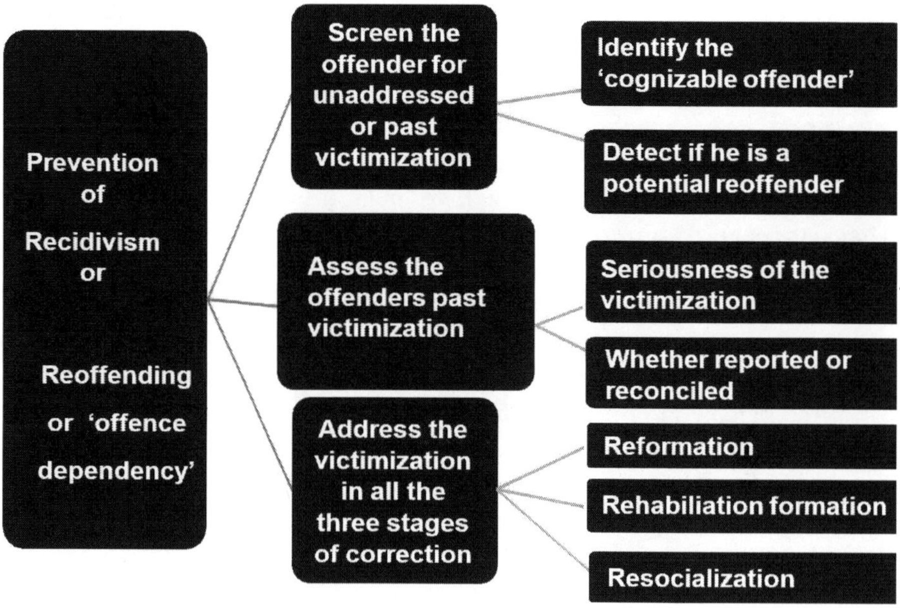

Figure 3: Recidivism Prevention (Shekhar, 2019)

Reduce Recidivism and Reoffending

These studies reveals that a large proportion of the incarcerated persons have some sort of victimization that has not been reconciled with or other childhood victimization related challenges that have contributed to their offending behavior. Reformation includes introspection, a look into his past for any residual anger or unaddressed victimization Resocialisation arranges some victim perpetrator mediation or some kind of mediation with the perpetrator if contactable to assist them in the ventilation of their anger and frustration associated with the unaddressed victimization. In order to assist these offenders and prevent recidivism, a two week program that delves into their past and addressees their past victimization to appropriate them and rehabilitate these offenders.

These incarcerated persons with past history of unreported or unaddressed victimization are also prone to 'offence dependency', which is like drug dependency or alcohol dependency. They cannot but help venting their anger by committing offence that may or may not be related to their victimization. The researcher has coined a term for this – people with this 'offence dependency'. These incarcerated persons, with unreconciled victimizations are 'cognizable offenders', which means that they are potential, perceptible or clearly identifiable offenders. The bright side is that this knowledge, could be used constructively, to design an intervention that could be a solution to prevent this group of people from reoffending or from committing another crime.(Shekhar 2019).

The three R's -- Reformation, Resocialization and Rehabilitation are the purpose of any penal policy. Reformation - includes introspection, a look into his past for any residual anger or unaddressed victimization; Resocialization - A program should be developed, to help the victim understand that what happened to him or her is not the norm but a one off incident and his offending behavior is not going to address that issue. Rehabilitation - arranges some kind of a mediation with the perpetrator if contactable and to assist them in the ventilation of their anger and frustration associated with the victimization; Rehabilitation is the reintegration into society of a convicted person and the main objective of modern penal policy, to counter habitual offending, also known as criminal recidivism These incarcerated persons with past history of unreported or unaddressed victimization are also prone to 'offence dependency', which is like drug dependency or alcohol dependency, something that is un uncontrollable urge to commit an offence. The need to lead a law abiding life in the society has to be understood through specially designed programs

Also, these studies reveals that a large proportion of the incarcerated persons have some sort of victimization that has not been reconciled with or other childhood victimization related challenge that has contributed to their offending behavior. Since these persons are 'cognizable offenders', which means that they are potential, perceptible or clearly identifiable potential offenders. From the findings of these various researches, lead us to think that this knowledge may be used to combat reoffending and reduce recidivism among released incarcerated persons

Revisiting the literature of Von Hentig 1948 and Fattah 1999. The researcher has revisited the existing literature, interpreted it based on the findings of these studies among victimised incarcerated persons. The researcher has attempted to extend the meaning of term 'victim' used by Von Hentig and Fattah and replace the term 'victim' with the term 'victimization'. Von Hentig (1948) addressed involvement in the crime event by centering on victim vulnerabilities, which was stated to be outdated, and lacked support. These studies confirm that one of the vulnerabilities is the propensity of the victim to become an offender. (Hentig, 1948) Motives for criminal behaviour do not develop in a vacuum (Von Hentig, 1948). They come into being through drives and responses, reactions and interactions, to the victimisations. Von Hentig (1948) made the most significant impact by introducing the notion of doer-sufferer interaction. Here the doer and the sufferer are both inside one person. He proposed to take the victim as one of the determinants here we take the victimisation in a crime event where he noted a nefarious symbiosis (evil relationship) existed between the two. This maybe interpreted as the evil relationship between victimization and offending behavior. His work had the most significant impact because it highlighted the importance of the roles of the victim, here victimization in the understanding of crime.

The commission of a crime is the outcome of a process where many factors are at work. In most cases, crime is not an action, but a reaction or an overreaction to external environmental stimuli. Often the criminal act is not an isolated gesture but the denouement of a long or brief interaction with the victim here the unreconciled victimization within himself. In such cases, it is not possible to understand the act fully without analysing the chain of interactions that led to the perpetrations. It is scientifically unsound to examine and analyse the offender's act in isolation from the dynamic forces that have prepared, influenced, conditioned or determined it (Fattah, 1991) Here we may interpret the victimization as the dynamic force that has prepared, influenced, conditioned or determined the offending behaviour

People who have been incarcerated account for one in five of all crimes. Nearly three in five incarcerated persons are re-convicted within two years of leaving prison. Offending by ex-incarcerated persons costs society at least £11 billion a year. This all tells us we are failing to capitalise on the opportunity prison provides to stop people offending for good. We need to make sure that a prison sentence punishes the offender, but also provides the maximum opportunity for reducing the likelihood of re-offending. That means we need to redouble efforts to rehabilitate incarcerated persons back into society effectively. There is now considerable evidence of the factors that influence re-offending. Building on criminological and social research, the Social Exclusion Unit (SEU) has identified nine key factors: education, employment, drug and alcohol misuse, mental and physical health, attitudes and self-control, institutionalisation and life-skills, housing, financial support and debt, and family networks. (The Social Exclusion Unit, 2002)

Why do we fail to break the cycle of reoffending & recidivism? In spite of all the efforts inside the prison for reformation, resocialization and rehabilitation and all the other efforts to prevent them from reoffending after they are released? As recommended by the SEU, most after care programs pay attention to the nine key factors – education; employment, drug and alcohol misuse, mental and physical health, attitudes and self-control, institutionalisation and life-skills, housing; financial support and debt; and family networks. Nevertheless reoffending g and recidivism still challenge the criminal justice system in most countries today .So, what is wrong?

Are we only looking for solutions outside? Outside the incarcerated person? Should we not look inside the person? Healing needs to happen on the inside of the person, for all the other external programs to be successful. Who are the perpetrators and who are the ones who reoffend? We need to ask the 5Ws and 2Hs about the victimization. WHAT? WHO? WHEN? WHERE? WHY? HOW? HOW MUCH residual anger revenge.

What was the type of victimization they were subjected to? What was the type of succor they received? Who was the victimizer? Who did they report to? If at all they did report, why did they not share this experience? When did this occur? When did they share their experience of victimization? Where did the victimization occur? Where did they look for assistance? How much did this victimization experience impact their daily life? How much of assistance did they receive? How much difficulty did they experience? How much residual anger because of the lack of support?

Ian Loft in an article on how people become criminals stated that an offender is a victim of circumstances. Could the unreconciled past victimization be the circumstance? Is a victim who is not reconciled with his/ her victimization more vulnerable to becoming a criminal?

Hentig's Victim Precipitation Theory explains the basic premise is that 'victims may initiate, either actively or passively, the confrontation that leads to their victimization' (Siegel, 2006). Siegel (2006) developed a more elaborate victim precipitation theory. The victim precipitation theory suggests that some people cause or initiate confrontation that may lead to that person being victimized. Siegel (2006) notes that precipitation could be active or passive. 'Active precipitation occurs when the victim behaves aggressively or provocatively or even is the first to attack. Passive precipitation occurs when victims unknowingly threaten or encourage the offender. ' So generally, this theory is talking about victims surely did something that initiated or stimulated the following crimes that happened to them; Victims strongly linked back to criminals and crimes. For a vast majority of violent offenders, the crime does not take place in a vacuum. By the same token, the victim and the suspect are not always so clearly defined. In many instances, the final result is the end to what was a series of events leading up to that ultimate episode (violence). An example of this would be a person that is assaulted or killed after years of physically abusing their spouse or child. This example also lends itself to the second point made in that line between victim and suspect can be somewhat unclear (Dietrich, 2008).

Revisiting this theory and interpreting the victim precipitation theory as the victimization precipitation theory, we may say that : There are two types of victimization precipitations – direct and indirect. Direct – when the victim acts in retaliation and commits an offence against the perpetrator, as an act of vengeance or as a vigilantism having not been provided any succor, in the immediate aftermath of his victimization. Indirect – but internalizes it and in the future commits offense or offences against persons other than the perpetrator, resembling the perpetrator or with the same profile. The irony is that, in the case of active or passive victim precipitation, when the perpetrator is injured, they have the legal safeguards to protect them like the self defense clause, general exception or the battered woman syndrome phrase. But in the case of the outcome of their actions direct or indirect, against any persons, because of their inability to cope with their victimization, they are hapless and fall into the clutches of the criminal justice system – as offenders – as victim turned offenders. Thus is the vulnerability of the victims who have not received any victim assistance and are not reconciled with their victimization and are unable to cope with their victimization. This unaddressed victimization leads them to become offence dependent. They have the urge to commit offence against their perpetrator or against any other person, who may or may not bear a resemblance to their perpetrator. It is then, when these victims are still struggling to cope with the impact of their victimizations, the inevitable happens. These victims fall – fall, hook, line and sinker, from the frying pan, of being a victim, into the fire of being an offender!

And their ordeal with the Criminal Justice System begins or continues – as offenders, as recidivists. From the frying pan, into the fire!

Road Ahead

Prepare a program for incarcerated persons, with victimologists and psychologists to delve into their past history of victimization address in the most appropriate way through various interventions such as counseling, anger management or desensitization techniques and remove the residual anger form the victims. The program needs to delve into the past history of victimization .We need to ask the 5Ws and 2Hs about the victimization. WHAT? WHO? WHEN? WHERE? WHY? HOW? HOW MUCH residual anger and revenge?

Obtain the necessary permission from the prison authorities to utilize this intervention program among incarcerated persons who have suffered victimizations in the past and assist the incarcerated persons to reconcile with their past victimization. Long term studies on incarcerated persons who have served their sentence and undergone the program, to study their reoffending behavior and reduce their offence dependency in their attempt to reconcile with their victimization.

Conclusion

These studies measured five types of childhood victimization - crime victimization, caretaker abuse, peer and sibling abuse, sexual abuse and indirect victimization – and found significant evidence for all of them among all the incarcerated persons and the results of these studies revealed that early victimization of the convicted person, and the unaddressed victimization had in some way contributed to his offending behavior. Thus, these studies have answered questions like – Following victimization is there a causal path towards criminalization? Are the victims who are not reconciled with their victimization more susceptible to become a criminal or engage in offending behavior? These studies also unearthed some answers for the control of reoffending behavior and recidivism. To that end, these studies were able to touch its goal of using the findings to provide a doable, to address the challenge of not only crime prevention in general, but also to tackle reoffending behavior and reduction of recidivism in particular.. Now armed with this knowledge, the researcher has suggested ways to prevent reoffending or to reduce recidivism. A model was evolved in the treatment of offenders and to help in the rehabilitation programs. This model addresses the incarcerated person's victimization and help in reconciliation thus preventing future reoffending or recidivism. Hopefully this will prevent the falling of the person from the frying pan into the fire and will reduce the number of victim turned offenders!

References

[1] Agnew Robert. (1985). Social Control Theory and Delinquency: A Longitudinal Test. Criminology, Vol. 23, No.1 (1985), pp. 47-61.

[2] Agnew, R. (1992). Foundation for a General Strain Theory. *Criminology* 30(1), 47-87. *And the Community*, 15(1),15-30.

[3] Akers, Ronald L. (1985). Deviant behavior: A social learning approach (3rd ed.). Belmont, CA: Wadsworth.

[4] Akers, Ronald L. (1998). Social learning and social structure: A general theory of crime and deviance. Boston: Northeastern University Press. (PDF) Social Learning Theory. Available from: https://www.researchgate.net/publication/321167448_Social_Learning_Theory [accessed Nov 01 2019].

[5] Anderson, E. (1999). Code of the Street, New York: Norton

[6] Becker, G.S. (1968). Crime and punishment: An economic approach. *Journal of Political Economy*, 76(2), Behavior by Girls Reporting Violent Victimization: A Prospective Study. *Arch Pediatr Adolesc Med.* 2005; 159: 731-739.

[7] Beecher (2007) Hoodie or goodie? New research reveals ways to break the cycle of violence among young people available at http://www.victimsupport.com/vs_england_wales/about_us/press_releases/press_releases_current/#ss6

[8] Brennen, B.H. (2011, November). Causes of Crime. Sounds of Encouragement: Helping people smile again.

[9] Broidy, L.M., Daday, J.K., Crandall, C.S., Sklar, D.P., &Jost, P.F. (2006). Exploring demographic, structural, and behavioral overlap among homicide offenders and victims. *Homicide Studies*, 10, 155-180.

[10] Buckle (1857). History of civilization in England. Published: London, J. W. Parker and son, 1857-61. London, J. W. Parker and son, 1857-61.

[11] Burke (2012) Life, Rape and Death in an Indian City, *The Hindu*, September 14, 2013.

[12] Cohen, L.E. and M. Felson (1979). Social Change and Crime Rate Trends: A Routine Activities Approach. *American Sociological Review*, 44, 588-608. correlates of witnessed Ehrlich, I. (1973). Participation in Illegitimate Activities: A Theoretical and Empirical Investigation, *Journal of Political Economy*, 81(3), 521-565.

[13] Crime: The Effects of Witnessing Violence, Traumatic Victimization, and Other Stressful Life Events. *Journal of Research in Crime and Delinquency* 2002, 39: 214.

[14] Criminal Statistics and the Construction of Crime March 2012 DOI: 10.13140/RG.2.1.4956.6485/1. In book: Oxford Handbook of Criminology Edition: 5th, Chapter: 8, Publisher: Oxford University Press Editors: Mike Maguire, Rod Morgan, Robert Reiner.

[15] Cullen, F.T., Unnever, J.D., Hartman J.L., Turner M.G., Agnew R. (2008). Gender, Bullying Victimization, and Juvenile Delinquency: A Test of General Strain Theory. *Victims and Offenders*, 3(4), 346-364.

[16] David J. Smith and Susan McVie (2003). Theory and Method in the Edinburgh Study of Youth Transitions and Crime, *The British Journal of Criminology*, Vol. 43, No. 1, pp. 169-195, Published by: Oxford University Press https://www.jstor.org/stable/23638922.

[17] Eitle David & Turner, Jay R. (2002). Exposure to Community Violence and Young Adult.

[18] Ellis, L., Beaver, K.M., & Wright, J. (2009). Handbook of Crime Correlates. Academic Press.

[19] Entorf, H. (2012). Expected Recidivism among Young Offenders: Comparison of Specific Deterrence under Juvenile and Adult Criminal Law, forthcoming in *European Journal of Political Economy*.

[20] Entorf, Horst (2012). Certainty and Severity of Sanctions in Classical and Behavioral Models of Deterrence: A Survey.

[21] Estévez & Emler (201). Adolescent and youth offending behavior available at https://www.uv.es/lisis/estevez/12-7IJCHP.pdf

[22] Fagan Abigail, A. (2005). The Relationship between Adolescent Physical Abuse and Criminal Offending: Support for an Enduring and Generalized Cycle of Violence. *Journal of Family Violence*. Vol. 20, No. 5 (October, 2005), pp. 279-290.

[23] Fagan Jeffery, Piper Elizabeth. S, Cheng Yu-The. (1987). Contributions of Victimization to Delinquency in Inner Cities. *The Journal of Criminal Law and Criminology* (1973), Vol. 78, No. 3 (Autumn, 1987), pp. 586-613.

[24] Farrington, D. (1989). Early Predictors of Adolescent Aggression and Adult Violence. *Journal of Family Violence*, 20, 279-290.

[25] Farrington et al. (2012). School bullying, depression and offending behaviour later in life: An updated systematic review of longitudinal studies. Stockholm: Swedish National Council for Crime Prevention.

[26] Fattah, Ezzat A. (1999). The Vital Role of Victimology in the Rehabilitation of Offenders and their Reintegration into Society. Paper presented at the *112th International Training Course of UNAFEI*, Japan, Apr. 12 – Jul. 2, 1999.

[27] Fehr E, Gächter S (2002). Altruistic punishment in humans. *Nature* 45: 137-140.

[28] Foreman-Peck, J., and S.C. Moore (2010). Gratuitous Violence and the Rational Offender Model. *International Review of Law and Economics*, 30(2), 160-172.

[29] Garoupa, N. (2003). Behavioral Economic Analysis of Crime: A Critical Review. *European Journal of Law and Economics*, 15(1), 5-15. 26

[30] Gottfredson & Hirschi (1990). A General Theory of Crime, Stanford, CA: Stanford University Press.

[31] Hartline, Sharon E. (1997). Battered Women Who Kill. *Journal of Social Philosophy*, Vol. 28, No. 2, Fall 1997, 56-67.

[32] Hay, C. and M.M. Evans (2006). Violent victimization and involvement in delinquency: Examining predictions from general strain theory, *Journal of Criminal Justice*, 34(3), 261-274.

[33] Hentig, H.V. (1941). Remarks on the interaction of perpetrator and victim, *Journal of Criminal Law, Criminology, and Police Science*, 31, 303-309.

Hentig, H. V. (1948). The Criminal and His Victim. New Haven: Yale U. Press.

[34] Hindelang, M.J., M.R. Gottfredson and J. Garofalo (1978). Victims of Personal Crime: An Empirical Foundation for a Theory of Personal Victimization, Cambridge: Ballinger. http://www.fbi.gov/about-us/cjis/ucr/ucr-statistics-their-proper-use

[35] Hume, D. (1978). A Treatise of Human Nature, Oxford: Oxford Clarendon Press (original published in 1739).

[36] Ian Loft (2009). How People become Criminals. Retrieved from http://www.helium.com/items/1360240-how-people-become-criminals

[37] Jacobs, B.A., and R. Wright (2010). Bounded Rationality, Retaliation, and the Spread of Urban Violence, *Journal of Interpersonal Violence*, 25(10), 1739-1766.

[38] Jacobs, B.A., and R. Wright (2010). Bounded Rationality, Retaliation, and the Spread of Urban Violence, *Journal of Interpersonal Violence*, 25(10), 1739-1766.

[39] Jacques, S., and R. Wright (2008). The victimization-termination link. *Criminology*, 46(4), 1009-1038.

[40] Klevens Joanne, Duque Luis Fernando & Ramírez Clemencia. (2002). The Victim-Perpetrator Overlap and Routine Activities: Results From a Cross-Sectional Study in Bogotá. *J Interpers Violence 2002*, 17: 206.

[41] Kreuter E.A. (2006). Victim vulnerability – An Existential-Humanistic Interpretation of a Single Case Study, p. 24. Nova Science Publishers, Inc.

[42] Kubrin, C.E., and R. Weitzer (2003). Retaliatory Homicide: Concentrated Disadvantage and Neighborhood Culture, *Social Problems*, 50(2), 157-180.

[43] Levitt, S.D., and S.A. Venkatesh (2000). An Economic Analysis of a Drug-Selling.

[44] McAdams, R.H. and T.S. Ulen (2009). Behavioral Criminal Law and Economics, in: N. Garoupa (ed.): *Criminal Law and Economics*, Edward Elgar Publishing,403–425

[45] Meyer, S. (2007). Sozialkapital und Delinquenz, Doctoral Dissertation, Darmstadt University of Technology, http://elib.tu-darmstadt.de/diss/000833.

[46] Molnar Beth E., Browne Angela, Cerda Magdalena, Buka Stephen L. (2005). Violent.

[47] Monfardini, C. and R. Radice (2008). Testing Exogeneity in the Bivariate Probit Model: A Monte Carlo Study, *Oxford Bulletin of Economics and Statistics*, 70(2),271-282.

[48] Mustaine, E.E., & Tewksbury, R. (2000). Comparing the lifestyles of victims, offenders, and victim-offenders: A routine activity theory assessment of similarities and differences for criminal incident participants. In Jennings et al. A Longitudinal Assessment of the Victim Offender Overlap (pp 2148). *J Interpers Violence 2010* 25: 2147.

[49] Muster, Nori Treating the Adolescent Victim – Turned – Offender. Adolescence, v27, Eric publications 1992.

[50] Nofziger Stacey & Kurtz Don (2005). Violent Lives: A Lifestyle Model Linking Exposure to Violence to Juvenile Violent Offending. *Journal of Research in Crime and Delinquency* 2005, 42: 3.

[51] Ousey, G.C., P. Wilcox and B.S. Fisher (2011). Something Old, Something New: Revisiting Competing Hypotheses of the Victimization-Offending Relationship Among Adolescents, *Journal of Quantitative Criminology*, 27, 53–84.

[52] Ousey, G.C., P. Wilcox and S. Brummel (2008). Déjà vu all over again: Investigating Temporal Continuity of Adolescent Victimization, *Journal of Quantitative Criminology*, 24, 307-335.

[53] Papadopoulos, G. (2011). The Relationship between Immigration Status and Victimization. Evidence from the British Crime Survey, mimeo, University of Essex, paper presented to the European Economic Association meeting in Oslo. Parents' Views About Child Sexual Abuse Prevention Education. J

[54] Pauwels Lieven J.R., Svensson Robert (2011). Exploring the Relationship between Offending and Victimization: What is the Role of Risky Lifestyles and Low Self-Control? A Test in Two Urban Samples. *Eur J Crim Policy Res* (2011) 17: 163–177.

[55] Report by the Social Exclusion Unit (2002). Reducing Reoffending.pdf https://www.bristol.ac.uk/poverty/downloads/keyofficialdocuments/Reducing%20Reoffending.pdf

[56] Rivera, Beverly; Widom, Cathy Spatz.(1990). Childhood Victimization and Violent Offending Violence and Victims. Vol. 5, no 1, pp. 19-35(17).

[57] Schreck, C.J., Stewart, E.A. & Osgood, D.W. (2008). A Reappraisal of the Overlap of Violent Offenders and Victims. *Criminology*, 46: 871–906.

[58] Schreck, C.J., E.A. Stewart and B.S. Fisher (2006). Self-control, victimization, and their influence on risky lifestyles: A longitudinal analysis using panel data. *Journal of Quantitative Criminology*, 22, 319-340.

[59] Schreck, C.J., E.A. Stewart and D.W. Osgood (2008). A Reappraisal of the Overlap of Violent Offenders and Victims, *Criminology*, 46(4), 871-904.

[60] Shekhar B & Somasundaram, Vijaya S. (2016). Victimisation Survey among Adolescents of Three Districts in Tamil Nadu, University Publication, ManonmaniamSundaranar University, Tirunelveli. Tamil Nadu, January, 2016.

[61] Beulah Shekhar, S. Raja, Vijaya Somasundaram (2015). The Victim Turned Offender an Empirical Study in Palayamkottai Central Prison, *155 The Indian Police Journal*, October-December, 2015 l Vol. LXII l No. 3.

[62] Shekhar B (2012) Victims of the System – Crime as a Cause of Crime in Dimensions of Violations & Victimization, ed. pp. 395-406, ISBN No: 978-93-81402-27-6 Publication Division, Manonmaniam Sundaranar University, November 2012.

[63] Shekhar B (2015). Creating safe space for Women & Child Victims of Crime, ISBN: 978-81-906687-2-96, University Publication, Manonmaniam Sundaranar University, Tirunelveli. Tamil Nadu, January.

[64] Shekhar. B & Raja S. (2012). Victimization Survey in the Prison the Victim Turned Offender Dimensions of Violations & Victimization, ed. pp. 395-406, ISBN No: 978-93- 81402-27-6, Publication Division, Manonmaniam Sundaranar University, November 2012.

[65] Shekhar B. (2015). Toward A Victim Justice System – A New Vision of Justice for Crime Victims, ISBN: 978-81-906687-3-6, University Publication, Manonmaniam Sundaranar University, Tirunelveli. Tamil Nadu, December, 2015.

[66] Shekhar B. (2019). A study on victim turned offender among the prisoners in eight central prisons in Tamil Nadu, in the book Criminology & Victimology – Through the Looking Glass, MSU Publication, 2019, ISBN 9789381402658.

[67] Shekhar B., Sundar, Somasundaram (2014). Victimization as a Cause of Crime with Volume 8, Number 1, ISSN 2156-6194 in International Perspectives in Victimology, The Press at California State University, Fresno, CA 93740-8024, USA, March 1, 2014, *Journal International Perspectives in Victimology.*

[68] Simons, R.L., and C.H. Burt (2011). Learning to be Bad: Adverse Social Conditions, Social Schemas and Crime, *Criminology*, 49(2), 553-598.28

[69] Singer, S. (1981). Homogeneous victim-offender populations: A review and some research implications, *Journal of Criminal Law and Criminology*, 72,779-88.

[70] Smith & Thornberry (1995). The Relationship between Childhood Maltreatment and Adolescent Involvement in Delinquency. *Criminology*, Vol 33, Issue 4, pp. 451-481, November 1995.

[71] The Federal Bureau of Investigations: Uniform Crime Reports (2011). Uniform Crime Reporting Statistics: Their Proper Use, January 2011.

[72] The Indian Express: Journalism of Courage. Village woman bobbitises oppressing husband in bed. Retrieved from http://www.indianexpress.com/news/village-woman-bobbitises-oppressing-husband-in-bed/429998/

[73] Von Hentig, H. (1940). Remarks on the interaction of perpetrator and victim. Journal of CriminalLaw, Criminology and Police Science. Vol. 31, No. 3 (Sep. - Oct., 1940), pp. 303.

[74] Von Hentig, H. (1948). The Criminal and His Victim,Studies in the Sociology of Crim. New Haven: Yale University Press.

[75] Walker Lenore E. (1979). The Battered Woman, p. 10. Harper & Row, Publisher, Inc.

[76] Widom C.S. (1989). The Cycle of Violence. *Science*, Vol. 244, April 1989, 160-165.

[77] Wilcox, P., D.C. May and S.D. Roberts (2006). Student weapon possession and the fear and victimization hypothesis: Unraveling the temporal order, Justice Quarterly, (23), 502-529.

[78] Wolfgang, M.E. (1958). Patterns in criminal homicide, Wiley, New York.

[79] Seigel, L (2006) Criminology, 9th Edition, Belmont. CA: Thomas Wadsworth.

Chapter XI

Towards Rural Victimology: Perspective on Rural Crime

YOSHIKO TAKAHASHI

Introduction

There are significant shortages in the study of rural crime and victimization because crime and violence are often framed as urban matters. Along with the public perception of rural communities as stable and immune to crime, overall, rural crimes are identified less frequently than urban crimes in the United States. When comparing the national statistics for urban and rural regions, the violent crime rates in rural areas are much lower than those of urban areas. According to the National Crime Victimization Survey (NCVS) in 2014, a vast majority of rapes and sexual assaults occurred in urban and suburban areas (55% for urban and 35% for suburban).Rural areas accounted for 10% of all rape and sexual assaults, 6% of robberies, and 18% of aggravated assaults (Office for Victims of Crime, 2017). However, scholars studying rural regions have been alarmed that rural communities and residents pose unique challenges because of geographical dispersion and a lack of resources. The objectives of this paper are to describe the characteristics and socioeconomic status of rural residents and explore how those rural factors affect victimization in specific crimes. Throughout the paper, I take notice to the distinct needs of rural victims and call attention to the need to reconsider existing victimological theories, research, and practices.

Rural Demographics and Characteristics in America

Rural can be defined in many ways. The term has been used for unincorporated areas, villages, small towns, townships, countries, states, and even countries or agricultural regions (Weisheit &Donner meyer, 2012). The U.S. Census Bureau defines rural as any population, housing, or territory not in an urban area (Ratcliffe, Burd, Holder, & Fields, 2016).

According to the American Community Survey released from the U.S. Census Bureau, ruralincludes97% of the nation's land area with about 60 million people. Among those rural residents, 9%, or 5.3 million, lived in completely rural counties from2011 to2015 (U.S. Census Bureau,2016). When comparing rural residents against urban counterparts, rural residents were much older than urban residents(median age 51 for rural versus45 for urban) and prime-age (ages 25–54) workers have declined in rural areas (Pew Research Center, 2018). Rural residents were less educated than urban residentswith35% of urban and 31% suburban residents having a bachelor's degree or more education, whereas only 19% of rural residents have such a degree. Rural households had lower median household income than urban households ($52,386 versus $54,296).

The same survey also portrays the views of problems faced by communities. Despite rural stereo types that little crime and social issues occur in rural communities, both urban and rural residents identified drug addiction as a pressing problem (50% for urbanresidentsversus46% for rural). Although the percentage is much lower than urban residents (35%), one fifth of rural residents (20%) say that crime is a major problem in their community. Some distinct problems are accessibility to public transportation (43%), availability of jobs (42%),accessibility to high-speed Internet (24%), and good doctors and hospitals (23%) (Pew Research Center, 2018).As expected, gun ownership is much more prevalent in rural areas: 46% of rural adults say they own a gun compared to28% of suburban adults and 19% of urban adults. Notably, rural residents are more likely to own guns but are less likely to use guns in the commission of a crime. (Weisheit &Donner meyer, 2012).

When comparing crime rates in urban and rural regions, both the Uniform Crime Report (UCR) and the National Crime Victimization Survey (NCVS) show that cities with a larger population in general have higher crime rates than suburban and rural areas. For example, motor vehicle theft occurs 2.2 times more frequently in urban areas than in rural areas (Office for Victims of Crime, 2017). However, the official crime statistics do not reveal the full story. Research has shown that certain segments of rural populations suffer from violence at a much higher proportion than urban and suburban ones. Furthermore, geographic and social factors in rural areas make rural residents more susceptible to certain types of crimes. The section below highlights crimes for which rural residents are more vulnerable due to social isolation, lack of opportunity, and poverty.

Rural Youth Violence and Substance Abuse

School violence is often perceived as an urban problem as reported school crimes in urban and suburban areas have higher percentages than rural areas (35 per 1,000 urban students, 36 for suburban and 18 for rural) (Zhang, Musu-Gillette, & Oudekerk, 2016). Contrary to the general assumption that rural schools are more resilient to school violence, rural schools in fact face similar problems such as bullying, gang activities, and substance abuse as urban schools (Weisheit, Falcone, & Wells, 2006). Furthermore, rural youth reported more risk-taking behaviors including frequent tobacco use, sexual intercourse, weapon carrying, and higher rates of pregnancy than urban youth (Weisheit et al., 2006). Along with existing challenges in rural schools, rural youth experience many stressing factors that do not exist in urban and suburban environments. For example, the availability of such community and school resources as extracurricular activities, and social networks beyond family and relatives for rural youth, are significantly limited. Furthermore, rural areas are more homogeneous than urban areas, and consequently, rural youth have fewer opportunities to interact with diverse ethnic groups to understand different cultures and backgrounds. Lack of diversity and limited social interaction could explain the high prevalence of school violence and victimization in rural schools. According to the 2014 National Crime Victimization Survey, youth ages 15–17 in rural areas experienced violent victimization 3.9 times more than urban youth and 4 times more than suburban youth in the same age group. Furthermore, in 2013, 12% of LGBTQ students who live in rural areas reported that they had been physically assaulted because of their sexual orientation, which is about 1.5 times as many victims as in urban or suburban areas (Office for Victims of Crime, 2017).

Rural youth would benefit from school-based anti-bullying and mentoring programs and extracurricular activities that promote awareness of and respect for diversity and enhance a sense of belonging to the school. As the offender and the victim and her parents will likely know each other, alternative solutions such as mediation and other restorative justice practices could be particularly effective in rural settings. Finally, more research is needed to explain why rural youth ages 15–17 have a higher violent victimization rate than urban youth in the same age group.

Drug and Alcohol Use in Rural America

Methamphetamine ("meth") emerged as a national concern in the United States in the early 21st century. Methamphetamine can be snorted, smoked, injected, or consumed orally, which makes the users initially feel increased energy, wakefulness, awareness, and ability to concentrate followed by anxiety, sleeplessness, paranoia, and decreased appetite (Garriott, 2016). Methamphetamine has emerged as a major problem in rural areas for both production and consumption. For example, a study of inmates in Kentucky found that 30% of inmates from rural communities reported prior use, whereas a little more than 10% of those from urban communities mentioned so (Warner & Leukefeld, 2001). In the National Institute of Justice (NIJ)'s Arrestee Drug Abuse Monitoring (ADAM) program conducted in rural Nebraska (Herz, 2000), rural arrestees were mentioned that Methamphetamine is easy to obtain mainly from friends and family members (Herz, 2000).

Along with consumption, methamphetamine production is another concern in rural areas. The production of methamphetamine can be large scale, but it is also ideal for as mall-scale meth lab, which could be in cars, homes, outbuildings, or hotel rooms (Garriott, 2016). A rural area has the advantage of being able to avoid detection as the production process creates a chemical odder. Furthermore, the geographic isolation of rural areas makes it easy to dump the 5–6 pounds of chemical waste used to produce every pound of methamphetamine (Garriott, 2016). The challenge to curtail methamphetamine production is to control the accessibility of the needed ingredients and materials such as plastic tubing and anhydrous ammonia, which can be easily purchased from local farm supply stores. Efforts have been made to pass anti-meth legislation and develop a program such as the Meth Watch Program, which helps to identify signs of meth production (Garriott, 2010). Yet, challenges remain as to social and economic problems in rural areas contributing to meth consumption and production.

A recent prominent public health concern in America is opioid-related mortality. According to the Centers for Disease Control and Prevention (CDC), opioid-related deaths totaled45,838 in2016, a 400% increase from1999. The opioid crisis has affected both urban and rural areas, yet rural areas face three major distinct challenges: infrastructure, demographics/ socio economics, and social networks. In terms of infrastructural factors, hospitals and treatment centers are often dispersed across large geographic areas and are not easy to access if one wants to have detoxification treatment for opioid addiction or medication-assisted treatment. Furthermore, longer travel times and the availability of public transportation are significant obstacles for those who seek support services (Rigg, Monnat, & Chavez, 2018). As to socioeconomic factors, the rural population consists of many military veterans, older adults, persons with disabilities, and the poor, and those are populations susceptible to drug addiction (Van Gundy, 2006). Furthermore, rural residents are more likely to experience high-risk injuries such as farming, fishing, construction, and mining and suffer from chronic pain. The economic disadvantages of rural areas areanother concern as that creates a sense of hopelessness and decay in a community. Finally, in terms of social factors, rural residents tend to have a large family and strong kinship and social networks, which could facilitate sharing, selling, and trading prescription drugs; typical diversion sources of pharmaceutical opioids are known to be family members, relatives, and friends (Eaton, 2017).

Given those rural-specific challenges, in addressing drug and substance epidemics in rural areas, efforts must aim to provide better services and advocacy to rural residents. Examples are implementing mobile clinics and telehealth and utilizing virtual treatment programs. Above all, providing better opportunities and revitalizing economies in rural communities would be the ultimate solutions to reducing substance abuse in rural regions.

Rural Subculture and Violence Against Rural Women

When discussing violence against rural women, the rural subculture cannot be overlooked. Research has shown that rural areas are governed by strong informal social control (Donner meyer &De Keseredy, 2014). The traditional group cohesion and strong peer support mechanism among rural men are usually considered as positive protective factors. However, rural women are more susceptible in responding to intimate partner violence because of this. Another important factor in rural culture is gun ownership. Nearly 6 in 10 rural Americans have a gun in their household (Pew Research Center, 2018). Rural gun owners possess rifles for hunting, but handgun ownership among rural residents is also higher than among urban dwellers. The idea of gun ownership has been engrained into rural cultural values and norms. Websdale (1998) argued that the justification for acquiring firearms for hunting and self-protection might include "a code among certain men that accepts the casual use of firearms to intimidate wives and intimate partners" (p. 10). Hall-Sanchez (2014) echoes that male peer support, which is an integral part of hunting subculture, promotes the use of weapons to intimidate, threaten, control, and hurt their female partners. Particularly, separation/divorce is a dangerous transition for rural women. Interviewing 43 rural women in Ohio, De Keseredy and Schwartz (2009) found that 58% of respondents noted that their perpetrators had guns, and some threatened to use the guns when the women attempted to leave their partners. Such violence could be escalated into a feud by the rural peer subculture, and separation/divorce could be perceived as a masculinity failure and result in lost status among one's peers (Donner Meyer & De Keseredy, 2014).

Furthermore, geographic and physical isolation make it particularly difficult for rural women to report cases to the police. It is generally assumed that rural areas are more cohesive and friendly. Contrary to such a common assumption, rural abused women in fact experience considerable isolation and loneliness (Websdale, 1998). Because of a lack of public transportation and large distances between houses, battered women can find it difficult to see friends or engage in a social life. Furthermore, those women tend to be isolated from any service allies including childcare, healthcare, and schooling, which makes it difficult for the abuse to be identified.

The strong informal social control also affects women's reporting behavior. There is a tendency in rural communities to keep community problems to themselves given the rural culture of cooperation and self-sufficiency, a greater reliance on informal social control, and mistrust of government. Given such community norms, rural women are reluctant to report cases to the authority (Weisheit et al., 2006).Law enforcement practices also affect women's willingness to report. Gagne (1992) noted that police and prosecutors are reluctant to take action due to traditional rural views about man's authority over his wife and the home as a sanctuary, making women less willing to report cases to authorities. Finally, the officer's relationship to the victim and the perpetrator could affect the response to domestic violence. In a small town setting, it is likely that the officer personally knows the husband and/or the wife. When the officer is related to or friends of women, the officer is more willing to enforce the law, whereas if officer is a classmate or acquaintance of the husband, he becomes sympathetic to the husband (Weisheit et al., 2006).

Solutions to address violence against rural women would require understanding multiple layers of obstacles for those women and establishing partnerships to expand community resources to help provide an array of services. Ultimately, the most important solution could be a revitalized economy and the availability of skilled jobs for rural women.

Rural crimes and Victimization Related to Agricultural

Agricultural theft is a major concern for farmers. Common types of agricultural theft include stolen crops, livestock, pesticides, timber, and agricultural machines and tools. Such rural-specific victimization has not been fully understood due to the underreporting of incidents and lack of research (Barclay, 2016). A few studies have indicated that the cost of victimization is significant to farmers. Earlier studies showed approximate

$1 million in annual losses from the theft of avocado, lime, and mango fruit in Florida, timber and vandalism in western Washington, and $2 million in annual losses from pesticide theft and $30 million in annual thefts from California farmers (Weisheit et al., 2006). To better understand agricultural theft, California recently passed SB 224, which will create a new category for grand theft of agricultural property in conjunction with a rural crime prevention program. There is a continued need for ongoing research in this area to bring more awareness of the problem. Other areas of concerns related to farmers are trespassing on farms, ranches, dairies, and other agricultural enterprises. For example, a recent study of agricultural crimes in Georgia surveying 415 Georgia Farm Bureau members indicated that 44% of the respondents had been a victim of trespassing, followed by theft (33.4%), illegal dumping of refuse (30.1%), poaching (27.5%), and vandalism (16.3%) (McIntyre, Prine, & Knowles, 2018). A challenge remains to reduce trespassing as there is a public misconception that wide-open spaces are public lands, and we need to explore better ways to designate land as private or public.

Along with crimes related to agriculture, an area to address is the victimization of migrant workers. A majority of farmworkers—at least 60%—are undocumented migrant workers who contribute to the economy. Yet, there is lack of advocacy for their poor working and housing conditions. In many of the cases, even their most basic needs, such as clean and sufficient drinking water on the job and clean bathrooms, are not provided by their employers. Less than half of farmworkers interviewed in 2015–2016 reported that they had health insurance despite the fact that agriculture is one of the most dangerous occupational sections (Barclay, 2016). Beyond work-related injuries, farmworkers are susceptible to serious health problems because of exposure to pesticides; inhaling dust from moldy hay or straw, grain, or tobacco; and working in dangerously hot weather. Furthermore, due to stressful working conditions, 40% of farmworkers nationally are depressed and 30% experience anxiety (La Cooperativa, 2011). Work-related injuries and sickness are a major concern for the safety and well-being of farmworkers, and advocacy is needed to gain access to primary healthcare services, mobile health clinics, and other means to provide adequate medical care for them.

Nationally, women make up 32% of the agricultural workforce, according to the National Agricultural Workers Survey (NAWS) 2015–2016. Women on farms are often sexually or verbally abused by their employers. In California's Central San Joaquin Valley, a 2010 survey of 150 farmworker women found that 80% had experienced some form of sexual harassment. Because the issue is so pervasive, women refer to the fields as the "Green Motel" or "fil de calzon" (fields of panties) (Ramchandani, 2018). Those women have suffered silence, afraid to report incidents. Moreover, in many situations, they lack information of available resources or have difficulty accessing services because of limited English-language capability. For example, a monitoring system such as the Coalition of Immokalee Workers' (CIW)

Fair Food Program is an innovative partnership among farmers, farmworkers, and retail food companies that could help improve the quality of working conditions for workers. Finally, to support women in the fields, service programs should address the holistic needs of women including free legal services, counseling, housing and transportation assistance, and education.

Moving Forward

This paper described how a distinct rural environment affects the victimization of rural residents, in some cases more severely than in urban areas. The numerous facts presented here in indicated that there is a great need to raise awareness of rural crimes and victimization. When looking at the root causes of rural crimes, many challenges are found for rural residents that are similar to those for urban residents, yet the resources for rural victims are limited. Throughout the paper, it has been discussed that the ultimate solution for rural crime is to improve the social and economic conditions of rural residents. For example, better educational and job opportunities for rural women would help reduce violence against rural women. This paper also revealed that rural victims face specific challenges that are distinct to rural areas. For example, geographic isolation makes it difficult for rural victims to access services and rural cultural norms and strong informal social control prohibit women from revealing their victimization and seeking assistance. More research is needed on effective and innovative programs tailored to the unmet needs of rural victims. Finally, other rural crimes issues not included in this paper, such as illegal hunting, farm animal abuse, illegal dumping, and human trafficking, are equally important for victimologists to address.

References

[1] Barclay, E. (2016). Farm victimization: The quintessential rural crime. In J. Donnermeyer (Ed.), *The Routledge International Handbook of Rural Criminology* (pp. 107-115). Routledge: Abingdon, Oxford, UK.

[2] Donnermeyer, J.,&DeKeseredy, W. (2014). Rural criminology: New directions in critical criminology. Routledge: Abingdon, Oxford, UK.

[3] DeKeseredy, W., & Schwartz, M. (2009). Dangerous exits: Escaping abusive relationships in rural America. New Brunswick, NJ: Rutgers University Press.

[4] Eaton, J. (2017, May 18). The new opioid dealers. *AARP Bulletin*.

[5] Gagne, P.L. (1992). Appalachian women: Violence and social control. *Journal of Contemporary Ethnography*, 20, 387–415.

[6] Garriott, W. (2010). Targeting the local: Policing clandestine methamphetamine production in a rural US community. *Canadian Journal of Law and Society*, 25(1), 1–19.

[7] Garriott, W. (2016). Methamphetamine and the changing rhetoric of drugs in the United States. In J. Donnermeyer (Ed.), *The Routledge International Handbook of Rural Criminology* (pp. 275-283). Routledge: Abingdon, Oxford, UK.

[8] Hall-Sanchez, A. (2014). Male peer support, hunting, and separation/divorce sexual assault in rural Ohio. *Critical Criminology*, 22(4), 495–510. Retrieved from http://www.aarp.org/health/drugs-supplements/info-2017/selling-prescription-medications-opioids.html

[9] Herz, D. (2000). Drugs in the Heartland: Methamphetamine use in rural Nebraska [Research Brief]. National Institute of Justice, U.S. Department of Justice Office of Justice Programs: Washington, DC.

[10] La Cooperativa (2011). Health issues for migrant worker. *Farm Labor Information Bulletin*, 21, 7.

[11] McIntyre, R., Prine, N., & Knowles, F. (2017, June). An exploratory assessment of agricultural crimes in Georgia. *International Journal of Rural Criminology*, 3(2), 157–175.

[12] Office for Victims of Crime (2017). Urban and rural victimization. *National Crime Victim's Rights Week Resource Guide: Crime and Victimization Fact Sheets*, Washington, DC.

[13] Pew Research Center (2018). Social and demographic trends. Retrieved fromhttps://www.pewsocialtrends.org/

[14] Ramchandani, A. (2018). There's a sexual-harassment epidemic on America's farms. *The Atlantic*. Retrieved from https://www.theatlantic.com/business/archive/2018/01/agriculture-sexual-harassment/550109/

[15] Ratcliffe, M., Burd, C., Holder, K., &Fields, A. (2016). Defining rural at the U.S. Census Bureau: American Community Survey and Geography Brief. U.S. Census Bureau: Washington, DC.

[16] Rigg, K., Monnat, S., & Chavez, M. (2018). Opioid-related mortality in rural America: Geographic heterogeneity and intervention strategies. *International Journal of Drug Policy*, 57, 119–129.

[17] U.S. Census Bureau (2016). New Census data show differences between urban andrural populations. Retrieved from https://www.census.gov/newsroom/press-releases/2016/cb16-210.html

[18] Van Gundy, K.T. (2006). Substance abuse in rural and small town America. *A CarseyInstitute Report on Rural America*. Durham, NH: Carsey Institute.

[19] Weisheit, R., &Donnermeyer, J. (2012). Change and continuity in crime in rural America. Create Space Independent Publishing Platform: Scotts Valley, CA.

[20] Weisheit, R., Falcone, D., & Wells, L. (2006). Crime and policing in rural and small-town America (3rd ed.). Long Grove, IL: Waveland Press, Inc.

[21] Warner, B., & Leukefeld, C. (2001). Rural-urban differences in substance abuse and treatmentutilization among prisoners. *American Journal of Drug and Alcohol Abuse*, 27(2), 265–280.

[22] Websdale, N. (1998). Rural woman battering and the justice system: An ethnography. Thousand Oaks, CA: Sage.

[23] Zhang, A., Musu-Gillette, L., &Oudekerk, B. (2016). Indicators of school crime and safety: 2015. U.S. Department of Education, U.S. Department of Justice Office of Justice Programs: Washington, DC.

Chapter XII

Teaching Victimology: Yesterday, Today and Tomorrow – A South Australian Perspective

MICHAEL O'CONNELL

Over the past six decades, concern for victims of crime has grown dramatically, as has the discipline – perhaps social science – known as Victimology. Developments in the measurement of victimisation, awareness of the short-comings in criminal justice response to victims, and knowledge on what works, on what does not and what is showing promise in relation to assisting victims deal with the effects of crime have driven an array of law reforms and procedural changes across Australia. Academics have also advanced theoretical frameworks in better understanding why some individuals and groups are victimised as well as confirmed victims' needs and expectations.

Scholars, such as Professor K Chockalingam of India have been at the forefront in both research and advocacy to improve outcomes for victims of crime. This chapter on teaching Victimology in Australia is dedicated to him. It focuses on the evolution of training and education in South Australia because that state took the lead in the 1980s. Before doing so, it outlines the development of victim assistance and victims' rights in that state as it was against a backdrop of such that discussions on Victimology as an academic endeavour began. The chapter summarises the status of Victimology in Australia today then speculates on its future.

Development of Victim Assistance and Victims' Rights

In the 1960s and 1970s, South Australia was not a leader in law reform or procedural change to benefit victims of crime. In 1969, for instance, it became the third state to introduce a state-funded victim compensation scheme. It was not a pioneer either in setting up shelters for women and children escaping domestic violence or establishing a rape crisis centre and medical services for victims of sex offences. Similarly, in 1979 it followed others when a group of families bereaved by homicides gathered to form a self-help group, which soon became known as the Victims of Crime Service (VOCS). VOCS, under the stewardship of its first executive officer Ray Whitrod, aimed "to provide support for victims, and to press for reforms in the criminal justice system" (Whitrod 1986, p. 296).

As that decade closed, however, South Australia assumed a lead and has in many ways done so since. In 1980 an Inquiry into Victims of Crime commenced. The committee comprised senior staff of the criminal justice agencies, the women's advisor to the Premier and the executive officer for the VOCS. The chair was Peter Grabosky the Director of the Office of Crime Statistics. After seven months, the committee produced a report, which was released in 1981. It was the first victim-centric review of an Australian criminal justice system; and, according to Whitrod (1986), the first in the world to probe the needs of victims of crime. The committee made sixty-five recommendations that both the Liberal Attorney-General, Hon. Trevor Griffin MLC and the Labor Shadow Attorney-General, Hon. Chris Sumner MLC undertook to implement as opportunities arose.

This report appeared before the widely acclaimed report of the USA President's Task Force on Victims of Crime (1982). Both reports pointed to a plethora of feelings of injustice. They made common observations about the criminal justice system being a source of secondary victimisation, and the imbalance between resources expended on offenders as compared to those available to victims. Both reports also acknowledged that victims should be protected; the criminal justice system should become more responsive to victims' needs; and, victims need assistance to deal with the effects of crime. These reports fuelled debate on victims' rights, which are integral, said Mawby (1988, p. 133) for the majority of victims for whom "crime is an irritant rather than a crisis". Notably, four years on in South Australia and in the USA, significant reforms had happened, and more were happening.

The pace of reform and the magnitude of change in the 1980s in South Australia was, in a relative sense, remarkable. In 1981 South Australia hosted the first National Symposium on Victims of Crime at which several speakers contended that many of the problems for victims in the criminal justice system stemmed from insensitivity fuelled by police, lawyers' and judges' ignorance. They added that it was absurd that these people were not educated on how to properly deal with the human suffering they faced almost daily; and, recommended better training and education.

In September 1985, the Hon Chris Sumner as then Attorney-General introduced the state's and Australia's first declaration on victims' rights. He modelled the declaration on the Declaration of Basic Principles of Justice for Victims of Crime and Abuse of Power(1985) drafted earlier that year at the United Nations Congress on the Prevention of Crime and Treatment of Offenders, Milan Italy. Hon Chris Sumner had led the Australian delegation during the sessions on victims of crime at the Congress(Sumner 1985; see also Grabosky 1985).Thus, South Australia became one of the first jurisdictions in the world to endorse the United Nations declaration – in fact, it did so two months before the General Assembly resolved likewise to endorse it.

Furthermore, the Government of South Australia by Cabinet direction required all government departments to the extent reasonably practical to give effect to the declaration on victims' rights. Via the Attorney-General, it also mapped out an array of legislative reforms, including amendments to the state-funded victim compensation scheme, such as raising the maximum sum payable to $50,000, setting up a dedicated fund to ensure money was readily available to pay compensation to victims of crime and pay for other assistance, and introducing victim impact statements – yet another Australian first.

Government departments responded. For example, in 1986 the South Australia Police gazetted the declaration then issued a Police Commissioner's Office Circular 'Victims of Crime' (1988) with specific guidelines on how police staff were to respond to victims and their rights; and in 1987 the police established a Victims of Crime Branch to coordinate its victim-oriented activities (Woodberry 1989).It also successfully piloted a Victim Contact Officer (Litster, Russo & Helbig 1988), and soon after appointed the inaugural Victim Impact Statement Coordinator (O'Connell 2009). The police were transitioning from are active force to a community service and revisiting the prevention of crime as its primary purpose. In 1987 the Commissioner of Police David Hunt (1987) asserted that the process of victimisation involves: crime causation; the crime; and, the effects of the crime. He linked this process to crime prevention in Victims Past, Victims Future (South Australia Police 1987). Like Schneider (1985), the police highlighted the importance of reducing the number of "victimogenic situations" (Schneider 1985, P.15). Other departments followed, such as the Department of Correctional Services (1988).

The Government in addition determined to ground its reforms on inquiries and research findings. In the mid-1980s, task forces were charged with examining responses to domestic violence (South Australia Domestic Violence Council 1987) and child sexual abuse (South Australian Government Task Force 1986). The Government felt these victims were "in need of close attention" (Office of Crime Statistics 1988, p.4)Amendments to the state-funded compensation scheme were informed by a survey of victims of crime (O'Connell 2015). Reforms to the criminal justice system were informed by another survey of victims of crime (Gardner 1990), which was based on that conducted by Shapland, Willmore and Duff in England (Shapland et al 1985). The Government also planned an evaluation of victim impact statements, which did not begin until the early 1990s (see Erez, Morgan& Roeger 1994). Additional data came from national crime victim surveys (for example, Australian Bureau of Statistics 1986)

The Government as well drew on the momentum to reform other laws. It, for instance, gave prosecutors the power to ask courts to review bail decisions; broadened rape laws; abolished unsworn statements in all cases; introduced new offences to counter threatened and actual violence; and amended sentencing laws. It also supported the transition in policing and promulgated a state-wide crime prevention plan, Together against Crime. Although the Labor Government and Liberal Opposition emphasised an association between victims' rights and crime control, neither exploited, as happened in the USA (Dubber 2002), the 'war on crime' rhetoric.

The flurry of initiatives and activities served as the backdrop for discussions on training and educating those who deal with victims. Professionalisation became the catch cry of those urging agencies to tackle their failures to meet victims' needs (O'Connell 2015). Higher standards of service required reflective practitioners. Some scholars and practitioners recognised that higher education could play a central role to enhance the knowledge and skills of those dealing with victims by advancing the new discipline known as Victimology.

Teaching Victimology: Yesterday

In 1986 in South Australia discussions began on the introduction of Victimology as a core subject for students undertaking the Graduate Diploma in Public Sector Management (Justice Administration) and those undertaking the Associate Diploma in Business (Justice Administration), as well as an elective for students undertaking the Bachelor of Business. In the mid-1980s Victimology was a relatively new subject in Australia but it had been taught in Canada, United States of America, England and other European countries. As Dussich (2003, p. 6) said, for instance, Victimology had been taught in the United States since the mid-1960s "as subtopics to existing courses in Criminology, Sociology, Psychology, and social work".

Beniamin Mendelsohn, a Father of Victimology, first argued for a penal victimology, which, as the opposite of Criminology, would study victims of crime but later he favoured a general Victimology, which would be the study of all victims (Dussich 2003; O'Connell & Hayes 2019). Notwithstanding, given the political imperatives, the scope of the Victimology subject in South Australia was agreed to be victims of crime (Bishop 1986). Its purpose was to develop analytic perspectives and techniques for understanding the ways victims are dealt with by police, prosecutors, courts staff, the magistracy and the judiciary.

Then Attorney-General, the Hon. Chris Sumner, who introduced the state's first Declaration on Victims' Rights, drove the development of Victimology as a formal academic subject. He collaborated with Harold Weir, the Justice Administration Coordinator, Elton Mayo School of Management, Institute ofTechnology. Mr Weir worked with fellow members of the School's Advisory Panel on Justice Administration, including Ray Whitrod, the executive director of the Victims of Crime Service (VOCS) and member of the World Society of Victimology. Among the first students were David Hunt, Commissioner of Police, Gary Byron, State Courts Administrator and John Dawes, Chief Executive for the Department of Correctional Services.

Graduate Diploma in Public Sector Management (Justice Administration)

The Graduate Diploma was designed for students with professional interests in the administration of justice (Weir 1986). Victimology was taught over two semesters. The aim of Victimology 1G was "To develop an understanding of the concepts, legislation and practices of Victimology in criminal justice processes". The aim of Victimology 2G was "To examine cross-cultural theories and practices in the area of Victimology and techniques for evaluating victim services". Table 1 shows the syllabus for each.

The Graduate Diploma ran over two years, and after students graduated the course was postponed.

Associate Diploma in Business (Justice Administration)

The Associate Diploma was designed for students seeking to become senior administrators the public sector, but the Justice Administration stream was reserved for police, courts staff and correctional services officers. Victimology was one of four subjects Justice Administration students were required to complete. It covered the development of Victimology and theoretical fundamentals, victims in crime causation and control processes, the victimisation process, the effects of crime and treatment, restitution and compensation, and the plight of victims of particular offences, including 'groups at risk' and victims of sex offences.

The Associate Diploma in Business (Justice Administration) ran for several years; however, in 1990 the Institute of Technology merge with over tertiary institutions to form the University of South Australia. To coincide with the merger, responsibility for the Associate Diploma transferred to the state's Technical and Further Education Colleges (TAFE). The Adelaide TAFE campus established a Justice Studies Department and a new Associate Diploma Justice Studies was introduced.

Associate Diploma Justice Studies

Once again, the Hon. Chris Sumner, Harold Weir and Ray Whitrod played a central role in developing Victimology as a core subject in the new Diploma. They were helped by other members of the committee of the Australasian Society of Victimology, including then Commissioner of Police, David Hunt (Hunt 1990).

Instead of a textbook, Mr Weir and Mr Whitrod wrote five booklets that TAFE published. Each booklet covered a component of the subject, which students were expected to complete over three weeks, that is fifteen weeks in total. These booklets were used for students class attendance and distance education students.

Initially, Harold Weir and Ray Whitrod taught Victimology, but on Mr Whitrod becoming unwell, Mr Weir asked Michael O'Connell who was then the inaugural Victim Impact Statement Coordinator, to co-lecture. On Mr Weir's retirement, TAFE opened Victimology to all justice studies students. It employed a senior police officer, Peter Woite, as the principal lecturer on Victimology but Mr O'Connell continued to lecture on theoretical Victimology. Mindful of the principles of pedagogy (see Bishop & Jerin 2014), Woite and O'Connell combined practical, thought provoking exercises with lectures on theoretical concepts and objective analysis of research findings, among other sources. Such said, they endeavoured to traverse the divide between education and training, especially for students from criminal justice agencies such as the police. As Dussich (2003, p12) states,

> Education is primarily theoretical, abstract and functions to describe phenomena and/or to explain causality. Training is primarily practical, applied and functions to impart skills which result in the acquisition of competencies.

This quote is apt because on the turn of the century, TAFE tasked Michael O'Connell, as an expert and adult educator, to rewrite the Victimology curriculum as competency based. This became necessary as the national training framework was adopted across Australia and the focus was on competency-based training and education. O'Connell, however, insisted on keeping theoretical perspectives, so the subject kept educative elements, rather than become out-service training for police, correctional service officers, and court staff. Student appraisals confirmed students' want for knowledge rather than 'rope learning' of law and procedure.

Figure 1 states the aim and summarises the syllabus for the subject. It is evident that the educational aspect succumbed, at least partially, to the training aspect. Nevertheless, that the police continued to complete the subject as a core subject of promotion to Sergeant or above remained a constant and yet another first for South Australia.

Police Training

Coinciding with the advance in Victimology, the South Australia Police introduced lessons on victims' rights, victim impact statements and dealing with victims for recruits, and for those already graduated, a series of in-service training courses were offered. Such training aimed to avoid the exacerbation of victim suffering and trauma; and, to ensure police staff respected victims' rights. Key stakeholders contributed; for example, in one-year VOCS staff participated in training over 1,000 from cadets to commissioned officers (Paterson 1992), which equated to over one quarter of the department's staff.

Like training was adopted by all police services in Australia in the 1990s, and as well the Australasian Police Commissioners' Conference charged a working group with auditing the victimological training and education in each department. All Commissioners acknowledged the police have an obligation to weigh and examine all issues cautiously, and to always remember fundamental legal tenets such as the presumption of innocence and the rule of law. However, they also concluded that the police may have been serving the criminal justice system rather than those who suffered as a result of crime. They recognised that the police are in a unique position to observe trauma and suffering of victims of crime (Hunt 1987; 1988; see also NCVAW 1993). Moreover, respecting victims' rights and assisting victims, like other people, in times of crisis, are central to the shift from crime-fighter to service provider (O'Connell 2009). In 1995, the Commissioners agreed to 'victims of crime' as a standing item on the annual agenda.

Listening to victims has an impact on police, an effect that can make listening difficult. Although references to vicarious trauma were far less evident at the time. As the 1990s closed, several speakers (Wilson 1991; Eijkman 1991; O'Connell 1991) raised concerns about police becoming victims at a national conference convened by the Australasian Society of Victimology. Eijkman (1991) pointed to the implications for education in policing. Charles Sturt University, which offered a Bachelor of Justice (Policing Studies) via correspondence to police across Australia, introduced a psychology on policing subject on personal well-being that grappled with some of the concerns, including police as victims. This subject partnered another that dealt with contemporary issues in policing, such as domestic violence, child abuse and sexual violence.

In 1998 the Attorney-General, Hon Trevor Griffin MLC commissioned a Review on Victims of Crime. He recruited a police officer and lecturer on Victimology, Michael O'Connell, to lead the review, which resulted in a three-volume report. Among the reviewers' tasks was an examination of training on victims' rights, needs and assistance in South Australia. They recommended (Justice Strategy Unit 1999):

> "Police should continue to receive compulsory initial and ongoing training and education on Victimology, including how to respond to victims empathically and constructively, and in a culturally sensitive manner" (Rec 19).

> "All agencies that have contact with victims (no matter whether that agency provides exclusively service for victims) should ensure their staff is adequately training on victim issues" (Rec 44).

The then Commissioner for the South Australia Police, Mal Hyde, endorsed the bulk of the recommendations impacting police. He agave an undertaking to keep victimological issues central in recruit training, and he undertook to keep Victimology as a core subject in the Advance Diploma on Policing, which was integral to promotional scheme. His undertakings have prevailed to this day with each subsequent Commissioner pledging to maintain the leadership in the field of Victimology first shown by David Hunt in the mid-1980s.

Each year 2001 to 2006, Victimology students completed exit surveys (O'Connell 2009). Most of these students were police officers. Most students stated that the studying Victimology was worthwhile. Some police students elaborated on their views; for example,

> "Very interesting [I am] thinking differently to when I came in."

> "As a police officer, I got a lot of benefit from completing [Victimology]."

> "Interesting and informative."

> "Victimology really highlighted to me the deficiencies in [the police] handling and understanding of victims."

The students' positive appraisal and comments do not necessarily indicate that police treat victims better. Real education is more than raising awareness and imparting knowledge. Real education should bring about changes in interpersonal behaviour such as listening respectfully to victims through to victim-centric changes in procedures governing police activities. On this point, three senior police officers – one assistant commissioner and two superintendents –each observed fifteen or more years after completing Victimology that they valued what they learnt and tried to act accordingly. One superintendent added that as a student he thought much of the subject was "crap" but as a far more experienced officer he wished he had listened more closely and had such realisation earlier.

Regarding other agencies, the commitment to training and education has been mixed. Court staff rarely, if ever, participate in the TAFE Justice Studies programme. Correctional Services withdraw more than a decade ago, to pursue professionalisation via a degree course offered by the University of South Australia, which was adapted from a course devised in New South Wales specifically for correctional staff. Rape and Sexual Assault Services staff had in-service training for its social workers and medical staff, which continues. This agency is also a member of National Association of Services against Sexual Violence (NASASV) and adheres to it 'standards of practice, including training standards (for example, NASASV 2015). The Education Department approved the inclusion of a module on victims and the law in the Legal Studies curriculum for Year 11 students, which led to the module being available, not compulsory, to students in South Australia and the Northern Territory (O'Connell 2005).

Post the Review on Victims of Crime, and considering gaps in child protection, South Australia Police, Public Prosecutors and Families SA staff collaborated with TAFE SA to develop a Certificate course on Child Protection. The course was embedded in the Code of Practice for the Investigation of Child Abuse and Neglect. The police commitment was not questioned; however, prosecutors argued they need only attend those lessons pertinent to their role in the criminal justice system, and some Families SA social workers challenged the value of course given their existing qualifications. Eventually, all agencies withdrew from the joint course; and, instead, the police introduced an internal course for officers specialising in the investigation of child abuse. Likewise, the police introduced an internal course for officers dealing with victims of domestic violence. These courses have been revised and restructured to accommodate findings of Coronial inquests into the deaths of Zahra Abrahimzadeh, a victim of domestic violence, and Chloe Valentine, a victim of criminal child neglect, as well as the recommendations of Royal Commissions (for example, Royal Commission into Families SA and Royal Commission into Institutional Responses to Child Sexual Abuse).

Victimology: Today

At the National Conference on Victims of Crime in 2000, Professor Arie Frieburg (2000, p.) observed that universities and other educational institutions could provide education and training to improve the skills of those working with victims of crime. He pointed out that universities could also provide an independent monitoring and evaluation service to ensure that victim support services are effective, and especially are not harmful.

Notably, there was no and still is no Bachelor of or major in Victimology. An exception happened in the mid-1990s when the University of Melbourne and the Victoria Government's Victim Referral and Assistance Scheme collaborated to develop a post-graduate course on victim services.

An audit revealed that there was a lack of training for VRAS referral staff and for the psychologists working under the scheme. VRAS and university staff determined that specialised training was needed for psychologists who treated victims of crime, so VRAS sponsored a position in the university for an initial period of three years to develop a course on victim services. University staff reviewed courses offered elsewhere, including 'summer institute' offered at the California State University, Fresno that covered four subjects: domestic violence; victimology, community services dealing with victims, and law and policies regarding victim services. The review also examined the Victim Assistance Program at Washburn University, including the intensive course covering concepts of victim assistance, an historical review of victims, ecological perspectives of victimisation, attitudes towards violence and victimisation, impact of stress, trauma response, barriers to services, the justice system and victims, victims of specific victimisations such as sexual assault, and victim advocacy.

Commencing in 1999, the University of Melbourne's School of Criminology began a course comprising six subjects, including Victimology; assessment and treatment of victims; organisational issues, such as service delivery methods; Criminology; and, special needs groups. Those who designed the course expected it would evolve, and not look the same after a few years (Frieberg 2000). It did not evolve, VRAS funding ended and the state's political environment changed.

Today, in the tertiary education sector, Victimology is taught as a subject or module in at least one university in most states in Australia (see Figure 2). The syllabi are like that proposed in 1986 for the Institute of Technology and later adapted by TAFE. Theory still plays a critical role in helping students make sense of the victimisation process, the effects of criminal victimisation and so on. Dussich (2003, p. 13) says, "[such] grounding in the potential causes of victimization can provide the student with a framework to critique victim policy, reduce victimization risk, and appreciate the broader context of victimization risk as criminal justice agents, first responders, and service providers".

In 2015, the World Society of Victimology's (WSV) triennial international symposium on Victimology was held in Perth, Western Australia. The only time prior that Australia hosted the symposium was in 1994 in Adelaide when a concurrent session was dedicated to training and education on Victimology. In 2015, consistent with a practice introduced in 2003, the symposium coincided with a one-off course on Victimology, victim assistance and criminal justice, which was jointly convened by the University of Western Australia, Tokiwa University and the WSV. The course comprised two full days of lectures, four days of the symposium and two extra days for students' presentations. Given the diversity of the lectures, which included theoretical perspectives, victims of crime, victims of abuse of power and victims of disaster, the course as a whole was more akin to General Victimology than Penal (or Criminal) Victimology.

Since 1984, the WSV organises international courses on Victimology. The first course on Victimology, victim assistance and criminal justice, which is based in Croatia, celebrated its 35th year in 2019. Similar courses have been organised in Asia (Japan, Indonesia and India) since 1998; in South Africa since 2003; and, less frequently in Latin-South America (for example, San Salvador 2001, Caracas 2002, and Bogotá 2013). A course was held in the USA in 2006, and the course held in 2018 will be held biannually. A one-off course was held in 2012 in the Netherlands to coincide with the triennial symposium. The WSV's Executive Committee, including Professor K Chockalingam,in 2015 endorsed an 'Education Policy' that lists the core topics it requires for a course on Victimology, victims' rights and victim assistance (or similar in title).

These are:

- The history of Victimology
- Theoretical issues and perspectives
- Victimological research methods and findings
- The process of victimisation
- The importance and practice of 'evidence-based' victim support and assistance
- Victims and criminal justice, including victims' rights

Later, Professor Chockalingam as the Chair of the WSV Standards and Norms Committee commenced a review of that policy. Although some articles of the policy were amended to accommodate changes in the structure of some courses, the core topics were not altered.

Victimology: Tomorrow

The victimological field has expanded considerably since discussions happened in South Australia in the mid-1980s. The study of Victimology as an academic discipline is now possible in a few Australian universities; however, there is no major or dedicated degree in that subject. Yet, it is possible to attain a PhD with an emphasis on a contemporary issue for victimologists (see, for example, Flynn 2010; Braun 2014;McKinley 2015; Iliadis 2017; Holder 2018). Across Australia there are academics specialising in one or more of theoretical, applied and forensic victimology. There are few, but an increasing number of, textbooks dedicated to victimological issues; however, there is no uniquely Australian textbook solely on Victimology. Two of Australia's leading Criminology textbooks – both in their 5th edition – have had a chapter on victims and criminal justice since first published (Prenzler & Hayes 2019; Palmer, de Lint & Dalton 2016).

The exact direction of Victimology cannot be predicted, so some of that following is speculative. The core and common topics, such as the process of victimisation, will likely continue to shape Victimology for years to come. There are too many victims of crime and too many victims who are treated ambivalently by those from whom they seek assistance. There is still much to learn about the efficacy of treatment, and so on. Despite the steps taken to train and/or educate police, lawyers, social workers, psychologists and others, Victimology remains in the main an add-on - compulsory for police officers in some jurisdictions but optional for other police and other professionals.

Victimology tomorrow will need to adapt. As crime mirrors the existing political, social, economic and technological structures, as any of these changes, so will the form and sources of victimisation, among other things. Already the perpetrator can be in one country, commit a crime in another on a victim in yet another country. E-crime will necessitate a cross-border, culturally competent Victimology. Mass violence (including terrorism) is more prevalent, and studies are revealing both the similarities and differences of the impact on victims, compared to victims of other violence. Victims' rights as human rights is a developing discourse in Australia (Kirchengast 2017), so a future topic will be victims of abuse of power. Australia's near neighbours, Indonesia and New Zealand have endured repeated natural disasters. Indonesia has a charter on the rights of victims of natural disasters, so the effects of disasters on victims and their rights and needs will likely feature in future curricula. Victim service providers will require knowledge and skills in online outreach services and triage trauma techniques for victims of all manner of sources of victimisation, some of which are yet to be known. Reciprocal training of victim service practitioners from different countries is already happening but it will be more common, which will necessitate common standards in training as well as education in the ever-expanding field of Victimology.

One thing will, however, remain constant – people will always be at the heart of Victimology.

Table 1

Victimology 1G	*Victimology 2G*	*Victimology*
Aim: To develop an understanding of the concepts, legislation and practices of Victimology in criminal justice processes.	**Aim:** To examine cross-cultural theories and practices in the area of Victimology and techniques for evaluating victim services.	**Aim:** To provide the participant with a knowledge and comprehension of the scope, concepts, theories and practices of Victimology with an emphasis on criminal victimisation, and the application victimological principles and processes in the justice sector.
Objectives: Students who complete this subject should be able to: • Interpret and apply relevant Statutes and Regulations; • Explain the philosophical bases of Victimology; • Understand the extent and types of Victimology and the characteristics of victims; • Evaluate proposals for policy formulation and	**Objectives:** Students who complete this subject should be able to: • Demonstrate an understanding of the results of government enquiries into Victimology in France 1982, USA 1982, Canada 1983; • Appreciate the central elements of the United Nations Declaration of Basic Principles of Justice for Victims of Crime and Abuse of Power (1985) and the political assumptions	

Victimology 1G	*Victimology 2G*	*Victimology*
implementation relevant to victims in Australia's criminal justice systems	and problems involved in their implementation; • Devise efficient evaluation techniques for Victimology policy and research proposals; • Understand cultural differences in traumatic stress reactions, therapeutic and preventive measures; • Specify types of crimes that are most fear-provoking in various communities.	
Syllabus: 1. History, theory and development of concepts of Victimology overseas, in other Australian states and in South Australia. 2. The South Australian Government's 17 principles, the Statutes Amendment (Victims of Crime) Act 1986, and Criminal Injuries Compensation Act 1978. 3. The preparation of Victim Impact Statements, the role of police and correctional services officers, and the use of VIS ibn court processes. 4. The interactionist perspectives; types of victims and vulnerability	**Syllabus:** 1. Introduction of the various applications of the interactionist analytical perspectives to provide a holistic explanation of criminal/ victim relationships; different interpretations of the concept of 'victim'. 2. Overseas attitudes of individuals and governments; their differences and agreements. 3. The revision and extension of crime categories beyond those of violence; methods of data collection and information processing., 4. The history and development of the involvement of the United Nations organisations in Victimology theories and principles; extent	**Syllabus:** 1. The nature and concerns of victimology. 2. Sources of victimological information and empirical data. 3. The theoretical basis for victimology. 4. The victimisation process 5. The effects and consequences of victimisation. 6. Crime victims and the criminal justice system. 7. Criminal justice practitioners and crime victims. 8. Services for crime victims 9. Compensation and restorative justice. 10. Victims with special needs – Families bereaved by Homicide; Road

Victimology 1G	*Victimology 2G*	*Victimology*
rates; victim resistance, degrees of provocation and facilitation; and, organisations as victims of crime. 5. Impact on individuals and communities; restitution, compensation and retribution; and, prevention programmes. 6. National and state surveys; data from on-government organisations; unreported crimes; and, reasons for reluctance to report.	to which Australian proposals and methods of implementation differ from those of other countries. 5. Comparative research studies of individual and social victimisation processes, consequence and remedies; the functions of adversarial and inquisitorial judicial processes in relation to victims and courts.	Crash / Trauma; Sexual Assault (including child victims); Domestic Violence

Table 2

University	*Course & Subject Name*	*Aims*	*Content*
Open & Griffith (QLD)	Bach Criminology & Criminal Justice Victimology	Students who complete this subject should be able to: 1. "... examine the ways that victims of crime interact with the criminal justice system and apply research and theory to understand ways to balance victim and offender rights"; 2. "... provide a working knowledge of the theories that explain victimisation risk"; 3. "... critically review the research about crime victims and to enable students to become intelligent consumers of this research"	1. Introduction, History, Course Overview 2. Effects of Victimisation on Individuals 3. Measuring, Prevalence & Patterns of Victimisation 4. Victimisation Theories 5. Effects on Communities and Third Parties 6. Repeat Victimisation 7. Victims and the CJ System 8. Specific Forms of Victimisation 9. Specific Forms of Victimisation 10. Contemporary Issues

University	*Course & Subject Name*	*Aims*	*Content*
Bond (QLD / NSW)	Bach of Criminology Forensic Victimology	Students who complete the subject should be able to: 1. Explain "the theories of victimisation and the role of the victim in the criminal justice system". 2. "Apply these theories to case studies and criminal justice issues". 3. Critically examine the issues of victimisation, "including false reporting and false victims of the criminal justice system among others". 4. Take responsibility for their feelings and actions, and for the consequences of their choices on self and others.	1. The study of victims 2. Rationales for forensic victimology 3. Empirical evidence to identify victims of crime 4. Psychological Aspects of Victimity 5. Intimate Partner Violence 6. Workplace and School Violence 7. Victims of Homicide 8. Sexual Violence 9. Victim Services 10. Victims of the criminal justice system 11. Future of victimology
University of New South Wales	Graduate Diploma & Master of Criminology Graduate Diploma & Master of Law Critical Victimology	Students who complete the subject should be able to: 1. Understand the reasons for "the removal of the victim from the criminal justice system". 2. Critically evaluate the international and domestic reforms initiated to give victims greater recognition in criminal justice systems.	1. Perspectives on victims of crime as participants in the criminal justice system. 2. The victim of crime as a causative force in the evolution of criminal law, the decline and rise of the victim in criminal justice; the development of victim rights and human rights; and, the status of the victim in law, as well as a participant of criminal proceedings. 3. The theories of victimisation and impact of these theories on policy and practices.

University	*Course & Subject Name*	*Aims*	*Content*
Newcastle (NSW)	Bach Social Science Victimology	Students who complete this subject should be able to: 1. Develop a theoretical and practical understanding of the victim in criminology (including victimology) 2. Apply this knowledge in a vocation setting, using relevant case examples to demonstrate their understanding.	1. The scope of victimology as a discreet discipline within criminology, and its role within allied disciplines (such as social work, law, and psychology) 2. Context of the term 'victim' through the discussion of various definitions (legal, social, etc.) 3. The costs of victimisation 4. Victim typologies; including victims targeted on the basis of; age, gender, or ancestral origin 5. The victim's position in a modern criminal justice system
University of New England (NSW)	Bach of Criminology Bach of Criminal Justice Bach of Laws Victimology	Students who complete this subject should be able to: 1. Understand the position and role of victims of crime in criminal justice systems; 2. Understand the victim in criminological contexts.	1. The history of victimology; 2. The rise of victim movement; 3. The nature and extent of criminal victimisation; 4. The victimisation of specific groups; 5. The consequences of victimisation; 6. The relationship between the victim and criminal justice system; 7. The victim's rights in the criminal justice system.
Southern Cross (NSW)	Bach Law & Legal Studies Bach of Laws Ass Degree Law Bach Business Victimology	Students who complete this subject should be able to: 1. Articulate the fundamental concepts, principles, and theories of victimology. 2. Examine the evolution of crime victims' rights.	1. The theories of Victimology 2. The scope, assumptions and concerns of victimology 3 Empirical evidence on criminal victimisation 4. Responses and reactions to criminal victimisation and its impact.

University	*Course & Subject Name*	*Aims*	*Content*
		3. Critically evaluate the current topics and themes in the field of victimology including victims as participants in criminal justice systems, victims' role in sentencing, the needs of various classes of victims, and non-adversarial justice (e.g. restorative justice). 4. Explore the scope of and types of victims that should be included in the study of victimology.	5. Victims and criminal justice, including the evolution of victims' rights internationally and domestically. 6. Victims' relationships with police, prosecutors, court officials and corrections staff 7. Comparative approaches to criminal justice (including non-adversarial justice) 8. Victims' needs and victim assistance. 9. Reparations, including restitution (offender responsibility) and compensation (state and/or third-party responsibility)
Charles Sturt (NSW)	Bachelor of Policing Bachelor of Policing (Investigations) Bachelor of Public Safety and Security Diploma of Policing Investigations Diploma of Investigations Theoretical, Applied and Forensic Victimology	Students who complete this subject should be able to: 1. Apply the principles and practices of victimology to improve outcomes for people they encounter in dealing with criminal victimisation, including the investigation of criminal offences.	1. The scope and theories of victimology, and its role in the investigation of crime; 2. Direct and indirect victims of crime; 3. The functions of a Family Liaison Officer; 4. Strengths and weaknesses of witness information, and obtaining accurate and credible evidence to assist investigations and prosecutions; 5. Victims' rights and the investigator's obligations; 6. Groups at risk / vulnerable victims, including elderly, children, people with disability and culturally and linguistically diverse people.

University	*Course & Subject Name*	*Aims*	*Content*
La Trobe (VIC)	Bach of Criminology	Students who complete the subject should be able to: 1. Examine the concept of 'victim' in domestic, regional and international contexts 2. Apply the theoretical perspectives and practical understandings of victimology.	1. Contemporary issues in victimology, including the definition of victim, the concept of an 'ideal victim' and its impact on people's perception of victimhood. 2. Victimological theories. 3. The impact of victims' rights on common law/ adversarial and civil law/inquisitorial justice systems, and alternative approaches to criminal justice (including restorative justice) 4. The application of victimology in legal and social contexts.
University of South Australia (SA)	Bach of Criminal Justice Victimology	Students who complete this subject should be able to: 1. Understand the prevalence and impact of victimisation, and responses (of offenders, the criminal justice system and society more broadly) to victims of crime.	1. The evolution of victimology in 'social science'. 2. Victimisation statistics and other sources of data. 3. Victims' rights - relevant legislation. 4. Societal constructs that influence responses and attributions to victims of crime domestically and internationally.
Edith Cowan (WA)	Bach of Criminology & Justice Bach of Arts (Psychology, Criminology & Justice) Victimology	Students who complete this subject should be able to: 1. Explain the historical and current perspectives about victims and criminal justice; 2. Critically evaluate the main theories of victimology; 3. Critically discuss the sources and methods of attaining victim data for empirical research;	1. Defining victims, victimisation and victimology. 2. Victimological research – crime statistics, victim surveys and studies on victims. 3. Victims and criminal justice (with a focus on the Victims of Crime Act 1994). 4. Children as victims. 5. The gender nature of victimisation (for

University	*Course & Subject Name*	*Aims*	*Content*
		4. Explain the evolutions of victims' rights in domestic, regional and international contexts; 5. Examine the short- and long-term effects of crimes on victims and others; 6. Explain the victimisation process and the impact of the criminal justice system on victims of crime; 7. Critically evaluate the effectiveness of victim impact statements having regard for the victim's right to access to justice and the victim's well-being and sense of fairness; 8. Demonstrate an understanding of justice, including natural and social justice.	example, gender-based violence). 6. Restorative Justice and other non-adversarial approaches to justice. 7. Special victim groups/ groups at risk. 8. The effects of criminal victimisation, including the psychological impact. 9. Significant others as secondary victims. 10. Victims' role in sentencing, including Victim Impact Statements. 11. Victims' rights, victims' needs and criminal justice, and procedural safeguards.
Australian National University (ACT)	Victimological issues taught within Criminology subjects.		
University of Tasmania (TAS)	Victimology a topic within a Criminology subject		
University of Canberra (ACT)	Victimology a topic within a Criminology subject		

Sources: Bond University <https://bond.edu.au/subject/crim12-210-forensic-victimology>; Charles Sturt University <https://www.csu.edu.au/handbook/handbook19/subjects/JST345.html>; Edith Cowen University <https://handbook.ecu.edu.au/unit_outline.asp?UCID=7597&V=1.01>; Griffith University <https://www.open.edu.au/subjects/griffith-university-victimology-grf-ccj214>; La Trobe University <https://www.latrobe.edu.au/students/your-course/subjects/current/lst2vic-victimology>; Newcastle University <https://www.newcastle.edu.au/course/CRIM1020>; South Cross University <https://www.scu.edu.au/study-at-scu/units/law00120/>; University of New England <https://my.une.

edu.au/courses/2020/units/CRIM207>; University of New South Wales <https://www.handbook.unsw.edu.au/postgraduate/courses/2019/JURD7422/>; University of South Australia < https://online.unisa.edu.au/courses/165261/2020 >

References

[1] Australian Bureau of Statistics (1986). Victims of Crime: Australia – 1983. Catalogue No. 4506.0. Canberra: Australian Bureau of Statistics.

[2] Bishop, N.R. (1986). Letter – dated 26th November to Chris Bitter, Secretary to the Attorney-General, Attorney-General's Department, Adelaide, South Australia.

[3] Braun, K. (2014). The Role of the Victim in Criminal Proceedings in Australia and Germany – A Comparison. PhD thesis: University of Queensland.

[4] Committee of Inquiry on Victims of Crime (1981). Report. Adelaide: Department of the Attorney-General.

[5] Dubber, M.D. (2002). Victims in the war on crime: The use and abuse of victims' rights. New York: New York University Press.

[6] Dussich, J. (2003) History, Overview & Analysis of American Victimology and Victim Services Education. In *Exploration of Higher Education and Professional Practice – Proceedings of the first American symposium on Victimology*, Kansas City, Kansas, January. Retrieved <https://studylib.net/doc/8197906/the-proceedings-from-the-first-american-symposium-of-vict...>

[7] Eijkman, H. (1991). Police as victims of crime: Implications for police welfare services & education. *Journal of the Australasian Society of Victimology*, Special Edition.

[8] Erez, E., Morgan, F. & Roeger, L. (1994). Victim Impact Statements in South Australia: An Evaluation. Research Report Series C, No. 6. Adelaide: Office of Crime Statistics, Attorney-General's Department, South Australia.

[9] Fisher, B.S. & Jerin, R.A. (2014). Introduction: The Evolution of Victimology: Pedagogy, Research, Services, and Advocacy. *Journal of Criminal Justice Education*, 25, pp. 403-404.

[10] Flynn, A.(2010). Secret Deals and Bargained Justice: Lifting the Veil of Secrecy Surrounding Plea Bargaining in Victoria. Unpublished PhD thesis: Monash University.

[11] Frieberg, A. (2000). Working Together to Improve Services for victims of crime. In M. O'Connell (Ed.), *Victims of Crime: Working Together to Improveservices – Conference Proceedings*, pp. 22-35. Adelaide: Institute of Justice Studies.

[12] Gardner, J. (1990). Victims and Criminal Justice, Attorney-General's Department, Research Report, Series C, South Australia.

[13] Grabosky, P.N. (1985). Crime Victims in Australia. In L. Jorgensen & J. Sandry (Eds.), *Seventh United Nations Congress on the Prevention of Crime and Treatment of Offenders*, Milan, 26 August – 6 September, 1985: Australian discussion papers, pp. 61-89. Canberra: Australian Institute of Criminology.

[14] Hayes, H. & Prenzler, T. (2019). An Introduction to Crime and Criminology, 5th Edition. Frenchs Forest, NSW: Pearson Prentice Hall.

[15] Holder, R. (2018). Just Interests: Victims, Citizens and the Potential for Justice. Cheltenham: Edward Elgar.

[16] Hunt, D.A. (1987). Victims of Crime: Towards a preventive approach – An Australian police perspective. Adelaide: South Australia Police.

[17] Hunt, D.A. (1990). Victims of Crime, national / international perspective. *Journal of the Australasian Society of Victimology*, 1(1) May, pp. 11-14.

[18] Kirchengast, T. (2017). Victimology and victims' rights: International comparative perspectives. Sydney: Routledge.

[19] Iliadis, M. (2017) Accessing Victims' Rights within the Adversarial Process: The Viability of Legal Representation for Victims in the Prosecution Process. Unpublished PhD thesis: Monash.

[20] Justice Strategy Unit (1999). Review on Victims of Crime – Report One. Adelaide: Attorney-General's Department, South Australia.

[21] Lister, J., Russo, M. & Helbig, K. (1988). Report on the Victim Contact Officer Trial. Confidential. South Australia Police.

[22] Mawby, R.I. (1988). Victims' needs or victims' rights: alternative approaches to policy-making. In Maguire, M. and Pointing, J. (Eds.), *Victims of Crime—A New Deal.* Milton Keynes: Open University Press.

[23] McKinley, A. (2015). Homicide Solvability and Applied Victimology in New South Wales, 1994-2013. Unpublished PhD thesis: Bond.

[24] NASASV (2015). Standards of Practice Manual for Services against Sexual Violence, 2nd Edition. Sydney: National Association of Services against Sexual Violence.

[25] O'Connell, M. & Hayes, H (2019). Victims, criminal justice & restorative justice, In H. Hayes & T. Prenzler (Eds.), *An Introduction to Crime and Criminology*, 5th Edition (pp. 327-350). Frenchs Forest, NSW: Pearson Prentice Hall.

[26] O'Connell, M. (1991). Police Victimisation: A Misunderstanding of the Role of the Police. *Journal of the Australasian Society of Victimology*, Special Edition.

[27] O'Connell, M. (2005). Victims' rights impacting the educational system in South Australia. *The Victimologist*, 9(1), April, pp. 1 & 5.

[28] O'Connell, M. (2009). Implementing Victims' Rights – A case study on the South Australia Police. In F Willem Winkel, PC Friday, GF Kirchhoff & RM Letschert (Eds.), *Victimisation in a multidisciplinary key: Recent advances in Victimology*. Wolf Legal Publishers: Netherlands.

[29] O'Connell, M. (2015). Evolution of Victims' rights and victim assistance, in D. Wilson & S. Ross (eds), *Crime, victims and policy* (pp. 240-277). Palgrave: London UK.

[30] Palmer, D., de Lint, W. & Dalton, D. (2016). Crime and Justice: A Guide to Criminology, 5th edition. Sydney: Thomson Reuters.

[31] Paterson, A. (1992). Report to Council, December 1992. Unpublished. Adelaide: VOCS.

[32] President's Task Force on Victims of Crime (1982). Final Report. Washington, DC: U.S. Government Printing Office.

[33] Schneider, H.J. (1985). The present situation of Victimology in the world. In H.J. Schneider (Ed.), *The Victim in an International Perspective*, pp. 11-37. Berlin: Walter de Gruyter.

[34] Shapland, J. Willmore, J, & Duff, P. (1985). Victims in the criminal justice system. England: Gower Publishing.

[35] South Australia Police (1988). Police Commissioner's Office Circular No. 478 'Victims of Crime'. Adelaide: South Australia Police.

[36] South Australia Police Department (1987). Victims past, victims future: A South Australian police perspective. Adelaide: South Australia Police.

[37] South Australian Government Task Force (1986). Child sexual abuse: Final report. Adelaide: South Australian Health Commission.

[38] Sumner, C.J. (1985). Victims of crime. Paper presented at the Seventh United Nations Congress on the Prevention of Crime and Treatment of Offenders, Milan Italy, 26 August – 6 September.

[39] United Nations (1985). Declaration of Basic Principles of Justice for Victims of Crime and Abuse of Power. Resolution adopted by the General Assembly, A/Res/40/34.

[40] Victims of Crime Response Group (1986). Statutes Amendment (Victims of Crime) Act 1986 and the Rights of Victims Bill: Recommendations towards implementation in the South Australian Department of Correctional Services. Adelaide: Department of Correctional Services.

[41] Wilson, C. (1991) Police as victims of crime. *Journal of the Australasian Society of Victimology*, Special Edition.

[42] Weir, H. (1986). South Australian Institute of Technology. Proposal for a graduate diploma in criminal justice administration with "Victimology" as a unit, second draft dated 9 July.

[43] Whitrod, R. (1986). Victimology – The Study of Victims – in Australia. In D. Chappell & P. Wilson (Eds.), *The Australian Criminal Justice System: The Mid 1980s*. North Ryde: Butterworths.

[44] Woodberry, J. (1989). A nation charter on victims' rights: Minimising the risk of victimisation and recognition of victims' rights as fundamental tenets of crime prevention. Paper prepared at the direction of the South Australian Commissioner of Police, D.A. Hunt, for presentation at the Australasian Police Ministers' Council, 24 November 1989. Adelaide: South Australia Police.

Chapter XIII

Reparation: Doing Justice for Victims

JO-ANNE WEMMERS & ROUGUIATOU BALDE

Introduction

Peace is not only a celebratory event at the end of a war. It is an ongoing and challenging process because factors that have fostered destructive conflict in the past and provoked war can remain part of the socio-political culture and undermine post-conflict peace (Opotow, 2012). For peace to be lasting it is important to foster social harmony and reconciliation (Staub, 2005). Transitional justice refers to processes and mechanisms used to address past abuses and ensure accountability, which serve justice and achieve reconciliation (Ambos, 2009; *Report of the Secretary General,* 2004).

Reconciliation refers to mutual acceptance by groups of each other, which is crucial for the prevention of new violence. It reflects a changed psychological orientation toward the other, where victims and perpetrators come to see the humanity of one another, accept each other and see the possibility of a constructive relationship in which the past no longer defines the future (Staub, 2005). It establishes or re-establishes a positive, cooperative relationship among the individuals and groups estranged by the harms they inflict on one another (Deutsch, 2011). Healing enables victims to lead better lives and contributes to reconciliation, thus reducing the likelihood of violence by them. Reparation, which can be either symbolic (e.g. an apology) or material, is a necessary pre-condition for reconciliation (Heylen, Parmentier, & Weitekamp, 2010).

Justice is intrinsically concerned with individual wellbeing and societal functioning and, therefore, it is especially pertinent for reconciliation (Deutsch, 1975). Survivors of mass violence desperately want justice as it affirms the moral order, thereby increasing feelings of safety and restoring trust in others (Staub, 2005; Wemmers, 2014). Law is a social force and legal procedures impact the lives of the individuals that they touch (Austin & Tobiasen, 1984). *Therapeutic jurisprudence* (Wexler & Winnick, 1996), *emotionally intelligent justice* (Sherman, 2003), and *trauma-informed approaches to law* (Randall & Haskell, 2013) are examples of what can be called a growing movement to recognize the impact of legal intervention on the emotions of victims, offenders and communities. Unjust procedures employed in resolving conflict and determining reparations may undermine confidence in the institutions that establish and implement the policies and rules regulating conflict and hinder reconciliation (Deutsch, 2011).

The creation of the International Criminal Court (ICC) by the international community was meant to put an end to impunity and to bring justice to victims of crimes against humanity, genocide and war crimes (Annan, 1998; Robbins, 1998). Unlike its predecessors, the Ad-hoc Tribunals for the Former Yugoslavia and the Rwanda Tribunal, the ICC includes provisions for victim reparation. Upon conviction, the Rome Statute allows the Court to make an order against an offender regarding reparation. Specifically, Article 75.1 of the Rome Statute specifies that, "the Court shall establish principles relating to reparation to, or in respect of, victims, including restitution, compensation and rehabilitation". Significantly, Article 75 recognizes that reparations may take many different forms. However, the Rome Statute does not clearly specify the goal of reparation (Dwertmann, 2010). While some experts within the ICC hoped the Court would develop general principles or guidelines, others favoured the idea that principles would emerge from the decisions of the Court (Wemmers, 2014). In practice, the Court has not established a single set of general guidelines for reparation and instead, different Chambers of the Court have taken decisions on reparation and, in each case, offered a justification for their decision. Thus, principles of reparation have begun to emerge through the jurisprudence of the Court (Carayon, 2017).

This has not put an end to the debate and critics argue that the case-by-case approach to reparations has resulted in inconsistent jurisprudence, divergence in practice and a lack of clarity for victims (Redress, 2018). Important questions are what is the goal of reparation and how should it be distributed? Should reparation focus on victims' needs and healing the individual victim? Or should it focus on reconciliation and healing the community? Should it focus on holding the offender accountable for victims' losses? Or should it focus on all of these goals and is it possible to serve different goals at the same time? In the following we will examine three decisions on reparation by the various Chambers: 1) The Lubanga decision by Trial Chamber I; 2) the appeal decision in the Lubanga case and 3) The Katanga decision by Trial Chamber II. Our analysis focuses on these decisions because they address key questions about the objective of reparation and how it should be distributed. After a discussion of reparations and the ICC, distributive justice theory is presented and the implications for systems of reparation are addressed.

Reparations and the ICC

The first decision by the Court regarding reparation was by Trial Chamber I (TC I) in the case against *Lubanga*, published on 7 August 2012 (*The Prosecutor v. Thomas Lubanga Dyilo*, 2012). This was a landmark decision by the Court that, for the first time in the ICC's history, established principles for reparation. According to the Court, reparation has two main purposes: to repair harm and to hold the offender to account. However, the Court goes on to specify that in this particular case, reparation should also relieve suffering, deter future offending and promote reconciliation (*The Prosecutor v. Thomas Lubanga Dyilo*, 2012).

In forming their decision, the judges took into consideration the expert opinions of those working with victims at the Trust Fund Victims (TFV) and several non-governmental organizations. These experts highlighted the importance of collective reparation for reconciliation, favouring victim support programs that promote healing, and in particular target vulnerable victims (*The Prosecutor v. Thomas Lubanga Dyilo*, 2012). The offender, Thomas Lubanga Dyilo, was indigent and had benefitted from legal aid throughout the trial. Therefore, the judges decided to not order reparation from the offender. Instead, the Court focused on using monies available to the TFV through donations, and explicitly focused reparations on victims of the situation, thus putting aside the individual interests of victims of the case, whose victimizations were included in the charges against the offender and for which he had been convicted (*The Prosecutor v. Thomas Lubanga Dyilo*, 2012). TC I emphasized the role of the TFV regarding 'victims of crimes within the jurisdiction of the Court' (Art. 79) in order to justify its broad view of eligible victims. Significantly, it went beyond the victims in the case against *Lubanga* and included victims of the larger conflict in the Democratic Republic of Congo (DRC). Specifically, they included victims of sexual violence, a crime that had not been included in the charges against *Lubanga*, and for which the ICC's Prosecutor had been strongly criticized by human rights groups (*The Prosecutor v. Thomas Lubanga Dyilo*, 2012; Wemmers, 2014). While they were not part of the case against *Lubanga*, the victims of sex crimes were widely recognized as victims of the war in the DRC and attempts to have sexual violence added later to the charges against *Lubanga* were unsuccessful (De Brouwer, 2009; Pena & Carayon, 2013). With its focus on healing, and broad scope, this first decision reflects a needs-based approach to the distribution of reparations by the Court.

This decision by TC I was, however, appealed by the defence as well as by victims who had participated in the case against *Lubanga*. In its decision, published on March 3rd 2015, the Appeals Chamber concurred that the two main purposes of reparations are to repair the harm caused to the victims and to hold offenders to account, and that reparations should secure, whenever possible, *reconciliation*. While the Appeals Court recognized that collective reparations may be awarded concurrently with individual reparations and that the two are not mutually exclusive, it upheld the lower court's decision to award only collective reparations, arguing that there is likely a high number of victims who did not participate in the trial proceedings (*The Prosecutor v. Thomas Lubanga Dyilo*, 2015). However, the Appeals Court shifted the scope of reparations from victims of the situation to victims of the case, by limiting the eligible victims to those directly linked to the charges for which *Lubanga* had been found guilty (*The Prosecutor v. Thomas Lubanga Dyilo*, 2015). Victims of the situation, whose victimization was not the result of an offence for which the offender had been found guilty, such as victims of sexual violence, were excluded from reparation.

The Appeals Chamber insisted, however, that regardless of an offender's lack of financial means, reparation orders must address the convicted person's monetary liability for the harm (*The Prosecutor v. Thomas Lubanga Dyilo*, 2015). It also produced a new list of principles on reparations (*The Prosecutor v. Thomas Lubanga Dyilo*, AnxA 2015). These principles guided the decision of the Appeals Chamber and were later reiterated by TC II in its decision regarding reparation in the *Katanga* case (*Le Procureur c. Germain Katanga*, 2017).

The Appeals Court recognized the risk of resentment among victims and the danger that it poses for reconciliation, which had preoccupied TC I. It argued that individual reparations should be awarded in a way that avoids creating tensions and divisions within the relevant communities (*The Prosecutor v. Thomas Lubanga Dyilo*, 2015). The Appeals Court further specified that awards should be proportionate to the harm, injury, loss and damage as established by the court. This was later reiterated by TC II, in the *Katanga* case, which, following the principles developed by the Appeals Chamber, argued that reparations should be proportional to the harm suffered by the victim in order to promote reconciliation between the offender and victims (*Le Procureur c. Germain Katanga*, 2017).

These decisions draw attention to the principles or values that underlie the distribution of outcomes and the effects of different distributive principles. The Appeals Chamber and TC II assume that reconciliation is promoted when reparation is distributed on the basis of equity, focusing on the harm suffered by individual victims of the crimes for which the offender was convicted, and the offender's degree of responsibility for their suffering. Alternatively, TC I took a broad, need-based approach to reparations, focusing on collective reparations, and healing. This raises the question whether it is preferable to focus on collective reparations that are distributed according to the needs of victims within the community, or whether the distribution of reparations should be proportional to the harm inflicted on victims by the offender, or, alternatively, the distribution of reparations should be divided equally among victims? Which of these distributive principles or some combination of all three principles should guide decisions about the distribution of reparation by the Court? These questions are at the heart of Deutsch's work on distributive justice.

Distributive Justice Theory

Distributive justice (DJ) is helpful in order to understand how to distribute reparations in a way that is fair and promotes reconciliation. The distribution of conditions, goods, outcomes and other resources, which affect the wellbeing of individual members of a group or community, is at the heart of DJ (Deutsch, 1975; Lind & Tyler, 1988; Streicher, Frey, & Osswald, 2012). DJ theory identifies criteria that lead you to feel you receive a fair outcome (Deutsch, 2000). These are general standards for allocating benefits or burdens among the members of a group or community (Druckman & Albin, 2011). Fair outcomes can foster effective social relations and promote individual wellbeing, which is important for reconciliation (Dutsch, 2011; Druckman & Wagner, 2016). DJ is particularly salient when we consider crimes against humanity, genocide and war crimes, where entire groups may be systematically victimized, creating large numbers of victims and severely harming intergroup relations.

Early work on distributive justice focused on equitable distributions. According to Adams (1965), social behaviour is affected by beliefs that the allocation of benefits and costs within a group should be equitable, and outcomes should be proportional to the contributions of group members. Hence, those members who have given up the most should receive the most benefits. This approach is represented in equity theory, which considers a distribution fair when one's outcomes are proportional to one's inputs (Walster, Berscheid & Walster, 1973). Equity theory assumes that people are rational, economic beings who are motivated by self-interest and the desire to maximize their gains. Applying this logic to victims, one might expect that more compensation would be paid to those victims who suffered greater losses.

However, people do not judge their situation in absolute terms but by comparing it to the situation of those around them. Equity theory ignores the interactional character of exchange relationships (Deutsch, 1985). Research on *relative deprivation* shows that social comparisons are important for feelings of justice, and in order for people to feel deprived when they lack some resource it is important that they feel that they deserve that resource (Crosby, 1976; Lind & Tyler, 1988). In other words, failure to receive compensation will in itself not lead to feelings of injustice, *unless* the person feels that they deserve compensation and they see comparable others obtaining compensation. Research on political and social discontent (e.g. rioting) has suggested that people's comparisons with others are heavily dependent on their views about justice (Lind & Tyler, 1988). Thus, a distribution based on equity will not always be considered fair and this will depend on the context.

Perhaps the most prominent researcher in the area of distributive justice is Morton Deutsch, who, inspired by the events of the Second World War and the desire to promote world peace, spent much of his professional life studying the factors that affect cooperation and competition (Deutsch, 2015). Recognizing the importance of relative deprivation, Deutsch, argued that what is considered a fair distribution will vary depending on the circumstances confronting the groups and the specific characteristics of the individuals making up the group. Deutsch identifies three essential values, which can be used as a basis of distributive justice: *equity, equality* and *need.* Based on extensive empirical research, Deutsch identified the conditions under which each of these values of fair distribution is relevant and their consequences for social relations including peace and reconciliation. According to Deutsch, the goal of the distribution largely determines which values will be employed as the basis of justice (Deutsch, 1985). When the moral or ethical standard for a fair distribution is violated, injustice occurs (Byrnes & Cropanzano, 2001). While other researchers have also identified distributive principles since Deutsch's early publications, his work is particularly relevant for transitional justice because it has been extensively studied across cultures, and contexts, including intergroup reconciliation (Byrnes & Cropanzano, 2001; Johnson, Johnson & Roseth, 2018).

Equity, is the dominant principle of DJ in cooperative relationships in which economic productivity is the primary goal (Deutsch, 1975). The rationale behind the equitable distributions is that assigning scarce resources (e.g. money) to those most able to use them is likely to result in the largest production and, therefore, is socially equitable. As we saw, an equitable distribution is proportional to one's input, contribution or costs: The more one gives, the more one should get. In the context of criminal victimization, an equitable distribution might be proportional to the victim's losses or, more precisely, relative to the offender's responsibility for their losses. Hence, an equitable outcome for the victim might proportionally increase the victim's gains by ordering compensation against the offender or, decrease the offender's gains by imposing punishment.

Although equitable distributions promote economic productivity within society, Over the long run, this equity principle is likely to be dysfunctional for the wellbeing of the group (Deutsch, 1975). Deutsch warns that equitable distributions tend to foster the introduction of economic values in all aspects of social life, which results in a diminished quality of life. A proportional distribution may be equitable, however, it would not promote collective or individual healing but foster competitiveness, selfishness and possibly lead to clashes within the group. In contrast, distributive systems based on equality and need are associated with more cooperative feelings (Deutsch, 1975; 1983).

In cooperative relations, where the fostering of personal development and personal welfare is the common goal, the dominant principle of distributive justice is need is need. In other words, when reparation aims to promote individual well-being and healing, need is an essential value for distribution. Need-based distribution means that the most needy victims should receive the most reparation regardless of issues of offender liability. Trauma limits the functioning of the individual, including their capacity to work and engage in social interactions (Berger, 2015). Healing enables victims to lead better lives. A needs-based approach recognizes the importance of fundamental human needs, such as basic physiological needs, the need for security and the need for a positive social identity. In the context of criminal victimization, where the aim of reparation is to promote the personal healing and welfare of victims, a fair distribution would be need-based.

Deutsch further specifies that in cooperative relations, the fostering or maintenance of positive social relations is the common goal. The dominant principle of distributive justice in cooperative relations is *equality*. He defines enjoyable social relations as relationships in which one feels respected and esteemed by others (Deutsch, 1975). This coincides with a human rights approach in which the dignity of all individuals is recognized (Ignatieff, 2001; Wemmers, 2012). Deutsch (1975) emphasizes that equality does not mean that everyone must always receive the same outcome. More importantly, equality means the equal divine or moral value of everyone in the community is affirmed. Equality promotes cooperative feelings towards others, and is associated with durable peace agreements and social cohesiveness (Deutsch, 1975). As we saw, reconciliation refers to the mutual acceptance by groups of each other. In order to promote reconciliation, reparations ought to be distributed based on the principle of equality.

Sometimes all three goals are important and in such situations, the three principles (equity, equality and need) can be applied in a way that is either *mutually supportive or mutually contradictory* (Deutsch, 2000). In a mutually supportive application, equity, equality and need-based distributions are combined in a way that is positive and promotes social harmony. The equity principle means recognizing individual differences in contribution or sacrifice and honouring those who make exceptional contributions. At the same time, in order to generate social harmony, no individual distinctions are made between those who are recognized and those who are not. The equal social value of everyone in the community is acknowledged as the community honours its members who made unique sacrifices. The equal worth of every individual leads to special help for those who are especially needy. The idea is to create a win-win situation in which one person's gain does not mean that the other group members have lost something.

In contrast, conflict is created when the principles of DJ are applied in a way that is mutually contradictory. For example, if the equity principle is applied in a manner that suggests those who lost more are generally more worthy and entitled to better treatment, then social harmony and cohesion are impaired. It becomes a win-lose situation in which one person gets all and the others get nothing. At the same time, if the equality principle leads to a uniformity in which the value of exceptional individual contributions or sacrifices is denied, then productivity as well as social cohesion is diminished. As Deutsch points out, 'it is a delicate balance that often tilts too far in one direction or the other' (Deutsch, 2015).

In addition to the principles of DJ, Deutsch draws our attention to the *scope of justice* (Deutsch, 1975, 2011; Opotow, 2012). This refers to who is and is not entitled to justice, or more accurately, fair outcomes and fair treatment, based on inclusion or lack of thereof in one's moral community (Opotow, 2012). It acts like a psychological boundary for fairness (Opotow, 2012). Those who are inside of one's scope of justice are considered worthy of dignity and respect. However, for those who are outside the boundary, the same considerations of fairness do not apply. As a result, they may be treated in ways that would be considered immoral if people within the boundary were so treated. Lesser forms of moral exclusion include the marginalization of certain social groups such as religious and ethnic minorities, and women (Deutsch, 2011). According to Opotow (2012), our scope of justice can change over time and this can affect intergroup conflict and peace. Restricting the scope of justice limits the applicability of justice and can support destructive intergroup conflict and violence while enlarging of the scope of justice widens the applicability of justice and supports mutual respect, constructive approaches to conflict and the potential for peaceful intergroup relations.

Implications for Reparations at the ICC

DJ is highly relevant to the question of reparation at the ICC. Transitional justice processes and mechanisms, such as the ICC, aim to address past victimizations and achieve reconciliation (Ambos, 2009); Report of the Secretary General, 2004). How the ICC distributes reparations will impact the individuals and the communities before the Court and its ability to contribute to lasting peace. In the following we will consider the goals of reparation specified by the Court and their application within the framework of DJ.

Repair Harm

An important goal of reparation is to repair the harm caused to victims. Neither the Rome Statute or the Rules of Procedure and Evidence provide a definition of harm (Redress, 2018). The Appeals Chamber in the Lubanga case defines harm as material, physical or psychological hurt, injury and damage, which may be indirect but must have been personal to the victim (*The Prosecutor v. Thomas Lubanga Dyilo*, AnxA 2015).

If the harm suffered as a result of victimization translates directly into needs, then this would correspond with a need-based distribution: The greater the need, the more resources victims would have access to. As we saw, a need-based distribution promotes personal welfare and development, and is associated with cooperative feelings. However, while the harm caused by the offence is related to the victim's needs, it is not the same thing. Victims' personal resources will determine whether, and to what extent a consequence of victimization translates into a need. To illustrate, imagine two victims of robbery who each had $100 stolen from them. One victim is wealthy and the loss is something that he can easily absorb. However, the other victim is poor and the loss means that he will be unable to buy groceries or pay his rent. The importance of personal resources with respect to consequences and needs is not limited to financial resources and applies equally to psychological as well as social resources. Moreover, those most at risk of victimization are often socially vulnerable (Wemmers, 2017). The victim's personal history and their situation at the time of the victimization will affect how the crime impacts them (Hill, 2009).

When reparation is proportional to the harm caused, the distribution of reparations follows the equity principle. According to Deutsch, equitable distributions promote economic productivity and foster economic values in all aspects of social life. In the *Katanga* case, TC II considered the material and pecuniary losses suffered by each victim in the case and attached a monetary value to it in order to calculate the total monetary value of the harm suffered by the defendant's victims (*The Prosecutor v. Thomas Lubanga Dyilo*, 2015). In their decision, the judges indicated that reparations should be proportional to the harm suffered by the victim in order to promote reconciliation (*The Prosecutor v. Thomas Lubanga Dyilo*, 2015). However, the judges' assumption that proportional distribution will foster positive social relations is highly questionable in view of the above research on DJ.

Moreover, in this approach to the distribution of reparations, wealthier victims are poised to receive more reparations than poorer victims simply because they have more to lose. If pre-existing social inequality was a contributing factor to the violence, an equitable distribution could effectively maintain social injustice, which would add to the conflict (Maniriqué, 2014). In addition, because consequences and needs are not the same, focusing on harm means that the most needy victims may be overlooked. Hence, while equitable, a proportional distribution would not necessarily be perceived to be just, and would not promote individual or collective healing or positive social relations. By ignoring victims' needs, one risks creating an environment in which vulnerability is not recognized. Rather than promote healing, focusing on economic values may result in a diminished quality of life, by creating competitiveness, selfishness and conflict within the group.

The Lubanga case, in which the Trial Chamber I ordered symbolic collective reparations, provides an example of a need-based distribution. This had been appealed by some of Lubanga's victims who sought individual reparations, however, the Appeals Chamber maintained that the ruling was appropriate because there was likely a high number of victims who did not participate in the trials proceedings (*The Prosecutor v. Thomas Lubanga Dyilo*, 2015). Subsequently, the new Trial Chamber II approved plans by the TFV in relation to symbolic collective reparations (*The Prosecutor v. Thomas Lubanga Dyilo*, 2016). in the form of construction of community centres and a mobile program to reduce stigma and discrimination against former child soldiers, and service-based reparations (*The Prosecutor v. Thomas Lubanga Dyilo*, 2017) in the form of physical and psychological rehabilitation, vocational training and income-generating activities. These collective programs offer the direct and indirect victims of the crimes for which Lubanga was convicted (i.e. child soldiers) access to services (Redress, 2018).

The collective, service-based reparations address victims' physical, psychological and social needs. In terms of DJ, need-based distributions promote personal development and healing. Deutsch maintains that the satisfaction of basic needs, such as basic physical and mental health as well as the need for safety, is a necessary precondition for reconciliation. Unless victims' posttraumatic stress is substantially relieved, reconciliation may be difficult to achieve at more than a superficial level (Deutsch, 2011). The satisfaction of basic psychological needs is vital for the healing process, and constitutes a necessary precondition for lasting peace (Staub, 2003; Wemmers & De Brouwer, 2011; Robins, 2017). The frustration of basic human needs gives rise to social conflict, while distributive justice systems based on need are associated with cooperative feelings (Staub, 2003). Hence, a need-based distribution of reparations is important for reconciliation.

Hold to Account

A second goal of reparations identified by the Court is to hold the offender to account. Accountability is important for victims and is a key component of transitional justice (Parmentier, 2003). Not only does it confirm the offender's responsibility for the crime, in doing so it establishes the victim's innocence (Christie, 1986; Holstein & Miller, 1998). In addition to recognizing the harm caused by the offender, it transfers the burden of shame from the victim to the offender (Herman, 2007). Holding offenders to account shows the victim that somebody cares about what happened to them (Wemmers, 2017). It provides a public denunciation of the offender's behaviour as well as validation of the victim by the community. Victims of violence may feel that the crimes were intended to dishonour and isolate them and, in such cases, actively seek the restoration of their honour and standing (Herman, 2007). Accountability is not synonymous with punishment or revenge but rather with recognizing the offender's responsibility and finding him guilty (Herman, 2007; Erez, 1999). Hence, for victims, accountability is a rich and multidimensional concept.

The ICC's approach to accountability is narrowly centred on the offender. Unlike victims, for whom accountability reflects recognition of their innocence as well as the offender's responsibility, the ICC approaches this objective in terms of a narrow, highly legalistic and abstract notion of liability. Following this approach, the Court distributes reparation using the *equity* principle: The more a person is liable for the harm caused, the greater their responsibility to repair that harm.

For example, in the *Katanga* case, TC II argued that because Germain Katanga was found to be complicit in the crimes committed against the victims, this diminished his responsibility to make reparations to the victims (*Le Procureur c. Germain Katanga,* 2017). Therefore, while the Court calculated that all together the victims in the case had suffered $3,752,620 USD in damages, because of his diminished responsibility, the Court ordered Mr. Katanga to pay only $1,000,000 USD in damages to the victims (*Le Procureur c. Germain Katanga,* 2017).

In the Lubanga case, as mentioned earlier, Thomas Lubanga Dyilo was found guilty by Trial Chamber I, however, because he was insolvent, the judges did not order him to make reparation to his victims. The Appeals Chamber insisted that even if an offender is insolvent, the court must establish the offender's liability. The Appeals Chamber recalled that the scope of a convicted person's liability is proportionate to the harm caused and his participation in the commission of the crimes for which he has been guilty (*The Prosecutor v. Thomas Lubanga Dyilo*, 2015). A new court, Trial Chamber II was given the task of assessing Lubanga's legal liability and ruled that he was liable for $10,000,000 USD (*The Prosecutor v. Thomas Lubanga Dyilo, 2017*). However, as Lubanga was judged to be insolvent, reparations would be financed by donations to the TFV.

Reconciliation

The third goal of reparation identified by the Court is reconciliation. Reconciliation is based on mutual acceptance by groups of each other and the (re-)establishment of positive, cooperative relationships among the individuals and groups divided by the harms they inflict on one another. According to DJ, equality is dominant when social harmony, cohesiveness, or fostering enjoyable social relations is the primary emphasis. Equality is, therefore, very important for the ICC and its goal to promote reconciliation and prevent new violence from erupting.

A clear example of the use of the equality principle to distribute reparations to victims can be found in the reparation order imposed by TC II in the *Katanga* case. The Court indicated that the $1,000,000 USD, which it had ordered from Mr. Katanga, was to be distributed equally among the 300 victims of the case. The Court decided that each victim of the case would receive an individual reparation of $250 USD, which symbolized Katanga's responsibility for their suffering (*Le Procureur c. Germain Katanga,* 2017).

Multiple Goals

Reparation at the ICC serves multiple goals: harm reduction, accountability and reconciliation. Fair distributions can serve multiple goals and, according to Deutsch, it is possible to apply more than one principle of distribution at once. However, special attention must be given to how these principles are combined. When combined together the interaction may change how they impact social relationships. In order to be constructive, fair and contribute to lasting peace, the principles governing the distribution of resources should be applied in a way that is mutually supportive and not mutually contradictory. In other words, it has to create a win-win situation rather than a win-lose situation.

As we saw, TC II explicitly combines two distinct principles of distributive justice (equity and equality) in its reparation order in the *Katanga* case. After determining the losses suffered by victims and the proportional responsibility of the offender for their suffering, the Court then divided reparations equally among all of 300 victims. The Court ordered symbolic reparations of $250 USD to be paid to each of the 300 victims of the case (*Le Procureur c. Germain Katanga,* 2017). The equal distribution of reparation recognizes all 300 victims of the case equally.

However, the equality principle emphasizes the sameness or uniformity of victims and fails to recognize the value of unique individual contributions or sacrifices by victims. Deutsch warns us that if the equality principle is applied in a way that denies the value of unique individual contributions, then social cohesion is impaired. Equity, rather than equality, allows for individual differences in the distribution of resources. While equitable distribution can lead to conflict competition between victims, if done properly, it can provide a sense of justice to victims. Although the decision by TC II recognizes the relative responsibility of the offender, it fails to recognize the unique sacrifices of individual victims or the needs of victims.

In the context of criminal victimization, equality can mean recognizing the humanity in each individual (Wemmers, 2012). Equality does not necessarily mean that everyone will receive the same reparation but recognizes the equal moral value of victims. Victims' needs should also be considered and special attention should be given to those victims who are the most needy (Wemmers, 2017). While the collective service-based reparations ordered in the Lubanga case, focus on victims' needs, they also provide equal access to services. Hence, they effectively apply two principles of distribution and combine them in a way that is mutually supportive for all victims of the case.

Scope of Justice

In addition to the principles of distribution, the *scope of justice* also has to be taken into consideration. Victims of crime seek recognition and are very sensitive to issues of fairness and equality (Shapland, 1985; Wemmers, 2017). Victims perceive how authorities treat them as a reflection of their value or standing and they are very sensitive to the suggestion that some victims are more valuable than others (Wemmers, 2010; Bradford, 2011; Feldthusen, Hankivsky, & Greaves, 2000). If the equity principle is applied in a way that suggests that some human beings are more worthy than others and are entitled to superior treatment, this would constitute moral exclusion. *Moral exclusion* occurs when there are differences in how categories of people are treated and this creates stress and impairs social harmony (Opotow, 2012).

The question of which victims are eligible for reparations by the ICC is controversial. As we saw, TC I included reparations for victims of the situations before the Court, however, this was later rolled back by the Appeals Court, which chose to limit reparations to victims of the case. Hence, the Court has created two groups of victims: victims of the case who are eligible for reparation and victims of the situation who are not, even though they may have experienced tremendous suffering during the armed conflict and have significant needs (Bitti, 2011). Restricting the scope of justice limits the applicability of justice and can support destructive intergroup conflict.

While the difference between victims of the situation and victims of the case is significant from a legal perspective, from the victims' standpoint it may seem arbitrary and, hence, unfair. Victims of the case have not necessarily sacrificed more than other victims. They simply belong to the lucky few whose offender was charged and prosecuted by the ICC. There are numerous factors that influence which offenders the ICC tries and the precise nature of charges laid against them and often these factors have nothing to do with the legitimacy of the victim. As we saw in the *Lubanga* case, witnesses provided ample evidence of sexual violence, but sexual violence was not included in the charges against Lubanga and attempts to have sexual violence later added to the charges were unsuccessful (Pena & Carayon, 2013).

Failure to recognize victims is an important source of secondary victimization as it sends the message to victims that they are not respected and valued members of society (Wemmers, 2017). If victims of the situation feel that, like victims of the case, they too deserve reparations then they are likely to feel that their exclusion is unfair. When victims fail to receive the validation and respect that they seek, this can hinder victims' recovery from crime (Symonds, 1980; Campbell, Wasco, & Ahrens, Sefl & Barnes, 2001; Cyr, 2008; Wemmers, 2013). By creating two groups, the reparations system is under stress and the unequal treatment of victims may antagonize their suffering and create a sense of injustice.

In equality, there is no hierarchy of victims, only a hierarchy of needs. The equal moral worth of every individual leads to special help for those who are especially needy. In post-conflict settings victims' needs can be overwhelming and seem endless, however, some needs are more important than others (Staub, 2003; Maslow, 1968). Basic physiological needs are considered primary because they are key to the survival of the individual. The next level is the need for safety and security, which is followed by higher level needs such as the need for recognition and respect (Wemmers & De Brouwer, 2011; Robin, 2017). Following violent conflict, reconciliation may be difficult to achieve unless the post-traumatic stress is substantially relieved (Deutsch, 2011). Victim rehabilitation is a form of reparation, which includes medical and psychological care as well as legal and social services (United Nations *Basic Principles and guidelines on the Right to a Remedy and Reparation for Victims of Gross Violations of International Human Rights Law and Serious Violations of International Humanitarian Law, 2005*). In a mutually supportive application of the principles of DJ, the humanity of all victims is recognized, while recognizing the responsibility of offenders, as well as the needs of the most vulnerable victims. The relationship between the goal of reparation, DJ values and the implications for the Court are summarized in Table 1.

Table 1: Overview of Reparative Goals, DJ Values and Implications for the Court

Goal of Reparation	*DJ value*	*Implications for the Court*
Reconciliation: building positive social relationships	Equality	Recognize the equal moral value of all victims
Repair harm: human dignity and development	Need	Focus on reparation in terms of victim rehabilitation
Accountability: liabilty	Equity	Risks creating competition between victims

Conclusion

Peace is an ongoing and challenging process. Injustice breeds conflict and in order to promote peace and reduce the risk of renewed violence, it is important to develop fair rules, institutions and other resources for managing such conflicts constructively and justly. It is of great importance that reparations do not further contribute to the tensions between groups, adding insult to injury. This means being sensitive to concerns about fairness and applying principles of DJ in a way that is mutually supportive. Specifically, the distribution of reparations should be done in a way that respects the equal moral worth of all victims while recognizing the responsibility of the offender, acknowledging victims who have made particularly important sacrifices for the community and, at the same time, helping those who are especially needy.

Currently, the ICC's heavy reliance on equity as a basis for the distribution of reparations, together with the exclusion of victims of the situation, risks creating competition among victims. In order to contribute to reconciliation rather than conflict, reparations should emphasize equality and need as principles of distribution and the Court should widen its scope of justice. Reparations can continue to serve multiple goals, however, the Court needs to be attentive to how it combines principles in order to promote social harmony and personal development.

This paper highlights the importance of thinking in terms of the strategic implications of the use of particular distribution rules rather than normative conceptions of justice. Those who apply the law, including judges, need to be aware of how their application of the law can impact victims and victimized communities. Further research on the strategic role of justice processes in the post-conflict setting is needed in order to extend existing theories of distributive justice to an analysis of social change.

References

[1] Adams, J. S. (1965). Inequity in Social Exchange. In Leonard Berkowitz (Ed.), *Advances in Experimental Social Psychology*, Vol 2, pp. 267-299. New York, NY: Academic Press.

[2] Ambos, K. (2009). The Legal Framework of Transitional Justice: A Systematic Study with a Special Focus on the Role of the ICC. In Kai Ambos, Julie Large and Marieke Wierda (Eds.), *Bulding a Future on Peace and Justice: Studies on Transitional Justice, Peace and Development The Nuremberg Declaration on Peace and Justice*, pp. 19-103. Berlin: Springer Verlag.

[3] Annan, K. (1998). Overview, Rome Statute of the International Criminal Court. Retrieved June 12, 2017 from http://legal.un.org/icc/general/overview.htm

[4] Austin, W. & Tobiasen, J.M. (1984). 'Legal Justice and the Psychology of Conflict Resolution'. In Robert Folger (Ed.), *The Sense of Injustice: Social Psychological Perspectives*, pp. 227-274. Plenum Press, NY.

[5] Berger, R. (2015). *Stress Traumatic and Posttraumatic Growth: Social Context, Environment and Identities*. New York NY: Routledge.

[6] Bradford, B. (2011). Voice, neutrality and respect: Use of Victim Support services, procedural fairness and confidence in the criminal justice system. *Criminology and Criminal*, 11(4), pp. 345-366.

[7] Bitti, G. (2011). Les droits procéduraux des victimes devant la Cour pénale internationale, *Criminologie*, 44(2), pp. 63-98.

[8] Byrnes, Z.S. & Cropanzano, R. (2001). The History of Organization Justice: The Founders Speak. In Russell Cropanzano (Ed.), *Justice in the Workplace: From Theory to Practice*, Vol. 2, pp. 3-26. Mahwah, NJ: Lawrence Erlbaum Associates, Publishers.

[9] Campbell, R., Wasco, A.M., Ahrens, C.E., Sefl, T., & Barnes, H.E. (2001). Preventing "the second rape": Rape survivors' experiences with community service providers. *Journal of Interpersonal Violence*, 16(12), pp. 1239-1259.

[10] Carayon, G. & O'Donohue, J. (2017). The International Criminal Court's Strategies in Relation to Victims, *Journal of International Criminal Justice*, 15(3), pp. 567-591.

[11] Christie, N. (1986). The Ideal Victim. In Ezzat. A. Fattah (Ed.), *From Crime Policy to Victim Policy*, pp. 17-30. Basingstoke, UK : MacMillan.

[12] Crosby, F.J. (1976). A model of egoistical relative deprivation, *Psychological Review*, 83(2), pp. 85-113;

[13] Cyr, K. (2008). Empowerment et système de justice pénale: L'expérience des victims d'actes criminels. (PhD diss., Université de Montréal).

[14] De Brouwer, A-M. (2009). What the International Criminal Court has achieved and can achieve for victims/survivors of sexual violence, 16(2), *International Review of Victimology*, 183-210.

[15] Deutsch, M. (1975). Equity, Equality, and Need: What Determines Which Value Will be Used as the Basis of Distributive Justice? *Journal of Social Issues*, 31(2), pp. 137-149.

[16] Deutsch, M. (1983). Current Social psychological Perspectives on Justice, *European Journal of Social Psychology*, 13, pp. 305-319.

[17] Deutsch, M. (1985). *Distributive Justice*. New Haven: Yale University.

[18] Deutsch, M. (2000). Justice and Conflict. In Morton Deutsch and Peter T. Coleman (Eds.), *The Handbook of Conflict Resolution: Theory and Practice*, 41-64. San Francisco, CA: Jossey-Bass Inc.

[19] Deutsch, M. (2015). A Career That Spans the Life of a Social Psychologist. In Peter Coleman (Ed.), *Conflict, Interdependence and Justice: The Legacy of Morton Deutsch*, pp. 1-21. New York: Springer.

[20] Deutsch, M. (2015). Justice and Conflict. In Peter Coleman (Ed.), *Conflict, Interdependence and Justice: The Legacy of Morton Deutsch*, pp. 95-118. New York: Springer.

[21] Druckman, D. & Albin, C. (2011). Distributive Justice and the Durability of Peace Agreements, 37(3), *Review of International Studies*, pp. 1137-1168.

[22] Druckman, D. & Wagner, L.M. (2016). Justice and Negotiation, *Annual Review of Psychology*, 67, pp. 387-413.

[23] Dwertmann, E. (2010). *The Reparation System of the International Criminal Court*. Leiden NL: Brill.

[24] Erez, E. (1999). Who's Afraid of the Big Bad Victim? Victim Impact Statements as Victim Empowerment and Enhancement of Justice, *Criminal Law Review*, pp. 545 -556.

[25] Feldthusen, B., Hankivsky, O., & Greaves, L. (2000). Therapeutic Consequences of Civil Actions for Damages and Compensation Claims by Victims of Sexual Abuse.' *Canadian Journal on Women and Law*, 12, pp. 66-116.

[26] General Assembly resolution 60/147, *United Nations Basic Principles and guidelines on the Right to a Remedy and Reparation for Victims of Gross Violations of International Human Rights Law and Serious Violations of International Humanitarian Law* (16 December 2005). Retrieved from https://www.ohchr.org/EN/ProfessionalInterest/Pages/RemedyAndReparation.aspx

[27] Herman, J.L. (2005). Justice From the Victim's Perspective', *Violence Against Women*, 11(5), pp. 571-602.

[28] Heylen, B., Parmentier, S. & Weitekamp, E. (2010). The Emergence of 'Holistic Reconciliation': Lessons Learned from Victims and Offenders Inside the South African Truth and Reconciliation Commission. *International Perspectives in Victimology*, 5(1), 1–12, pp. 1-12.

[29] Hill, J. H. (2009). *Working with victims of crime: A manual applying research to clinical practice*, 2nd edition. Ottawa, ON: Department of Justice Canada.

[30] Holstein, J.A. & Miller, G. (1990). 'Rethinking Victimization : An Interactional Approach to Victimology', *Symbolic Interaction*, 13(1), pp. 103-122.

[31] Ignatieff, M. (Nov-Dec 2001). 'The Attack on Human Rigths. *Foreign Affairs*, 80(6), pp. 102-116.

[32] Johnson, D. W., Johnson, R.T., Tjosvold, D. & Roseth, C. (2018). Morton Deutsch: Celebrating His Theorizing and His Research. *Negotiation and Conflict Management Research*, 12(1), pp. 1-14.

[33] *Le Procureur c. Germain Katanga*, Ordonnance de réparation en vertu de l'article 75 du Statut, (ICC-01/04-01/07-3728), La Chambre de Première Instance II, 24 mars 2017, §20-30.

[34] Lind, E.A. & Tyler, T.R. (1988). *The Social Psychology of Procedural Justice*. New York, NY: Plenum Press.

[35] Maniriqué, G.R. (2014). Lands, wars and restoring justice for victims. In Jo-Anne Wemmers (Ed), *Reparation for Victims of Crimes Against Humanity*. Oxon UK: Routledge.

[36] Maslow, A. (1968). *Toward a psychology of being* (2nd edition). New York, NY: Van Nostrand Reinhold.

[37] Opotow, S. (2012). The Scope of Justice, Intergroup Conflict, and Peace. In Linda R. Tropp (Ed.), *The Oxford Handbook of Intergroup Conflict*, pp. 72-86. Oxford UK: Oxford University Press.

[38] Parmentier, S. (2003). Global Justice in the Aftermath of Mass Violence, *International Annals of Criminology*, 41(1), pp. 203-224.

[39] Pena, M. & Carayon, G. (2013). Is the ICC Making the Most of Victim Participation?, *International Journal of Transitional Justice*, 7(3), pp. 518-535.

[40] Raymond, E. (2010). Justice pour les crimes contre l'humanité : point de vue et attentes des victimes (Master, diss., Université de Montréal, 2010).

[41] Redress. (20 June 2018). *Making Sense of Reparations at the International Criminal Court : Background paper*, Lunch talk. Retrieved August 16, 2018 from https://

redress.org/news/lunch-talks-on-victims-rights-on-the-20th-anniversary-of-the-rome-statute/

[42] *Report of the Secretary General – United Nations, General on the rule of law and transitional justice in Conflict and Post-conflict Societies*, 23 August 2004, UN Doc. S/2004/616.

[43] Robins, S. (2017). Failing Victims? The Limits of Transitional Justice in Addressing the Needs of Victims of Violations, *Human Rights and International Legal Discourse*, pp. 41-58.

[44] Shapland, J., Wilmore, J. & Duff, P. (1985). *Victims in the criminal justice system.* Aldershot, UK: Gower Publishing.

[45] Sherman, L.W. (2003). Reason for Emotion: Reinventing Justice with Theories, Innovations and Research – The American Society of Criminology, 2002 Presidential Address, *Criminology*, 41(1), pp. 1-38.

[46] Staub, E. (2003). Notes on cultures of violence, cultures of caring and peace, and the fulfilment of basic human needs, *Political Psychology* 24 (1), pp. 1-21.

[47] Staub, E. (2005). Constructive Rather Than Harmful Forgiveness, Reconciliation and Ways to Promote Them After Genocide and Mass Killing. In Everett L. Worthington (ed.) *Handbook of Forgiveness* (pp. 443-459). New York: Routledge.

[48] Streicher, B., Frey, D. & Osswald, S. (2012). Forming Fairness Judgments. In Elisabeth Kals and Jürgen Maes (Eds.), *Justice and Conflicts: theoretical and empirical contributions*, pp. 185-198. Heidelberg: Springer.

[49] Symonds, M. (1980). The Second Injury, *Evaluation and Change, Special Issue*, 36-38.

[50] *The Prosecutor v. Thomas Lubanga Dyilo*, Decision establishing the principles and procedures to be applied to reparations, (no. ICC-01/04-01/06-2904), Trial Chamber I, 7 August 2012.

[51] *The Prosecutor v. Thomas Lubanga Dyilo*, Judgment on the appeals against the 'Decision establing the principles and procedures to be applied to reparations' of 7 August 2012 with AMENDED order for reparations (Annex A) and public annexes 1 and 2, (ICC-01/04-01/06-3129), Appeals Chamber, 3 March 2015, §157.

[52] *The Prosecutor v. Thomas Lubanga Dyilo*, Order for Reparations (amended) (ICC-01/04-01/06-3129-AnxA 03-03-2015 1/20 NM A A2 A3) Appeals Chamber, 3 March 2015.

[53] *The Prosecutor v. Thomas Lubanga Dyilo*, approving the proposed plan of the Trust Fund for Victims in relation to symbolic collective reparations (ICC-01/04-01/06-3251), Trial Chamber II, 21 October 2016, § 14-17.

[54] *The Prosecutor v. Thomas Lubanga Dyilo*, Order approving the proposed programmatic framework for collective service-based reparations submitted by the Trust Fund for Victims (ICC-01/04-01/06-3289), Trial Chamber II, 6 April 2017, § 16-17.

[55] *The Prosecutor v. Thomas Lubanga Dyilo*, Rectificatif de la 'Décison fixant le montant des réparations auxquelles Thomas Lubanga Dyilo est tenu' (ICC-01/04-01/06-3379-Red-Corr 21-12-2017 1/125 RH T), Chambre de Première Instance II, 21 décembre 2017, §268.

[56] Walster, E., Berscheid, E. & William Walster, G.W. (1973). New Directions in Equity Research, 25(2), *Journal of Personality and Social Psychology*, pp. 151-176.

[57] Wemmers, J. (2010). The Meaning of Justice for Victims. In Shlomo Giora Shoham, Paul Knepper, Martin Kett (Eds.), *International Handbook of Victimology*, pp. 27-42. (Boca Raton: CRC Press.

[58] Wemmers, J. (2012). Victims' Rights are Human Rights: The importance of recognizing victims as persons. *Temida*, 15(2), pp. 71-84.

[59] Wemmers, J. (2013). Victims' experience in the criminal justice system and their recovery from crime, *International Review of Victimology*, 19(3), pp. 221-233.

[60] Wemmers, J. (2014). Restoring Justice for victims of crimes against humanity. In Jo-Anne Wemmers (Ed.), *Reparation for Victims of Crimes Against Humanity*, pp. 38-50. Oxon: Routledge).

[61] Wemmers, J. (2017). *Victimology*. Toronto: University of Toronto Press.

[62] Wemmers, J. & De Brouwer, A-M. (2011). Globalization and Victims of Crime. In Rianne Letschert and Jan J.J. Van Dijk (Eds.), *New Faces of Victimhood: Globalisation, Transnational Crimes and Victim Rights*, pp. 279-300. Dordrecht NL: Springer.

[63] Wexler, D. B. & Winnick, B.B. (1991). *Essays in Therapeutic Jurisprudence*. Durham, NC: Carolina Academic Press.

[64] Wexler, D & Winnick, B. J. (1996). *Law in a Therapeutic Key: Developments in Therapeutic Jurisprudence*. Durham, ND: Carolina Academic Press.

[65] Winnick, B. (2011). Therapeutic Jurisprudence and Victims of Crime. In Edna Erez, Michael Kilchling and Jo-Anne Wemmers (Eds.), *Therapeutic Jurisprudence and Victim Participation in Justice*, pp. 3-14. Durham, NC: Carolina Academic Press.

Chapter XIV

Victims of Caste-Based Discrimination: A Human Rights Perspective

ARVIND TIWARI

Introduction

Liberty, equality, justice and human dignity are the basic principle of contemporary society. Although injustice discrimination and inequality are social phenomenon, their nature and extent differ from society to society. At the same time there have been constant efforts to fight these problems in human history. Indian society is no exception to this. However, injustice inequality violence and discrimination in India exist in the worst form by way the social stratification and hierarchy that are directly linked to religion and caste. Caste plays its role in both ways i.e. as a system and as an institution (NCTE, 2003).

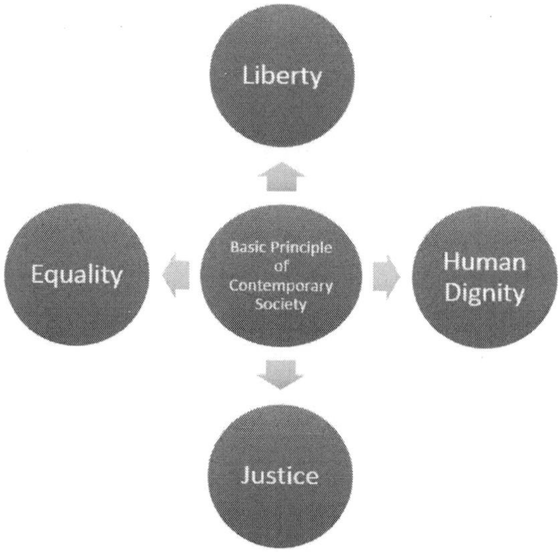

Caste is a system of social stratification, which lies at the very root of social structure of most social groups in India. By social structure, we mean the persistent pattern of social interaction existing within and among social groups. These patterns of interaction are guided by the *normative system* of the society. Caste structure is thus a pattern of social behaviour in which groups and individuals are guided by prescribed set of norms, values and sanctions. The groups and individuals occupy specific statuses within and in relation to other groups. In this system individuals are born into a certain caste and thereby acquire the role and status associated with that caste identity.

Sociologists have defined caste or (as locally referred to) *'jati'* as a "hereditary, endogamous, group, which is usually localised. It has a traditional association with an occupation, and a particular position in the local hierarchy of castes. Relations between castes are governed, among other things by the concepts of pollution and purity, and generally maximum commensality, i.e. interliningoccurs within the caste" (Srinivas 1962:3).

The main features of caste system are:

- Hierarchy,
- Endogamy,
- Association with a hereditary occupation,
- Restrictions on food and social intercourse,
- Distinction in custom, dress and speech, and
- Civil and religious disabilities and privileges enjoyed by different sections of the society. (Ghurye 1950)

In contemporary literature schedule caste/tribes is also referred as 'Dalit'.

Who is Dalit?

There has been an intense debate on this question, resulting in two important view points:

- That all socially politically and economically oppressed sections of the society are Dalits;
- That Dalits consists of only those sections of Indian society that suffered as 'untouchables'. Both the viewpoints are correct in their own ways. But, the untouchables suffer the worst form of discrimination at all levels. While the first viewpoint has the strength of focusing on the wider process of exploitation, it may not adequately represent and reflect the social discrimination to which the untouchables have been subjected. For this reason, the Indian constitutions provides a schedule for these castes and mandates that all the organs of the government treat the Dalits as a special category and enforce their rights with greater care and commitment (Hargopal, 2002).

State and Social Inclusion of Scheduled Caste and Scheduled Tribes

The Indian Constitution has provided various statutory and legal safeguards for SCs and STs. The Scheme of the Constitution reflects a three-pronged strategy for changing the status of SC and ST based on the traditional social order. In this write up dalit is interpreted as SCs and STs.

Protection

Knowing that mere granting of universal adult franchise would not automatically empower the SCs and STs., the Constitution provided for reservation of seats in the Parliament and State Legislative Assemblies (Articles 330, 332, 334) for the Scheduled Castes (SCs) and Scheduled Tribes (STs).

A range of legal/regulatory measures, for enforcing equality and removing disabilities, providing punitive action against physical violence inflicted on SCs and STs and eliminating customary arrangements, which deeply hurt their dignity and person, have been enacted. Given below is a comprehensive list of these measures:

- Protection of Civil Rights (Anti-Untouchability) Act, 1955.
- Bonded Labour (Abolition) Act, 1976
- Scheduled Castes and Scheduled Tribes (Prevention of Atrocities) Act, 1989
- Employment of Manuel Scavengers and Construction of Dry Latrines (Prohibition) Act, 1993.

Untouchability and related human rights violations are also crimes defined as punishable crimes; both Central and state governments are required to intervene and punish those who commit these crimes. Crimes against Dalits are crimes under the Indian Penal Code and under special laws such as the Protection of Civil Rights (Anti-Untouchability) Act, 1955, and the Scheduled Castes and Scheduled Tribes (Prevention of Atrocities) Act, 1989. By enacting these laws, and by defining dehumanizing acts against Dalits as punishable crimes, it is expected that others will be prevented from committing similar crimes.

Autonomous watch-dog institutions such as the National Commission for Scheduled Castes were established (Article 338) to safeguard the guaranteed interests, rights and benefits of Dalits and to report to the President of India on the working of safeguards and measures taken by state governments. For effective implementation of the safeguards, the National Human Rights Commission (NHRC), the National Commission for Women, and the National Commission for SafaiKarmacharis were created to re-address specific areas of vulnerability, including issues related to the violation of Dalit rights.

Protection against Atrocities	Protection of Civil Rights (Anti-Untouchability) Act, 1955.
	Employment of Manuel Scavengers and Construction of Dry Latrines (Prohibition) Act, 1993.
	Scheduled Castes and Scheduled Tribes (Prevention of Atrocities) Act, 1989.

Compensatory Discrimination

Acknowledging the need for positive action against discrimination, the Constitution not only prohibits discrimination by the State on grounds of religion, race, caste, sex or place of birth, but also empowers the Central and the State Governments to make special provisions in favour of the SCs and STs to overcome existing disabilities and advance social justice. To deal with the entrenched inequalities and discriminatory practices, enforcement of reservation provisions in public services, representative bodies and educational institutions (Article 15[4] and 16[4]) have been made. All disabilities and restrictions based on caste and race in the matter of access to public places and resources have been removed by legislations.

Development

Measures to bridge the gap between SCs and STs and other communities in their economic conditions and social status, by making special allocation of resources (for instance, Special Component Plan), and distribution of benefits are required to be made by law. In addition, India is a signatory to various international covenants and conventions on human rights and non-discrimination. These include:

- Universal Declaration of Human Rights 1948;
- International Covenant on Civil and Political Rights, 1966;
- International Covenant on Economic, Social and Cultural Rights, 1966;
- International Convention on Elimination of all Forms of Racial Discrimination, 1965;
- Convention on Elimination of all forms of Discrimination against Women, 1979;
- Convention on Rights of Child, 1989;
- ILO Convention No. 29: Forced Labour Convention, 1930;

- ILO Convention No. 111: Discrimination (Employment and Occupation) Convention, 1958; and
- ILO convention No.107: Indigenous Peoples Convention, 1957.

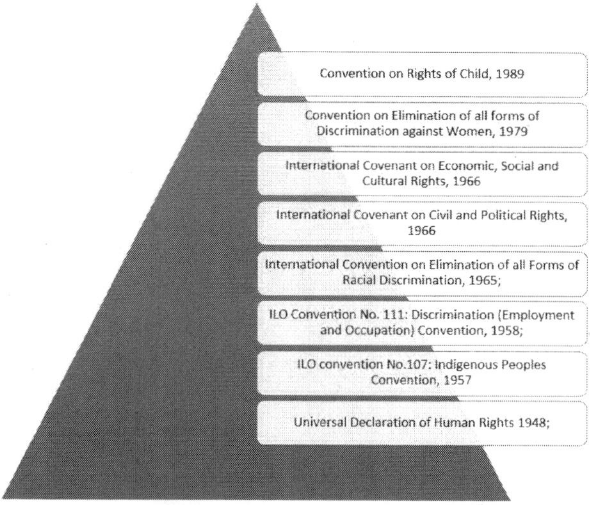

The picture that emerges from above is positively reassuring as far as law and mandatory State action are concerned. Though some progress has been achieved in the elimination of caste-based discrimination in society, particularly in education and economic development, there are miles to go. The challenge lies in the vigorous implementation of the full range of existing Constitutional provisions and laws.

Exploring Untouchability Practices by the State Machinery

Caste, as a system of exploitation, does influence the State machinery. The recent book entitled *Untouchability in Rural India* (Shah, Mander, Thorat, Deshpande and Baviskar, 2006) is perhaps the first nation-wide survey of untouchability practiced in rural India. It also brings forth discriminatory practices by government functionaries and deserves to be discussed here in detail. While 27.6 per cent of the Dalits surveyed are prevented from entering police stations and 25.7 per cent from ration shops, 33 per cent public health workers refuse to visit Dalit homes, and 23.5 per cent of Dalits still do not get letters delivered to their homes. Segregated seating for Dalits was found in 30.8 per cent of the self-help groups and cooperatives, and in 29.6 per cent of the Panchayat offices surveyed. In 14.4 per cent of the villages, Dalits were not permitted to enter the Panchayat building. They were denied access to polling booths, or forced to form separate lines in 12 per cent of the villages surveyed.

Dalit settlements are most often segregated from the main village. Such traditions have been reproduced by the government, when building Indira Awaas housing colonies for Dalits or by non-governmental organisations during the post-2001 earthquake reconstruction programmes in Gujarat. The large majority of Dalits is landless. In a few cases where they are landowners, they are denied access to water for irrigation in more than one-third of the villages. In 21 per cent of the villages, they were denied access to grazing lands and fishing ponds, and violent upper-caste opposition was reported when Dalits encroached onto or were allotted government lands for cultivation or housing.

The study by Shah and Others (2006) also reports discrimination against Dalits in the labour market. Normally, Dalits are coerced into agricultural labour under unfavourable working conditions, and sometimes even into bondage. In the lean agricultural season, when work is scarce for all, upper-caste workers are preferred and Dalits are excluded. In 25 per cent of the villages, Dalits were paid lower wages than other workers and payment of their wages were delayed. Dalits are also subjected to much longer working hours, as well as verbal and physical abuse, not just in 'feudal' states like Bihar, but also notably in 'progressive' states like Punjab. In 37 per cent of the villages, Dalit workers were paid wages from a distance to avoid physical contact. District-level government functionaries of the Labour Department took no cognizance of the above violations. Untouchability was found to extend to consumer markets as well. Dalit producers in 35 per cent of the villages were barred from selling their produce in the local markets. Instead, they were forced to sell in the anonymity of distant urban markets where caste identities blur.

This imposes additional burdens of cost and time, and reduces their competitiveness. Caste-taboos apply particularly to products like milk. In as many as 47 per cent of the villages with cooperatives, Dalits were not allowed to sell milk to the cooperatives or private buyers. In 25 per cent of the villages, they were prevented from buying milk from cooperatives. District Deputy Registrars of cooperatives were completely in the dark about such practices. Dalits are, therefore, not only disproportionately burdened with poverty to start with, but they are also restricted from accessing natural resources as well as the markets for their products. Caste discrimination in labour and consumer markets condemns them to lower wages with harder work in an uncertain employment environment. In nearly half of the surveyed villages (48.4 per cent), Dalits were denied access to water sources. In over a third, the shopkeepers kept the goods bought from the Dalits segregated and asked the Dalits to keep the money on the floor to avoid physical contact. In teashops, Dalits were denied seating and were served in separate cups.

Intolerance of displays of well-being or public celebrations by Dalits result in banning wedding processions on roads passing through houses of upper castes; at times, violence is unleashed if Dalits defied the ban. In 10–20 per cent of the villages, Dalits were not even allowed to wear fashionable clothes or sunglasses. They could not ride bicycles, smoke in public, unfurl their umbrellas, wear footwear on public roads, or stand without their head bowed. Restrictions on their entry into Hindu temples averaged 64 per cent in 11 states, ranging from 47 per cent in Uttar Pradesh to 94 per cent in Karnataka. None of these have spurred government functionaries to take action against the perpetrators.

Untouchability persists even in death. In nearly half of the villages surveyed, Dalits were debarred from access to cremation grounds. In Maharashtra, Dalits have their own cremation grounds in the eastern side of the village, so that the upper-castes are not polluted by the winds that pass from the West to the East. Local-level government functionaries take the easy way out by providing separate cremation/burial grounds for the Dalits.

The discrimination does not end here. Worse forms of discrimination are practiced among various constituent Dalit castes themselves. For example, the scavengers are segregated and required to do odd jobs such as removing human excreta, cleaning dry latrines, cleaning of roads, and so on. Other Dalit castes do not share food, water, and so on, with them. Though these Dalits seldom protest against this humiliation, increasing awareness and empowerment of some sections among Dalits have manifested in resistance to suppression. Apart from the discriminatory practices described above, other human rights violations against Dalits are as follows: threats against contesting in an election; refusal of demand for higher wages; disputes arising during sowing and harvesting operations; disputes arising from removal of crops from the granary after harvesting; protest against occupation change; denial of the services of the village barber or priest; discrimination in schools; denial of access to public transport; forcing them to do manual scavenging; bonded labour; violence against Dalit women (rape, parading them naked in public, and so on) for violating caste norms; marriage with non Dalits; forcing Dalit women into the devdasi system, and so on. Some of these human rights violations against Dalits are manifest, while others are subtle. Often, violence against Dalits takes brutal forms against not just individual Dalits, but against whole groups of Dalits. Atrocities against a whole group of people, such as massacre, rape, and burning of settlements are more manifest forms of violence. More subtle methods like social boycott are intended to block their access to basic necessities and services.

Exploitation Through Gendered Lens

Dalit women constitute 16.3 per cent of India's total female population and 47.96 per cent of the total SC population (India: Office of the Registrar General, 2001). Around 81.45 per cent of them live in rural areas, while they constitute only about 12 per cent of the urban population. The triple burden of caste, class, and gender effectively ensures that Dalit women are the furthest removed from legal protections. Dalit women have to share the economic burden of the family on equal terms with those of men and, in addition, the entire household burden as well. They get married early and have to experience frequent pregnancies. They experience a higher number of child births than upper-caste women do. Dalit women bear the brunt of their entire community to the lack of access to basic services. They have to shoulder the responsibility of collecting fuel wood and water, and, at times, even edible articles from long distances. They are typically the last in the family to take food where men and children of the family receive higher priority. Most of them have nutrient deficient food. Access to education and health facilities is poorer than the male members of their community. While there is a general literacy gap between Dalits and members of general category, the gap is even wider between Dalit women and men. The position is worse in the states of Bihar, Madhya Pradesh, Rajasthan, and Uttar Pradesh. The hardship of many Dalit women is even more pronounced because a large number of Dalit households are women-headed — either due to the husband's desertion or alcoholism. This places the entire burden of running the household on their shoulders.

Dalit women constitute a major workforce of the national economy. As per an estimate, nearly 89.5 per cent of all adult Dalit women participate in some productive labour (National Campaign on Dalit Rights, 2002). Nearly 31.6 per cent of all children from Dalit communities are child workers, and Dalit girls constitute perhaps the largest segment of that child labour. In urban areas, they also function as hawkers, scrap collectors, petty traders, and so on, besides earning their livelihood as domestic helps, or as labourers in the construction industry, earthwork, beedi-/agarbatti-making, candle-making, as well as in garment and embroidery work. Employment in these sectors are characterized by low and irregular wages, irregular work, absence of social security, vulnerability to sexual exploitation, and dependency on middlemen and employers. Women labour, in general, irrespective of caste, are relatively underpaid and unrecognized and labeled as unskilled. These disabilities may be operating even more adversely against Dalit women. Dalit women are engaged in manual scavenging in large numbers. In fact, when an entire family is engaged in scavenging, it is the women members who share the larger load of work. It has also been experienced that where benefits have been extended to families for the elimination of manual scavenging through development programmes specifically targeted at them, it is usually the men of the family who have taken advantage of the scheme by giving up manual scavenging work and taking to alternative occupations. But the women continue to do manual scavenging for to enhance the household income (NHRC, 2002).

Dalit women also bear the brunt of violence against their community. The number of rapes committed against Dalit women has shown an increasing trend (India: National Crime Records Bureau [NCRB],). Upper-caste militias use Mass rape as a weapon to break the morale of the entire community. Rape is used as a political instrument and Dalit women become the target of the anger and wrath of the dominant castes. Dalit women are singled out for other indignities like being paraded naked by upper-caste people even for petty disputes. They are also subjected to prostitution in the name of religion, such as the Devdasi system where girl children between 6–8 years and mostly belonging to Dalit families are dedicated to God.

These children cannot marry, are raped by temple priests and upper caste men; and are eventually auctioned off to urban brothels. In times of extreme hardship, women are forced to sell their bodies for sheer survival (A.N. Sinha Institute of Social Sciences, 2002). According to certain superstitious beliefs, certain mishaps in the family are attributed to witchcraft and women; usually Dalit women, are branded as witches, publicly humiliated, grievously assaulted, and at times brutally murdered. Traditional healers/customary religious chiefs also lend support to such practices. Though disaggregated data is not available, benefits of various development programmes, such as distribution of land and other productive assets have, by and large, gone to Dalit males and, therefore, have not helped in improving the status of Dalit women within the family, as well as outside the family. Where women have been targeted for poverty alleviation in the family, the level of investment in projects selected for them is far lower as compared to those for men. Though the government has issued specific instructions to allot land in joint names, both as exclusive and joint ownership with their spouses, data on land and assets allotted to Dalit women is not readily available.

The Scheduled Castes and Scheduled Tribes (Prevention of Atrocities) Act, 1995, provides for transport and other expenses of the victims to be met to enable them to attend court hearing. In the case of women, provisions for expenses of an escort to accompany them are made; as well as provisions for covering of loss of wages during days attending hearings. However, it has been found that many sections of the rules of the Act are not implemented in majority of the cases, including provisions for travel and maintenance expenses. Often women, having no economic independence, simply do not have the money to pursue a case; if their family does not support them in pursuing the case, they drop it.

In-Built Bias in State Response

According to the NCRB, the year 2016 witnessed an increase in crimes against Dalits—40,801 as against 38,670 in 2015. In 20016, there were 2,540 cases of rape of Dalit women and 1,149 cases of causing hurt to Dalits. These figures indicate the areas of vulnerability of Dalits. Cases registered under Protection of Civil Rights (Anti-Untouchability) Act showed a drastic decline of 42.6 per cent in 2004 over 2003.

As proving untouchability is difficult under the Protection of Civil Rights (Anti-Untouchability) Act, the Scheduled Castes and Scheduled Tribes (Prevention of Atrocities) Act, 1989, was enacted bringing new types of offences under its purview, providing for more stringent punishment and giving the law more teeth. But law enforcement authorities generally book cases under the Indian Penal Code or under the Protection of Civil Rights (Anti-Untouchability) Act—both much milder laws—and are reluctant to file cases under the stringent provisions of the Scheduled Castes and Scheduled Tribes (Prevention of Atrocities) Act, 1989. This often enables the culprits to go scot-free.

Despite being charged with a Constitutional mandate to promote social justice, various grassroots-level government functionaries in India continue to practice untouchability and human rights violations against Dalits. Not registering a case, registering a case only under political pressure or in response to mass protest, or when the victim or her/his relatives insist on registering a case, law enforcement authorities use brutality to dissuade them from registering a case. Officials often act under the influence of political parties or dominant social groups who want to keep the Dalit communities suppressed. In numerous clashes between caste groups, the police have regularly sided with members of the upper-caste groups. While the Dalits can complain about non-registration of FIRs to higher authorities, action taken on the basis of such complaints is often too late and fails to provide direct protection against threats and harassment. It is also reported that social activists who are fighting against caste discrimination are subjected to attack and harassments—both by the State and other powerful interests.

Other methods of harassment include the filing of apparently false criminal cases under Section 151 of the Indian Penal Code, which allows the police to detain people they suspect may commit a crime, as a preventive measure, to detain Dalit rights defenders. Incidents of members of one upper caste forcing a Dalit member to register a case against members of another upper caste to settle scores under these laws have also been reported. Later, after the scores have been settled between the upper castes, the Dalit complainant has been made to withdraw the case. It also happens that at the time of registering a case, Dalits are recorded as aggressors instead of victims, and therefore, cases are registered against the Dalits, instead of the perpetrators.

At the investigation stage, delay at every stage is a common feature. Harassment and intimidation of witnesses for deposing against upper-caste perpetrators delays the process of recording statements and collecting evidence. Delays in conducting post-mortems and/or falsification of post-mortem reports are also not unknown tactics used to delay and/or distort the investigation process. Role of local functionaries such as the *talati*, police *patil*, *gram sevak*, and others in delaying the registration and investigation of the case cannot be overlooked. All these functionaries and the local media are known to be hand-in-glove with upper caste elites in rural areas. In urban areas, the scenario is not much different. Sometimes, the investigation is delayed because social boycott is difficult to prove and the concerned authorities are ignorant of the procedures. Law enforcement authorities fumble due to ignorance of the procedures to be followed, thereby enabling the upper castes take advantage of the situation. Victims who actually manage to lodge a complaint face a bigger obstacle. Failure to follow through with cases is alarmingly apparent at the lowest echelons of the judicial system. Statistics speak for themselves: out of the 40,789 Scheduled Caste and Scheduled Tribe (Prevention of Atrocities) Act cases pending in the courts in 2015, only 4,497 were brought to trial and total pendency is 91 percent. Such a delay is endemic to the Indian judicial system. Further, the 2016 NCRB report shows that 76,998 persons were arrested in cases of atrocities against Dalits, and 65,924 were charge-sheeted. But trials were completed only in 14,615 cases, indicating the seriousness, or lack thereof, with which these cases are treated by the criminal justice system.

The Sessions Courts, which conduct these cases, are often overloaded with a number of different kinds of 'priority' cases, virtually guaranteeing that none of these cases receive the attention they are mandated to receive. Although the Scheduled Caste and Scheduled Tribe (Prevention of Atrocities) Act mandated the creation of Special Courts to circumvent this problem, only two states have created separate Special Courts in accordance with the law. In other states, the existing Sessions Courts have been designated as Special Courts, while still being asked to process their usual caseloads. Once the case is filed in the court, the police consider that their job is over, and there is slackness in following the case through. Judicial delay is just one cause of the low conviction rate. The time lapse between the case being registered and the trial means that the witnesses, who are often poor, face intimidation, turn hostile resulting in the case becoming too weak for a conviction. The long wait also results in many plaintiffs losing interest. Judicial bias against Dalits is rampant and unchecked, and court decisions frequently bear the mark of such bias. As these are cognizant non-bailable crimes, the accused are treated leniently. In the case of victims held under false charges, they are given conditional release and are harassed. Out of the 14,554 cases in which trial were completed under the Scheduled Castes and Scheduled Tribes (Prevention of Atrocities) Act in 2016, only a paltry 3,752 cases resulted in a conviction and 10,802 ended in acquittals. The conviction rate in cases tried under the Indian Penal Code and Scheduled Caste and Scheduled Tribe (Prevention of Atrocities) Act—25.8 per cent convictions in 2016. Of the total 40,801 crimes against Dalits reported in the country in 2016, Madhya Pradesh accounted for about 4922; Rajasthan 12.6 per cent; and Uttar Pradesh 25.6 per cent. Only in recent times, has the reportage of crimes against Dalits shown an increase in these states. The conviction rate in Uttarakhand was 57.1 per cent in 2016—the highest in India that year.

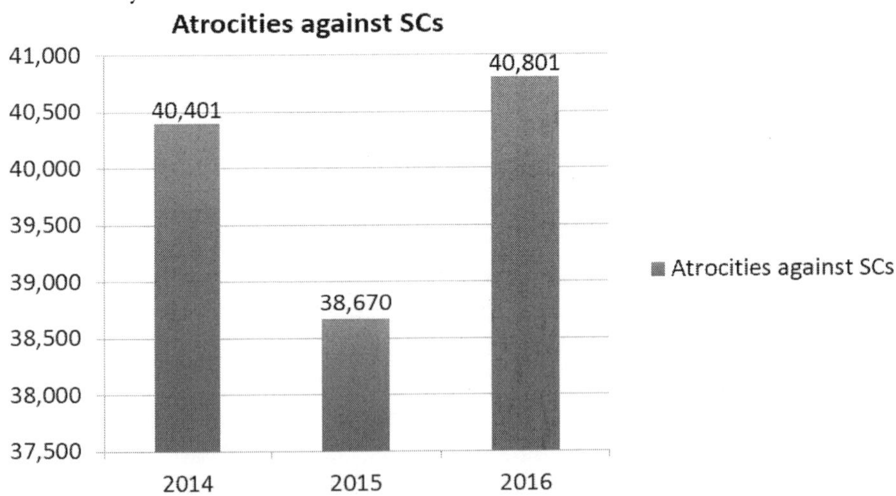

Source: Crime in India 2016, NCRB

It is tempting to attribute increased reportage to the political awakening of Dalits in these states, which has compelled the establishment in these states to register the cases. It is difficult to say if there is a pattern in the geographical distribution of the incidents and registration of crimes against Dalits based on one year's figures. It is necessary, however, to look at the trends over the last one or two decades to confidently conclude that Dalits are breaking their silence, and are reporting crimes on the one hand, and that things have changed for the better, on the other hand. The fact that the establishment is registering the incidents is an official acknowledgement of social reality. Some attribute the non-implementation of legal provisions to caste-based politics perpetrated by political parties with the connivance of vested interests; others blame the Dalits themselves for neglect of education. Yet others find the State apparatus not showing sufficient interest in implementing the anti-discrimination laws and in promoting officially proclaimed affirmative action programmes. Local self-governments are also blamed for their continued denial of equal opportunities to Dalits. Whatever be the reason for the malaise, it is a matter of concern that, despite progressive laws and an egalitarian Constitutional scheme, the plight of Dalits in Indian society continues to be miserable (Menon, 2003: 5).

Social Exclusion

The concept of "Social exclusion" in social science literature is of recent origin. Social exclusion is a complex and multidimensional concept having social, cultural, political and economic ramifications. These dimensions are interwoven. The relations of social exclusion can be differentiated in several ways. One can talk of systemic or constitutive exclusion, which is inbuilt in hierarchical social system. It excludes certain communities from interaction and access to social resources through social arrangements, normative value systems and customs. The exclusion based on caste is one example. Patriarchy is another example. Such systemic exclusion is reinforced by instrumental exclusion, which is embedded in the economic structure and the macro-economic policies associated with them. Members of certain groups by virtue of not having particular marketable assets/capabilities and facilities/ linkages are excluded from opportunities to add/improve their capabilities. For example, those who are asset less (landless in the rural area) do not get adequate useful education to improve skills and enhance their capabilities. Such exclusion leads to other kinds of deprivation, which, in Amatya Sen's words, "lead to the impoverishment of the human life through their casual consequences (such as the denial of social and economic opportunities that would be helpful persons involved)." The consequences of macroeconomic policies such as poverty, unemployment and involuntary migration exclude the victims from economic, cultural and political activities. Systemic exclusion reinforced by instrumental exclusion, supports structures of hegemony.

The study of such hegemonic structures is all the more, important in the Indian context where institutional inequality and discrimination has been a pervasive feature of our society. This has prevented a large segment of the population especially those on the margin of the society from access to rights and privileges enjoyed by the dominant sections of society. Overcoming 'exclusion' constitutes the most elementary pre-requisite for the building of a democratic society, the goal with which our freedom struggle was fought, and the tacit social impact on the basis of which modern India has come into being. This concern is the centre of our Constitution. Indian Constitution provides equality to all citizens irrespective of caste, creed, region and gender. It also directs the State to take various measures to remove the different forms of discrimination, inequality and thereby helps to eradicate social exclusion. Without attaining this objective, an integrated and united nation cannot be built on a sound footing. The potentialities and limitations of such protective measures need to be studied carefully. The Tenth Plan recognized that marginalization; exclusion, persecution of people on account of social, religious, caste and gender adversely affect developmental outcomes. The State is committed to instituting a National Charter to ensure social justice to deprived communities like Scheduled Castes, Scheduled Tribes, other backward castes and minorities. (UGC xii plan guidelines for establishment of centres in universities for study of social exclusion and inclusive policy).

The Preamble to the Constitution identifies securing social, economic and political justice for all citizens as one of its key objectives. Access to fair, quick and speedy justice is a constitutional guarantee recognized under Article 14, which lays down the principle of non-discrimination by assuring every person of the right to equality before the law and equal protection of laws and Article 21, which guarantees that no person will be deprived of their life or personal liberty except in accordance with procedure established by law.

It is the responsibility of all organs of the state to ensure that the administration of justice is made easily accessible and affordable for the common man. Yet we find that courts in the country are burdened on account of the large number of cases that are pending before them, often leading to delays in the delivery of justice. The socially and economically weaker sections of society are the ones who suffer the most on this account. Very often they do not have the capacity or the resources to face prolonged legal disputes causing them to either forgo their rights or settle for less than their due share. One example of this can be seen from the large number of undertrial prisoners, many of whom belong to the marginalized sections of the society. Securing the timely release of such persons is an important facet of upholding the rule of law, which is why they have the first right to obtain timely and free legal aid from the state.

Conclusion and the Way Forward

Given this context of State apathy, Scheduled Caste and Scheduled Tribes have no one to turn to except themselves when their human rights are violated. With untouchability persisting unashamedly in state institutions like schools and police stations, in public spaces like temples and shops, in farms and markets, and in homes and hearts, Dalits still live in India waiting hopelessly and sometimes in anger, for the long-betrayed dawn of equality.

Presented below are some recommendations, which need to be implemented for a better protection of human rights of Scheduled Caste and Scheduled Tribes in India:

1. Human rights violations against Scheduled Caste and Scheduled Tribes invokes three actors—the State and its agents, the civil society, and victims of human rights violations. The task of the State is to de liver what is al - ready pro vided in the Constitution, laws and developmental schemes. The State Legislature, Executive and Judiciary play vital roles in the prevention of human rights violations against Dalits.
2. The Scheduled Caste and Scheduled Tribe (Prevention of Atrocities) Act, 1989, has the potential to bring about change by sending out the message that human rights violations against Dalits will not go unpunished. The implementation of the Scheduled Caste and Scheduled Tribe (Prevention of Atrocities) and other legislations, however, de pend largely on the ability and willingness of the police to follow proper procedure, over come caste biases, and use of forensic tools to en sure equitable jus tice for Dalits. In fact, police re forms should be an integral part of the agenda for Dalit organisations to pre vent human rights violations against Dalits.
3. The State should take adequate steps to ensure that Dalits are able to enjoy the equal rights on community lands and other common property resources and their right to access common water resources, temples, public trans port, and so on, are not restricted.
4. Watch dog in institutions like the National Commission for Scheduled Castes, National Commission for Scheduled Tribes, National Com mission for Women, National Commission for Safai Karmacharis,

and the NHRC should be strengthened in terms of sufficient powers (administrative and financial autonomy) to make them effective instruments of delivery of justice. Civil society organisations should conduct the social audit of the recommendations made by the various Commissions mentioned above to curb human rights violations against Scheduled Caste and Scheduled Tribes

5. At the grass roots level, Panchayats have an important role to play in protecting the human rights of Scheduled Caste and Scheduled Tribes contrary to expectations; however, Panchayats are often found to join the ruling elite in oppressing the Dalits. This trend needs to be reversed by facilitating active participation of Scheduled Caste and Scheduled Tribes in Panchayats through awareness building for local Scheduled Caste and Scheduled Tribes leaders, in particular, and masses, in general.
6. Recommendations made by the NHRC in its Report on Prevention of Atrocities Against Scheduled Castes should be implemented without any delay.
7. The Scheduled Castes and Scheduled Tribes (Prevention of Atrocities) Act remains largely on paper. Out of total cases under the Act, less than one-third are brought to trial. The conviction rate under the Act is very low due to faulty investigation made by the police and harassment of victims and witnesses during the entire process of justice delivery. It is, there fore, required that victims and witness protection programmes be introduced in the law.
8. It is urgently required that the members of Scheduled Castes and Scheduled Tribes should gain awareness about their rights and entitlements, use available channels and mechanisms to obtain justice when found with violation, and increase their presence in all levels—political, business, bureaucracy, police, judiciary, promote organisations and build alliances that support their struggle, and ac quire new skills to negotiate a respectable deal for themselves. Civil society organisations, academia, Dalit and women's organisations, the media, and concerned citizens can take up issues relating to violence against Dalits to the State, bureaucracy and judiciary through various means. In this regard, proper execution of regulatory and developmental programmes would be helpful to curb human rights violations against Dalits.

It is a matter of serious concern that even after nearly seven decades after Independence, more than 160 million Dalits in the world's largest democracy remain at risk of their human rights being violated on the basis of the caste into which they are born by the State — the guarantor of rights. Inherent attitudinal change in the government and civil society is required to give meaning to the Constitutional guarantees of equality and freedom to citizens who have remained at the fringes of Indian society.

References

[1] A.N. Sinha Institute of Social Studies (2002): Musahar: A Socio-Economic Study, Patna.

[2] Address by Hon'ble Minister of Law & Justice at the Inaugural Session of 12th All India Meet of State Legal Services Authorities on 21st March, 2015 at Ranchi, Accessed from http://lawmin.nic.in/mino/s_index.htm).

[3] Ghurye G. S. (1950) (1957)'Caste and Class in India'Bombay: popular book depot.

[4] Hargopal, G. (2002): Rights and Dalits; Law and Reality, *Journal of National Human Rights Commission*, New Delhi, Vol. 1, p. 1.

[5] IGNOU: Unit 20, 21 caste – structure and regional patterns IGNOU reading material. http://www.ignouhelp.in/ignou-eso-12-study-material/liberty, equality.

[6] Mumbai Mirror, 2006, Conspiracy of Silence, December 4, 1–4.

[7] Mandar, H. (2006): Freedom's Just Another World. *The Hindustan Times*, August 15.

[8] Menon, M. (2003): Keynote Address on 'Protection of Human Rights Against Racial Discrimination and Related Tolerance: An Indian Perspective'. In *Report on National Seminar and Public Consultation on Racism, Racial Discrimination, Xenophobia and Related Tolerance*, New Delhi: National Human Rights Commission & National Law School of India University.

[9] National Crime Records Bureau (2016): Crime in India, New Delhi: Ministry of Home Affairs, Government of India.

[10] National Human Rights Commission, (2004): Report on Prevention of Atrocities Against Scheduled Castes, New Delhi.

[11] Shah, G., Mander, H., Thorat, S., Deshpande, S. and Baviskar, A. (2006): Untouchability in Rural India, New Delhi: Sage Publications.

[12] Srinivas, M.N. 1962. *Caste in Modem India and other Essays*. Asia Publishing House: Bombay.

[13] Tiwari. A (2007): Human rights violations against dalits a case of failed state? *The Indian Journal of Social Work*, Mumbai, Volume 68, Issue 1, p.73-87.

[14] UGC XII plan guidelines for establishment of centres in universities for study of social exclusion and inclusive policy.

Chapter XV

Workplace Violence in the Indian Academia: An Examination of Harassment, Abuse and Bullying in the Universities

K. JAISHANKAR

Introduction

Workplace Violence is an issue that erupted, since, the humans started settling down in one place for want of food and shelter. The sharing of resources became a problem, and violence was the refuge of the humans. In sharing the resources, there were violence within groups, between groups and individuals. Later in ancient times, the division of labor created rift among the haves and have-nots and slavery became a norm in the industrial age (Anthony, 1977, p. 20), where violence became embedded with work. Also, work was not a welcome affair as the Greeks, Hebrews and Judeo Christians felt work as a curse and Political Philosophers such as Plato, Aristotle, Max Weber, and Marx (Anthony, 1977; Berenstein, 1988; Hill, 1992, 1999) felt that work is the exploitation of the poor by the elite and this exploitation resulted in Workplace violence. Stark (2009, para 1-11) examines this issue as:

> The Greek word for work was ponos, taken from the Latin poena, which meant sorrow (Tilgher, 1930, p. 3) and the Traditional Judeo-Christians believed that man was placed in the Garden of Eden "to work it and take care of it" (Genesis 2:15; Holy Bible, NIV, 1973). The Greeks believed that a person's prudence, morality, and wisdom was directly proportional to the amount of leisure time that person had. For the Romans, work was to be done by slaves, and only two occupations were suitable for a free man—agriculture and big business. Philosophers such as Plato and Aristotle made it clear that the purpose for which the majority of men laboured was in order that the minority, the élite, might engage in pure exercises of the mind—art, philosophy, and politics (Tilgher, 1930, p. 5). Max Weber, the German economic

sociologist, coined the term the Protestant ethic. The key elements were diligence, punctuality, deferment of gratification, and primacy of the work domain (Rose, 1985, p. 29). From a Marxist view, what actually occurred was the development of a religious base of support for a new industrial system which required workers who would accept long hours and poor working conditions (Anthony, 1977; Berenstein, 1988; Hill, 1992, 1999) and this also caused workplace violence [*sic*].

Though, in the information age, humans became knowledge workers (Stark, 2009) and placed themselves appropriately in elite workplaces, their instinct to involve in violence never died. Workplaces became prone to violence as workplaces are guided by rules and regulations which many of the workers tend to break and involve in workplace deviance and violence. Modern Workplaces are not devoid of violence, as in 1939/1940 itself, Sutherland defined White Collar Crime as "a crime committed by a person of respectability and high social status in the course of his occupation." So, violence in workplace is not restricted only to low or middle level occupations and it is now it is endemic in modern workplaces.

The U.S. Occupational Safety and Health Administration (OSHA, 2011, p. 5) categorized workplace violence into four types:

1. *Type 1—Criminal Intent:* Violent acts by people who enter the workplace to commit a robbery or other crime—or current or former employees who enter the workplace with the intent to commit a crime.
2. *Type 2—Customer/Client/Patients:* Violence directed at employees by customers, clients, patients, students, inmates or any others to whom the employer provides a service.
3. *Type 3—Co-worker:* Violence against co-workers, supervisors, or managers by a current or former employee, supervisor, or manager.
4. *Type 4—Personal:* Violence in the workplace by someone who does not work there, but who is known to, or has a personal relationship with, an employee.

There was a notion that workplace violence only included physical violence (NIOSH, 2002). However, Engel (1989, p. 29) defined Workplace Violence as "*Any act of physical, verbal or psychological threat or abuse, assault or trauma on an individual that results in physical and/or psychological damage.*" This definition placed verbal, psychological threat, abuse, and psychological damage equal to physical violence. Though modern workplaces are prone to physical violence it is psychological violence that occur more and its impact is higher on the victims. The International Labor

Office (2002, p. 3) pointed out the impact: "Although a single incident can suffice, psychological violence often consists of repeated, unwelcome, unreciprocated and imposed upon action which may have a devastating effect on the victim" (cited in Keim & McDermott, 2010, p. 168).

Though, workplace violence existed, research on workplace violence, especially with the inclusion of psychological violence was mostly done in the late 80's and early 90's (Leymann, 1990). Also, there were many researches on workplace violence that occur in many organizations, but there are no or less studies on workplace violence in the academia. Even though the researchers belonging to academia did research on workplace violence in other places they failed to do research on their own workplaces (Keashly & Neuman, 2010). Keashly and Neuman (2010, p. 49) analyses the reasons for the failure:

> This is an interesting oversight for a number of reasons. First, it stands in contrast to reliable evidence of other forms of hostile and demeaning behaviors on campus such as student and faculty incivility in the classroom (e.g., Braxton & Bayer, 2004). Second, the quality of interpersonal relations, such as collegiality, is an important factor in retention of faculty (Norman, Ambrose, & Huston, 2006). Third, the extensive literature on conflict and misconduct in higher education (Cameron, Meyers, & Olswang, 2005; Euben & Lee, 2006; Holton, 1998) highlights the structural and interpersonal opportunities for disagreement and potentially for hostility in such settings. Finally, the academic environment has a number of organizational and work features that increase the likelihood of hostile interpersonal behaviors (Neuman & Baron, 2003; Twale & De Luca, 2008).

The growth of workplace violence in the academic setting needs to be analyzed in detail. Notably, there are little or less studies in this area from western perspectives and there is a total vacuum in the Indian context on the research on workplace violence in the academia. The present chapter is an attempt to analyze and examine the issue of workplace violence in the Indian academia from a holistic perspective.

Universities as Workplaces and Workplace Violence in Universities

Though, universities are workplaces like any other organizations (Hasse et al., 2008), it is not recognized in that fashion by laymen, as Universities are Ivory Towers which only few could enter or interact and many of the public are unaware of the activities of the universities or its employees. Universities are considered to be places of idealism and Merton (1942) provided some ideals to knowledge workers in the University. He asserted that "Communism, Universalism, Disinterestedness, Organized Scepticism" should form a part of the work in the Universities (Merton, 1942). "In the Mertonian ideal, scientific communities should not compete, but share scientific results" (Hasse, et. al, 2008, p. 10). However, Universities now have become work places of cutthroat competition and faculty members involve in various forms of workplace violence including bullying, harassment, mobbing and abuse, to attain their goals such as research funding, administrative and academic positions.

Hasse et al. (2008, p. 10) placed this issue effectively in comparative perspective: "Universities are very competitive workplaces, unlike private enterprises where companies compete against each other to make the best research results; it seems that as universities become more competitive, scientists compete increasingly more against each other than other research groups in the same field." Entering and sustaining academia needs more political skills than scientific skills. Bourdieu (1990, p. 59) points this out: "Scientific skills are not enough; one must also have the support of mentors and develop a 'feel for the game'". Academic politics take dangerous propositions, at times. Harvard University Professor Neustadt once explained: "Academic politics is much more vicious than real politics," "We think it's because the stakes are so small" (Boston Globe, 1992).

There are varied personalities in the academia, the good, bad and the ugly. Perlmutter (2010) has given a vivid presentation on the typology of trouble makers. "These are the 'turfmaster' (easily offended when someone offers a contrary opinion relating to their area), the 'prickly pear' (nursing chips on their shoulder), the 'big bully' (essentially cowards), 'Dr Chaos' (with a fondness for random battles), the 'deal maker' (horse traders by temperament), and the 'smiler' (duplicitous and manipulative)" (Prondzynski, 9 November 2010, para 2). Though, the manipulative and aggressive knowledge workers form a miniscule of the Universities, they are the one who destruct the growth of the universities by involving in workplace violence in the forms of bullying, harassment, mobbing and abuse.

Apart from faculty members involving in bullying and harassment, the support staff or the so called Non-teaching staff (in the Indian parlance) do involve in workplace violence spoiling the tranquility of workplace. There is always a rift between the faculty members and the support staff. The support staffs think that they are superior as they maintain and manage the files of the faculty members and the faculty members think that they are superior to them by position and hierarchy. This conflict often ends in workplace violence. There are also instances where support staffs involve in violence among themselves. Many support staff feel that they are treated in an unfair manner by the faculty members and their profession is not treated at par with teaching and research and academics gain more recognition than them (US Chronicle of Higher Education, 2003). Also, many a times support staffs involve in strikes and sometimes vandalize the University infrastructure.

Thomas (2005, pp. 273–288) did a research on bullying among the support staff in UK and found that many support staff experience bullying. This study found that:

> A total of 42 employees responded, 19 reporting experiencing one or more forms of bullying in the previous two years, while 17 had witnessed colleagues being bullied. The top four bullying tactics ranked in terms of frequency of reporting were undue pressure to produce work, undermining of ability, shouting abuse, and withholding necessary information. When bullying occurred it was likely to be by a line manager. Major findings are that headaches, loss of confidence, loss of self-esteem, fatigue/listlessness, and stress are the most commonly reported health consequences of being bullied, and that these syndromes are associated with a decrease in workplace morale, increased stress at home, and propensity to seek alternative employment (para 3).

Also, students do involve in violence and that is not a new trend. Mass shootings in University campuses which has become common in United States is a rare phenomenon and it is also a rare in other countries. However, other forms violence in the campus has become normalized across the globe. For e.g., most of the students in the university campuses in the world have experienced/experience "stalking, harassment, vandalism, physical assault, sexual assault and other forms of interpersonal violence, and suicide" (Davies & Evans, 2010, para 3). In one way students are victims, however, in some cases they are perpetrators. There are instances, where, professors are bullied, stalked or killed by students (*Mytelka*, September 24, 2011). Some of the students have now resorted to online bullying and stalking their teachers (Halder & Jaishankar, 2013).

Workplace Violence in the Indian Universities

Violence in the Indian University Campuses is not a new phenomenon. Starting from issues of strikes by students, support staff, faculty members to sexual harassment and bullying within chambers and laboratories, workplace violence in the Indian universities has become a day to day occurrence. There is a need to analyze the workplace violence in the Indian Universities from a holistic perspective. Though, the issue of sexual harassment in the Indian University campuses has formed as one of the largest media fodder, other issues like bullying, mobbing and emotional abuse has been sidelined. The following analysis of workplace violence in Indian universities is done based on the typology of workplace violence developed by the U.S. Occupational Safety and Health Administration (*OSHA*, 2011, p. 5).

Workplace Violence against University Authorities and Faculty Members

University authorities and Officials like Vice Chancellor, Registrar and other Professors who involve in the University administration are often targets both by the public, students, and faculty members. Since they are the symbols of University and power centres, many of the agitators attack them or their offices. In 2006, Arson and Vandalists attacks were done by students on the residences of the Vice-Chancellor and the Proctor in Meerut University on an issue of answer copies scandal (*Times of India*, August 15, 2006). In the violence prone Osmania University, the issue of Telangana state is burning and the Vice chancellor became a target of attack of the students (*DNA*, February 20, 2010). In another incident, the Bangalore University (BU) Vice-Chancellor was attacked by a group of students with a wooden stick (*The Indian Express*, 20th December 2011). A group of politically agitated students vandalized the Patna University Vice Chancellors house, pelted stones and hurled abuses on him and other officials of the University (Mishra, August 15, 2012). In Thiruvallvar University of Tamil Nadu, the Vice Chancellor's office became the victim of arson. The arson was done by some unknown miscreants who have burnt many important files (*The New Indian Express*, 20th September 2013). The safety of the University authorities such as Vice Chancellor is always at question in Indian Universities. In a gruesome incident, a Principal of a Private Engineering College in Keezha Vallanad in Tuticorin district of Tamil Nadu was brutally murdered by three students, using knives. The students killed the Principal for suspension of one of the students for his delinquent behavior in the campus (Joseph & Sudhakar, October 10, 2013).

Apart from the university authorities, faculty members also take the ire of the students and the public. A mob attacked Allahabad University professor and his colleague on an alleged mistreatment of a disabled student. The mob also damaged the room of the Professor and properties worth more than 10 lakhs were vandalized (*Times of India*, November, 30, 2013). In Osmania University, some faculty members were attacked by the students and the university authorities did not take action against the students and the faculty members protested by resigning from the administrative posts such as chairman, dean and HOD (*India Education Review*, 20 December 2012).

There are many cases of bullying of teachers by colleagues and students, which however, is not reported to the police/media for various reasons. The author of this chapter is aware of the following case where a student abused a teacher online and the case is provided in Halder and Jaishankar (2013, p. 391).

In this case, the student – perpetrator was a university graduate student aged about 25 years. Angered by the charges of misbehavior, he targeted some of the university faculties with sharp verbal abuses. When he found that his victims, the faculties were nonchalant, he took to circulating SMSs with extremely derogatory remarks. To increase his audience, he finally took to Google hosted social media. He started posting extremely derogatory remarks about the faculties, often calling them names and threatening with dire consequences. Even though his 'posts' were repeatedly reported by the victims and their acquaintances, the social media neither recognized such posts as 'hate messages', nor took any action against the perpetrator for posting inappropriate contents. When the perpetrator finally copied a picture of one his victims from a website which spoke about his (the victim's) scholarly achievements, and posted the same along with further derogatory remarks about him, the victim lodged a strong complaint with the social media. Even though the social media further refused to take down the post on the ground that it does not recognize the mischievous activity as an offensive post, the perpetrator finally took down the post after he was informally warned by the police, who was alerted by other faculty members.

Apart from students harassing teachers, it is also the colleagues, who harass the teachers more than the students. Many a times there are issues of rumor mongering, harassment, abuse of junior colleagues by the senior colleagues who are jealous or competitive. It is not only attack of one against one, it is one against many and Westhues (2004) calls this as mobbing and it is more dangerous than single person harassment (Keashly & Neuman, 2010). Though, cases of bullying are not reported, sexual harassment of women teachers is now reported. In a case of altercation, in the University business School of Punjab University a woman assistant professor filed a complaint against the chairperson of the department and one another colleague (Rahi, May 10, 2013). An another case, the Indian Institute of Management, Indore, a woman assistant professor filed a complaint against a colleague on sexual harassment (PTI, Feb 23, 2013), which was later found to be false complaint and she was sacked by the Institute (*Indian*

Education Review, 30 April 2013). In a case of discrimination and sexual harassment, an assistant professor of the Department of Journalism and Mass Communication who belongs to the Scheduled Caste community, complained against her ex-head of the Department, that, "he harassed her for the last two years and instigated some male students to pass lewd remarks about her" (*The Hindu*, March 24, 2013, para 2). In a prominent sexual harassment case at Post Graduate Institute of Medical Education and Research, Chandigarh, "an assistant professor in the department of biochemistry was sacked for sexually harassing a woman colleague" (*Times of India*, Dec 18, 2012, para 1). Notably, there are mixed cases of sexual harassment in the Indian Academia. While much importance is given to sexual harassment of women students, it can be seen that less importance are given to cases of women faculty members, owing to the reason, that, some women faculty members have used the sexual harassment laws / guidelines as a weapon to settle scores against their male colleagues.

Workplace Violence Against Students and Research Scholars

When it comes to violence against students and research scholars it is found that they are more affected by gender harassment issues, than non-sexual harassment issues, though the later is considered trivia by many, as even many male students die in group clashes inside the university campuses. Safety of women in the University campus in India is one of the most discussed issues, though, there is less action from the sides of the University corridors, and the victimization continues (Irfan, November 6, 2013). Campus killings are largely associated with United States, however, in a horrendous attack, a student of Jawaharlal Nehru University (JNU) attacked his female classmate with an axe and committed suicide (Gohain & Shekhar, Aug 1, 2013). An internal study, post attack by the JNU student, found that 53% of JNU women student face sexual harassment. "Of the 529 students who participated in the study, 21% declared themselves to be in an abusive relationship, 53% stated that they had to face sexual harassment 'once in a while', and 96% were upset over the July 31 incident" (Irfan, November 6, 2013, para 4), in which the male student attacked the female student with an axe.

There are many cases of sexual harassment of female students by their professors in the Indian University campuses. A research scholar of the Department of Zoology, Mysore University, attempted suicide after she was sexually harassed by her professor and the university has suspended the professor (Balakrishnan, March 10, 2011). There is a case of sexual harassment in the authors' University itself. A chemistry professor was suspended as students protested that the professor sexually harassed students and if they don't oblige he would threaten them with dire consequences if they report it to University authorities (*Times of India*, April 29, 2012). A research scholar from the Department of Economics of Gulbarga University complained that she was sexually harassed by an associate professor of the department and the university authorities tried to put the issue under the carpet by trying to intimidate her and provide her with bribe to withdraw the case (*The Hindu*, December 14, 2013). In a typical case of sexual harassment of a female research scholar, the Indian Institute of Technology suspended a professor. The professor sexually harassed her while she accompanied him on an academic visit to Poland (Janardhanan, Dec. 25, 2013).

Apart from sexual violence, mentioned above, there are incidents where many male students are killed, or wounded or bullied by their fellow students. But the issue here is highlighting it. Though there are no studies or much newspaper reporting, the issue of violent attacks on male students is a reality. However, more priority to the student victims of sexual violence as they are the unprotected and vulnerable persons on the campus.

Workplace Violence Against Support Staff

There are many incidences of support staff involving in violence in the campus for demanding hike in salary or regularization of services and also they are victimized by the authorities. However, this type of victimization is seen from a holistic perspective and it is presumed that the victimization is precipitated by the support staff themselves. But there are cases of interpersonal violence, especially, sexual harassment of support staff both by the administrative officials as well as teachers. In a case of Sexual harassment, a support staff of National University of Juridical Sciences, Kolkata, filed a First Information Report against her colleague who tried to make physical advances and continuously tortured her by threatening to pour acid on her (Ganz, 29 July 2013). The accused in this case was arrested by the police only after six months (*India Today*, December 27, 2013). In another case of the same University, another support staff complained that she was "was receiving lewd emails and objectionable proposals from a senior staffer in the registrar's department for over a year" (Shrivastava, 19 July 2013). The issue of workplace violence against support staff needs to evaluated or researched further as there is less literature in this area.

Discussion and Conclusion

Ironically in India, workplace violence in the academia has not been given much attention. The preventive laws are scattered in different legal provisions ranging from physical attack to verbal abuse; for example, physical attack including causing minor injuries to causing culpable homicide or even murder by anyone may attract penal punishments irrespective of the gender, age or caste or class of the accused. While such violence in the workplace like universities / colleges can attract compensation from the organization or the institution based on the work agreements or contract, not much examples are there in India on compensating victims for workplace bullies, stalking, creating gross defamation throughout the campus by the institution or the organization. Nonetheless, such acts can be made directly punishable against the offender and the institution plays little role in actually compensating the victim. In such cases, the entire burden of proof lies on the victim. Depending upon the evidences provided by the victim the institution can take up preliminary investigations which may result either in suspending the offender from his/her role played in the institution till the offender offers satisfactory clarifications and/or apology to the victim or terminating his/her services.

When a victim is woman, she may have several legal options to seek justice; this may include Prevention of Sexual Harassment at Workplace Act, 2013, which includes, several non physical acts, such as passing sexual comments including sending offensive messages through digital communication technology; or the Criminal Amendment Act, 2013 which has included voyeurism, stalking including cyber stalking etc as offences in the Indian Penal Code, or provision prohibiting word, gesture etc to harm the modesty of women (S.509 of the IPC), or the Indecent representation of women (Prevention) Act in case the victim is harassed by ways described in the said provision, or Sections 67 and 67a of the Information Technology Act (2000, amended in 2008) if the victim is subjected to obscenity or sexually explicit materials conveyed by digital/information technology, etc. But this does not mean that the victim can always avail the benefits more smoothly and quickly than her male counterparts. Fear of Gender discrimination in the workplace may play a crucial role in preventing the victim from reporting the harassment, especially, when she fears for loss of job or blocking of her promotions.

In India due to the gender sensitive drafting of several laws many activities have become illegal only when it is committed by a man against woman. The law becomes blind when the victim is a male and the harasser is a female, or when the victim and harasser both are females. Indian laws provide little solace to the victims of non-physical workplace violence, especially, if the victim is a male. The problem becomes critical when the victim is a faculty and the harasser is either a student (Halder & Jaishankar,

2013) or group of students or a female faculty member working in the same institute. While in the first case, the student harasser can generate more hatred by involving false charges against his victim which can claim the victim's job especially if the charges involve taking bribes for exam papers, or sexual harassment against girl students, in the second case, many often the enquiring authority may be more lenient or biased towards the complainant harasser than listening to the defenses of the male victim. Further, women centric anti-stalking laws or anti-voyeurism laws play important role in escalating the problem of the male victims.

Now many of the universities in India have started creating policy guidelines for protecting their employees and students. This should be welcomed. Especially, many universities have now created sexual harassment prevention committees and the recent law on sexual harassment will provide clear cut guidelines for the universities to move further positively in this direction. However, there are no universities which is viewing bullying or mobbing by the faculty members, students, and support staff as a big issue. Bullying or mobbing by the students is named as ragging or eve teasing in India and it is not highlighted in the same vein as done in developed nations. Bullying and mobbing is a reality in the Indian university workplaces and it spoils the academic environment. It is high time that Indian academia seriously views mudslinging, rumor mongering, emotional abuse, bullying and harassment (non-sexual) and includes them as a form of workplace violence along with sexual harassment. Also, empirical researches should be done in this area to get a holistic perspective on workplace violence in the Indian universities.

References

[1] Anthony, P. D. (1977). *The ideology of work.* Great Britain: Tavistock.

[2] Balakrishnan, D. (Mar 10, 2011). Mysore University girl alleges sexual harassment. *CNN-IBN.* Retrieved on 20th January 2014 from http://ibnlive.in.com/news/mysore-university-girl-alleges-sexual-harassment/145422-3.html

[3] Bernstein, P. (1988). The work ethic: Economics, not religion. *Business Horizons,* 31(3), 8-11.

[4] Boston Globe. (1992 July 13). *Fighting for turf and soothing egos* [City Edition]" by Martin F. Nolan, Quote Page 9, Boston, Massachusetts. (ProQuest).

[5] Bourdieu, P. (1990). *The Logic of Practice.* Cambridge: Polity Press.

[6] Braxton, J. M., & Bayer, A. E. (1999). *Faculty misconduct in collegiate teaching.* Baltimore: Johns Hopkins University Press.

[7] Cameron, C. A., Meyers, L. A., & Olswang, S. G. (2005). Academic bills of rights: Conflict in the classroom. *Journal of College and University Law,* 31, 243–290.

[8] Davies, J., & Evans, M. (2010). Preventing Violence on College Campuses: Seven Considerations for Parents. Retrieved on 20th January 2014 from http://counseling.uoregon.edu/dnn/ParentsFamilies/PreventingViolenceonCollegeCampuses/tabid/164/Default.aspx.

[9] DNA (February 20, 2010). Osmania univ vice-chancellor's car attacked, students take out rally. Retrieved on 20th January 2014 from http://www.dnaindia.com/india/report-osmania-univ-vice-chancellors-car-attacked-students-take-out-rally-1350256.

[10] Engel, F. (July/August 1989). Violence, Crime and Trauma at Work: An Overlooked Problem. *EAP Digest*, 29-33.

[11] Euben, D. R., & Lee, B. A. (2006). Faculty discipline: Legal and policy issues in dealing with faculty misconduct. *Journal of College and University Law*, 32, 241–308.

[12] Ganz, K. (29 July 2013). NUJS staffer files FIR over colleague's acid attack threat & sex harassment, after admin inaction. Retrieved on 20th January 2014 from http://www.legallyindia.com/201307293870/Law-schools/nujs-sex-harassment-fir

[13] Gohain, M. P., & Shekhar, R. (Aug 1, 2013). Armed with knife, axe and gun, boy attacks girl in JNU, then kills self. Retrieved on 20th January 2014 from http://articles.timesofindia.indiatimes.com/2013-08-01/delhi/40960366_1_jnu-aiims-classroom

[14] Halder, D., & Jaishankar, K. (2013). Targeting teachers in the social networking sites: An analysis from legal and criminological perspectives. In K. Jaishankar & N. Ronel (2013). (Eds.), *Proceedings of the Second International Conference of the South Asian Society of Criminology and Victimology (SASCV)*, pp. 390-392. Tirunelveli, India: SASCV & Department of Criminology and Criminal Justice, Manonmaniam Sundaranar University. ISBN: 978-81-906687-5-0.

[15] Hasse, C. et al. (2008). *Draw the Line! Universities as workplaces for male and female researchers in Europe*. Understanding Puzzles in the Gendered European Map (UPGEM). Estonia, Tartu: Tartu University Press.

[16] Hill, R.B. (1992, 1999). Historical Context of the Work Ethic. Retrieved on 15th January 2014 from http://workethic.coe.uga.edu/historypdf.pdf

[17] Holton, S. A. (Ed.). (1998). *Mending the cracks in the ivory tower: Strategies for conflict management in higher education*. Bolton, MA: Anker.

[18] Holy Bible: New International Version (NIV). (1973). Grand Rapids, Mich.: Zondervan.

[19] *India Education Review* (20 December, 2012). 112 faculties of Osmania Univ resign to protest attack, demand judicial probe. Retrieved on 20th January 2014 from http://www.indiaeducationreview.com/news/112-faculties-osmania-university-resign-protest-attack-demand-judicial-probe

[20] *India Today* (December 27, 2013). NUJS official held for sexually harassing female colleague. Retrieved on 20th January 2014 from http://m.indiatoday.in/story/nujs-official-held-for-sexually-harassing-female-colleague/1/333241.html

[21] *Indian Education Review* (30 Apr 2013). IIM-I sacks lady professor over 'false' sexual harassment allegation. Retrieved on 20th January 2014 from http://www.

indiaeducationreview.com/news/iim-i-sacks-lady-professor-over-false-sexual-harassment-allegation

[22] International Labour Office (2002). Framework guidelines for addressing workplace violence in the health sector. Geneva: International Labour Office, International Council of Nurses, World Health Organization, and Public Services International. Retrieved on 20th January 2014 from http://www.ilo.org/public/english/dialogue/sector/papers/health/guidelines.pdf

[23] Irfan, H. (November 6, 2013). 53% JNU women face sexual harassment, says survey. Retrieved on 20th January 2014 from http://www.dnaindia.com/india/report-53-jnu-women-face-sexual-harassment-says-survey-1914238

[24] Janardhanan, A. (Dec 25, 2013). IIT-Madras suspends professor after student alleges sexual harassment. Retrieved on 20th January 2014 from http://articles.timesofindia.indiatimes.com/2013-12-25/india/45561020_1_complaints-committee-sexual-harassment-inquiry-committee

[25] Jeanmarie, K., & McDermott, J. C. (2010) Mobbing: Workplace Violence in the Academy. *The Educational Forum*, 74(2), 167-173. DOI: 10.1080/00131721003608505

[26] Joseph, P. P. P., & Sudhakar, P. (October 10, 2013). Vengeful students murder principal. *The Hindu*. Retrieved on 20th January 2014 from http://www.thehindu.com/news/national/tamil-nadu/vengeful-students-murder-principal/article5220580.ece?ref=relatedNews

[27] Keashly, L., & Neuman, J. H. (March 2010). Faculty Experiences with Bullying in Higher Education: Causes, Consequences, and Management. *Administrative Theory & Praxis*, 32(1), 48–70.

[28] Leymann, H. (1990). Mobbing and psychological terror at workplaces. *Violence and Victims*, 5, 119–126.

[29] Merton, R. K. (1942). *The Sociology of Science: Theoretical and Empirical Investigations*. Chicago: University of Chicago Press.

[30] Mishra, B.K. (August 15, 2012). Patna University students attack vice-chancellor house. *Times of India*. Retrieved on 20th January 2014 from http://articles.timesofindia.indiatimes.com/2012-08-15/patna/33215755_1_pu-office-students-owing-allegiance-pu-campus

[31] Mytelka, A. (September 24, 2011). Graduate Student Who Killed His Professor Gets 15-Year Sentence. Retrieved on 20th January 2014 from http://chronicle.com/blogs/ticker/graduate-student-who-killed-his-professor-gets-15-year-sentence/36651.

[32] National Institute for Occupational Health. (2002). *Occupational Hazards in Hospitals*. DHHS (NIOSH) Pub. No. 2002-101. Retrieved on 20th January 2014 from http://www.cdc.gov/niosh/docs/2002-101/#5]

[33] Neuman, J. H., & Baron, R. A. (2003). Social antecedents of bullying: A social interactionist perspective. In S. Einarsen, H. Hoel, D. Zapf, & C. L. Cooper (Eds.), *Bullying and emotional abuse in the workplace: International perspectives in research and practice* (pp. 185–202). London: Taylor & Francis.

[34] Norman, M., Ambrose, S., & Huston, T.A. (2006). Assessing and addressing faculty morale: Cultivating consciousness, empathy, and empowerment. *Review of Higher Education*, 29, 347–379.

[35] OSHA (2011). US Department of Labor, Occupational Health and Safety Administration. Directive CPL 02-01-052: Enforcement Procedures for Investigating or Inspecting Workplace Violence Incidents. Retrieved on 20th January 2014 from http://www.osha.gov/pls/oshaweb/owadisp.show_document?p_table=DIRECTIVES&p_id=5055.

[36] Perlmutter, D.D. (November 7, 2010). Spotting Your Enemies. US Chronicle of Higher Education. Retrieved on 20th January 2014 from http://chronicle.com/article/Spotting-Your-Faculty-Enemies/125289/?sid=wb&utm_source=wb&utm_medium=en

[37] Prondzynski, v. F. (9 November 2010). Grappling with academic politics. Retrieved on 20th January 2014 from http://universitydiary.wordpress.com/2010/11/09/grappling-with-academic-politics/

[38] *PTI* (Feb 23, 2013). Indian Institute of Management professor files sexual harassment complaint against colleague. Retrieved on 20th January 2014 from http://www.samachar.com/Indian-Institute-of-Management-professor-files-sexual-harassment-complaint-against-colleague-ncwwMxhcfhe.html

[39] Rahi, B. (May 10, 2013). Following altercation, UBS woman prof slaps sexual harassment case against 2 colleagues. *The Indian Express*. Retrieved on 20th January 2014 from http://archive.indianexpress.com/news/following-altercation-ubs-woman-prof-slaps-sexual-harassment-case-against-2-colleagues/1113837/0

[40] Shrivastava, P. (19 July 2013). NUJS committee postpones staff sexual harassment hearing by a month. Retrieved on 20th January 2014 from http://www.legallyindia.com/201307193851/Law-schools/nujs-committee-postpones-staff-sexual-harassment-hearing-by-a-month

[41] Stark, S. (June 18, 2009). A Brief History of Work. Retrieved on 15th January 2014 from http://www.slideshare.net/stevenstark/a-brief-history-of-work

[42] Sutherland, E.H. (1939). White-Collar Criminality. Thirty-fourth Annual Presidential Address delivered at Philadelphia, Pa., Dec. 27, 1939 in joint meeting with the American Economic Society (its Fifty-second).

[43] Sutherland, E.H. (1940). White-Collar Criminality. *American Sociological Review*, 5(1), 1-12.

[44] *The Hindu* (December 14, 2013). Probe sought into sexual harassment case. Retrieved on 20th January 2014 from http://www.thehindu.com/todays-paper/tp-national/tp-karnataka/probe-sought-into-sexual-harassment-case/article5458106.ece

[45] *The Hindu* (March 24, 2013). Dalit professor alleges harassment by colleague, students. Retrieved on 20th January 2014 from http://www.thehindu.com/news/national/dalit-professor-alleges-harassment-by-colleague-students/article4542459.ece

[46] *The Indian Express* (20th December 2011). Students attack Bangalore Varsity VC on campus. Retrieved on 20th January 2014 from http://www.newindianexpress.com/cities/bangalore/article237116.ece.

[47] *The New Indian Express* (20th September 2013). Miscreants break into TU V-C's chamber, burn files. Retrieved on 20th January 2014 from http://www.newindianexpress.com/states/tamil_nadu/Miscreants-break-into-TU-V-Cs-chamber-burn-files/2013/09/20/article1792985.ece.

[48] Thomas, M. (2005). Bullying among support staff in a higher education institution, *Health Education*, 105(4), 273 – 288. Retrieved on 11th January 2014 from http://www.emeraldinsight.com/journals.htm?articleid=1509710.

[49] Tilgher, A. (1930). Homo faber: Work through the ages. Translated by D.C. Fisher. New York: Harcourt Brace.

[50] *Times of India* (Apr 29, 2012). Students protest sexual harassment by university professor. Retrieved on 20th January 2014 from http://articles.timesofindia.indiatimes.com/2012-04-29/madurai/31475950_1_girl-students-committee-against-sexual-harassment-protest

[51] *Times of India* (August 15, 2006). Meerut varsity shut down after students attack. Retrieved on 20th January 2014 from http://articles.timesofindia.indiatimes.com/2006-08-15/india/27800060_1_chaudhary-charan-singh-university-meerut-varsity-students-attack.

[52] *Times of India* (Dec 18, 2012). PGI prof sacked for 'sexual harassment' of colleague. Retrieved on 20th January 2014 from http://articles.timesofindia.indiatimes.com/2012-12-18/chandigarh/35889721_1_sexual-harassment-manju-wadwalkar-pgi

[53] *Times of India* (November, 30, 2013). Mob attacks Allahabad University professor, vandalizes campus. Retrieved on 20th January 2014 from http://articles.timesofindia.indiatimes.com/2013-11-30/allahabad/44595308_1_mob-attacks-angry-mob-varsity-authorities

[54] Twale, D.J., & De Luca, B.M. (2008). Faculty incivility: The rise of the academic bully culture and what to do about it. San Francisco: Jossey-Bass.

[55] US Chronicle of Higher Education (31 January 2003). Bullying destroyed my self worth. Retrieved on 20th January 2014 from 'http://www.timeshighereducation.co.uk/174440.article.

[56] Westhues, K. (2004). Workplace mobbing in academe: Reports from twenty universities. Lewiston, NY: Edwin Mellen Press.

Chapter XVI

Victimology and Victim Service Education and Training: An Amerian Perspective

JOHN P.J. DUSSICH

History

In some victimological historical discussions, three influences often voiced come from: the spirit of the times, *zeitgeist,* the spirit of the place, *ortgeist,* (Walker, 2003) and I would add, the spirit of the people, *menschgeist.* One can observe the synergistic confluence offered by these German words in these three influences in the following discussions. Victimology arrived in the United States with little notice, mostly from the first articles by: Beniamin Mendelsohn from Rumania (1937), Hans von Hentig from Germany (1948), Willem Nagel from the Netherlands (1949) and Henri Ellenberger from Switzerland (1954). They all mostly wrote in the European criminological tradition. However, Mendelsohn began from a criminal attorney perspective. Yet, no only did he go on to coin the term "victimology" but he also developed this term beyond its focus on crime victims to include all forms of victimization with his term "general victimology". This concept embodies victims of disasters, wars, genocides (especially from the Holocaust), traffic accidents, crimes and human rights violations. The evolution of victimology in the USA most remained within the framework of penal victimology with works from Marvin Wolfgang (1958, Walter Reckless (1967) and Stephen Schafer (1968). These early victimology developments occurred within the context of such social forces as: the post-war II" baby boom"(children fathered by returning soldiers born between 1946 to1964) that largely contributed to the crime wave of the sixties and seventies (during the time they became teenagers). Later, came the civil rights movement and its method of civil disobedience in the mid-sixties. Then was the Vietnam War, with its anti-war demonstrations and the Post Traumatic Stress Disorder experiences of its veterans. The feminist movement considered the condition of female victims and their lack of empowerment. Ultimately, the focus on social problems and the search for fresh solutions by federal government grants. These social influences brought about an awareness crime victims which had a major effect on the expansion of victimology and victim services.

The early appearance of victimology in the mid-1960s at universities has been a component of existing courses such as in: psychology, sociology, criminology social work, political science and law. As the subject of victimology expanded victimology texts appeared thereby justifying the creation of stand-alone course teaching victimology as a separate discipline. The majority of these courses for both training and education were only about victims of crime. Two victim-related events attracted much attention in the US. The first was the enactment of a Victim Compensation Law in California in 1965; and, the second was the launching of systematic crime victimization surveys across the nation in 1966. These two activities drew from and supported each other. The new compensation program created a need for empirical data to help establish its guidelines and it also used survey data to identify better victims who were in greater need of compensation. The surveys gathered evidence about the entire universe of crime victimization: the "dark figure" of crime victims who had not been officially reported to the police as well as those who had been reported. Thus, for the first time, information was available elucidating the numbers and the character of both types of victims, thereby justifying the need for a wide range of individualized services. University researchers were the main resources for these victimization surveys. In particular the leaders were: Wesley Skogan, Jim Garofalo, Michael Hindelang, and Michael Gottfredson. All published extensively and were frequent guest professors lecturing at universities around the nation. They dramatized the plight of crime victims with their hard data and formed the basis for a new kind of respect for the victim movement. Their research started in the late sixties, continued through the seventies and on into the eighties. Other authors who made significant contributions to the awareness and understanding of special types of victimizations, but who were not researchers, criminologists nor academicians, were: Vincent Fontana who wrote about child abuse (1973); Susan Brown miller who wrote about rape (1975); Frank Carrington who wrote about victim rights (1975); and, Del Martin who wrote about battered wives (1976). Victimology and victim services evolved dramatically in the early 1970s. By a time lag of three to five years, this was followed by the education of college students who wanted to learn about crime victims and by volunteers and new practitioners who wanted to help victims recover. These early initiatives were at first tentative, vague and exploratory. Another feature of these early efforts to learn about crime victims was the resistance to change in academe and in government. Encouragement, organization and clarity came about when the First International Symposium on Victimology was held in Jerusalem in 1973 followed by the publication of its proceedings a year later by Israel Draplin and Emilio Viano with a five-volume to me. This event and its proceedings significantly stimulated the serious study of crime victims, especially in the US. At this point the movement was further accelerated with the formation of various victim service organizations, particularly the National Organization for Victim Assistance (NOVA) in 1976 in Fresno, California launched by me, then a young scholar who had just completed his Ph.D. at the Florida State University a year earlier. This organization served to organize victim service providers nationwide by hosting annual conferences where practitioners could meet and share their skills and experiences, it began to train crisis responders, advocates and professionals, and it also published authoritative manuals, monographs and books on all aspects of victim assistance in a non-academic setting and format. Simultaneous to these mostly organizational, academic, and governmental initiatives were the early victim programs that spread throughout the country in the mid-1970s.

These were two general types: *grassroots efforts* which directly and quickly supported all types of crime victims – especially children and women; and, *prosecutor-based victim/witness programs* primarily concerned with helping prosecutors successfully try defendants and ease the suffering of victims as they fulfilled their witness responsibilities. These programs were initially hosted by the National District Attorney's Association in 1974 to enhance the cooperation of victims as witnesses. Most of the persons who came to work in both these type programs were a mixture of victim-survivors, social workers, untrained volunteers, psychologists, sociologists, pre-law and social work student interns, nurses and retired police officers. All were thirsty for the knowledge needed to help victims recover. The sad irony was that there was little information available at that time. The result was confusion, frustration and many victims who were not helped, in some cases, injured further. The need for a body of educational and training materials was serious and compelling. The development of the early university victimology courses was mostly due to the zeal of such persons as Stephen Schafer at the Florida State University and later at North eastern University, Richard Knudten at Marquette University, William McDonaldat Georgetown University, Joe Hudson and Burt Galaway at the University of Minnesota, Robert Denton at the University of Akron, Eduard Zeigenhagen at the State University of New York, Emilio Viano at the American University, LeRoy Lamborn at Wayne State University, and me, fist at the University of Southern

Mississippi and then at the California State University – Fresno, covering a period from about 1968 to about 1982.Another giant step forward was the publication of victimology textbooks that greatly facilitated the teaching of complete victimology courses. The first American book was by produced by Eduard Ziegenhagen (1977), then Andrew Karmen (1984), and later William Doerner (1994) and Harvey Wallace (1998). Today, my estimation is that the number of victimology texts is in the upper double digits.

From the onset of program development in the mid-1970s, victim service training was first offered within the larger victim assistance programs to prepare victim care providers who were both paid and volunteer staff. Also, most of the victim NGOs offered periodic training events and usually provided certificates of attendance for short term training for a day, over a weekend or for a five-day week. One of the key innovators in victim assistance was James Rowland, the Chief Probation Officer in Fresno County, California who created the first Victim Impact Statement in 1976. This VIS required all the local probation staff to collect data about victims to assess the impact of a crime. This report was then given to the judge at sentencing. In that same year, I launched NOVA in Fresno. Over the next six years these developments prompted victim sensitive programs and academic interest in educating students for eventual employment by these new victim service agencies, especially in: Ft. Lauderdale, Florida; Fresno County, California; Pima County, Arizona; St. Louis, Missouri; Akron, Ohio; and, Rochester, New York. In 1982 I was hired by the California State University, Fresno and subsequently created the first regular certificate program for victim advocates at CSUF in the 1983/4 academic year (Walker 2003).

In 1992 the California State University, Fresno, created the first Victimology Major in the nation. This program later became the model for other interested universities which eventually joined forces and, in 1995, became part of a nation-wide consortium referred to as the National Victim Assistance Academy providing a standardized curriculum and annual training. These were: the California State University, Fresno; Washburn University in Topeka, Kansas; University of South Carolina, Charles ton, South Carolina; and the University of New Haven, West Haven, Connecticut (Walker 2003). Most of the victimology and victim assistance courses were exclusively about victims of crime. However, despite Mendelsohn's call for broader victimology and its recent greater acceptance, most courses were still *not* called General Victimology. Most courses were called simply "Victimology" or "Victims of Crime," and were exclusively focused on the study of crime victims, their role within the criminal justice process and were offered within departments of criminology or criminal justice. The early university-level courses, as well as those for training practitioners, were mostly presentations of basic concepts in crime victimology. They covered the various types of crime victims, with descriptive statistics that had been gleaned from the early victimization surveys completed up to that time. These courses also tried to reconcile the often-conflicting needs of the criminal justice system with the needs of the victim. Today, these courses are much more sophisticated and now provide students and practitioners with information from more advanced studies. They teach about the findings of roughly sixty years of research, some even deal with a broader range of victims, including victims of traffic accidents, war, hate crimes, human rights violations, disasters, refugees, and genocides; however, the emphasis is still with crime victims.

Additionally, today's courses provide more sensitive and effective responses to alleviate suffering and prevent the escalation of trauma. There is much more psychological information on the formation of trauma, phobias and a range of dysfunctional behaviors and the protocols to treat these conditions. The result of this greater sophistication is more success in helping to restore victims to a level of functionality sooner. One of the most widely disseminated and used book, especially by the victim services community was, *New Directions from the Field: Victim Rights and Services for the 21st Century*, organized and published by the Office for Victims of Crime, Office of Justice Programs, U.S. Department of Justice in 1998. Of special significance are sixteen recommendations from Chapter Six, these are the following:

- Reach diverse constituencies of crime victims
- Conduct community needs assessments to identify underserved victims
- Establish comprehensive community-wide services
- Develop standards of service
- Expand basic training and continuing education
- Create a national commission for certification and accreditation standards
- Increase public awareness of victim issues and services
- Conduct evaluation studies of victim services
- Adopt a code of ethics for victim service providers
- Develop statewide crisis response teams
- Create interagency response protocols
- Establish national hotline/state hotlines
- Integrate technology into all levels of victim services
- Comply with the requirements of the Americans with Disabilities Act (ADA)

- Conduct media training on victims' issues, and
- Include crime victims in all aspects of program development, planning, implementation, and oversight (Edmunds 2003 p. 36-7).

Functional Overview

People who work with victims need at least two basic things: the *understanding* about how people respond to a victimization in all its aspects (prior, during and after the injury); and, the resources to help ease the suffering of victims and facilitate their recovery. *All the research, all the changes in laws, all the programs, all the training and education are of little value if at the end of the day, victims are not again made whole. Victimology is not an exercise to amuse the curious, it is not an activity to enhance the careers of scholars, and it is not a ritual to soothe the conscience of politicians. In the final analysis, it is a sincere endeavor to improve the human condition.* Thus, as academicians in victimology our prime objectives must focus on these two simple goals: to cause understanding about victims, and to teach students the skills and information so that they have the resources to bring about victim recovery. "The transfer of 'knowledge to practice' is an essential aspect of the alliance of institutions of higher education and the victim services profession" (Gaboury 2003, p. 26).

Over the past four decades it is clear that victimology has indeed evolved significantly in that direction. At first victimology was a voice of concern by scholars and practitioners to recognize the plight of crime victims who were in large part being taken for granted by the criminal justice system and by society. Then victimology widened to include a variety of research efforts to document the extent of the victimization phenomenon in all its aspects. Finally, the information from this research was used to prompt changes in the laws and practices as to how victims should be responded to. As a part of the human social experience victimology began to be taught in departments of psychology, sociology, criminology, law, anthropology, social work, and political science. As this emerging field took form, its size and complexity grew; and, the need to diversify this educational process became apparent. Public awareness, the needs of the criminal justice system and the social responsibilities of responding to the conditions of many forms of victimization demanded more information and more attention. This was not only for the greater understanding by the community and at the university level to enlighten students about the theories of life, but also as an integral part of the training process for practitioners in this new craft. The early trainers and educators were the pioneers in victimology, teaching about how to confront the chaos of victim trauma and crime response simultaneously. Searching for solutions with almost no traditions, training, funding, or awareness by the public, by the media and by the criminal justice system. Eventually the topic of victimology took on the character of a discipline with elaborate definitions of its unique words, clarification of its often conflicting and confusing concepts and special processes, with the creation of taxonomies of its various forms, and the generation of theories to explain the dynamics of victimization. Not only was a new discipline. emerging, but also anew profession was emerging.

The typical victimology course topics included: the history of victimology, its basic concepts, compensation and restitution, sexual assault, child abuse, domestic violence, elderly abuse, victimization surveys, the victim and the criminal justice system, victim rights, mediation and reconciliation, victim program development and management, crisis intervention, victim organizations, and, the future of victimology and victim services. Of course, this learning process inherited most of its character from generic pedagogy; however, the uniqueness of victimology and victim services also had a variety of needs which required different educational/ training approaches. Some of the special features of victimology included: the synergism of the theory/practice paradigm, the multidisciplinary fusion of ethics, law, sociology and psychology; the organizational dynamics of program development, management and evaluation; the understanding of how to utilize volunteers and survivors effectively, and, the missionary zeal for rendering aid to those in dire need.

Victimology has gone beyond just dispensing information to the masses, it has also become a *bona fide* learning enterprise. It now has concerns for: resource materials, qualified teachers, comprehensive curricula, effective methods of delivering information, creating theories and practices that address both the needs of the society as well as the needs of the victims, and concerns over the social relevance of what is being taught. One of the first workshops about teaching victimology was held prior to the World Society of Victimology's Xth International Symposium on Victimology in Montreal, Canada in 2000. These same issues were articulated, and suggestions were made to continue these discussions. The theme of the symposium was one of the outcomes of a workshop. Another workshop was planned in Germany in 2003 called "Curricula in Victimology and Victim Assistance" hosted by Gerd Kirchhoff and Elmar Weitekampin Mönchengladbach, Germany. Also, later that same year at the WSV's XIth International Symposium on victimology in South Africa, this theme was again given a place in the schedule of topics. It was a long time in coming; however, we had the opportunity to seize the moment for the first time in history, we captured this subject and produced a summary that led to improvements in the way we taught victimology at universities and in the way we trained practitioners. Thus, the important linkage between victim services and teaching was needed and was established. It now forms a bedrock of standards for the effective and efficient delivery of services to facilitate victim recovery; and, also supporting information for the career of victim advocates.

Pedagogical Analysis

The process of victimology learning has two basic forms: *educational* and *training*. Each of these forms has different characteristics. Education is primarily theoretical, abstract, and functions to *describe* phenomena and/or to explain *causality*. Training is primarily practical, applied and functions to impart skills that result in the acquisition of competencies. The prime challenges of victimological education are: to promote student understanding of the victimization/recovery phenomenon; to help reconcile the judgmental legal absolutes with the non judgmental behavioral realities; and, to effect the acquisition of contextual information so that in its totality students will obtain mastery in the comprehension of all aspects surrounding victimization. The prime challenges of victim services training are: to promote understanding of the role of victims within both the criminal justice system and the community; to ensure that competencies are learned that will effectively help to reduce victim suffering and to bring about timely recovery; and also, to provide the student with organizational skills so that they can deliver their services effectively, efficiently and ethically.

Victimological Education is first theoretical in character, aimed at understanding victimization and is found primarily at universities and other institutions of higher learning. It is general and abstract and has the dual responsibility to *describe* and *explain* the quantitative, qualitative and contextual information mostly using simple statistics, percentages and rates to classify the various forms of victimizations and related behaviors. The first focus is on the nature of victimization as an injurious action visited upon humans and uses descriptive nouns, numbers and adjectives to explain what, how, whom, when, and where victims are threatened, injured and killed. The second focus is to understand the systemic responses to victimization, which includes the moral, social and organizational processes which serve the needs of the community as well as the needs of the victim so that societal harmony is facilitated. The third focus is on the causal variables surrounding the phenomenon of victimization and recovery. These include such questions as what makes some persons more or less vulnerable, what makes some victims recover sooner, some later and some not at all. The fourth focus is contextual and considers the social-cultural and organizational environment within which victimization and recovery occurs and includes: history, religion, norms, ethics, laws, management, community, and economics.

Victim Services Training has two basic responsibilities; the first is *to qualify persons in the basic skills* needed to operate within a given job specification. Examples would be: a victim telephone hotline operator; a crisis responder for crime victims; or, a volunteer victim advocate. Some countries/states have created standardized curricula with uniform requirements and qualification tests leading to certification and in some cases, licensure; these specify the types of information and skills that must be learned prior to working in specific roles where direct contact with victims exists. Usually these type standards are rigid because these roles involve levels of responsible decision- making and the objectives include avoiding the exacerbation of victim suffering and trauma; and, to ensure problem-free processing at the organizational level. The second responsibility of training is to provide *advanced skill acquisition* to enhance role effectiveness and efficiency and to be able to accept greater responsibility to promote organizational goals and serve the interests of victim recovery. Ironically this type of training is less standardized and is often offered by the many NGOs as short-term events for a day, a weekend or for one week where the requirement for a certificate is usually attendance and participation. These forms of training usually reflect the orientation of the respective NGOs. The exceptions are specific types of licensure training where closely regulated tests determine entrance into a profession, such as with clinical psychology and social work. The products of training are the ability to make triage decisions at first contact with victims, perform crisis intervention, short-term counseling, and long term therapy. Training is mostly *practical* and *specific* in its character, aimed at providing every-day skills for those individuals working in the many systems, within the scope of laws and rules, and are mostly found at local victim assistance programs, training centers associated with universities and government academies. This type of learning environment involves teaching the methods for processing victims as they meet government and non-government entities, like the police, prosecutors and courts as well as the local rape crisis centers, spouse abuse support groups, coalitions for victim empowerment and victim/ witness centers. The goal of this form of learning is to reflect organizational missions and therefore, are usually taught internally by senior members of each organization and/or by imported experts. The objectives, standards and methods used are dictated by the respective organizational mandates. Ideally, the goals of the training are to help expediently eliminate victim suffering and return victims into society as recovered functioning citizens again. Realistically, this form of learning is more oriented at organizational needs; and, it often operates from a narrower frame of reference linked to the special orientation of that organization.

Students and Teachers

Who are the people who are drawn to the study of the teaching about and the healing of victims? I am reminded of the observation about the motives of psychology students for selecting their major because of the desire to understand their problems. I think many people have entered both academic programs and joined service programs as volunteers because they had some direct victim experience as either a victim or a witness. Of course, there may be a host of other reasons as well: coincidence, personality, job assignment, religion, to mention a few. Among those who have been victims, gathering information about one's own experience is a normal healthy way to cope and to hasten recovery. A natural progression after gathering information for oneself is to realize a larger potential: that this unique knowledge is a valuable commodity that can benefit others. Also, the gathering of knowledge about one's own major life event is often an empowering feeling that significantly offsets the hopelessness and helplessness that usually accompanies the aftermath of victimization. Thus, another natural progression is to continue learning and sharing, first about their own victimization and recovery, and then about related victimizations and recoveries. These activities are precursors to selecting victimology courses, obtaining volunteer training, giving testimonials, proselytizing about the victim's cause, offering direct aid to victims, and conducting research and teaching.

The Future

Victimology education and training offer a bright prospect both for those interested in studying victims and those interested in helping victims. At the university level, there will be the full spectrum of professional education in the field of victimology, at the baccalaureate, masters and doctorate levels. At the practitioner level there will be standardization and licensure with requirements for regular and standardized refresher training. The likely scenario in the near future will be that specializations will develop for the major traditional sub-areas within victimology and victim services. Some of these will likely be Female Victimization and Recovery Services; Victimization and Recovery Services of Abused Elders; Victimization and Recovery of Children; Victimological Theories; Research Methods for Victimization and Recovery; Rights and Legal Issues of Victims; Psychological Protocols for Victim Injury and Trauma; and, Victim Program Management. Then there will likely be the newer victim topics such as those dealing with: Victims of Terrorism; Victims of Abuse of Power; Victims of Disasters; Victims of Computer Fraud; Refugee Victims; Victims of Religious Prosecution; Police as Victims; Victim Outreach Services; Victim's Role in the Restorative Justice Model; Triage Trauma Techniques for Victims; and, Victims of Sexual Harassment.

In the not so distant future, I see: a nation that provides needs-based services to all victims regardless as to the origin of the victimization, services that are provided by highly trained personnel who have licenses based on national and international standards; professional victimology education that leads to a career in either teaching, research or direct services; a victimology that has the victim in the center of its concerns; standardized victimology curricula offered in all major universities; a victimology that accepts a comprehensive theory which explains all forms of victimization and the process of recovery; a victimology that also emphasizes preventing victimization with a primary focus on the identification of vulnerable groups; a victimology that also has a balance of academic offerings equal to criminology; a victimology that is restorative for all persons involved; and finally, a victimology and victim services that is accountable for its teachings and its services through the medium of empirical student evaluation. I am convinced that these possibilities are on our horizon and will be the great challenges of the next generation of victimologists.

Conclusions

While this article has mainly presented the view of a US scholar, it is applicable to most other nations, especially those with common law traditions. The cultures, laws, attitudes, and behaviors of those from other countries ultimately will dictate which policies, education, training and philosophies will be applied to their treatment of victims. The realization that we now live within a global community and many features of our respective societies are being blended; as international and global ideas, attitudes and behaviors become dispersed, ways to problem solve at the societal level provide the opportunity to learn from each other. In a speech I made at the California State University, Sacramento, in 2017 concerning globalization and criminal justice education, was subsequently made into an article; I would like to quote myself and relate those comments to victimization and victim services education and training:

> Embracing and applying the concept of globalization offers a quantum leap to criminal justice educators and a broader range of criminal justice information and options. The current availability of all kinds of valuable information about criminals; victims; criminal justice systems; human rights; criminal, civil and religious laws; and social institutions from around the world is unprecedented. Thus, a university criminal justice teacher today has extensive research and practical resources available to compare the American criminal justice system with those of many other countries, thereby greatly enhancing the scope and relevance of his or her academic work and significantly broadening his or her own career as well as those of his or her students. The best example of a vast database is at the Vienna-based headquarters of the United Nations' Office on Drugs and Crime (UNODC): the primary agency of the UN that deals with criminal justice issues and provides all their key documents in English, Spanish, Russian, French, Arabic, and Chinese. It is important to note that a large percentage of the nongovernment organizations that participate at UN events are staffed by college professors of criminal justice, sociology, psychology, political science, and law (Dussich 2019, ch. 12).

References

[1] Brownmiller, Susan (1975). 'Against Our Will: Men, Women and Rape'. Simon and Schuster Inc. New York.

[2] Carrington, Frank G. (1975). 'The Victims'. Arlington House, New Rochelle, New York.

[3] Doerner, William G. and Steven P. Lab (1994). 'Victimology'. West Publishing. St. Paul, Minnesota.

[4] Drapkin, Israel and Emilio Viano (1974). Editors 'Victimology: A New Focus, Society's Reactions to Victimization', Lexington Books, Massachusetts.

[5] Dussich, John P.J. (2003). 'History, Overview and Analysis of American Victimology and Victim Services Education, in Exploration of Higher Education and Professional Practice', *Proceedings of the First American Symposium on Victimology*, January. Kansas City, Kansas, January.

[6] Dussich, John P.J. (2019). 'Globalizing Criminal Justice Education: Building Cultural Bridges for Career Enhancement' in *Critical Issues in Criminal Justice; Historical Perspectives*, First Edition, Ernest Uwazie, Jennifer Noble, Ryan Getty, and Mercedes Valadez (eds.) Cognella Academic Publishing, Chapter 12, pp. 229-244.

[7] Edmunds, Christine N. (2003). 'The Field of Victim Services, in Exploration of Higher Education and Professional Practice', *Proceedings of the First American Symposium on Victimology*, January. Kansas City, Kansas, January, pp. 36-37.

[8] Ellenberger, Henri (1954). 'Psychological Relationships Between the Criminal and the Victim'. *Zeitschriftfür Psychotherapie und PsychologischeMedizin*, Edition 1, Volume 4, Stuttgart.

[9] Fontana, Vincent O. (1973). 'Somewhere a Child is Crying'. Macmillan Publishing Company'. New York, New York.

[10] Gaboury, Mario T. (2003). 'Role and Current Status of Higher Education and Research in Victim Services, in Exploration of Higher Education and Professional Practice', *Proceedings of the First American Symposium on Victimology*, January. Kansas City, Kansas, January, p. 26.

[11] Karmen, Andrew (1984). 'Crime Victims'. Brooks/Cole Publishing Company. Monterey, California.

[12] Martin, Del (1976) Battered Wives. Glide Publications, San Francisco,California.

[13] Mendelsohn, Beniamin (1937). 'Methode a utiliser par la defenseurpurles recherchesconcertant la personalite du criminal. Revue de Droit Penal et deCriminologie et Archives Internationals de medicine legale', Pari. 877-891.

[14] Nagel, Willem Hendrik (1949). 'De criminaliteit van Oss'. De Sikke, Antwerpen, The Netherlands.

[15] 'New Directions from the Field: Victim Rights and Services for the 21st Century', published by the Office for Victims of Crime, Office of Justice Programs, U.S. Department of Justice, U.S. Government Printing Office, Washington, D.C. (1998).

[16] President's Task Force on Victims of Crime (1982). 'Final Report', Government Printing Office, Washington, D.C., December.

[17] Reckless, Walter (1967). 'The Crime Problem. Appleton-Century-Drafts', New York, New York.

[18] Schafer, Stephen (1968). 'The Victim and His Criminal: A Study inFunctional Responsibility'. Random House, New York, New York.

[19] Von Hentig, Hans (1948). 'The Criminal and His Victim: Studies in the Sociobiology of Crime'. Yale University Press, New Haven, Connecticut.

[20] Walker, Steven D. (2003). 'History and Development of Academic Programs in Victimology and Victim Services, in Exploration of Higher Education and Professional Practice', *Proceedings of the First American Symposium on Victimology*, January. Kansas City, Kansas, January.

[21] Wallace, Harvey (1998). 'Victimology: Legal, Psychological, and Social Perspectives'. Allyn and Bacon, Needham Heights, Massachusetts.

[22] Wolfgang, Marvin E. (1958). 'Patterns in Criminal Homicide'. University of Pennsylvania Press, Philadelphia, Pennsylvania.

[23] Ziegenhagen, Eduard A. (1977). 'Victims, Crime, and Social Control'. Praeger Press. New York, New York.

Chapter XVII

Asian Women and Violent Crime Victimization in USA

XIN REN

Asia is the largest and most populous continents in the world. Thirty percent of lands and sixty percent of the world population are in Asia (the World Population Review, 2019). It also has the fastest growth rates of population in the world. China and India are the two most populous countries in Asia as well as in the World. China counts for 31.69% of Asian total population and 18% of the world population while the percentages for India is 29.36% and 17.5% (ibid., 2019). Due to China's effective birth control policy and result of lower birth rates between 1980 and 2016, it is estimated that India will surpass China's population by 2022 with 1.45 billion people. Asian population also counts for largest immigrant group in the globe mainly moving to Europe and the North American like the United States and Canada.

Asian population is ranked as number 3 populous ethnic/racial group in the United States with 16.61 million people (Wolfram Alpha, 2019). The Asian population, tracing origins to 19 Asian countries, grew 72% between 2000 and 2015, the fast growth rate of any ethnic/racial group in the Unites States. Among the Asian Americans from 19 origins of Asian countries, Chinese, Indians and Filipinos are the three largest ethnic groups as Chinese count for 24% of total Asian population, Indians count for 20% and Filipino count for 19 percent (PEWRsearch.org, 2019). It is projected that by the year of 2055, Asians will become the largest immigrant group (38%) in the United States, surpassing Hispanic population (33%) (FEWResrach.org, 2019). This largest immigrant group also has its shares in crime and victimization (ibid, 2019). This chapter will discuss some important characteristics of victimization of Asian female population in the United States.

The Asian population, in general, tend to have lower rates of victimization than people of other races and ethnicities in the Unites States. While Asians, including Native Hawaiians and Pacific Islanders, count for 4% of the US population, they were victims of 2% of nonfatal violent crimes and 3% of property crimes (Harrell 2009). The victimization rate for Asians in the United States was 10.6 for nonfatal violent crimes and 115.3 per 100,000 populations for property crimes, while it was 24.1 and 162.3 per 100,000 populations for the non-Asian population between 2003 and 2006 (Harrell 2009). However, in an examination of victim–offender relationships, Asian victims were more likely than the non-Asian victims to experience violent crime by strangers (Harrell 2009). This stranger-on-stranger relationship is especially more prevalent for Asian female victims. While non-Asian women reported 66.2% of violent crime committed against them by someone they knew beforehand (including intimate partners, relatives, or acquaintances), Asian female victims reported 51.5% of violent crime committed against them by strangers. Stranger violence against Asians, especially Asian women, has been a widespread public safety concern in Asian communities across the United States. Violent offenders such as rapists and robbers often target Asian women because of the perceived submissiveness of Asian women (Fuchs 2016).

Asian Female Victims and Human Trafficking

The 2016 Global Slavery Index (p. 20; global-slaveryindex.org) found that there are nearly 45.8 million victims of human trafficking in 167 countries worldwide. Of that 45.8 million, 58% of victims live in the following five Asian countries India, China, Pakistan, Bangladesh, and Uzbekistan (UNODC 2010). A previous report from the United Nation Office on Drug and Crime (UNODC) also reported that 66% of human trafficking victims were women (UNODC 2010). Various sources have found that international migrant workers have the highest vulnerability for both labor and sexual exploitation. Of those international migrant workers, *domestic servitude and the commercial sex industry* are two major employment sectors that heavily recruit Asian women workers. A recent survey conducted by the International Labor Organization (ILO) reports that the majority of Southeast Asian migrant domestic workers (between 56% and 84%) are women (Vanek et al., 2014). Because of a high illiteracy rate, poverty, and lower employability among Asian migrant domestic female workers, these women are likely to be illegally employed and work in isolated, private homes; consequently, they are often subject to the worst form of exploitation and abuse. In response to mounting international condemnation of domestic worker exploitation, some governments in the Asian region have sought to improve protections for this vulnerable group. The Philippines, Hong

Kong, and Singapore have increased government agencies' inspection of private businesses and domestic employers to reduce possible exploitation and abuse. Following the execution of two Indonesian domestic maids who had killed their male employers in self-defense against rape in Saudi Arabia in 2015, the Indonesian government issued a travel ban on domestic workers applying for permits to work in several countries in the Middle East (Quiano and Whiteman 2015).

Trafficking Asian women for sexual exploitation has long cultural roots in history. During World War II, the Japanese army brutally kidnapped and raped hundreds of thousands of Asian women from China, Korea, and the Philippines, and forced at least 200,000 Asian women to work as Asian comfort women in Japanese army brothels, a government-sponsored crime of sex trafficking against humanity (Theradical 2013). Between 1860 and 1930, Japanese government shipped more than 10,000 Japanese women as young as 14 years old to South Asia countries and forced them to work in the government-ran brothels. Japanese author Yamazaki Tomoko's book "Sandakan Brothel No.8" documented the miserable experiences of one of the eight brothels in Sandakan, a red light district in Borneo, Malaysia. Many of these former sex workers dies and are buried at the Japanese Cemetery on a hillside overlooking the town (Yaolin, Huo, 2019).

In sex trafficking cases, 85% of victims are women. Of those female victims of sex trafficking in the United States, Asian women account for about 27% of cases (Polaris Project 2017); a much smaller percentage of trafficking cases than Hispanic and African American women (USDOJ 2014). A previous report from the United Nation Office's on Drug and Crime (UNODC) also reported that 66% of human trafficking victims were women (UNODC 2010). Various sources have found that international migrant workers have the highest vulnerability for both labor and sexual exploitation. Of those international migrant workers, *domestic servitude and the commercial sex industry* are two major employment sectors that heavily recruit Asian women workers. A recent survey conducted by the International Labor Organization (ILO) reports that the majority of Southeast Asian migrant domestic workers (between 56% and 84%) are women (Vanek et al., 2014).

Because of a high illiteracy rate, poverty, and lower employ- ability among Asian migrant domestic female workers, these women are likely to be illegally employed and work in isolated, private homes; consequently, they are often subject to the worst form of exploitation and abuse. In response to mounting international condemnation of domes- tic worker exploitation, some governments in the Asia region have sought to improve protections for this vulnerable group. The Philippines, Hong Kong, and Singapore have increased government agencies' inspection of private businesses and domestic employers to reduce possible exploitation and abuse. Following the execution of two Indonesian domestic maids who had killed their male employers in self-defense against rape in Saudi Arabia in 2015, the Indonesian government issued a travel ban on domestic workers applying for permits to work in several countries in the Middle East (Quiano and Whiteman 2015).

In sex trafficking cases, 85% of victims are women. Of those female victims of sex trafficking in the United States, Asian women account for about 27% of cases (Polaris Project 2017); a much smaller percentage of trafficking cases than Hispanic and African American women (USDOJ 2014).

Asian Women and Domestic Violence

Asian women are disproportionally represented among victims of domestic violence. Due to the traditional cultural role of Asian women and their lower social status in society, Asian women are often targeted by various crimes, such as robbery, domestic violence, sexual assaults, and human trafficking. Reportedly, 21 to 55% of Asian women report experiencing intimate physical or sexual abuse during their lifetime (Yoshihama and Dabby 2015); and 23 to 38% of Asian women respondents knew someone who had experienced domestic violence (Yoshioka and Dang 2000). For married Asian couples, Asian women who earn more income than their husbands are more likely to report domestic violence or sexual assault experiences than wives whose incomes were lower than their husbands' (Zahnd et al. 2010). In 2010, the California Health Interview Survey (CHIS) assessed a wide range of health topics including domestic violence with a random sample of adult residents, aged 18 to 65, across the state. The CHIS found that foreign-born Asian women (7%) were less likely to experience intimate partner physical or sexual violence than US-born Asian women (13%). A similar pattern was also observed among foreign-born Latinos (11%) in comparison with US-born Latinos (18%) (Zahnd et al., 2010). In an attempt to explain these findings, Yoshihama et al. (2011) used a more socio-culturally inclusive measure. Their studies found an 18% increase in the reported rate of physical abuse (the reported victimization went up to 52%), compared to the rate obtained using the Conflict Tactics Scale (CTS), a widely used measure in domestic violence study which found only 34% victimization (Yoshihama et al., 2011; Yoshihama, Bybee, and Dabby 2012). This finding is indicative that foreign born women, Asian or non-Asian, are less likely to either recognize the physical punishment as domestic violence or less likely to reveal their experience of domestic violence in survey or interview.

Another unique characteristic of domestic violence among Asian female victims is the surprising finding of domestic abuse by their in-laws. In two separate studies, Raj et al. (2006) and Yoshioka and Dang (2000) found that 5.9% and 6.6% of Asian female respondents reported emotional abuse by their in-laws. A similar finding was also observed in other studies where 28.5% of participants (McDonnell and Abdulla 2001) in Project AWARE (Asian Women Advocating Respect and Empowerment) and 13% of Asian respondents (Lyon, Bradshaw, and Menard 2011) identified in-laws as the persons committing the abuse. The percentages reported in these studies are considerably higher than that reported by other racial and ethnic groups: Hispanics/Latinos, 4%; Whites, 3%; and African Americans/Blacks, 1%.

The traditional Asian culture and community highly value interpersonal relationships which delineate roles and status relationships as based on gender, social roles, economic hierarchy, and power differences. There is communal expectation that individuals, especially women, will conform and perform within their roles based on age, gender, and social class (Lee 1996). Family disputes are frequently settled within families or clans, often with the help of senior family members or clan chiefs who serve as mediators. Divorce is highly stigmatized in Asian cultures (Lee 1996). When marital problems, such as domestic violence, do occur, outside intervention is strongly discouraged for fear that this will bring shame and dishonor to the family. In many Asian cultures, women are expected to remain silent about their suffering, be perseverant, and accept abusive behaviors from those with high status in the family hierarchy (Ho 1990). Due to this cultural orientation, Asian female victims in domestic violence are far less likely to report their victimization to police and to seek for outside help and assistance than their other racial and ethnic counterparts (Dabby 2017). Cho and Kim's studies (2012a, 2012b) among Korean American victims of domestic violence also report that Asian victims of domestic violence are four times less likely to use mental health services than their White, Black, and Latino counterparts.

Asian Female Victims and Sexual Assault

Although the National Crime Victimization Surveys indicate a lower rate of rape or sexual assault for Asian women and Pacific Islanders (Harrell 2009), Asian women are far more likely to be sexually attacked by a stranger than non-Asian women. Asian women are stereotyped as being docile, and are seen as "easy targets" for sexual violence. Such stereotypes possibly prompt people to blame Asian women for not sticking up for themselves. The violence is often understood as a result of their perceived submissiveness and passive attitudes. A study of sexual abuse in the South Asian immigrant community conducted between 1991 and 1996 found that 60% of the women interviewed reported being forced to have sex with their husbands against their will and 90% of Indian women in a chemical dependency treatment program said they were victims of rape and childhood sexual abuse. The most recent survey on sexual violence against Asian American women provides more detailed information. Among female participants, 53.5% reported that they experienced some type of sexual violence at some point in their lives, which is higher than the national estimates of 29.5% of Asian or Pacific Islander females and 44.6% of females overall (Black et al., 2011). About 12.4% reported that they have been forced to engage in sexual relations with another individual; 17.3% reported experiencing sexual harassment; 31.7% reported unwanted touching in a public place; and 25.2% reported feeling pressured to engage in an unwanted sexual act (Black et al., 2011). People between ages 10 and 29 seemed most vulnerable to sexual violence. That age range reported the highest frequency of sexual violence. More than half of the participants who were survivors experienced their first sexual violence when they were teenagers. The most prevalent forms of sexual violence were unwanted touching (31.7%), pressure to engage in an unwanted sexual act (25.2%), sexual harassment (17.3%), and sexual assault (12.4%). More than one-third of all participants personally knew someone who experienced sexual violence at least once or more in their lifetime. Of those, 70% knew two or more victims, which potentially indicates that the majority of Asian American and/or immigrant communities are not directly affected by sexual violence experiences (Black et al., 2011).

Victimization Assistance Issues

The National Immigrant Women Project conducted a large scale research on police responses to violent crime against immigrant women victims in 2013. The study surveyed 722 agencies over 22,000 cases of immigrant women victims between January 2008 and March 2013 covering 49 states. Among the women victims whose case reviewed in the survey, Asian female immigrant victims reported higher levels of domestic violence (50.9%) than other forms of victimization – sexual assault (13.2%), child abuse (7.3%), homicide (9%), stalking (10.1%), elderly abuse (3.1%), kidnapping/false imprisonment (2.8%), extortion (1.9%), and human trafficking (1.8%). One of most shocking findings is widespread police inaction in responding to these violent crimes against immigrant woman victims. Reportedly, in domestic violence, police did not file any report in 83.4% of cases due to language communication problems even though the victims had visible injuries which would provide for probable cause to mandate an arrest for domestic violence. In sexual assault cases, the police failed to file any report in 51.3% of cases even though 60.8% of victims had visible injuries which were observed by the police. In human trafficking cases, the police failed to file any reports in 67.8% of cases while 91.5% of the victims had visible injuries observable by the naked eye and 18.6% of victims could not physically move due to their severe injuries (Lee et al. 2013). Besides cultural bias and stereotyping of Asian women, a language barrier is often cited by the experts in victim services and police investigators as the major reason for delayed assistance or non-assistance for Asian female victims. In 2005, the California Commission on Access to Justice points out that the "Lack of comprehension is perhaps the greatest single barrier to justice. A failure to understand the system, the law or the language of legal proceedings renders justice incomprehensible at best. At worst, it can result in severe injustice" (California Commission on Access to Justice 2005). In an investigative report by the Civil Right Division of the US Attorney General's Office, the investigation found that Los Angeles County Court and California Judicial Council had failed to provide adequate language assistance programs in all foreign languages, except Spanish language (US Department of Justice 2016), even though a multimillion dollar fund allocated for state language assistance programs was unused.

It is clear that Asian women victims of violent crime face many cultural, social and legal challenges in reporting crime victimization, accessing equal justice and protection in criminal justice system and receiving assistance and help from legal, social and human service system and medical and health care professionals.

References

[1] Black, M. C., Basile, K. C., Breiding, M. J., et al. (2011). The national intimate partner and sexual violence survey. NISVS 2010 Summary Report. National Center for Injury Prevention and Control, Centers for Disease Control and Prevention, Atlanta, GA.

[2] California Commission on Access to Justice. (2005). Executive summary: Language barriers to justice in California. Report. http://www.calbar.ca.gov/ Portals/0/ documents/accessJustice/2005_Language-Barriers_Executive-Summary.7.2.12.pdf

[3] Cho, H., and Kim, W.J. (2012a). Intimate partner violence among Asian Americans and their use of mental health services: Comparisons with White,

Black, and Latino victims. *Journal of Immigrant Minority Health*. Published online. DOI: 10.1007/s10903- 012-9625-3

[4] Cho, H., and Kim, W.J. (2012b). Racial differences in satisfaction with mental health services among victims of intimate partner violence. *Community Mental Health Journal*, 48(1): 84–90.

[5] Dabby, C. (2017). A-Z advocacy model: Asians and Pacific Islanders build an inventory of evidence-based practice. *Asian Pacific Institute on Gender-based Violence*. https://www.api-gbv. org/resources/a-z-advocacy-model-report/

[6] Fuchs, C. (2016). Man faces 12 years for hate crime robberies against Asian women. NBC News, October 27. Harrell, E. (2009). *Asian, Native Hawaiian, and Pacific Islander Victims of Crime*. Special Report NIJ225037.

[7] Bureau of Justice.

[8] Ho, C.K. (1990). An analysis of domestic violence in Asian American communities: A multicultural approach to counselling. *Women & Therapy*, 9(1–2), 129–150. DOI:10.1300/j015v09n01_08

[9] Huo, Yaolin (2019). Ugly Shame in Japanese Modern History. In *World Chinese Weekly*, October 30, 2019. https://mp.weixin.qq.com/s/-mCNpTG5 ZSRyZthlyXqCHg.

[10] Lee, E. (1996). Asian American families: An overview. In M. McGoldrick, G. Giordao, and J.K. Pierce (Eds.), *Ethnicity and Family Therapy* (pp. 227–247). New York: Guilford Press.

[11] Lee, N., Quinones, D.J., Ammar, N., and Orloff, L.E. (2013). National survey of service providers on police response to immigrant crime victims, U visa certification and language access. National Immigrant Woman Advocacy Project: American University, Washington College of Law.

[12] Lyon, E., Bradshaw, J., and Menard, A. (2011). Meeting survivors' needs through non-residential domestic violence services and supports: Results of a multi-state study. National Institute of Justice.

[13] McDonnell, K.A., and Abdulla, S.E. (2001). Project AWARE (Asian Women Advocating Respect and Empowerment): Research Project. *Asian/Pacific Islander Domestic Violence Research Project*, Washington, DC.

[14] Polaris Project (2017). 2017 hotline statistics. https://polarisproject. org/2017statistics

[15] PEWResearch.org (2019). Key Facts about Asian Americans: A Diverse and Growing Population. https://www.pewresearch.org/fact-tank/2017/09/08/key-facts-about-asian-americans/

[16] Quiano, K., and Whiteman, H. (2015). Saudi Arabia executes second Indonesian maid in one week. *CNN*, April 17.

[17] Raj, A., Livramento, K.N., Santana, C.M., et al. (2006). Victims of intimate partner violence more likely to report abuse from in-laws. *Violence Against Women*, 2006(12): 936–949. DOI:10.1177/1077801206292935

[18] Theradical, M. (2013). Japan's crimes against humanity: Asian comfort women of WWII. *China Daily Mail: Human Rights and Social Issues*, May 18.

[19] The World Population Review (2019). 'Asian Population 2019'. Worldpopulationreview.com.

[20] United Nations Office of Drugs and Crime (UNODC) (2010). *Global Report on Trafficking in Persons.* Vienna: UNODC.

[21] US Department of Justice (USDOJ) (2014). Attorney General's annual report to congress and assessment of US government activities to combat trafficking in persons fiscal year 2013. US Department of Justice.

[22] US Department of Justice (2016). Complaint No. 171-12C-31 investigation of the superior court of California, Los Angeles County and Judicial Council of California. Civil Rights Division, Washington, DC.

[23] Vanek, J., Chen, M., Carre, F. et al. (2014). Statistics on the informal economy: Definitions, regional estimates and challenges. WIEGO working papers. ILO-WIEGO.

[24] Wolfram Alpha (2019). Asian Population in the United States. WolframAlpha.com

[25] Yoshihama, M., Bybee, D., and Dabby, C. (2012). Life course trajectories of intimate partner violence and health care seeking among Asian women. *Poster Session presented at National Conference on Health and Domestic Violence*, March 30, 2012. San Francisco, California.

[26] Yoshihama, M., and Dabby, C. (2015). Factors and stats report: Domestic violence in Asian and Pacific Islander homes. *Asian Pacific Institute on Gender Based Violence.* https://vawnet.org/material/facts-stats-report-domestic-violence-asian-pacific- islander-homes

[27] Yoshihama, M., Yunomae, T., Tsuge, A., Ikeda, K., Masai, R. (2011). Violence against women and children following the 2011 Great East Japan Disaster: Making the invisible visible through research. *Violence Against Women.* Published online. DOI:10.1177/1077801218802642

[28] Yoshioka, M., and Dang, Q. (2000). Asian family violence report: A study of Chinese, Cambodian, Korean, South Asian and Vietnamese communities in Massachusetts. *Asian Task Force Against Domestic Violence*, Boston.

Chapter XVIII

Expansion of the Punishment for Money Laundering Terrosrism and Immigration

MIGUEL ABEL SOUTO

The Big Bang and the Expansion of the Crime of Money Laundering

The crime of money laundering since its creation has been expanding unceasingly in Bolivia, Ecuador, Germany, Italy, Mexico, Peru, USA, etc. (Abel Souto, 2017).

When the "expansion" of the punishment for money laundering is taken into consideration a simile is being made: just as the universe was created, it is said, with the Big Bang and its ongoing expansion so the crime of money laundering since its creation has been expanding unceasingly (Abel Souto, 2016a, pp. 1-183).

I made a unattended call to the legislature to moderate its intervention in money laundering (Abel Souto, 2009, pp. 243 and 244), which has preferred to add, with the organic laws 5/2010, 1/2015 and 2/2015, three additional reforms to the already long list of modifications on money laundering (Abel Souto, 2005a, pp. 5-26; Zaragoza Aguado, 2011, pp. 1154 and 1155), that undermine the legal certainty and the consideration of criminal law as *ultima ratio*. This criminal policy goes to a "breakneck speed" and continues to accelerate, despite being reported a long time ago (Hassemer, 1994, p. 1369; 1998, p. 217). These constant reforms violate the legal security or "the spirit of the mean", of which He (2010, pp. 7 and 8) speaks, citing Cheng Hao and Chen Yi, scholars of Chinese Song dynasty, who believed that the doctrine of the mean includes to be steady, "steadiness means not to be changeable" and "is the law of the world".

First of all, organic law 5/2010, in the initial clause contained in article 301.1, regarding the requirement for the knowledge that the goods have their origin "in a crime", changes these words by the formula "in a criminal activity", "without being clear the objective pursued" (Manjón-Cabeza Olmeda, 2010, p. 340) with the replacement, speech which is attributed expansion effort and, in principle, wider than the previous noun "crime"

(Fernández Teruelo, 2010, pp. 318, 319 and 324), it seemed to allow the inclusion of the petty offenses made in preceding facts of money laundering, which would mean "an enormous enlargement of the field of this crime" (Muñoz Conde, 2010, p. 557). But the petty offenses should be excluded from previous facts on the basis of a literal, historical and systematic interpretation.

However, organic law 1/2015 of March 30, although says eliminating, doing away with the petty offenses, using Orwellian Newspeak, it actually transforms most of them into minor offenses in Spain, so that expands the preceding facts of money laundering.

To illustrate this point, a single euro from a previous petty offense of fraud, now a minor offense according to article 249 of the Spanish Criminal Code, becomes a material object capable of money laundering and preparatory acts of such fraud, before unpunished regarding petty offenses, are punished in accordance article 269. However, must be excluded here the punishment of money laundering by the principle of insignificance.

Moreover, the petty offences, now minor offenses, can not be included in the previous facts to the crime of money laundering because it limits the effectiveness of the norm (Flick, 1992, p. 1293; Terradillos Basoco, 2008, p. 261), and increases social costs (Flick, 1990, p. 1264) so intolerable and contrary to the principle of proportionality (Fernández Teruelo, 2010, p. 324; Manjón-Cabeza Olmeda, 2010, p. 341). Thus He (2010, p. 7) says that to achieve the purpose of defense of human rights "the penalty must adhere to the spirit of mean", which opposes to "any penalties that are extreme, excesive" and requires "moderateness and appropriateness" (2012, pp. 4 and 5).

Secondly, organic law 5/2010, after the reference in article 301.1 to the "criminal activity", which integrates the previous fact, added "committed by him or by any third person", which punishes expressly money laundering committed by those responsible for the previous fact in the way the majority interpreted the crime (Fernández Teruelo, 2010, p. 319) and "ditch one of the most controversial issues" (González Cussac and Vidales Rodríguez, 2009, p. 195). In this sense there was already a plenary agreement no jurisdictional of the Supreme Court of 18 July 2006 (Gómez Rivero, 2010, p. 540) admitting the self-laundering (Abel Souto, 2011a, pp. 15 and 16; 2011b, pp. 78-80, with references of various sentences).

But the punishment of self-laundering combined with new behaviour of possession or use, to the Criminal Code incorporated by organic law 5/2010, produces "strange consequences" (Quintero Olivares, 2010a, p. 13; 2010b, p. 109), even absurd (Castro Moreno, 2009, pp. 1 and 4), because this would imply that the person who has a painting or a jewel which he has stolen would now commit a new crime and the same applies to the individual using someone else´s car without permission (Quintero Olivares, 2010a, p. 13; 2010b, p. 109).

Not only that, but since the enlargement of the previous facts to the old petty offenses operated under organic law 1/2015, a new crime is also committed by anyone having or wearing a scarf worth 5 euros acquired through theft, a petty offense converted now into a minor offense according to article 234.2, and who uses an old moped, of very little value, which he subtracted, because the old petty offense has become a minor offense of theft of usage with no predetermined worth of article 244.1.

To avoid jeopardy (Martínez-Buján Pérez, 2015, pp. 580-579) the *typus* should be interpreted as meaning that the possession by the authors or participants in the preceding fact as money laundering is punishable only when this is not possible to sanction them for the previous crime (Quintero Olivares, 2010a, p. 20; 2010b, p. 110). It should exclude from the *typus* both the use and another kind of possessions on the basis of the principle of insignificance and teleological interpretation, taking into consideration the legally protected interest, requiring a significant impairment of the socio-economic order and appropriateness of behaviours to incorporate illegal capital to trade.

Thirdly, the reform of June 22, 2010 incorporated in the initial paragraph of article 301.1 of the Criminal Code the possession and use of criminal property as new forms of money laundering (Abel Souto, 2011a, pp. 17-27; 2011b, pp. 81-98). The possession and use behaviours were already covered, from the Criminal Code in 1995, through the formula "perform any other act to conceal or disguise the illicit origin, or to help the person who has participated in the infringement or infringements to evade the legal consequences of their actions". Now, however, they are also explicitly included in the Code (Muñoz Conde, 2010, pp. 554 and 556), but regardless of the purpose that guides a money launderer (Abel Souto, 2005b, pp. 93-102, 290 and 291; 2009, pp. 177-187 and 235; Blanco Cordero, 2011, p. 42; 2012, p. 437).

Thus, it seems that since organic law 1/2015 the Spanish offense of money laundering includes the carrier that among the things that moves sees the above-mentioned scarf with a anti-theft device, the person who takes care of this scarf in the cloakroom of an establishment and the garage worker who guards the old moped mentioned, knowledgeable of the subtraction, because article 301.1 punishes simple possession of property with knowledge that have their origin in an offense.

In addition, from the reform of June 22, 2010 the mere use of goods from a crime is incriminated, so that article 301.1 of Spanish Criminal Code, such as §261 II number 2 of the German StGB, seems covering surprisingly, who write a text with a subtracted computer, but much more astonishing that since organic law 1/2015, which transforms the old petty offense into a minor offense of theft (art. 234.2), if a person writes something with a subtracted pen he is considered a money launderer.

However, the Spanish offense of money laundering, as well as the German, should be "teleologically restricted" (Vogel, 1997, p. 356), which excludes of the article 301 of the Criminal Code, by reason of lack of typus, all material objects of insignificant quantity, as the "amount of cents" (Bottke, 1998, p. 11), under the principle of insignificance (Aránguez Sánchez, 2000, pp. 184, 185 and 248; Palma Herrera, 2000, pp. 350 and 351; Ragués i Vallès, 2001, p. 625; Terradillos Basoco, 2008, pp. 240 and 263) or of "minimal intervention" (Martínez-Buján Pérez, 2015, p. 565).

The same principle of insignificance applies to basic consumer acts, services or merchandise sales in everyday vital business (Aránguez Sánchez, 2000, pp. 184, 247 and 248), given how important it is for individuals to be able to transmit the money received and to use purchased goods (Lampe, 1997, pp. 131 and 132). The previous author who only has money originating from a crime "would prohibit almost the satisfaction of vital needs" (Barton, 1993, p. 161) and thus, his own survival (Blanco Cordero, 1997, p. 272), if behaviours directed to sustain life are not excluded from typus. Furthermore, it would be forcing any potential provider of goods or services "now to waive the settlement of accounts with uncontrolled money now to refrain traffic" (Bottke, 1995, p. 122), which limits so much economic rights of the citizen raising serious questions of constitutionality (Blanco Cordero, 1997, p. 290). According to He the penalty "to achieve the greatest value of defending human rights" must be "moderate, appropriate, fair, impartial, and free from excess and deficiency" (2010, p. 8), and these elements are not satisfied in the current case and also here would criminalize "behaviours which do not violate human rights, such unethical behaviours". The primary and main adjustments in response to crimes in the era of globalization requires decriminalization of "immoral behaviours or minor offences with petty violation against social orders" (2012, p. 4).

Fourthly, regarding the new aggravations laundering of profits from certain crimes against public administration, contained in articles 419-445 of the Penal Code, against land planning and urbanism (Abel Souto, 2011a, pp. 27-31; 2011b, pp. 98-103; 2013c, pp. 1-7; Ferré Olivé, 2013, pp. 389-391; Núñez Paz, 2013, pp. 267-279), the penalty is aggravated despite such increases gravity "do not have relevant general preventive effect" (Silva Sánchez, 2010, p. 5). Over this punitive "hardening" (Díaz y García Conlledo, 2013, p. 288) must be applied the penalty of imprisonment in the upper half for membership of an organization dedicated to money laundering of article 302.1 Penal Code (Lorenzo Salgado, 2013, pp. 235-237), so that the penalty can achieve "really high limits" (Muñoz Conde, 2013a, p. 376).

It can not be presumed that the amount of money laundered from these offenses exceeds the amount derived from other crimes. Neither are these aggravations justified by the legally protected interests (Berdugo Gómez de la Torre and Fabián Caparrós, 2010, p. 13), because they are the same values protected by the basic *typus*, since the Administration of Justice is interested in punishing any crime and the socio-economic order is not more damaged by the laundering of the proceeds of such crimes. Truly the laundered value determines a higher content of unfairness and it should aggravate the penalty (Palma Herrera, 2000, pp. 787 and 788), so the qualified *typus* would focus on the characteristics of the material object, the "magnitude" (Díaz y García Conlledo, 2002, p. 209) or obvious importance of the amount laundered, but not in the irrelevant nature of the predicate offense (Aránguez Sánchez, 2000, p. 316), since the foundation of the aggravation would reside in the greater flow of illicit goods (Faraldo Cabana, 1998, p. 150; Vidales Rodríguez, 1997, p. 142) put into circulation. From a technical standpoint, it is also unacceptable to increase the penalties for laundering according to the origin of goods, given that the autonomy of this crime would deny to attend the previous offense (Álvarez Pastor and Eguidazu Palacios, 2007, p. 356). The criminalization of money laundering would be deprived of independent material content and would simply be a reinforcement of the legally protected interest through the crime of which capital derives (Fabián Caparrós 1998, p. 194). Finally, the foundation of the aggravation underlies neither greater reproach, since the person who converts property linked to crimes against the public administration and urban planning is not guiltier than money launderers derived from other crimes (Palma Herrera, 2000, p. 785), nor international pressure, since no supranational instrument forces a heavier penalty of money laundering in these cases.

In conclusion, the excessive punishment of new aggravations, like "the abuse of any penalty", according to He (2010, p. 7), is a breach of the theory of human rights defense and a "serious violation of the value target".

Finally, the reform of June 22, 2010 adapted the punishment of money laundering to the innovative criminal liability of legal persons, but this model of responsibility was not required, because international agreements only require sanctions "effective, proportionate and dissuasive", so that administrative penalties were sufficient.

Recently organic law 1/2015 exempts all legal persons from criminal responsibility, in Article 31 bis.4, if they adopt a system of effective prevention, provision of doubtful usefulness, because in most cases the subsequent money laundering will demonstrate the ineffectiveness of the system.

This expansion in punishment of money laundering is taking place worldwide. Thus in Spain the organic law 1/2015 extended the previous facts of money laundering to the ancient petty offenses, now called minor offenses, and in China article 191 of the Criminal Code in 1997 punished money laundering from drug crimes, organized criminal syndicate nature or smuggling crimes, in 2001 terrorism was added to the list of preceding offenses of money laundering and in 2006 the previous facts were extended to crimes of corruption, bribery and disrupting the order of financial administration and financial fraud crimes (Yu, 2016, pp. 358 and 361).

What will be the next step? How long will our Criminal Code wait to punish money laundering from mere administrative infractions or civil wrongs?

Money Laundering and Terrorism

Terrorism is escalating around the world. After the terroristic acts in Paris and Brussels in 2015 there were "about 900 attacks in Iraq and Syria during the first quarter of 2016" (He, 2016, p. 1).

In 2017 Paris and London have once again become tragic protagonists, in addition to Nice, Manchester, Berlin and Stockholm; a few weeks ago, the terrorist barbarity hit the Ramblas in Barcelona and the Paseo de Cambrils. Although it might seem otherwise, in fact a Directive against terrorism was approved in 2017, the European Union is not the most affected region, but in other latitudes the fatalities are counted by hundreds, as in Afghanistan, Iraq, Syria, Somalia, Pakistan, Nigeria, Mali, Yemen, the Philippines, India or Egypt, with the last attack, for the moment, with more than 300 dead in the Sinai

In accordance with the resolution adopted by the General Assembly of United Nations on 1 July 2016 "any acts of terrorism are criminal and unjustifiable, regardless of their motivation, wherever, whenever and by whomsoever committed" (United Nations, 2016, p. 1), because as He says "are threatening innocents' lives, infringing people's basic freedom and human dignity and threatening international peace and security seriously" (He, 2016, p. 2), but United Nations also remember that in the fight against terrorism is necessary to ensure the "respect for human rights for all and the rule of law" (United Nations, 2006, p. 9).

Organic law 2/2015, also of March 30, introduces a new form of money laundering in article 576 of the Spanish Criminal Code, with a terrorist purpose, which distorts the legally protected interest by criminalization of money laundering, because it is not required that the goods used for terrorism are of illegal origin (Abel Souto, 2016a, pp. 125-132; Lorenzo Salgado, 2017).

However, "in the financing of terrorism, the wrongfulness of the conduct lies not in the source of the goods, but at the destination" (González Cussac and Vidales Rodríguez, 2009, p. 194).

Terrorism financing and money laundering must not be confused to extend onto money laundering the exceptional and reinforced protection of the prevention of terrorism. In recent years under the pretext of pursuing terrorism has been expanded the prosecution of money laundering, but the fight against terrorism can not become an excuse to control absolutely all citizens and to destroy the guarantees of the rule of law (Ferré Olivé, 2009, pp. 164 and 165).

Both human rights and the principles of legal certainty and proportionality prohibit criminalization, by connivance with terrorism, normal behaviour in a democratic society, because the reason of state can not prevail over the reason of law (Grupo de Estudios de Política Criminal, 2013, pp. 9, 11, 15 and 20).

Immigration and Money Laundering

First of all, inhuman trafficking and illegal immigration (FATF, 2011b, pp. 1-84) are one of the most lucrative criminal phenomena (FATF, 2011a, p. 19) and obviously they are connected with money laundering.

Secondly, the sector of foreign exchange and money remittance also are connected with money laundering. FATF devoted a special report in 2010 to the sector of foreign exchange and money remittance, which demonstrated with the use of various examples, voluntary or unconscious, laundering activities and warned the detection at low compared to the volume of suppliers (FATF, 2010a, p. 7).

To illustrate this point there are several alternative delivery systems such as *hawala* (FATF, 2013, pp. 1-72) or *hundi*, informal funds transfer without moving based on a trust relationship, voucher systems in China and East Asia or changing the black market peso used by immigrants to send money to their countries (Collado Medina, 2010, pp. 480 and 481).

Thirdly, the detection and monitoring of transboundary movements of cash, despite being one of the oldest techniques of money laundering, it still continues to increase its volume significantly (FATF, 2010b, pp. 46 and 47; FATF, 2015, p. 3).

However, immigration and money laundering must not be confused to extend on immigration the exceptional and reinforced protection against money laundering. Border control can not become an excuse to control absolutely all citizens and to destroy the guarantees of the rule of law.

In conclusion, both human rights and the principle of proportionality also prohibit criminalization, by connivance with immigration, normal behaviour in a democratic society, because the reason of state can not prevail over the reason of law.

Last but not least, the Financial Action Task Force urges countries to ensure that their authorities impede or restrict the movement of cash which is potentially related to money laundering (FATF, 2012, pp. 25 and 99-102) and the United Nations Convention against corruption provides that "States Parties shall consider implementing feasible measures to detect and monitor the movement of cash... across their borders", but "without impeding in any way the movement of legitimate capital".

It has been said that the cash is the common medium of exchange in criminal transactions (Jurado and García, 2011, p. 172). In similar vein, the Spanish government, having more closely in mind its tax collection purposes, approved in 2012 a bill to combat tax fraud. The government limited to 2,500 euros cash payments (Ley 7/2012, article 7) and on 2017 the Spanish government will limit cash payments to 1,000 euros. So also France and Italy, and the Indian government banned on 2016 money notes of 500 and 1,000 rupees.

However, in order to escape the Charybdis of paper money we will find the Scylla of electronic money, because new payment technologies are not without risks that may thwart prevention and repression of money laundering (Abel Souto, 2012a, pp. 1-45; 2013a, pp. 266-284, 2016c, pp. 345-353; González Cussac and Cuerda Arnau, 2013, pp. 1-540).

For example, new technologies allow the realization of huge transactions instantly from remote locations, keeping the anonymity and without the involvement of traditional financial institutions (FATF, 1995-1996, p. 8).

In addition, traditional investigation techniques become ineffective or obsolete to new technologies: the problem of physical volume of money posed for launderers —to the point of leaving the paper money because of slow movement— is minimized with "electronic money", its rapid mobility, especially on the internet, difficult to trace the funds transferred and the unusual volume of data to analyze make it almost impossible to detect any suspicious activity (FATF, 1996-1997, pp. 28, 29 and 31).

Furthermore, behind the apparent dogma of the criminogenic character of cash hides a program that exceeds the fight against crime, further marginalizing those who earn less and allows control of the private sphere (Pieth, 1992, p. 27) and also allows immigration control.

References

[1] Abel Souto, M. (2002), *El blanqueo de dinero en la normativa internacional: especial referencia a los aspectos penales*, Servicio de publicacións e intercambio científico, Universidad de Santiago de Compostela, Santiago.

[2] Abel Souto, M. (2005a), "Década y media de vertiginosa política criminal en la normativa penal española contra el blanqueo. Análisis de los tipos penales contra el blanqueo desde su incorporación al Texto punitivo español en 1988 hasta la última reforma de 2003", *La Ley Penal. Revista de Derecho Penal, Procesal y Penitenciario*, No. 20, octubre, pp. 5-26.

[3] Abel Souto, M. (2005b), *El delito de blanqueo en el Código penal español*, Bosch, Barcelona.

[4] Abel Souto, M. (2009), "Conductas típicas de blanqueo en el Ordenamiento penal español", in Abel Souto and Sánchez Stewart, pp. 175-246 and 325-327.

[5] Abel Souto, M. (2011a), "La expansión penal del blanqueo de dinero operada por la Ley orgánica 5/2010, de 22 de junio", *La Ley Penal. Revista de Derecho Penal, Procesal y Penitenciario*, No. 79, febrero, pp. 5-32.

[6] Abel Souto, M. (2011b), "La reforma penal, de 22 de junio de 2010, en materia de blanqueo de dinero", in Abel Souto and Sánchez Stewart, pp. 61-109.

[7] Abel Souto, M. (2011c), "Luces y sombras en la reforma penal sobre drogas de 2010", *La Ley Penal. Revista de Derecho Penal, Procesal y Penitenciario*, No. 83, junio, pp. 61-86.

[8] Abel Souto, M. (2012a), "Blanqueo, innovaciones tecnológicas, amnistía fiscal de 2012 y reforma penal", *Revista Electrónica de Ciencia Penal y Criminología*, No. 14, pp. 1-45.

[9] Abel Souto, M. (2012b), "The Update of Penalty Concept and Adjustment of Crime in Money Laundering", *Antiriciclaggio*, No. 2/3, pp. 220-247.

[10] Abel Souto, M. (2013a), "Money laundering, new tecnologies and Spanish penal reform", *Journal of Money Laundering Control*, No. 16, 3, pp. 266-284.

[11] Abel Souto, M. (2013b), "Volumen mundial del blanqueo de dinero, evolución del delito en España y jurisprudencia reciente sobre las últimas modificaciones del Código penal", *Revista General de Derecho Penal*, No. 20, pp. 1-33.

[12] Abel Souto, M. (2013c), "Anti-corruption strategy in the global era and money laundering", *Fifth Session of the* International Forum on Crime and Criminal Law in the Global Era, Beijing, pp. 1-7.

[13] Abel Souto, M. (2014a), "Jurisprudencia penal reciente sobre el blanqueo de dinero, volumen del fenómeno y evolución del delito en España", in Abel Souto and Sánchez Stewart, pp. 137-201 and 309-317.

[14] Abel Souto, M. (2014b), "Drugs criminal policies in the global era and money laundering", *Sixth Session of the International Forum on Crime and Criminal Law in the Global Era*, Beijing, pp. 80-91.

[15] Abel Souto, M. (2014c), "El blanqueo de dinero como innovador instrumento de control económico y social", *Revista Cuatrimestral Europea sobre Prevención y Represión del Blanqueo de Dinero*, No. 1, pp. 11-65.

[16] Abel Souto, M. (2014d), "Política criminal sobre drogas en la era global y blanqueo de dinero", *Revista Cuatrimestral Europea sobre Prevención y Represión del Blanqueo de Dinero*, No. 2, pp. 9-22.

[17] Abel Souto, M. (2014e), "El blanqueo de dinero: problemática actual española, con anotaciones de Derecho comparado estadounidense", *Revista Cuatrimestral Europea sobre Prevención y Represión del Blanqueo de Dinero,* No. 3, pp. 7-56.

[18] Abel Souto, M. (2016a), *La expansión penal del blanqueo de dinero,* Centro Mejicano de Estudios en lo Penal Tributario, Méjico.

[19] Abel Souto, M. (2016b), "Expanding the crime of money laundering and countermeasures against global terrorism", *Eighth Session of the International Forum on Crime and Criminal Law in the Global Era,* Beijing, *Lex Russica,* No. 12 (121), pp. 125-132.

[20] Abel Souto, M. (2016c), "Cybercrime and money laundering ", in Kolaric, D. (ed.), *Thematic conference proceedings of international significance Archibald Reiss Dayss,* vol. 3, Academy of Criminalistic and Police Studies, Belgrade, pp. 345-353.

[21] Abel Souto, M. (2017), "La expansión mundial del blanqueo de dinero y las reformas penales españolas de 2015, con anotaciones relativas a los ordenamientos jurídicos de Bolivia, Alemania, Ecuador, Estados Unidos, Méjico y Perú", *I congreso de la Asociación Iberoamericana de Derecho Penal Económico y de la Empresa, Santa Cruz de la Sierra,* Bolivia.

[22] Abel Souto, M. and Sánchez Stewart, N. (2009) (coords.), *I congreso de prevención y represión del blanqueo de dinero,* Tirant lo Blanch, Valencia.

[23] Abel Souto, M. and Sánchez Stewart, N. (2011) (coords.), *II congreso sobre prevención y represión del blanqueo de dinero,* Tirant lo Blanch, Valencia.

[24] Abel Souto, M. and Sánchez Stewart, N. (2013) (coords.), *III congreso sobre prevención y represión del blanqueo de dinero,* Tirant lo Blanch, Valencia.

[25] Abel Souto, M. and Sánchez Stewart, N. (2014) (coords.), *IV congreso sobre prevención y represión del blanqueo de dinero,* Tirant lo Blanch, Valencia.

[26] Abel Souto, M. and Sánchez Stewart, N. (2017) (coords.), *V congreso sobre prevención y represión del blanqueo de dinero,* Tirant lo Blanch, Valencia.

[27] Álvarez Pastor, D. and Eguidazu Palacios, F. (2007), *Manual de prevención del blanqueo de capitales,* Marcial Pons, Madrid/Barcelona.

[28] Aránguez Sánchez, C. (2000), *El delito de blanqueo de capitales,* Marcial Pons, Madrid/Barcelona.

[29] Avilés Gómez, M. (2011) (coord.), *El enriquecimiento ilícito,* Editorial Club Universitario, Alicante.

[30] Barton, S. (1993), "Sozial übliche Geschäftstätigkeit und Geldwäsche (§261StGB)", *Strafverteidiger*, No. 3, pp. 156-163.

[31] Berdugo Gómez De La Torre, I. and Fabián Caparrós, E.A. (2010), "La «emancipación» del delito de blanqueo de capitales en el Derecho penal español", *Diario La Ley*, No. 7535, 27 de diciembre, pp. 1-19.

[32] Blanco Cordero, I. (1997), "Negocios socialmente adecuados y delito de blanqueo de capitales", *Anuario de Derecho Penal y Ciencias Penales*, tomo L, fascículo único, enero-diciembre, p. 263-291.

[33] Blanco Cordero, I. (2011), "El delito fiscal como actividad delictiva previa del blanqueo de capitales", *Revista Electrónica de Ciencia Penal y Criminología*, No. 13-01, pp. 1-46.

[34] Blanco Cordero, I. (2012), *El delito de blanqueo de capitales*, 3rd ed., Aranzadi, Cizur Menor.

[35] Bottke, W. (1995), "Teleologie und Effektivität der Normen gegen Geldwäsche", Teil 2, *Wistra*, No. 4, pp. 121-130.

[36] Bottke, W. (1998), "Mercado, criminalidad organizada y blanqueo de dinero en Alemania", traslated to Spanish by Soledad Arroyo Alfonso and Teresa Aguado Correa, *Revista Penal*, No. 2, pp. 1-15.

[37] Brooks, G. (2012), "Online gambling and money laundering: views from the inside", *Journal of Money Laundering Control*, Vol. 15, No. 3, pp. 304-315.

[38] Castro Moreno, A. (2009), "Reflexiones críticas sobre las nuevas conductas de posesión y utilización en el delito de blanqueo de capitales en la reforma del Anteproyecto de 2008", *Diario La Ley*, No. 7277, 5 de noviembre, pp. 1-12.

[39] Collado Medina, J. (2010), "El blanqueo de capitales: una aproximación", in Collado Medina, J. (coord.), *La investigación criminal y sus consecuencias jurídicas*, Dykinson, Madrid, pp. 469-491.

[40] Cuesta Arzamendi, J.L. de la (2010) (dir.), *Derecho penal informático*, Civitas/ Thomson Reuters/Aranzadi, Cizur Menor.

[41] Díaz y García Conlledo, M. (2002), "Blanqueo de bienes", in Luzón Peña, D.-M. (dir.), *Enciclopedia penal básica*, Comares, Granada, pp. 193-221.

[42] Díaz y García Conlledo, M. (2013), "El castigo del autoblanqueo en la reforma penal de 2010. La autoría y la participación en el delito de blanqueo de capitales", in Abel Souto and Sánchez Stewart, pp. 281-299, 395 and 396.

[43] Díaz-Maroto y Villarejo, J. (2009), "Recepción de las propuestas del GAFI y de las Directivas europeas sobre el blanqueo de capitales en el Derecho español", in Bajo Fernández, M. and Bacigalupo Saggese, S. (eds.), Política criminal y blanqueo de capitales, Marcial Pons, Madrid, Barcelona and Buenos Aires, pp. 21-66.

[44] *Directiva (UE) 2017/541 del Parlamento Europeo y del Consejo, de 15 de marzo de 2017, relativa a la lucha contra el terrorismo y por la que se sustituye la Decisión marco 2002/475/JAI del Consejo y se modifica la Decisión 2005/671/JAI del Consejo*, in *Diario Oficial de la Unión Europea*, L 88, 31 de marzo, pp. 6-21

[45] Fabián Caparrós, E.A. (1998), *El delito de blanqueo de capitales*, Colex, Madrid.

[46] Faraldo Cabana, P. (1998), "Aspectos básicos del delito de blanqueo de bienes en el Código penal de 1995", *Estudios Penales y Criminológicos*, No. XXI, pp. 117-165.

[47] *FATF (1995-1996), Report, Reviewing money laundering methods and counter-measures,* in http: //www.fatf-gafi.org (accessed December 2017).

[48] *FATF (1996-1997), Report, Issues concerning new payment technologies,* in http: // www.fatf-gafi.org (accessed December 2017).

[49] *FATF (2010a), Report, Money laundering through money remittance and currency exchange providers, June,* in http: //www.fatf-gafi.org (accessed December 2017).

[50] *FATF (2010b), Report, Money laundering using new payment methods, October*, in http://www.fatf-gafi.org (accessed December 2017).

[51] *FATF (2011a), Annual report 2010-2011,* in http://www.fatf-gafi.org (accessed December 2017).

[52] *FAFT (2011b), Report, Money laundering risks arising from trafficking in human beings and smuggling of migrants, July*, in http://www.fatf.gafi.org (accessed December 2017).

[53] *FATF (2012), International standards on combating money laundering and the financing of terrorism & proliferation. The FATF recommendations, February*, in http://www.fatf-gafi.org (accessed December 2017).

[54] *FATF (2013), Report, The role of hawala and other similarservice providers in money laundering and terrorist financing, October*, in http://www.fatf-gafi.org (accessed December 2017).

[55] *FATF (2015), Report, Money laundering through the physical transportation of cash, October*, in http://www.fatf-gafi.org (accessed December 2017).

[56] Fernández Steinko, A. (2012), "Financial channels of money laundering in Spain", *The British Journal of Criminology. An International Review of Crime and Society*, Vol. 52, No. 5, September, pp. 908-931.

[57] Fernández Teruelo, J.G. (2010), "Blanqueo de capitales", in Ortiz De Urbina Gimeno, I. (coord.), *Memento experto Francis Lefebvre. Reforma penal. Ley orgánica 5/2010*, Ediciones Francis Lefebvre, Madrid, pp. 313-334.

[58] Ferré Olivé, J.C. (2009), "Política criminal europea en materia de blanqueo de capitales y financiación del terrorismo", in González Cussac, J.L., pp. 163-179.

[59] Ferré Olivé, J.C. (2013), "El nuevo tipo agravado de blanqueo cuando los bienes tengan su origen en delitos relativos a la corrupción", in Abel Souto and Sánchez Stewart, pp. 389-391.

[60] Finklea, K.M. (2009), "Organized crime in the United States: trends and issues for congress", *Journal of Current Issues in Crime, Law & Law Enforcement*, Vol. 2, No. 1, pp. 9-40.

[61] Fisher, J. (2012), "The vulnerability of her majesty's revenue & customs to penetration by criminal actors", *Journal of Money Laundering Control*, Vol. 15, No. 2, pp. 153-161.

[62] Flick, G.M. (1990), "La repressione del riciclaggio ed il controllo della intermediazione finanziaria. Problemi attuali e prospettive", *Rivista Italiana di Diritto e Procedura Penale*, No. 4, pp. 1255-1273.

[63] Flick, G.M. (1992), "Le risposte nazionali al riciclaggio di capitali. La situazione in Italia", *Rivista Italiana di Diritto e Procedura Penale*, No. 4, pp. 1288-1298.

[64] Gless, S. (2012), "Strafverfolgung im Internet", *Schweizerische Zeitschrift für Strafrecht*, Vol. 130, No. 1, pp. 3-22.

[65] Gómez Rivero, M.C. (2010), *Nociones fundamentales de Derecho penal. Parte especial. (Adaptado al EEES)*, Tecnos, Madrid.

[66] González Cussac, J.L. and Cuerda Arnau, M.L. (dirs.) (2013), *Nuevas amenazas a la seguridad nacional. Terrorismo, criminalidad organizada y tecnologías de la información y la comunicación,* Tirant lo Blanch, Valencia.

[67] González Cussac, J.L. and Vidales Rodríguez, C. (2009), "El nuevo delito de financiación del terrorismo: consideraciones acerca de su necesidad y conveniencia", in González Cussac, J.L. (dir.), *Financiación del terrorismo, blanqueo de capitales y secreto bancario: un análisis crítico*, Tirant lo Blanch, Valencia, p. 195.

[68] González Rus, J.J. (2011), in Morillas Cueva, L. (coord.), *Sistema de Derecho penal español. Parte especial,* Dykinson Madrid, pp. 636-646.

[69] Grupo de Estudios de Política Criminal (1992), "Manifiesto por una nueva política sobre la droga", in *Una alternativa a la actual política criminal sobre drogas,* Imagraf, Málaga, pp. 9-14.

[70] Grupo de Estudios de Política Criminal (2010), "Propuesta alternativa en el ámbito de los delitos de blanqueo de capitales y encubrimiento", in *Una regulación alternativa contra la corrupción urbanística y otras conductas delictivas relacionadas,* Gráficas Luis Mahave, Málaga, pp. 63-70.

[71] Grupo de Estudios de Política Criminal (2013), "Manifiesto por una política criminal sobre terrorismo adaptada a los nuevos tiempos", in *Una propuesta de renovación de la política criminal sobre terrorismo,* Gráficas Luis Mahave, Málaga, pp. 9-20.

[72] Grupo de Estudios de Política Criminal (2014), *Autoevaluación. Política criminal de drogas,* 23 de mayo, in http://www.gepc.es, (accessed December 2017).

[73] Hassemer, W. (1994), "Gewinnaufspürung: jetzt mit dem Strafrecht", *Wertpapier Mitteilungen, Zeitschrift für Wirtschafts- und Bankrecht (Gastkommentar)*, p. 1369, translated to Spanish by Miguel Abel Souto (1998) as "Localización de ganancias: ahora con el Derecho penal", *Revista de Ciencias Penales,* Vol. 1, No. 1, pp. 217-220.

[74] He, B. (2010), *Resolution of the International Forum on Crime and Criminal Law in the Global Era on the "Theory of Human Rights Defense",* Beijing.

[75] He, B. (2012), *Fourth Session of the International Forum on Crime and Criminal Law in the Global Era*, Beijing.

[76] He, B. (2016), *Eighth Session of the International Forum on Crime and Criminal Law in the Global Era*, Beijing.

[77] Hugel, P. and Kelly, J. (2002), "Internet gambling, credit cards and money laundering", *Journal of Money Laundering Control,* Vol. 6, No. 3, pp. 57-65.

[78] Jurado, N. and García, R. (2011), "El blanqueo de capitales", in Avilés Gómez, pp. 159-193.

[79] Lampe, E.-J. (1994), "Der neue Tatbestand der Geldwäsche (§ 261 StGB)", *Juristen Zeitung*, No. 3, pp. 123-132, translated to Spanish by Miguel Abel Souto and José Manuel Pérez Pena (1997) as "El nuevo tipo penal del blanqueo de dinero (§ 261 StGB)", *Estudios Penales y Criminológicos*, No. XX, pp. 103-148.

[80] Levi, M. (2012), "Crimes of globalisation: some measurement issues", in JOUTSEN, M. (ed.), *New types of crime. Proceedings of the international seminar held in connection with HEUNI's thirtieth anniversary Helsinki 20 october 2011*, Heuni, Helsinki, pp. 107-115.

[81] *Ley 7/2012, de 29 de octubre, de modificación de la normativa tributaria y presupuestaria y de adecuación de la normativa financiera para la intensificación de las actuaciones en la prevención y lucha contra el fraude*, BOE del 30 de octubre.

[82] Lorenzo Salgado, J.M. (2011), "Reformas penales y drogas: observaciones críticas. (Especial referencia a la LO 5/2010, de modificación del Código penal)", in Muñoz Conde, F., Lorenzo Salgado, J.M., Ferré Olivé, J.C., Cortés Bechiarelli, E. and Núñez Paz, M.A. (dirs.), *Un Derecho penal comprometido: libro homenaje al prof. Dr. Gerardo Landrove* Díaz, Tirant lo Blanch, Valencia, pp. 631-679.

[83] Lorenzo Salgado, J.M. (2013), "El tipo agravado de blanqueo cuando los bienes tengan su origen en el delito de tráfico de drogas", in Abel Souto and Sánchez Stewart, pp. 223-249 and 377-379.

[84] Lorenzo Salgado, J.M. (2017), "El blanqueo de dinero procedente del narcotráfico, la protección del orden socioeconómico y la desnaturalización del bien jurídico en las modalidades de blanqueo con finalidad terrorista, introducidas por la Ley orgánica 2/2015, de 30 de marzo, por la que se modifica el Código penal", in Abel Souto and Sánchez Stewart, pp. 383-386.

[85] Manjón-Cabeza Olmeda, A. (2010), "Receptación y blanqueo de capitales (arts. 301 y 302)", in Álvarez García, F.J. and González Cussac, J.L. (dirs.), *Comentarios a la reforma penal de 2010*, Tirant lo Blanch, Valencia, pp. 339-346.

[86] Martínez-Buján Pérez, C. (2015), *Derecho penal económico y de la empresa. Parte especial*, 5th ed., Tirant lo Blanch, Valencia.

[87] Mata Barranco, N.J. de la (2010), "Ilícitos vinculados al ámbito informático: la respuesta penal", in Cuesta Arzamendi, pp. 15-30.

[88] Mills, J. (2001), "Internet casinos: a sure bet for money laundering", *Journal of Financial Crimen*, Vol. 8, No. 4, pp. 365-383.

[89] Moreno Alcázar, M.A. (2012), "Receptación y blanqueo de capitales", in Boix Reig, J. (dir.), *Derecho penal. Parte especial. Volumen II. Delitos contra las relaciones familiares, contra el patrimonio y el orden socioeconómico*, Iustel, Madrid, pp. 675-700.

[90] Muñoz Conde, F. (2010), *Derecho penal. Parte especial*, 18th ed., Tirant lo Blanch, Valencia.

[91] Muñoz Conde, F. (2013a), "El delito de blanqueo de capitales y el Derecho penal de enemigo", in Abel Souto and Sánchez Stewart, pp. 375 and 376.

[92] Muñoz Conde, F. (2013b), *Derecho penal. Parte especial*, 19th ed., Tirant lo Blanch, Valencia.

[93] Muñoz Conde, F. (2015), *Derecho penal. Parte especial,* 20th ed., Tirant lo Blanch, Valencia.

[94] Muñoz Conde, F. (2017), *Derecho penal. Parte especial,* 21st ed., Tirant lo Blanch, Valencia.

[95] Núñez Paz, M.A. (2011), "Tipologías criminales de blanqueo. Técnicas de comisión", in Abel Souto and Sánchez Stewart, p. 217.

[96] Núñez Paz, M.A. (2013), "El tipo agravado de blanqueo de dinero procedente de delitos urbanísticos", in Abel Souto and Sánchez Stewart, pp. 267-279, 393 and 394.

[97] Palma Herrera, J.M. (2000), *Los delitos de blanqueo de capitales,* Edersa, Madrid.

[98] Pérez Estrada, M.J. (2010), "La investigación del delito a través de las nuevas tecnologías. Nuevos medios de investigación en el proceso penal", in Cuesta Arzamendi, pp. 305-319.

[99] Pieth, M. (1992), "Zur Einführung: Geldwäscherei und ihre Bekämpfung in der Schweiz", in Pieth, M. (ed.), *Bekämpfung der Geldwäscherei: Modellfall Schweiz?,* Helbing & Lichtenhahn, Basel und Frankfurt am Main, Schäffer-Poeschel, Stuttgart, pp. 1-27.

[100] Quintero Olivares, G. (2010a), "Sobre la ampliación del comiso y el blanqueo, y la incidencia en la receptación civil", *Revista Electrónica de Ciencia Penal y Criminología,* 8 de marzo, pp. 1-20.

[101] Quintero Olivares, G. (2010b), "La reforma del comiso (art. 129)", in Quintero Olivares, G. (dir.), *La reforma penal de 2010: análisis y comentarios,* Aranzadi, Cizur Menor, pp. 107-110.

[102] Ragués i Vallès, R. (2001), "Lavado de activos y negocios *standard.* Con especial mención a los abogados como potenciales autores de un delito de lavado", in ROXIN, C., *Homenaje. Nuevas formulaciones en las Ciencias penales,* Lerner, Universidad Nacional de Córdoba, pp. 621-653.

[103] Ríos Corbacho, J.M. (2010), "Un acercamiento al perfil del delincuente urbanístico", *Revista General de Derecho Penal,* No. 14, pp. 1-31.

[104] Ruß, W. (1994), "Kommentar zum § 261 StGB", in *StGB Leipziger Kommentar. Großkommentar,* 11. neubearbeitete Auflage, Walter de Gruyter, Berlin, pp. 321-331, translated to Spanish by Miguel Abel Souto (1997) as "Comentario al parágrafo 261 del Código penal alemán: el blanqueo de dinero", *Dereito. Revista Xurídica da Universidade de Santiago de Compostela,* Vol. 6, No. 1, pp. 179-196.

[105] Shehu, A.Y. (2004), "Should gambling be a predicate for money laundering?", *Journal of Money Laundering Control,* Vol. 7, No. 3, pp. 254-260.

[106] Silva Sánchez, J.-M. (2010), "La reforma del Código penal: una aproximación desde el contexto", *Diario La Ley,* No. 7464, 9 de septiembre, pp. 1-13.

[107] Terradillos Basoco, J.M. (2008), "El delito de blanqueo de capitales en el Derecho español", in Cervini, R. *et al., El delito de blanqueo de capitales de origen delictivo. Cuestiones dogmáticas y político-criminales. Un enfoque comparado: Argentina-Uruguay-España,* Alveroni, Córdoba (República Argentina), pp. 203-274.

[108] Terradillos Basoco, J.M. (2012), *Lecciones y materiales para el estudio del Derecho Penal, vol. IV. Derecho penal. Parte especial (Derecho penal económico),* Iustel, Madrid.

[109] *The money laundering officer's practical handbook 2011* (2011), Compliance training products limited, Cambridge.

[110] United Nations (2006), *Resolution adopted by the General Assembly on 8 September 2006, The United Nations Global Counter-Terrorism Strategy, A/RES/60/288,* pp. 1-9.

[111] United Nations (2016), *Resolution adopted by the General Assembly on 1 July 2016, The United Nations Global Counter-Terrorism Strategy Review, A/RES/70/291,* pp. 1-15.

[112] Vidales Rodríguez, C. (1997), *Los delitos de receptación y legitimación de capitales en el Código penal de 1995,* Tirant lo Blanch, Valencia.

[113] Vidales Rodríguez, C. (2008), *El delito de enriquecimiento ilícito: su tratamiento en el marco normativo internacional y en la legislación comparada. Especial referencia a la legislación penal colombiana,* Center for the Administration of Justice, Florida International University, Miami.

[114] Vidales Rodríguez, C. (2012), *El delito de tráfico de drogas en la legislación penal costarricense. Su adecuación a la normativa internacional,* Center for the Administration of Justice, Florida International University, Miami.

[115] Vogel, J. (1997), "Geldwäsche – eine europaweit harmonisierter Straftatbestand?", *Zeitschrift für die Gesamte Strafrechtswissenschaft,* No. 2, pp. 335-356.

[116] Yu, J.-J. (2016), "Terrorism financing. China", *Revista Penal,*Vol. 38, julio, pp. 357-361.

[117] Zaragoza Aguado, J.A. (2011), in Gómez Tomillo, M. (dir.), *Comentarios al Código penal,* 2nd ed., Lex nova, Valladolid, pp. 1152-1182.

Author Index